A History of Middle New River Settlements and Contiguous Territory

ITB

DAVID E. JOHNSTON, at 60.

A HISTORY OF

MIDDLE NEW RIVER

SETTLEMENTS

AND CONTIGUOUS TERRITORY

By
DAVID E. JOHNSTON
AUTHOR OF
"FOUR YEARS A SOLDIER"

1906
STANDARD PTG. & PUB. CO.
HUNTINGTON, W. VA.

M. R.

Copyright 1906
BY
DAVID E. JOHNSTON

INTRODUCTION.

I have had in mind for several years to write and publish a history of Mercer County and its people, but finding on research and investigation that the settlement of the territory thereof and incidents connected with the life of its people are so interwoven with that of the people who first crowned and crossed the Alleghanies and made settlements on and along the upper waters of the Clinch, Sandy, Guyandotte, Coal, and other rivers and streams, that it will be necessary to broaden the scope of the work beyond what was at first intended.

Mercer County as originally created, and as it now exists, embraces territory which was formerly a part of that vast domain known as Augusta, later, and in succession, Botetourt, Fincastle, Montgomery, Greenbrier, Wythe, Monroe, Tazewell, and Giles Counties.

The early history of the County, and that of its settlers and people, is largely common all those who occupy the territory referred to.

Their long sufferings, dangerous encounters with the wild beasts and the savages, their patient endurance, their history during and after the close of the war between the States, their manly and heroic efforts to restore and reestablish their rights as citizens of a free Republic, not less renowned than their chivalric deeds in war, deserve a place in the annals of history to be handed down to succeeding generations, as examples of valor, heroism and fortitude worthy of emulation.

The desire usually possessed by civilized men to learn the history and character of their ancestors, who they were, and whence they came, excites regret that this history is the more often involved in obscurity; no one has thought it necessary to keep a correct record of the family.

Tradition alone, depended upon to supply the place of recorded facts, is often so obscured by the efflux of time and other causes, that it cannot always be relied upon as a safe guide to truth. Yet when tradition and known facts are closely coupled together, the former is greatly strengthened and becomes much more reliable.

Our ancestors who came across the mountains from the East and settled upon the Western waters were not, as a rule, college bred people; in fact, most of them had had few advantages along this line. They came bringing with them all their world's goods of which they were possessed, consisting usually of a horse or two, a cow, rifle gun, a dog, and such an amount of household furniture as could be carried on horses.

It is important as well as a matter of interest, that the deeds of heroism, and the dangers to which they were exposed, as well as the sufferings of those who won and redeemed this great wilderness country from the Savages and the wild beast, should be truthfully written. Already the time is here when the names of many of our ancestors who felled the forests, stood on the frontier, risked their lives, and endured untold hardships, have been forgotten. Their names should, as far as possible, be rescued from the obliteration of time and their illustrious deeds recorded upon the pages of history, lest they be forgotten or left to be preserved only in the indistinct memorials of tradition.

With this view and to this end, the author has undertaken, with the best lights and information obtainable by him, gathered from the most reliable sources attainable, to record the history of these people. It cannot and will not of necessity be full and accurate, and much that would be of great interest to those of the later generation has been lost and cannot be produced.

No attempt will be made to give a particular history of all the settlers of the New River Valley, or of the territory referred to, but will be confined to that portion of the said territory in which the first settlements were made along the Middle-New River and contiguous territory, and to record local inci-dents, coupling therewith biographical sketches of families.

DAVID E. JOHNSTON.

Bluefield, W. Va., 1905.

Middle New River Settlements.

Vast unexplored domain West of the Alleghanies—Crowning and Crossing the same—First White Man to see New River—First White Man West of this River—Origin of Name—Porter Settles at Mouth of East River—Salley, Howards and St. Clair on Middle-Lower New River—Clinche and Castle in Clinch Valley prior to 1748—Thomas Walker and party cross New River, 1748—Same year Draper's Ingles' settlement made—Adam Harman at Gunpowder Spring—1750 Dr. Thomas Walker and others on the Holstein and at Cumberland Gap—Christopher Gist on the Ohio and visits Mountain Lake—Philip Lybrook settles at Mouth of Sinking Creek—John Lewis and his son Andrew on the Greenbrier—James Burke discovers Burke's Garden—Samuel Culbertson on Culbertson's Bottom—Thomas Farley on New River—Builds a fort—James Ellison born in Farley's Fort—French and Indian War—Washington on the Ohio—Indian Depredations.

The country embraced by the New River Valley belonged, at the time the first settlements were made therein by white people, to that vast unknown domain in Augusta County, beyond the Alleghanies, which was sometimes erroneously called "West Augusta," stretching from the top of the Alleghanies Westward to the Mississippi River—if not to the uttermost sea.

The country at the time mentioned was a vast unexplored wilderness about which the people East of the Alleghanies had very vague and indefinite ideas. Immediately in and near this valley, about or a little before the white people came, the Canawhay tribe of Indians occupied the valley and plateau, now in Carroll and Floyd Counties, Virginia, and from the name of which tribe of Indians, the New and Kanawha Rivers took the name of Kanawha.

Where or when the upper part of this same river came to be called New River is not altogether agreed. The late Capt. Charles R. Boyd, upon the authority of Judge David McComas, says it was an Indian name meaning "New Water." Hardesty in his geographical history, says that "Captain Byrd, who had been employed in 1764 to open a road from the James River to where the town of Abingdon now stands, probably using Jefferson's map of Virginia engraved in France in 1755, and on which this river did not appear, named it New River. The late Major Jed Hotchkiss of Staunton, Virginia, attributed the name to a man by the name "New," who at an early day kept a ferry at or near where "Ingle's Ferry" was afterwards established.

The first white man who is supposed to have entered this valley, was Colonel Abraham Wood in 1654. Wood lived at the Falls of the Appomatox near where the present city of Petersburg, Virginia, now stands, and being, as said, of an adventurous turn of mind, obtained from the Government authority to open trade with the Western Indians. It is supposed, in fact stated, that Colonel Wood came over the Alleghanies at a place now and long known and called Wood's Gap in the present county of Floyd, and passed down Little river to the river now known as New River, and seeing a river flowing in a different direction from those up the course of which he had just traveled, he took it to be a new river and gave to it his own name "Wood's River," and it so appears on some of the oldest maps of Virginia.

So far as known, between the date of the discovery of this river by Colonel Wood, Captain Henry Batte in 1666, Thomas Batte and party in 1671, John Salling who was captured by the Indians and carried over this river to the West thereof in

1730, Salley, the Howards and St. Clair in 1742, Dr. Thomas
(3) Walker, and his parties in 1748-1750, are the only white
men that had seen or crossed New River, or penetrated this
vast wilderness country prior to 1748, unless it were the three
men whose names are hereinafter mentioned.

It is now more than a century and a half since the first
white settlement was made in the New River Valley. It has
been claimed, in fact conceded, that the first white settlement
was made in the year of 1748 by Ingles, Drapers and others
near where Blacksburg, in Montgomery county, Virginia, now
stands, but this claim is now and has been for many years
disputed and upon an investigation it appears from discover-
ies made at the mouth of East River at its junction with New
River in Giles County, Virginia, that in the year of 1780, when
Mr. John Toney (1) and his family, from Buckingham County,
Virginia, settled at that place, they found the decayed remains of a cabin and evidences that some of the land around
the same had been cleared, and nearby they found a grave with
a rough stone at the head, on which was engraved, "Mary
Porter was killed by the Indians November 28, 1742. (2) "Then
followed something respecting Mr. Porter, but the crumbling
away of the stone during the century and a half which has
elapsed since its erection, has rendered it illegible."—*Hardesty's Geographical His.* 405.

This Ingles-Draper settlement was called "Draper's Meadows," but we are told that the name was changed by Colonel
William Preston to "Smithfield," in honor of his wife, who
was a Miss Smith of Louisa County, Virginia.

While the "Draper's Meadows" settlement was not made
directly on the New River, it was not far away and the drain-
age of the waters in the vicinity is into this river.

---

(1). Built the brick dwelling house at mouth of East River, the
first brick house built in Giles County.

(2). This stone with engraving thereon often seen by Dr. Phillip H.
Killey and Mr. G. W. Toney.

(3). Upon the authority of Haywood, Vaughan of Amelia County,
Va., with a number of Indian traders crossed New River about Ingle's
ferry in 1740.

Adam Harman, who came with the Ingles, Drapers and others from Pattonsburg, in the Virginia Valley, shortly after the planting of the Colony, located, probably in the Spring of 1749, on New River at the place now known as Eggleston's Springs, but called by the early settlers "Gunpowder Spring," from the resemblance of its odor and taste to that of gun powder. This settlement of Harman, save that of Porter at the mouth of East River, is believed to be the oldest settlement made by white people in what is now the territory of Giles County.

Philip Lybrook, from Pennsylvania, but most likely born in Holland, and of whom we shall have occasion to hereafter speak, settled at the mouth of Sinking Creek on the New River, a short distance below Harman's settlement, about 1750. It is not believed that Lybrook, the correct spelling of whose name in his native tongue is "Leibroch," came with the Drapers Meadows settlers, but subsequently. His was the third settlement made by the whites in what is now Giles County.

It was upon Harman at Gunpowder Spring in April, 1749, that the Indians committed depredations by stealing his fur skins, but they remained peaceable and quiet until the breaking out of the French and Indian war in the year of 1753, which continued on the border for more than ten years.

It seems that Harman suspected a man by the name of Castle as being in league with and as prompting the Indians to steal his fur skins. Castle was at the time on a hunting expedition with the Indians, who were now friendly, in what is now called Castleswoods on the Clinch River in the Western portion of the now County of Russell. Harman obtained from a magistrate of Augusta County a warrant for the arrest of Castle, and with a posse, among them a large, stout, athletic man by the name of Clinche, who had been a hunter in that section, he set out to accomplish his purpose, but met with serious resistance from Castle and the Indians with whom he was engaged in hunting, and forced to beat a retreat, in which his man Clinche was thrown from his horse in crossing the river. Being a lame man from an attack of white swelling, the Indians supposing him disabled from the fall, one of them dashed into the river and seized him, but the great, strong man was an over match for his Indian enemy, and succeeded in drowning him, hence the name "Clinche River" was given, as the story goes. Dr. Thomas Walker in his journal kept of his journey to and through Cumberland Gap and return in 1750, says: "Clinche River was named for a hunter whose name was Clinche." It therefore seems altogether probable that, except Salling, Porter, Castle and Clinche were the first white men to cross the Middle-New River and to explore the territory West thereof. It is stated upon the authority of Mr. Virgil A. Lewis in his recent history, as well as by others, that in 1742, Salley, the Howards and St. Clair crossed the New River below the mouth of Greenbrier and passed over on to Coal River, to which they gave that name.

In the year of 1748 Dr. Thomas Walker, of Albemarle County, Colonel James Patton, Colonel John Buchanan, Colonel James Wood and Major Charles Campbell, from the neighborhood of Pattonsburg, on the James River, made an excursion into what is now known as Southwestern Virginia. The precise route this party traveled after leaving the New River, or how far they went Westward, seems to be left in doubt. This trip must not be confused with Dr. Walker's second one across the New River westward through Cumberland Gap and into Kentucky in 1750, in which his companions were Ambrose Powell, William Tomlinson, Colby Chew, Henry Lawless and John Hughes. This party on this trip in 1750 gave names, in some instances their own, to several mountains and streams, and on their return home came by way of the site of the present city of Pocahontas, Virginia, and along the Bluestone and Flat Top mountains near the present town of Hinton, and thence up the Greenbrier. See Appendix to "His. Southwest Virginia," by Summers.

From sketches taken from the diary of Dr. Walker and pub-

lished by Major Jed Hotchkiss some years ago, it appears that
Dr. Walker was the first white man to discover the great coal
deposit in the Flat Top region. In his dairy he says that near
the mouth of a small creek at the base of a mountain he discovered a large bed of stone coal lying to the north and northwest.

As already stated the Drapers Meadows settlement was
made in 1748. Whether the settlers made this location prior to
Dr. Walker's first journey across New River or after his return, does not certainly appear, but it is evident that some of
the parties who established themselves here must have had
some knowledge of the country before the date of settlement.

In 1750-1751 Christopher Gist, the employee of the Ohio
Company, explored the country west of New River through a
portion of Kentucky, returning through what is now Wise
County, Virginia, giving his name to a river now in that
County, as well also as a station, moving east along the watershed dividing the Clinch, Sandy and the Bluestone, he passed
through the territory of what is now the County of Mercer,
crossing New River about eight miles above the mouth of
Bluestone, and not far below the lower part of Culbertson's-
Crump's Bottom, now in Summers County, and on the 11th
day of May discovered on top of a very high mountain a lake
or pond about three-fourths of a mile long, northeast and
southwest, and one-fourth of a mile wide, which is supposed to
be what is now known as Mountain Lake, in Giles County, Virginia.—"His. So. W. Va.," Summers.

If tradition well authenticated is to be taken when supported by well attested evidence, then Christopher Gist never saw
Mountain Lake in Giles County. (1) The earliest settlers in
the vicinity of the lake and who lived longest, left the unbro-
ken tradition that when they first knew the place where the
lake now exists there was a deep depression between the mountains into which flowed the water from one or more springs

----

(1). If Gist really saw this lake in 1751, then it is evident that
water had escaped before 1768.

which found its outlet at the northeastern portion of the depression, and in this gorge or depression was a favorite salting ground in which the settlers salted their cattle by whose continual tramping the crevices through which the water from the springs found an escape, became closed and the depression began to fill with water. This filling began in 1804 and by 1818 the water in the depression had risen to about one-half its present height.

Kerchival in his "History of the Valley," at page 343 gives a conversation had by him in the year of 1836 with Colonel Christian Snidow and John Lybrook, which fully substantiates the statement above made, that the lake did not exist when the first settlers knew the place. To reconcile this statement with that of Gist it is fair to presume that after he saw this lake in 1751, the water had escaped through the crevices of the rocks and had disappeared before Snidow, Lybrook, and others saw it in about 1768, and that afterwards it repeated the process of refilling. It is reputed to be rapidly receding, having fallen several feet within the past two years.

In 1753, Andrew Culbertson settled on New River on what has been known since his settlement as Culbertson's, or Crump's Bottom, now in Summers County, formerly a part of the territory of Mercer County. This was the first white settlement made within the boundaries of Mercer County.

Andrew Culbertson, who lived in Pennsylvania, near to or where the town of Chambersburg is now situate, was compelled on account of the breaking out of the French and Indian war and fear of Indians to leave his land. He sold his claim to Samuel Culbertson, perhaps his brother. The country for some years was so infested with Indians from northwest of the Ohio, that the property appeared to be deserted and abandoned and in fact was. In the meantime other persons began to assert claim to the land, until finally the claims of all became vested in Thomas Farley who in March, 1775, procured the land to be surveyed, took a certificate thereof in order to obtain a grant from the Virginia Land Office, then expected to be shortly opened, and then assigned his right to James Burnsides. (Byrnside.)

Long litigation followed over the right and ownership to this land or a part thereof between the Culbertsons, Reid, and Byrnside.—*Wythe's Chancery Reports*, 150.

Thomas Farley from Albemarle County, Virginia, came to New River Valley shortly after the coming of Culbertson and immediately on locating on the land referred to, erected a fort near the lower portion of the bottom on the south bank of the river, near what is known as "Warford." (1)

This fort was known as Farley's and in which James Ellison, whose father came from the State of New Jersey, was born in May, 1778. The father of James Ellison was in the battle of Point Pleasant, and after his return to his home on Culbert- son's Bottom, was on the 19th day of October, 1780, while at work about a corn crib, attacked by a party of seven or eight Indians, wounded in the shoulder, captured, and carried some fifteen miles, escaping the day after his capture. In 1774 a woman was killed on Culbertson's Bottom, by the Indians, and about the same time a man by the name of Shockley, on a hill above the bottom, which still bears the name of "Shockley's Hill." •

The James Ellison spoken of, became a distinguished and successful Baptist minister, and was instrumental in planting a number of Baptist churches in this section, among them the Guyandotte Baptist church, in 1812, where Oceana, in Wyo- ming County, is now situated. He was, the father of the late Matthew Ellison, of Beckley, West Virginia, and who was re- garded the most distinguished Baptist preacher in this section in his day.

James Burke, who was one of the Drapers Meadows settlers, on a hunting exedition in 1753, wounded an elk and followed it through what is now called Henshue's Gap, into that beauti- ful body of magnificent land which has since borne the name of

(1). Shortly after the opening of Dunmore's war in 1774, a fort was erected at the mouth of Joshua's Run, on Culbertson's Bottom, called Fort Field.

Burke's Garden, about which and the discoverer more will
be said later on. The Indian (1) name for this beautiful land
was "Great Swamp."

————o————

CHAPTER II.

1753-1766

Exploring the Mississippi Valley—French and Indian War—
    Washington on the Ohio—Virginia Raises Troops—Colo-
    nel Fry Sick and Command Devolves on Washington—
    Fort Necessity—General Braddock Defeated on the Mon-
    ongahela—Depredations on the Virginia Border—De-
    struction of Drapers Meadows Settlers—Mrs. Ingles a
    Prisoner—Philip Barger Killed—Mrs. Ingles Escapes—
    Captain William Ingles and Governor Dinwiddie plan an
    Expedition Against the Ohio Indians—Major Andrew
    Lewis Ordered to raise a force for the destruction of the
    Indian Towns on the Ohio—Lewis Marches in February,
    1756, Crosses New River, North Fork of the Holstein,
    through Burke's Garden, over the head of the Clinch and
    on to the Sandy—Vaux's Fort Destroyed—1756 Settle-
    ments West of New River—Joseph Howe and Others on
    Back Creek West of New River, 1760—Indian Marauding
    Party Near Ingle's Ferry Attacked by Ingles, Harman
    and Others—Captain Henry Harman, Adam Harman—
    Herrman—One Branch of the Family from North Caro-
    lina and the Other from Virginia Valley—New River
    Lead Mines Discovered by Colonel Chiswell—Indian In-
    cursion into Jackson's River, Roanoke and Catawba Set-
    tlements—Pack, Swope and Pitman on the New River—
    Captain Audley Paul on Lower New River in 1763—Mas-
    sacres by Indians in Greenbrier Section in 1763—Butler,
    Carr and Others, Hunters on head of Clinch, 1766—This
    Year Family of John Snidow Settle at Mouth of Sinking
    Creek on the New River.

The Mississippi Valley was first explored and settled by the
French. They had a line of forts extending from New Orleans

---

(1). When first seen by white men, contained a large number of
acres of wet, marshy land, evidently once a lake. The waters flowing
out of Burke's Garden are the head springs of Wolf Creek.

to Quebec, one of which being Fort du Quesne, where Pittsburg now stands. The English were jealous of these movements, which jealousy at last ripened into open hostility, but before proceeding to open acts of war, the English sought to gain possession of the Western country by throwing a large white population into it by means of land companies, to whom large grants for land were made. The Ohio Company with a grant of 500,000 acres on the south side of the Ohio between Monon-gahela and the Kanawha; the Greenbrier Company, at the head of which was John Lewis of Augusta, obtained authority to locate 100,000 acres on the Greenbrier and its waters, and the Loyal Company, with a grant of 800,000 acres with authority to locate the same from the North Carolina line north and west.

Each of these land companies proceeded to locate their lands, and in 1751 Colonel John Lewis and his son, Andrew, afterward a distinguished General, surveyed the Greenbrier tract, including "Marlinton's Bottom," on the Greenbrier River, on which is now situate the town of Marlinton, the County seat of Pocahontas County, where they found Jacob Marlin and Stephen Sewell. The Loyal Company surveyed a large part of the lands granted to it, even extending its surveys into what is now Giles County, Virginia, about one of which tracts a controversy arose and was decided by the Supreme Court of Appeals of Virginia in July, 1834. *French vs Loyal Company*, 5th Leigh's R. 680.

The movements of the English were closely watched by the French, who, understanding their design, determined to defeat them.

They accordingly crossed Lake Champlain, built Crown Point, and fortified certain positions on the waters of the upper Ohio. In the year of 1752, on the Miami, a collision occurred between some of the French soldiers and the English traders and Indians, in which some of the Indians were killed and some of the whites were taken prisoners. This was the begin-ning of what is known as the French and Indian War, which resulted in the loss to France of all her territory east of the Mississippi.

Governor Dinwiddie of Virginia, arrived in that Colony in 1752, and viewing with alarm the encroachments of the French, dispatched George Washington on a commission to the French Commandant on the Ohio.

Washington left Williamsburg on the 31st day of October, 1753, and proceeded by way of Romney, in Hampshire County, where he remained one night, and finally reached the French post on the Ohio, made known his commission to the French Commandant, who replied that it "did not become him to discuss civil matters." Washington returned immediately to Williamsburg and reported the failure of his mission. Under instructions from the English goverument to raise a force of men to build and occupy two forts on the Ohio, the House of Burgesses voted 10,000 pounds and the raising of a regiment of men, the command of which was given to Colonel Joshua Fry as Commandant, with George Washington as Lieutenant-Colonel. Fry was taken sick on the journey and the command devolved upon Washington. These troops left Alexandria, Virginia, in April, and arrived at Will's Creek on the 20th of the same month, and on the 28th of May reached a place called Redstone, where they encountered a French and Indian force, which they attacked, killing ten and taking the rest prisoners. From these prisoners Washington learned that a large force of French and Indians were in his front; nevertheless he continued his march to the Great Meadows, where he halted and built a fort, calling it "Fort Necessity." On the third day of July, at 11 o'clock a. m., the enemy assailed Washington's works with vigor, and attempted to carry them by assault, but were repulsed with loss. The battle however, continued with great fury until well into the night. At the end of a nine hours engagement and after severe loss to the enemy, the French Commandant Count de Villiers, sent in a flag of truce, praising the gallantry of the Virginians, and offering to treat for a surrender of the works on honorable terms. His proposals were accepted, and the next morning the treaty was concluded, and the Virginians took up their line of march for their homes. The French and Indians numbered 1,000 men. (*Peyton's Augusta.*)

It seems that Washington on his march to the Great Meadows was joined by a Company of soldiers from South Carolina, who were with him at the surrender of Fort Necessity.

Being now fully satisfied that war was inevitable, the British cabinet encouraged the Colonies to unite for defense or aggression, as might be necessary, and a plan to this effect was duly signed in 1754.

In the Spring of 1755 the colonial forces attacked the French at four different points, Nova Scotia, Crown Point, Niagara, and on the Ohio River. Against the French on the Ohio, operations were conducted by General Braddock, who arrived from England in February of that year with two regiments. Virginia raised eight hundred men to join Braddock, who arrived at Alexandria, then called Bellhaven, and appointed Washington his aide-de-camp. Braddock dispatched one company of colonial troops under Captain Thomas Lewis of Augusta, to the Greenbrier country to build a stockade fort and prevent Indian raids on the white settlements in that region.

The captains commanding companies in the Virginia troops, which served under Braddock in his march to the Monongahela were Waggener, Cock, Hogg, Stephens, Poulson, Pemronny, Mercer and Stuart.

Braddock with his command of about twenty-two hundred men, left Alexandria on the 20th day of April, and crossed the Monongahela River on the 9th day of July, 1755, where he fell into an ambuscade of French and Indians. He was mortally wounded, and his army after sustaining fearful loss was routed and put to flight. But for the courage and bravery of Washington and his Virginians, Braddock's whole force would have been annihilated. The Colonial and British loss in this engagement was seven hundred and seventy-seven (777) killed and wounded.

This defeat spread wide alarm throughout Virginia, and aroused the people to renewed energies for the defense of the border.

It may here be noted that among the Virginians who survived this battle, and were afterwards distinguished in our annals, were Washington, Andrew and William Lewis, Matthews, Field, and Grant.

Following this disaster of Braddock and his army, devastations and inhuman murders were perpetrated by the French and Indians during the summer on the western borders of Virginia and Pennsylvania.

As a result of Braddock's defeat, the whole frontier of Western Virginia was thrown open to the ravages of the Indians, who crossed the Alleghanies and pushed into Augusta, the lower Valley and New River settlements, torturing and murdering men, women and children. Such was the distress occasioned by these butcheries that Washington in one of his letters to Governor Dinwiddie says, "The supplicating tears of the women and the moving petitions of the men melt me into such deadly sorrow, that I solemnly declare that if I know my own mind I could offer myself a willing sacrifice to the butchering enemy, provided that it would contribute to the people's ease."

During all the years, beginning with the year 1753 to 1763 the Indians continued their barbarities along the Virginia border. We must now turn to events transpiring in the New River valley.

Notwithstanding that Drapers Meadows settlement was far from the Ohio, and apparently safe from any probability of attack from any quarter, and although these settlers must have been aware that war was then being waged by the Indians against the whites, they took no reasonable precaution for their safety, but on Sunday, the 8th day of July, 1755, the day before Braddock's defeat on the Monongahela, they permitted themselves to be surprised by a band of marauding Shawnees from North of the Ohio, who killed, wounded and captured every person present. The killed were Colonel James Patton, Mrs. George Draper, Casper Barrier, and a child of John Draper, James Cull; wounded, Mrs. William Ingles, Mrs. John Draper and Henry Leonard, captured. After putting their plunder and the women and children on horses, they set fire to the buildings, and with their prisoners began their retreat to the Ohio, passing on their way, and not far from the scene of the tragedy, the house of Philip Barger, an old white haired man, whose head they cut off, put in a bag, and took it with them to the house of Philip Lybrook at the mouth of Sinking Creek, and where they left it, telling Mrs. Lybrook to look in the bag and she would find an acquaintance.

The morning of the attack upon the settlers of Drapers Meadows Colonel Patton had sent his nephew, young William Preston, over to Philip Lybrook's, on Sinking Creek, to get him to come over and help next day with the harvest, which was ready to cut. Preston and Lybrook instead of following the river, crossed the mountains, probably by the place where Newport, in Giles County, is now situated, and thus doubtless escaped death or capture. Of the facts and circumstances attending the attack on this settlement, the killing, wounding and capture of all present, of the journey of the prisoners to Ohio, the escape and return home of Mrs. Ingles, the writer is largely indebted to the authentic, pathetic account by the late Dr. John P. Hale, of Charleston, West Virginia, in his book "Trans-Alleghany Pioneers."

Just why the Indians did not disturb the families of Adam Harman and Philip Lybrook, whose settlements were immediately on the river and along the trace the Indians must have traveled in going to and returning from Drapers Meadows, cannot well be explained. These Indians with their prisoners passed down New River, crossing at the ford above the mouth of Bluestone, thence across what is called White Oak Mountain, the northeastern extension of the Flat Top, by way of where Beckley, in Raleigh County, is now situate, the old

Indian trail passed at what is now the junction of the principal streets of the town, and on to the head of Paint Creek
and down to the Kanawha. Thus it will be seen that they
passed over the territory of Mercer County. This trail up
Paint Creek, and either by Pipe Stem Knob or mouth of Big
Bluestone, was one of their frequently traveled ways to the
East River and New River settlements. Paint Creek took
its name from several trees standing thereon painted by the
Indians as one of their guides or land marks on their marauding expeditions into the white settlements and on their return they by marks on these trees would indicate the number
of scalps taken.

Governor Dinwiddie had on August 11th, 1755 been informed of the death of Colonel Patton and the destruction of the
Drapers Meadows settlement, as he refers to same in a letter
of that date to Captain Andrew Lewis.

Mrs. William Ingles who was captured by the Indians at
Drapers Meadows, and carried by them to their town North
of the Ohio, and later to Big Bone Lick, in Kentucky, escaped
in the fall of the same year with an old Dutch woman, and
they made their way up the Ohio, Kanawha and New Rivers
to the settlements. Evidently, from what subsequently happened, Captain William Ingles, the husband of Mrs. Ingles,
very shortly after her return, went to Williamsburg to lay
before Governor Dinwiddie the situation of affairs on the
border. Governor Dinwiddie writes on December 15th, 1755,
to Colonel Stuart and to Captains Hogg, Preston, Smith, Richard Pearis and Woodson, of the intention to take the Shawnee towns on the Ohio River, and in his letter to Preston
and Smith he refers to the bearer thereof as Mr. Ingles, who
evidently was Captain William Ingles, who, while at Williamsburg with the Governor, originated and planned the
Sandy expedition against the Shawnees whose towns were
situated on the lower side of the Scioto on the North bank
of the Ohio opposite the present city of Portsmouth. In about

1767 a great flood in the Ohio overran their towns and they moved up to Chillicothe.

Governor Dinwiddie in a letter to Major Andrew Lewis, dated February 6th, 1756, and which seems to have been written but a few days before the starting of the Sandy expedition, says: "The distance by Evans' map is not two hundred miles to the upper towns of the Shawnees, however, at once begin your march." This map was made by Lewis Evans, a copy of which can be found in the Library of Congress, and the distance estimated by Governor Dinwiddie from the farther settlements to the Shawnee towns on the Ohio River, at the mouth of the Scioto, was not far from correct.

Richard Pearis was a captain of militia of Augusta County and further had charge of a company of friendly Cherokee Indians. He is often referred to in the letters of Governor Dinwiddie. On page 266 of "The Dinwiddie Papers," note 161, Richard Pearis is described as an Indian trader, located on Holstein River, who acted as interpreter, and was afterwards commissioned a captain to command a company of Indians. The name is spelled in other instances, "Paris", and has respected representatives in Augusta County today. In a letter of Governor Dinwiddie's to Major Andrew Lewis, dated February 16th, 1756, he says: "I am glad the Cherokees are in so high spirits. I desire that you show proper regard and respect to the High Warrior and take care that Mr. Pearis behaves well and keeps sober."

It is undoubtedly true that Mrs. Ingles on her return from captivity in November, 1755, made known to her husband and others, the position of the Indian towns on the Ohio and of the expressed determination of the savages to destroy the white settlements along the New River valley. This led to Captain Ingles' visit to the Governor at Williamsburg to forestall the Indian plans by sending a force of troops to destroy them before they could strike a blow at the settlements.

Mrs. Ingles was not willing to remain on the New River nor even at Vaux's fort, on the Roanoke, nearby where

Shawesville now stands, but insisted that her husband should carry her to a place of greater safety for she was well aware that the Indians would repeat their visits to the settlements and that she and her friends would again be exposed to danger of death or capture.

The fears of Mrs. Ingles were well grounded, for on the very next day after the departure of herself and family from Vaux's fort, in the summer of 1756, it was attacked by the Indians, and the inmates were destroyed or captured and carried away, but two or three afterwards escaped.

The incursions made by the Indians into the frontier settlements and their depredations immediately after Braddock's defeat, led to the organization of the Sandy expedition, under the order of Governor Dinwiddie, and suggested and planned by Captain William Ingles, who accompanied the expedition. Colonel Washington sent Major Andrew Lewis from Winchester to take charge of the forces, which were to attack the Indian towns on the Ohio. Major Lewis' forces rendezvoused at Fort Prince George on the Roanoke, near where Salem, Virginia, now stands. The force consisted of about 340 men. Among the officers were Captains Peter Hogg, John Smith, William Preston, Archibald Alexander, Robert Breckinridge, Obediah Woodson, John Montgomery and ———— Dunlap, together with a company of friendly Indians under Captain Richard Pearis. The company commanded by Captain Hogg failed to attend at the appointed time, and Major Lewis after delaying a week for its arrival, marched forward, expecting to be overtaken by it.

It was important to the success of the expedition that it should not be discovered by the Indians until it was too late for them to take measures to thwart it; therefore, instead of taking the more public route by way of the Great Kanawha, Major Lewis selected the route most likely to keep his movements concealed from the enemy. While it would seem important, yet Major Lewis made no report of the expedition; if so it has not been published. Yet we are not without fairly full information on the subject. The author being so fortunate as to get a copy in part of Captain William Preston's journal, kept by him on this expedition, which will be hereinafter copied. The route by which Lewis with his men reached the mouth of the Sandy, has been stated by different writers, no two agreeing, and none strictly correct. See Withers. Bord. Warf. Hale's Trans-Alleghany Pioneers. Peyton's His. of Augusta. Lewis' His. of W. Va. His. Southwest Va. by Summers.

We will let Captain William Preston tell the story as written down by him at the time.

"Monday, ye 9th day of February, 1756,

"In persuance to ye orders of Major Lewis, dated the 4th inst., I marched from Fort Prince George, with my two Lieutenants, 2 Serjeants, 3 Corporals, and 25 Privates. We had one waggon load of dry beef, the wt. 2000 lbs. We traveled 15 miles the first day and lodged at the home of Francis Cyphers, on Roanoke, and early on Tuesday morning, being the 10th, we proceeded on our journey as far as Richd. Hall's, about 15 miles.

"Wednesday, the 11th, marched to New River; informed that Capt. Hog's compy was but a little behind us. As we marched by the Cherikee Camp we saluted them by firing off guns, which they returned in seeming great joy, and afterwards honored us with a war dance.

"Thursday, 12th, heard a sermon preached at Capt. Woodston's Camp, by Rev. Mr. Brown.

"Friday, 13th: reviewed by Major Lewis. The number reviewed was about 340, Indians included, being the Companies of Capt. C. Hog, Preston, Smith, Overton, Woodston, and Pearis, with the Cherikee Indians. Rev. Mr. Craig preached a military sermon, text in Deuteronomy. Two Captain's commissions given by Major Lewis to two head Cherokee Warriors named Yellow Bird and Round O.

"Sat. 14. A company of volunteers, 25 in number, under Capt. Delap (The name is indistinct in the Mss.) joined us.

"Sunday 15th, James Burk brot word that Robert Looney was killed nigh Alex Sawyers, and he had himself one horse shot and five taken away by the Shawnee Indians.

"Monday 16, 40 Indians and 60 white men under command of Capt. Smith and Woodston marched from fort in order to range the woods about Reed Creek; they are to march to Burke's Garden.

"Tuesday 17, Mr. Paul returned from the horse guard (This guard had been left to protect the crossing of New River.)

"Wednesday 18, Capt. Hog's company and Major Lewis march in afternoon.

"Thursday 19, Left Fort Frederick at 10 o'clock: 27 loaded pack horses, got to William Sawyer's: camped on his barn floor.

"Friday 20, Switched one of the soldiers for swearing, which very much incensed the Indian chiefs then present. Advanced to Alex Sawyers, met the Indians who went out with the first division, and Lieutenant Ingles who informed us of the burial of Robt. Looney. Some of our Indians deserted.

Sat. 21, Major Lewis, Capt. Pearis and the interpreter went to Col. Buchanan's place, where they met the Indians who had deserted us, and induced them to return, which they did.

"Sunday 22, Marched to John McFarland's.

"Monday 23, Marched over the mountain to Bear Garden, on North Fork of Holston's river. Lost sundry horses.

"Tuesday 24, Crossed two mountains and arrived at Burke's Garden. Had plenty of potatoes which the soldiers gathered in the deserted plantations.

"Wednesday 25, Remained in Camp.

"Burke's Garden is a tract of land of 5000 or 6000 acres, as rich and fertile as any I ever saw, as well watered with many beautiful streams, and is surrounded with mountains almost impassible.

"Thursday 26, Marched early, crossed three large mountains, arrived at head of Clinch. Our hunters found no game.

"Friday 27, Lay by on account of rain. Hunters killed three or four bears.

"Saturday 28, passed several branches of Clinch and at length got to head of Sandy Creek, where we met with great trouble and fatigue, occasioned by heavy rain, and driving our baggage horses down said creek, which we crossed 20 times that evening. Killed three buffalos and some deer.

"Sunday 29, In 15 miles passed the creek 66 times. Sundry horses were left, not being able to carry loads any further. Encamped at a cane swamp. This creek has been much frequented by Indians both traveling and hunting on it, and from many late signs I am apprehensive that Starnicker—the prisoners taken with him were carried this way.

"Monday 1st, of March (1756)

"Marched at 9 o'k. In 4 miles left the Creek to Eastward, passed a gap in high ridge, and came upon a branch, where we camped in a large bend in a prominent place. Sent Abrim Bledsher to hunt.

"Tuesday 2, Discovered recent signs of enemy Indians hunting camp: our Cherikees ranged the woods. Moved down the branch and came to the main creek where we camped. Put on half rations. Came into the Cole (Coal) land: crossed the river 8 times.

"Wednesday 3. Marched only 9 or 10 miles being much retarded by the river and mountains which closed in on both sides, which made our marching very difficult, and more so as each man had but half pound of flour and no meat but what we could kill and that was very scarce.

"Thursday 4, Lost many horses that wandered off and could not be found. Marched 6 miles. Hunters had no success, and nothing but hunger and fatigue appears to us.

"Friday 5, With great difficulty marched 15 miles: the river being very deep and often to cross, nearly killed the men, as they were in utmost extremity for want of provisions. My fourth horse expired.

"Saturday 6, As we encamped nigh the forks of the river, we only crossed the S. E. fork and encamped. The Cherikees made bark canoes to carry themselves down the river. Major Lewis had a large canoe made to carry the amunition and small remnant of flour. The men murmured much for want of provisions and numbers threatened to return home.

"Sunday 7, Marched to a place 6 miles below the forks of the river. Mountains very high and no appearance of level country, which greatly discouraged the men. The men were faint and weak with hunger and could not travel the mountains and wade the river as formerly, there was no game in the mountains, nor appearance of level country, and their half pound of flour would not support them, and that would soon be gone, and they intended to leave next morning and go home. I proposed to kill the horses to eat, which they refused. They said that might do to support them if they were on their way home, but it was not a diet proper to sustain men on a long march against the enemy. They finally agreed to make one more trial down the river.

"Monday 8, Proceeded down the river about 3 miles, where the mountains closed so nigh the water that we could not pass: went up a branch, crossed a very high mountain, and down another branch to the river, where we met a party of men who had been at the river and could not get down any further. Crossed another mountain to the head of another branch which we followed several miles to the river and camped. Some of the volunteers killed two elk, which they divided with us.

"Tuesday 9, The volunteers killed two buffalos and an elk, which helped us some, but the men are very faint and continue to murmur. Did not move this day waiting for Major Lewis, and the rest of the men who were left at the forks of the river, supposed 15 miles.

"Wednesday 10, Sent a messenger with a letter to Major Lewis to come at once, as the men were determined to desert and go home.

"Thursday 11th, 8 of Capt. Smith's men went off and Bledsher and ————.

"Friday 12, 8 or 10 of my Company being ready to leave, I was obliged to disarm them and take their blankets from them by force. Capt. Woodson arrived, with some of his company, and informed us that his canoe overset, and lost his tents and every thing of value. Major Lewis' canoe was sunk in the river and he and Capt. Overton and Lieut. Gun had to swim for their lives: they lost every thing of value, particularly 5 or 6 guns.

"Major Lewis, Lieut. McNeal and Mr. Chen arrived, and informed us of their shipwreck. He had seen Bledsher and 9 other men going off.

"Saturday 13th, Major Lewis ordered each Capt. to call his company together immediately, which was done. He made a speech to them, but they were obstinate.

"Major Lewis stepped off some yrads, and desired all that were willing to share his fate, to go with him. All the officers, and some privates, not above 20 or 30, joined him. Then Montgomery's volunteers marched off, and were immediately followed by my company and Smith's: 4 private men and my lieutenants stayed with me.

"Major Lewis spoke to Old Autocity, who was much grieved to see the men desert, who said that he was willing to proceed, but some of his warriors and young men were yet behind, and he was doubtful about them. Mr. Dunlap's volunteers went off in the afternoon.

"An account of miles marched each day on our journey to the Shawnees' towns.

	Miles.
"From F. P. George to Cyphers'	15
2nd day to R. Hall's	15
3rd day to F. A. Frederick	15
19th Feb. to Wm. Sawyers	20
20th Feb. to McCaul's	13
Sunday 22, to McFarland's	7
Monday 23 to Bear Garden	10
Tuesday 24 to Burke's Garden	9
Thursday 26, to head of Clinch	10
Saturday 28, to head of Sandy Creek	10
Sunday 29, down Sandy Creek	12
Monday 1st, March Sandy Creek	6
Tuesday 2, Sandy Creek	3
Wednesday 3rd, Sandy Creek	10
Friday 5, Sandy Creek	15
Saturday 6, Sandy Creek	2
Sunday 7, Sandy Creek	7
Monday 8, (Here the journal ends M,)	7

It will appear by a close examination of this journal by one fully acquainted with the territory from the head waters of the Clinch to the mouth of the Dry Fork of the Tug Fork of Sandy, where the Station of Iaeger on the line of the Norfolk and Western Railway now stands, over which territory the expedition passed, that it proceeded by way of one of the North branches of the Clinch through the farm of the late W. G. Mustard in Tazewell County, thence through Maxwell's Gap on to the waters of Horse Pen Creek, thence down the same to Jacob's Fork, and down the same to the Low gap or Cane Brake in the ridge dividing the waters of Jacob's Fork from Dry Fork, and a little South and West of the residence of Rev. R. B. Godbey, on Jacob's Fork, thence down the Dry Fork to its junction with the Tug or main fork.

Captain Hogg and his company finally overtook Major Lewis. At the same time a messenger arrived directing the return

of the expedition. It however proceeded to the mouth of the
Sandy, and some of the officers urged the crossing of the Ohio
river, but it was finally decided to obey the summons to return. The weather was extremely cold, snow having fallen
the march was a difficult one, and the men stopping at Burning Spring (Warfield) took strips of the hides of the buffalos
and broiled them in the burning gas. They cut them into
strips or thugs, hence the name of Tug River. On leaving the
spring they scattered through the mountains and many of
them perished, either frozen to death, starved or killed by the
Indians. They left however, some marks by the way, cutting
their names on trees on the route pursued by them, notably
at the forks of Big Coal and Clear Fork of that River, but
these trees have been destroyed in recent years.

As already stated, if Major Lewis ever made any written
report of this expedition, the author has been unable to find
it or any trace of it, and therefore we are without information
as to the number of men lost on the expedition.

The Indians had discovered that Lewis and his men were
on the Sandy or about the mouth of it, and some of them followed the whites for a distance on their way homeward.

A second Sandy expedition seems to have been contemplat-
ed, but for some reason abandoned.

Reference has already been made to that splendid body of
land situate in the southeastern part of the present County
of Tazewell, about fourteen miles from the Court House thereof and known as Burke's Garden. Colonel William Preston,
as we have seen from his journal, gives a short description of
this body of land. It appears that Lewis and his men saw
this Garden within less than three years after Burke had discovered it. Whether between 1753 and 1756 Ingles and Patton were therein surveying lands for the Loyal Company does
not certainly appear.

Burke moved with his family into the Garden in 1754, (1)

_____

(1) A white thorn bush, sprout from an older bush, at a spring,
near to the residence of Mr. Rufus Thompson, in Burke's Garden, is
pointed out as the spot where Burke spent his first night in the Garden.

cleared up some land, and planted a crop, including potatoes, and in the fall of 1755 was driven out on account of fear of Indians, and left his crop of potatoes in the ground which Lewis' men found the next spring and appropriated. Burke had killed a large number of deer, elk and bear, and had tanned a number of the hides, which he took with him when he left in the fall of 1755. On his way out with his family he camped one night in an old hunter's cabin near what is now Sharon Springs in the now County of Bland, Virginia. The Indians followed him, and on their way killed two hunters in their camp. On approaching Burke's cabin and seeing several horses, and the tanned hides rolled up in the cabin, they came to the conclusion that there were too many people for them to attack, and contented themselves with the cutting of the throat of one of Burke's horses. One of the evidences adduced that Burke had removed with his family to this Garden, and lived there in 1755, is, that no mention of him or of his family is made in the history of the destruction of the Drapers Maedows settlers by the Indians on the 8th day of July, 1755, while all the other settlers are accounted for. Burke was not killed in the Garden. He was living and seen by Captain Preston and his men on the 15th day of February, 1756, when he reported to Major Lewis the killing by the Indians of a man by the name of Robert Looney near Alexander Sawyer's. Burke with his family never returned to the Garden to live, first, because the Loyal Company claimed the land and had Ingles and Patton to survey it. Second, Burke got not one foot of it, and, third; he removed South where he died. Many of his descendants, among them the Snidows, of Giles County, still reside in the New River Valley, and they seem never to have heard of the story that Burke was killed in the Garden. Again Morris Griffith, the step son of Burke, who is reputed to have first seen the Garden, was captured at Vaux's Fort in the Summer of 1756, but escaped.

The failure of the Sandy expedition gave encouragement to the Indians and they prepared to assault more fiercely the border white settlements during the Spring, Summer and Fall months of 1756.

Vaux Fort situated on the Roanoke near where Shawesville Station on the line of the Norfolk and Western Railway Company now stands, was built prior to 1756, and destroyed in the early Summer of that year.

On September 8th, 1756, Governor Dinwiddie, (Dinwiddie Papers) writes to Captain Hogg as follows: "I received yours of the 25th ult., and observe you have made a beginning to build a fort near Vass's plantation, which is well. I am of the opinion that three forts are necessary, as the one you are constructing may be sufficient, as I hear Col. Washington is with you, counsel with him thereon." This letter shows that Colonel George Washington was with Captain Hogg on the Roanoke at Vass's Fort when the above letter was written.

From the beginning of the French and Indian war in 1753 up to the close of the war in the year 1763, the border country from the lakes to the mountains of North Carolina was scourged by Indian forays and incursions, and the few inhabitants were kept in almost constant fear.

Preston's Journal shows that several settlements had been made along Peak, Reed and other Creeks West of New River prior to 1756. Among the parties he names are William Sawyers, Alexander Sawyers, and John McFarland, and Dr. Walker mentions Samuel Stalnaker as on the Holston on the 24th of March, 1750, when he and Mr. Powell helped him to raise a house.

Hale in his Trans Alleghany Pioneers states that seven families were settled West of New River in 1754, but gives the names of but two, Reed and McCorkle.

The New River lead mines were discovered by Colonel Chiswell in 1757.

About the year of 1758 Joseph Howe, and a little later James Hoge settled in the Back Creek Valley.

In 1760 an Indian marauding party penetrated the New River settlements, and passing over into what is now Bedford

County, committed murders and other depredations and on
its return, reaching the vicinity of Ingles' Ferry, was attacked
by Captain William Ingles, Captain Henry Harman, (Harman Ms.) and others. One white man and six or seven Indians were killed, and this was the last Indian foray that ever
succeeded in penetrating so far into the interior. Captain
Henry Harman was a German, born in the Isle of Man, and
first settled in Forsythe County, North Carolina, where he
married Miss Nancy Wilburn, and removed to the New River
Valley about 1758, and settled first on Buchanan's Bottom
(the Major James R. Kent farm, below the present town of
Radford, Virginia); and from thence removed to Walker's
Creek in what is now Bland County, and shortly thereafter
to the Hollybrook farm on Kimberling in the same County.

This name Harman being German, was originally Herman,
and the family of this name that settled in the New River
Valley, except Adam Harman, and in Tazewell County, Virginia, were all from the State of North Carolina. Adam Harman and his family and all by that name that settled on the
Jackson River and in Western Virginia came from the Valley
of Virginia.

In the Fall of the year 1763, about fifty Indian warriors
ascended the Great Sandy, and passed over the present territory of Mercer County on to New River, where they separated,
forming two parties, one going towards the Jackson River,
and the other towards the Roanoke and Catawba settlements.

Pitman, Pack and Swope, trappers on New River, discovered
the trail of these Indians and the route they had taken, suspecting that they were preparing to attack the settlements
just mentioned, they set out, Pitman for Jackson's River and
Pack and Swope for Roanoke, but the Indians reached both
places ahead of them. After killing some people in the Jackson's River settlement and taking some prisoners, the Indians
began a hasty retreat towards the Ohio, pursued by Captain
Audley Paul with a company of twenty men from Fort Dinwiddie, and who followed the Indians up Dunlap's Creek over
on to Indian Creek and New River, to the mouth of Piney

Creek without discovering them, and Captain Paul started
on his return.

The party that had crossed over on to the Roanoke and
Catawba committed some depredations and murders, and captured three prisoners, a Mrs. Katherine Gun, a man by the
name of Jacob Kimberline (who was taken from a creek now
called Kimberling, a branch of Walker's Creek) and another
whose name is not given. This party was being pursued by
Captain William Ingles, Captain Henry Harman and their
men. On the night of the 12th of October, the Indians pursued by Ingles and Harman were discovered by Captain Paul
and his men about midnight, encamped on the North bank of
the New River opposite an island at the mouth of Turkey
Creek (now Indian Creek) in Summers County. Paul's men
fired on them, killed three and wounded several others, one of
whom threw himself into the river to preserve his scalp, the
rest of the party fled hurriedly down the river.

The Snidows came in 1766 and settled in the neighborhood
of Philip Lybrook, near the mouth of Sinking Creek; however
settlements had been made in the Greenbrier section of country by Marlin and Sewell in 1750, and some families came in
1762, but they were massacred by Indians in 1763, and reset-
tlements did not begin in that section until the year of 1769.

The Snidow family mentioned above, were Germans, and
came from Pennsylvania. John, the father, and head of the
family, had in 1765 visited the New River section, and Philip
Lybrook, whom it is supposed had been his neighbor in Pennsylvania. He returned for his family and started with them
for his new home in 1766, but on the road was taken suddenly
and violently ill, from which illness he died. His widow,
Elizabeth, with her children, made her way to the New River
home which had been selected and fixed upon by her husband.
This family later suffered from an Indian attack in which a
part of its members were killed and a part captured. This
family became one of the largest and most influential of the
settlers of the New River Valley.

Settlements began on the head waters of the Clinch in 1766-1767, but as there will be a chapter in this work devoted exclusively to the history of Tazewell County, in which these settlements were made, a statement in full in regard thereto is reserved to be stated in said chapter.

―――――o―――――

CHAPTER III.

1766-1774.

Formation Botetourt County from Augusta in 1769—Cooks, Keeneys and others on Indian Creek and the Greenbrier—Building Forts—Cooks on Indian Creek and Keeneys at Keeney's Knobs—Fort at Lewisburg built—John and Richard Chapman and McKensey settle at mouth of Walker's Creek—Snidows, Lybrooks and Chapmans build fort at the Horse Shoe—Absalom Looney from Looney's Creek explores upper Bluestone waters—Other settlers on the head of Clinch—John McNeil from the Virginia Valley locates at Little Levels—Accompanies General Lewis to the battle of Point Pleasant—Captain James Moore, Samuel Ferguson, the Peerys and others in the battle of the Alamance May 16th, 1771—In 1772 Evan Shelby at King's Meadows, and John Sevier from the Valley, on the Nolichucky—Refugees from the Alamance, from Fairfax County, Virginia, on the Watauga—Over mountain men —Back water men—Peace men—Fincastle County created and courts held at Lead Mines—Daniel Boone, family and party from the Yadkin—Squire Boone a Baptist minister, with the party—On their way to Kentucky are attacked by Indians and party scattered—Daniel and Squire winter near Castleswoods—Dunmore's War begins in the Spring of 1774—Daniel Boone in command of the frontier—Captain William Russell's company from the Clinch —Reece and Moses Bowen with Russell—Evan Shelby, his son Isaac and John Sevier also lead a company—Sevier from North Carolina but supposes he lives in Virginia—Governor Dunmore raises an army and commands northern division—General Andrew Lewis the southern division—March to the mouth of the Kanawha and battle of Point Pleasant—August 7th, 1774, Indians attack the Lybrooks and Snidows at Sinking Creek—Harman's fort —Shannons settle at Poplar Hill, 1774—Grant of Clover Bottom to Mitchell Clay.

Up to and including the year of 1769 the territory covering the New River Valley and the section of the country West thereof, was within the County of Augusta, but in November of that year a county called Botetourt was created, the act to be in effect January 31st, 1769.

The following are the boundary lines of the county of Botetourt as given in the Act: "That from and after the 31st day of January next ensuing, the said parish and county of Augusta be divided into two counties and parishes by a line beginning at the Blue Ridge, running north 55 deg. West to the confluence of Mary's Creek (or of South River) with the North branch of the James River; thence, up the same to the South of Kerr's Creek (Carr's Creek) thence, up said creek to the mountain; thence, North 45 deg. West as far as the courts of the two counties shall extend it."

By reference to the map of Virginia it will be seen that a line 45 deg. West extended from the mountain at the head of Kerr's Creek will reach the Ohio river at some point not far from the present city of Wheeling, and will cover largely that vast territory which had formerly belonged to Augusta County.

Between the years 1769 and 1774, settlements had been made by the Cooks from the Virginia Valley on Indian Creek (one of their number, John, being killed by the Indians), the Woods on Rich Creek, the Grahams on the Greenbrier, and others near Keeney's Knobs. Cook's Fort was on Indian Creek about three miles from New River, Wood's fort on Rich Creek on a farm recently owned by the family of John Karnes, and about 4 miles East of the present village of Peterstown in the County of Monroe. The Keeneys built Keeney's fort near Keeney's Knobs. The Snidows, Lybrooks, Chapmans and McKensey built Snidow's fort at the upper end of the Horseshoe farm on New River, in what is now Giles County. The Hatfields built Hatfield's fort on Big Stony Creek in the now county of Giles on the farm belonging to the late David J. L.

Snidow. The fort at Lewisburg was built in 1770. The Bargers built Barger's fort on Tom's Creek in the now County of Montgomery. Colonel Andrew Donnally built Donnally's fort. Colonel John Stuart built Fort Spring, and Captain Jarrett the Wolf Creek fort, the three last named on the Greenbrier waters.

In 1771 came John Chapman, Richard his brother, and their brother-in-law Moredock O. McKensey with their families from Culpepper County, Virginia, and located at the mouth of Walker's Creek on the New River. The Chapmans and Mc-Kensey, the latter a Scotsman, who had married Jemima, the only sister of the Chapmans, left their Culpepper home in November, 1768, crossed the Blue Ridge into the Valley of Virginia, and remained for more than two years on the Shen-andoah (then called the Sherando) River, and at some time in the year of 1771 fell in with the emigrant bands making their way further West, and even across the Alleghanies. John Chapman erected his cabin on the Northwest side of Walker's Creek at the base of the hill and near the bank of the creek. Richard Chapman and McKensey built on the river bottom above the mouth of the creek.

An adventurer by the name of Absalom Looney in 1771 left his home on Looney's Creek, now in the Rockbridge country, and came over the Alleghanies and explored the upper Blue-stone country, particularly a beautiful valley now in Taze-well County, Virginia, and which in part bears the name of its discoverer, being called "Abb's Valley." Looney remained in this valley and adjacent territory for two or three years, and had for his refuge and hiding place from the savages and wild beasts a cave or rather an opening in the limestone rocks, for it was not deep under ground. This hiding place was pointed out to the author by William T. Moore, Esq., whose grandfather settled nearby in 1777. The cave referred to is a few yards south of the spot whereon now stands Moore's Memorial Methodist Church. On Looney's return to his home he gave such glowing description of this valley that one of his neighbors, Captain James Moore, was induced to make a journey to see it. He came in 1776 or 1777 alone, from his home with no companians nor weapons, save his rifle gun, tomahawk and butcher knife, the hunter's usual weapons of offense and defense. Looney had furnished him such a description of the valley as to enable him to find the way without difficulty. Further description of Captain Moore's journey and settlement in this valley, and the destruction of his family by Indians will be related in the Chapter on the history of Tazewell County.

In 1773 John McNeil from the lower Virginia valley, settled in the Little Levels on the waters of the Greenbrier, now in Pocahontas County, West Virginia. McNeil accompanied General Lewis' army to the battle of Point Pleasant, and was a participant therein.

John Sevier of French extraction, who established and gave name to the town of New Market in the Valley of Virginia, and kept a store in that town, having made the acquaintance of Evan Shelby of King's Meadows, now Bristol, Tennessee-Virginia, made in 1772 a visit to Shelby, and went with him to the waters of the Watauga, finding there among the settlers persons who had fought in the battle of the Alamance, and some from the County of Fairfax, Virginia. These people later, together with settlers on the Holstein, were called by some, Backwater men, Over mountain men, and Peace men, as some of them at least opposed the war with Great Britain. But when the tug of war did come, they were almost without exception found on the American side, and many of them served in the patriot army. Sevier made up his mind to locate in this section, and accordingly did, fixing his residence upon the Nolichuckey, and he was afterwards known as, and called "Nolichuckey Jack." He was a brave, courageous and intelligent man, and figured extensively in the border wars, and in the formation of the State of Franklin, of which he was the Governor four years; and was afterwards Governor of the State of Tennessee for a number of years.

Owing to the remote settlements west of the Alleghanies
and along the New River waters and farther to the west,
and the difficulties the inhabitants had of reaching the courts
held at Fincastle in Botetourt County, the inhabitants petitioned the Legislature of Virginia for the formation of a
new county, the prayer of which petition was granted in
February, 1772. The county of Fincastle was created out
of Botetourt; with the following boundary lines as given in
the act creating same.

"That from and after the first day of December next, the
said county of Botetourt shall be divided into two distinct
Counties, that is to say all that part of said county within
a line to run up the east side of New River to the south of
Culbertson's Creek, thence, a direct line to the Catawba road,
where it crosses the dividing ridge between the north of the
Roanoke and the waters of New River; thence, with the top
of the ridge to the Bent, where it turns eastwardly; thence,
a south course to the top of Blue Ridge mountains, shall be
established as one distinct county and called and known by
the name of Fincastle; and that the other part thereof, which
lies to the east and north east of the said line, shall be one
distinct county and retain the name of Botetourt.

Daniel Boone from the Yadkin River, North Carolina, visited the Holstein settlements in 1760 and again in 1773, and
engaged in hunting along the waters of the Tennessee, performing his usual feat of "Cilling a bar," and proclaiming
the fact by inscribing it on a beech tree. Several trees are
said to have been found with similar inscriptions. A brief
sketch of the life of Boone is given by Dr. John P. Hale, in
the Trans-Alleghany Pioneers. It may be well to add, however, that in the fall of 1773 the Boones, with five other families
set out from their home on the Yadkin to go to Kentucky,
and were joined in Powell's Valley by William Bryan, their
brother-in-law, and forty other people. That while this body
of emigrants was leisurely traveling through the Valley, a
small company under James Boone, Daniel's eldest son, left

the main body and went to the home of William Russell to
procure provisions, and on the 9th of October James Boone
and his company, among the number being Russell's son, Henry, and two slaves, encamped a few miles in the rear of the
main body. At this point they were the next day waylaid by
a small party of Shawnee and Cherokee Indians, who were
supposed to be at peace with the white settlers. On the
morning of the 10th James Boone and his entire company
were captured, and after cruel torture were slaughtered. After this occurrence Daniel Boone's company broke up and returned to the settlements, and Daniel and his family returned
to the home of William Russell near Castleswoods on Clinch
river, and spent the winter of 1773-1774 in that neighborhood.
"Summers' His. South West Va." In addition to these statements made by Summers, it may be added upon well authenticated testimony that Squire Boone, a brother of Daniel, with
his family were with this party of emigrants and remained
over the same winter in the neighborhood of William Russell,
and his brother Daniel and his family. Squire Boone was
a Missionary Baptist minister, and during his stay at or near
Castle's-woods, planted the germ from which sprang Castle's-
woods Baptist church which exists to this day. Again it is
known that Squire Boone married the first white couple that
were married in Kentucky.

With the opening of the Spring of 1774 the Indians began
their depredations upon the border, and Governor Dunmore
began the raising and mobilizing of a Virginian army to punish the savages. The army was divided into two divisions, the
northern division was commanded by Dunmore himself, the
southern division commanded by Brg. General Andrew Lewis,
and its appointed place of rendezvous was at Camp Union
(now Lewisburg, West Virginia). To this southern division
belonged Colonel Wililam Christian's regiment of Fincastle
men, to which was attached a company from the lower Clinch
commanded by Captain William Russell, which in August,
1774, marched for the place of rendezvous, joining en route

on New River the regiment to which it belonged. It is believed that the line of march of Russell's company was up the Clinch and down the East river, passing the site of the present city of Bluefield, West Virginia. In Russell's Company were Reece Bowen, Moses Bowen, the latter dying from small pox on the expedition, and others from their neighborhood in the Cove, in the now County of Tazewell. Daniel Boone was left in command of Russell's fort and the border in the absence of Russell and his men. At this time Reece Bowen had a fort at Maiden Spring, which was located on the farm of Mr. Reece Bowen, a great grand son of the Reece Bowen, first above mentioned. In the absence of Captain Russell and his company, the neighbors of Reece Bowen had gathered in his fort, they were principally, if not altogether, women and children. Mrs. Bowen went out in search of her cows, and in a marsh she discovered Indian signs, immediately returned to the fort, and dressed up in male attire a negro woman, gave her a rifle gun, and caused her to walk to and fro in front of the door or gate to the fort. The ruse succeeded, and the fort was not attacked.

Between the years of 1765 and the Spring of 1774 there had been peace along the border -between the whites and the Indians. A difference of opinion exists as to the causes which led to Dunmore's War. Some have asserted that it had its origin in the murder of some Indians on the Ohio river both above and below Wheeling in the Spring of the latter mentioned year. Others suppose it to have been produced by the instigation of the British emissaries and the influence of Canadian traders. It it certain, however, that numerous outrages were committed upon the Indians by the whites, and the war was the natural outgrowth of the strained relations which had long existed between the Savages and the white colonists in their midst. Also immediately after the perpetration of the outrages, Indians in numerous bands and marauding parties attacked the border settlements and bloodshed and murder were the results.

One of these marauding parties left the north bank of the
Ohio river making their way up to the settlements of the Lybrooks, Chapmans and Snidows, and after prowling around
several days it was discovered by some of the settlers that they
were in the neighborhood, and thereupon most of the families
took refuge in the forts for safety. The family of John Chapman abondoned their house and went to the fort. The Indians
burned his house which was the second they had destroyed for
him. It has already been stated that the Chapmans, Lybrooks,
McKenseys and Snidows had a fort on the bank of New river,
at the extreme upper end of the farm now known as the Horse
shoe, and that Adam Harman had a fort or block house at Gunpowder Spring, in which his family and perhaps others had taken shelter. Philip Lybrook and a man by the name of Mc-
Griff had built their cabins in a little bottom just below the
mouth of Sinking creek on the farm lately known as that of
Croft or Hale, and were engaged in the cultivation of a small
crop of corn on the bottom lands. Mr. Lybrook had built a
small mill on the spring branch. As was the custom in that
day, when people were few in the country, for the young people
to assemble or get together on Sunday, and so it happened that
on Sunday the 7th day of August, 1774, that some of the children of Mrs. Elizabeth Snidow, who has heretofore been mentioned, and a young woman by the name of Scott went on a visit from the fort to Lybrook's and McGriff's. Mr. Lybrook was
busy about his mill, McGriff was in the house, and the young
people and the smaller children were at the river. Two of the
young men, a Snidow and Baltzer Lybrook, were out some distance in the river bathing, and three or four of the little boys
were playing in the water near the bank, and a young woman,
the daughter of Lybrook, was out in the river in a canoe with
some of the small children therein, when an Indian was discovered on the high bank overlooking the brink of the river,
and the alarm was given. The two young men in the river made
for the opposite shore, the Indians in the mean time began to
shoot at them. Being expert swimmers they turned upon their

backs their faces being turned to the Indians, enabled them to
watch their movments. The four small boys playing in the water near the edge of the river, were, viz. Theophilus Snidow,
Jacob Snidow, Thomas McGriff, and John Lybrook. There
were some deep gullies washed down through the banks of the
river, by way of which wild animals had made their way to the
river to get water, and when the little boys discovered the Indians, they attempted to escape by way of these breaks in the
bank, and as they did so the Indians would head them off. Finally an Indian stooped down and placed one hand on his knee
as a rest for his gun, and attempted to shoot one of the young
men in the river, and at this moment John Lybrook, a boy only
eleven years old, ran under the muzzle of his gun and made
for the house. So soon as the Indian fired, he pursued John,
and coming to one of the gullies which had washed out to about
the width of twelve feet, the Indian close upon him, John leap-
ed the gully, and the Indian finding he could not, threw his
lariat at him, striking him on the back of the head, at the same
time tumbling into the gully. By this time the two young men
in the river had reached the opposite shore, and were hidden
behind the trees, and discovering that John had safely crossed
the gully, they cried out to him,"Run John run,"and John ran,
and safely reached the house. While this was transpiring Miss
Lybrook, who was standing in the rear end of the canoe, was
pushing the same to the shore, when an Indian, who was hidden in the weeds on the bank of the river came to the water's
edge and reached out as the canoe touched the bank, and pulled the front end of it to the bank, and stepping therein, with
his war club began striking the little children over their heads
and taking their scalps. The rear end of the canoe being down
stream, and having floated near to the bank Miss Lybrook
sprang out and started to the house, the Indian pursuing her.
Her cries brought to her assistance a large dog, which seized
the Indian and finally threw him, but the Indian succeeded in
getting to his feet, and striking the dog with his club, but in
the meantime, the young woman made her escape. While a

part of the Indians were on the river shooting at the young men in the river, capturing the boys, and killing the children, a part of them had gone to the mill and the house. One shot Mr. Lybrook, breaking his arm and Mr. McGriff shot and mortally wounded one of the Indians, whose remains were years afterwards found under a cliff of rocks not far away from the scene of the tragedy. Three of the little boys, Theophilus Snidow, Thomas McGriff and Jacob Snidow were captured by the Indians and carried away by them, and after traveling with them for some two or three days, they formed a plan of escape, and that was to slip away at night. They reached Pipestem Knob, now in Summers County, and there camped for the night. During the night, and after all things had gotten quiet, two of the boys, Jacob Snidow, and Thomas McGriff slipped away from the camp, not being able to arouse the third boy without awaking the Indians, and thus they were compelled to go without him. After they had gotten a few hundred yards from the camp, knowing that they would probably be pursued, they crawled into a hollow log. In a few minutes thereafter the Indians discovering their absence raised an alarm and went in search of the runaways, and even stood on the log in which the boys were hidden, and in broken English cried "Come back, get lost." Not being able to find the boys, they gave up the hunt and returned to the camp. So soon as everything was quiet, the boys came out of their hiding place, struck through the woods, and made their way to Culbertson's bottom on the New River, where they were afterwards found by some of the scouts from the settlement, and who were in pursuit of the Indians. In this attack Mr. Philip Lybrook was wounded, three of his children, and a young woman by the name of Scott, two of the children, (small girls) of Mrs. Snidow were killed, and the three boys captured. The two young men who were in the river when the attack began, and had reached the farther bank ran across the ridges to the Gunpowder Spring, Harman's fort and halloed across the river to the people in the fort to bring a canoe and take them over, but the people being afraid they

were Indians refused to go. After waiting some time, the
young men being afraid of pursuit by the Indians, plunged into the river,and a young woman, seeing this insisted that they
were white men, ran to the river, jumped into a canoe, and
pushed into the river to met the swimmers, just in time to save
one of them, who was sinking the third time, and who no doubt
had taken a cramp by reason of exertion and overheating in
his run across the ridges. She carried them safely to the fort.
Who this young woman was, inquiry fails to disclose, and now
will never be known, but she deserves a place in history. Colonel William Preston was at the time of this attack, the commandant of the military district of Fincastle, and was then at
Draper's Meadows fort, then called Preston's fort, and writes
a letter about this incident on the 13th day of August, 1774,
which is as follows: "This summer a number of our people have
been killed and captured by the northern Indians. Thomas
Hogg, and two men near the mouth of the Great Kanawha,
Walter Kelly with three or four other persons below the falls
of that river, William Kelly on Muddy creek, a branch of the
Greenbrier river, and a young woman at the same time made
prisoner. One of the scouts, one Shockley, was shot in this
county and on Sunday the 7th of this inst., a party attacked the
house of one Laybrook (Lybrook), about 15 miles from this
place. Old Laybrook was wounded in the arm, three of his
children, one of them a sucking infant, a young woman, a
daughter of one Scott, and a child of one widow Snide (Snidow) were killed. They scalped the children, all but one, and
mangled them in a most cruel manner. Three boys were made
prisoners, two of whom made their escape the Wednesday following, and were found in the woods by the scouts. The Indians
were pursued by the militia, but were not overtaken." The
number of Indians in this marauding party numbered six, and
all this mischief was done by them in a very few minutes. The
Indians escaped with their prisoners though they were pursued,
by a company of men under a Captain Clendenin. The night of
the 7th of August was a sad one at the fort. Mrs. Snidow and

Mrs. Lybrook walked the floor throughout the night, weeping and wringing their hands, and saying that "they knew where the dead children were, but their hearts went out for the little boys, captives." The pursuing party followed the Indians down the New River until they met the escaped captives, and after listening to the story of their escape and calculating that the Indians were too far ahead to be overtaken, returned with the boys to the settlement, reaching there on the Wednesday after their capture on Sunday, much to the delight and joy of their mothers and friends. Theophilus Snidow, the other captive boy, was carried by the Indians to their towns north of the Ohio, and when he had reached his manhood returned to his people, but in delicate health with pulmonary troubles from which he shortly died. (Lybrook and Snidow Mss.)

Poplar Hill on Walker's creek in the now County of Giles was settled in the year of 1774 by Samuel Shannon, who came from Amherst County, Virginia. After a few years residence at that place Mr. Shannon removed to the vicinity of where Nashville, Tennessee, is now situated, leaving behind him his son Thomas, who is the ancestor of the Shannons of Giles County. This Thomas Shannon became one of the most prominent citizens of his day in the district in which he lived, both in civil and military affairs. Occasion will be presented to refer to him again as a captain in command of a company in the Revolutionary war.

In the Spring of 1773 a few individuals had begun to make improvements on the Kanawha river below the falls, and some land adventurers were making surveys in the same section. To these men Captain John Stuart, of Greenbrier, in the spring of 1774, had by direction of Colonel Charles Lewis, sent a messenger to inform them that apprehensions were entertained of serious trouble with the Indians and advising them to remove from that section. When Stuart's messenger arrived at the cabin of Walter Kelly at the mouth of Kelly's Creek on the Kanawha, twelve miles below the falls, he found Captain John Field Culpeper engaged in making surveys. Kelly at once sent his family to the Greenbrier valley under the care of a younger brother, but Captain Field, regarding the apprehension as groundless, determined to remain with Kelly. Very soon after Kelly's family had left the cabin and while yet within hearing of it, a party of Indians approached unperceived and shot Kelly, and rushed to the cabin where they killed a negro woman, and took prisoner a young Scotsman. Captain Field escaped and on his way to the Greenbrier settlement met Captain Stuart with a body of men, who on being informed of what had occured decided to return to the settlements and prepare them for defense.

In a few weeks after this another party of Indians came to the settlements in the Greenbrier section and killed Mr. Kelly, the brother who had conducted the family from Kanawha, and captured his neice. These outrages along the border impelled the Virginia government to take action to repress them, and to punish the Indians by the destruction of their towns north of the Ohio; and it was determined to raise an army for that purpose. The army destined for this expedition was composed of volunteers and militia, mostly from the counties west of the Blue Ridge, and consisted as already stated of two divisions. Lord Dunmore in person took command of the troops raised in Frederick and Dunmore (the latter now Shenandoah), counties and the southern division composed of different companies raised in Botetourt, Augusta and Fincastle with one company under Captain Field from the County of Culpeper, east of the Blue Ridge, and two companies from the Holstein and Watauga settlements under Captains Evan Shelby and Herbert, and a company under Captain William Russell from the Clinch, and an independant company from Bedford under Captain Buford. These latter companies formed a part of the forces to be commanded by Colonel William Christian. Near the first day of September the troops commanded by General Lewis rendezvoused at camp Union, now Lewisburg, and consisted of two regiments commanded by Colonel William Fleming of Botetourt, and Colonel Charles Lewis of Augusta, and numbering about four hundred men each. The third regiment, under Colonel William Christian, was composed as above stated. The force under General Lewis consisted of about eleven hundred men, and set out on its march to the mouth of the Kanawha on the eleventh day of Sepetember, 1774. The northern division of the army composed as herein before stated was under the immediate command of Colonel Adam Stephens. With this division was Lord Dunmore and Major John Connoly. Taking into consideration the forces already in the field under Major Augus McDonald and Captain William Crawford,this northern division numbered some twelve hundred (1200) men; along with which as scouts, were George Rogers Clark, Simon Kenton and Michael Cresap. The country between Camp Union and the mouth of the Kanawha river was a trackless forest so rough, rugged and mountainous as to render the march of the army exceedingly tedious and laborious. Captain Mathew Arbuckle, who had been on the Kanawha some years previous, became the guide for Lewis's army and after a march of several days it reached the Ohio river on the sixth day of October, and fixed its encampment on the point of land between that river and the Great Kanawha. Owing to some difference between General Lewis and Colonel Field as to priority of rank, and Field being in command of an independant volunteer company not raised by the order of Governor Dunmore, but brought into the field by his own exertion, after his escape from the Indians at Kelly's, induced him to separate his men from the main body of the army on its march and to take a different route or way than the one pursued by it, depending largely on his knowledge of the country to lead him by a practicable route to the river. While Field's company was encamped on the banks of the Little Meadow river, a branch of the Gauley, two of his men, Clay and Coward were sent out to hunt deer for the company and were attacked by the Indians, Clay was killed, but Coward made his way back to camp, first having killed one of the Indians. No doubt these Indians were simply spies watching the movements of Lewis's army and the one who escaped was able to make report to his fellows on the Ohio.

Early on the morning of Monday, the tenth (10) day of October, two soldiers left the camp and proceeded up the Ohio in quest of deer. When they had gone about two miles from the camp, they unexpectedly came in sight of a large number of Indians rising from their encampment, and who discovering the two hunters fired upon them and killed one. The other escaped unhurt, and running to the camp communicated the intelligence, "that he had seen a body of the enemy, covering four acres of ground as closely as they could stand by the side of each other." There is a difference in authors who have written upon the subject as to who these two men were. Withers in his Chronicles says, that they were James Mooney, of Russell's company, and Joseph Hughey, of Shelby's company, and that Hughey was killed by a shot fired by Tavenour Russ, a white renagade in Cornstalk's party; while, Haywood the author of the Civil History of Tennessee says, these men were James Robertson and Valentine Sevier, of Shelby's company. Both accounts may be correct in this, that there may have been four men out hunting deer, instead of two.

The main part of the army was immediately ordered out by General Lewis, one wing commanded by Colonel Charles Lewis and the other by Colonel William Fleming. Forming in two lines they had proceeded for a short distance when they met the Indians, and the fierce combat began which lasted throughout the day and finally resulted in the withdrawal of the Indian army. The loss on the part of the Virginians was severe in officers and men, being seventy five (75) killed and one hundred and forty (140) wounded.

The following gentlemen with others of high reputation in private life, were officers in the Battle of Point Pleasant. General Isaac Shelby, the first Governor of Kentucky, and afterwards secretary of war; General Evan Shelby one of the most favorite citizens of Tennessee;- Colonel William Fleming, and

acting governor of Virginia during the revolutionary war;-
General Andrew Moore, of Rockbridge, the first man ever elected in Virginia from the country west of the Blue Ridge to the
senate of the United States; Colonel John Stuart, of Greenbrier; General Tate, of Washington county, Virignia; Colonel William McKee, of Lincoln county, Kentucky; Colonel
John Steele, at one time governor of the territory of Mississippi; Colonel Charles Camron, of Bath; General Bazeleel Wells,
of Ohio, and General George Mathews, a distinguished officer in
the war of the Revolution, the hero of Brandywine, Germantown and Guilford, Governor of Georgia, and a senator from
that state in the Congress of the United States. The salvation
of the American army at Germantown is ascribed in Johnston's
life of General Greene, to the bravery and good conduct of two
regiments, one of which was commanded by General, then Colonel Matthews.

In this battle of Point Pleasant was John Sevier, who became a most distinguished citizen of Tennessee, and who upon
entering upon the expedition to Point Pleasant regarded and
believed himself to be a citizen of and living in Virginia, when
in fact, he at that time was within the territory of North Carolina.

Another distinguished man in this battle was Captain William Russel, in whose company was Reece Bowen, who distinguished himself in the battle at King's Mountain in which he
laid down his life for his country.

The battles of the Alamance and Point Pleasant were in re
ality the opening battles of the American revolution, but be
hind the battle of Point Pleasant, and which urged it on and
brought it about were British emissaries, who had doubtless
urged the Indians on to deeds of bloodshed and murder with
the view and set purpose of destroying the colonists.

No attempt has been made herein to give full details of this
last mentioned battle as this has been fully done by others.
Although a short respite occurred after the battle, the years following 1774 were filled with horrors beyond description. All

along the border settlements the savages made repeated forays, attacking the defenseless inhabitants, killing, plundering, burning and ravaging the country.

On the twenty fifth day of April, 1774, there was granted by Dunmore, Royal Governor of Virginia, to Mitchell Clay assignee of Lieutenant John Draper, a tract of eight hundred acres of land on the Bluestone creek in Fincastle county; this tract was then known and is still known as the "Clover Bottom," situated about five miles north of Princeton the present county seat of Mercer county. It is a very beautiful, rich body of bottom land, and one of the most valuable tracts to be found in this section of the country. By the terms of this grant, a copy of which is on file in the clerk's office of the county court of Mercer county, the grantee was to take possession of this tract of land within three years from the date of the grant. Mitchell Clay, at the date of the grant, lived in the county of Franklin, Virginia, and exchanged a negro woman and her children to John Draper for this land and took from Draper an assignment of the plat and certificate of survey, upon which the grant was issued to Clay as the assignee. The land script or warrant upon which the survey was based, was issued to Lieutenant John Draper for services rendered by him in the French and Indian war.

—————o—————

CHAPTER IV.

1775-1794.

Mitchell Clay and family settled on Clover Bottom—Mathew French and family settle on Wolf Creek—Declaration of the Fincastle men—Fincastle County abolished and Montgomery, Washington and Kentucky Counties created—Captain James Moore visits Abb's Valley—Peter Wright, the hunter, in the northern valleys of Peter's and East River Mountains—Greenbrier County created and its bounaries—Rev. John Alderson in the Greenbrier Valley—Joseph Cloyd settles on Back Creek—The family of

Colonel James Graham attacked by Indians—Donnally's
Fort attacked—Moredock O. McKensey and family at-
tacked by Indians—Captain Thomas Burke, Michael
Woods, John Floyd, and John Lucas in command of the
Forts 1777-78—Lybrooks, Chapmans, Snidows and others
on the frontier—Edward Hale and Joseph Hare in New
River Valley 1779—Tory uprising on upper New River
suppressed by Cloyd, Campbell, Crockett and Cleveland—
David Johnson and family, from Culpeper County, settles
in the New River Valley—Illinois County created—Thom-
as Ingles locates in Wright's Valley and removes to Burke's
Garden—In September 1779 John Pauley and wife and
others attacked by Indians on East River—1780, John
Toney and family, from lower Virginia, settle at the mouth
of East River—Family by name of Christian settle on East
River—John G. Davidson and Richard Bailey with their
families settle at Beaver Pond—William Wilburn and David Hughes, from North Carolina, and John and Benjamine
White, from Amherst County, Virginia, settle on Sugar
Run—Major Joseph Cloyd in October 1780 leads troops to
North Carolina and fights battles at Shallow Ford of Yadkin, Captain Geo. Pearis wounded—Battle of King's Mountain, part of Montgomery county men killed in this battle
under Lieutenants Reece Bowen and James Moore, Bow-
en killed in action—Battles of Wetzel's Mill and Guilford
court house—Captain Thomas Shannon leads a company
of New River Valley men in these battles—Captain Geo.
Pearis settles on New River in the spring of 1782—Adam
Caperton killed at Estill's defeat—The country alarmed
by the attack on Thomas Ingles, military called out—
Swarms of emigrants cross the Alleghanies in 1782-3-4
and settle in part in New River Valley, and others go to
Kentucky—Peters, Walker, Smith, Stowers and others
come in 1782—Indian raiding pary penetrate the Bluestone and upper Wolf Creek section, steal horses and escape—Mitchell Clay's family attacked by Indians at Clover Bottom in 1783—Captain Geo. Pearis kills an Indian
on New River—James Moore, Jr., captured by Indians
in Abb's Valley—New State of Franklin, effort to enlarge its boundaries by Campbell and others—Russell
county created in 1785—Captain James Moore and his
family attacked by forty Shawnee Indians in 1786 and
killed, captured and destroyed—1787, Federal Convention
assembles in Philadelphia, frames a Constitution and sub-
mits it to the States—1788, November 12th, Captain Henry
Harman and his sons fight a battle with the Indians on the
banks of the Tug—Harman's battle song—1789, William

Wheatley killed by Indians—Family of James Roark destroyed—1789, October, Mrs. Virginia Wiley captured—Indian marauding band on head of Clinch and Bluestone in 1790—Birth of Jonathan Bailey—Wythe County created—Family of Andrew Davidson captured by the Indians in 1791, Davidson's long search for his wife and her rescue—Upper Clinch and Bluestone raided by Indians in July, 1792, pursued by Major Robert Crockett, Gilbert killed and Lusk captured—Lusk and Mrs. Wiley escape in the fall of 1792—John G. Davidson murdered by Indians and a white man, one Rice, on the 8th day of March, 1793—Indians pursued, overtaken at Island of Guyandotte, skirmish follows—Petition of Robert Crockett, Joseph Davidson and fifty others to the Governor of Virginia—Alarm in the New River section and Governor calls out a military company under Captain Hugh Caperton which is stationed on the Kanawha, Daniel Boone the commissariat—Marauding party of Indans in 1793, the last on the waters of the upper Clinch and Bluestone—Wayne's great victory over the United Indian Tribes in Ohio on August the twentieth, 1794, brings peace to the Virginia Border—Swarms of land speculators and surveyors on the Ohio Waters, north and west of the settlements—Numerous and large grants of land to Robert Morris, the patriot and financier—Grants to Pollard, Hopkins, Young, McLaughlin, Moore and Beckley, Bliss, Dwight and Granger, Rutter and Etting, Dr. John Dillion, Dewitt Clinton, Robert McCullock, Wilson Cary Nicholas, Wilson, Pickett, Smith and others—Manners and customs of the border people, their religious life—Early Ministers.

Mitchell Clay (1) settled on the Clover Bottom tract of land hereinbefore referred to in the year of 1775. Save one, this was the first white settlement made within what is now the present territorial limits of Mercer County. Andrew Culbertson's settlement on Culbertson's Bottom, which was once a part of the territory of Mercer County, was made twenty years prior to that of Clay on the Clover Bottom. Clay and his family remained on this land undisturbed for a period of about eight years, but were finally attacked by the Indians,

(1) Richard Bailey, son of the elder Richard, the Settler, made about 1790 the first settlement at the mouth of Widemouth Creek on Bluestone, a few miles above where Clay settled in 1775.

part of the family killed, and one captured, a full account of which will be given herein later on.

In the year 1775 Mathew French and his family, from the County of Culpeper, Virginia, settled on Wolf Creek, about six miles from its mouth, now in Giles County, on what is known as the Boyd farm.

Settlements were made by the Bromfields on New River about the mouth of Big Stony Creek, in 1776, and the same year by the Hatfields on said Creek, on what is now known as the David J. L. Snidow place, where the Hatfields erected a fort. On Lick Branch, flowing into Big Stony Creek from the north, In the early days, there was a deer lick, and on an occasion it happened that a Bromfield and Hatfield went the same night to watch this lick, neither knowing that the other was there, or to be there. One took the other for a bear moving around in the brush and shot and killed him.

On the 20th day of January, 1775, the Freemen of Fincastle County assembled at Lead Mines, and made a declaration which was the precursor of that of July 4th, 1776, made by the Congress at Philadelphia. This declaration of the Fincastle men foreshadowing American independence was the first one made in America, and it so fully breathes the spirit of independence and freedom that it is here inserted in full:

"In obedience to the resolves of the Continental Congress a meeting of the freeholders of Fincastle County, in Virginia, was held on the 20th day of January, 1775, and who, after approving of the association formed by that august body in behalf of all the colonies, and subscribing thereto, proceeded to the election of a committee, to see the same carried punctually into execution, when the following gentlemen were nominated:

The Reverend Charles Cummings, Colonel William Preston, Colonel William Christian, Captain Stephen Trigg, Major Arthur Campbell, Major William Ingles, Captain Walter Crockett, Captain John Montgomery, Captain James McGavock, Captain William Campbell, Captain Thomas Madison, Captain Evan Shelby and Lieutenant William Edmondson. After the election, the committee made choice of Colonel William Christian for their chairman, and appointed Mr. David Campbell to be clerk.

The following address was then unanimously agreed to by the people of the County and is as follows:

To the Honourable Peyton Randolph, Esquire, Richard Henry Lee, George Washington, Patrick Henry, Junior, Richard Bland, Benjamin Harrison and Edmund Pendleton, Esquires, the delegates from this colony who attended the Continental Congress held at Philadelphia: Gentlemen: Had it not been for our remote situation, and the Indian war which we were lately engaged in, to chastise these cruel and savage people for the many murders and depredations they have committed amongst us, now happily terminated under the auspices of our present worthy Governor, his Excellency, the Right Honourable Earl of Dunmore, we should have before this time made known to you our thankfulness for the very important services you have rendered to your country, in conjunction with the worthy delegates from the other provinces. Your noble efforts for reconciling the mother country and the colonies, on rational and constitutional principles, and your pasifick, steady and uniform conduct in that arduous work, immortalize you in the annals of your country. We heartily concur in your resolutions and shall, in every instance, strictly and invariably adhere thereto.

We assure you, gentlemen, and all our countrymen, that we are a people whose hearts overflow with love and duty to our lawful Sovereign, George the Third, whose illustrious House for several successive reigns have been the guardians of the civil and religious rights and liberties of British subjects, as settled at the glorious revolution; that we are willing to risk our lives in the service of his Majesty for the support of the Protestant Religion, and the rights and liberties of his subjects, as they have been established by compact, Law and Ancient Charters. We are heartily grieved at the differences which now subsist between the parent state and the colonies, and most urgently wish to see harmony restored on an equitable basis, and by the most lenient measures that can be devised by the heart of man. Many of us and our forefathers left our native land, considering it as a Kingdom subjected to inordinate power; we crossed the Atlantic and explored this then wilderness, bordering on many Natives or Savages and surrounded by mountains almost inaccessible to any but those various Savages, who have insistantly been committing depredations on us since our first settling the Country. These fatigues and dangers were patiently encountered, supported by the pleasing hope of enjoying these rights and liberties which had been granted to Virginians, and denied us in our native country, and of transmitting them inviolate to our posterity; but even to this remote region the hand of enmity and unconstitutional power hath proceeded us to strip of that liberty and property with which God, Nature, and the Rights of Humanity have visited us. We are ready and willing to contribute all in our power for the support of his Majesty's Government if applied to considerately, and when grants are made by our own Representatives, but cannot think of submitting our liberty or property to the power of a venal British Parliament, or the will of a greedy ministry.

We by no means desire to shake off our duty or allegiance to our lawful Sovereign, but on the contrary shall ever glory in being the royal subjects of the Protestant Prince, descended from such illustrious progenitors, so long as we can enjoy the free exercise of our religion as Protestants, and of our liberties and properties as British subjects. But if no pacific measures shall be proposed or adopted by Great Britain, and our enemies will attempt to dragoon us out of these inestimable privileges which we are entitled to as subjects, and to reduce us to a state of slavery, we declare that we are deliberately determined never to surrender them to any power upon earth but at the expense of our lives.

These are real though unpolished sentiments of liberty, and in them we are resolved to live or die."

We are, gentlemen, with the most perfect esteem and re-gard,

Your most obedient servants,"
From the American Archives,4th Series, 1st Volume, page 1166

The men who made and promulgated this declaration were then, and afterwards became among the most distinguished cit-izens who crossed the Alleghanies, and were first and foremost in fomenting and sustaining our glorious revolution. Evidence is not wanting that between 1755 and 1758 some of these men, viz., the Crocketts, McGavocks and others, among them the Gra-hams, Tates and Sawyers had located in the section of country now in Pulaski and Wythe counties, but on account of Indian incursions were driven back into the Rockbridge country from whence they came, and that later they came again and remain-ed permanently. It is generally understood that the Crocketts McGavocks, Grahams and Sawyers were all of Scotch-Irish ex-traction. Among these people were found the bravest and most valiant soldiers in all our wars.

In October, 1776, the general assembly of Virginia by an act abolished the county of Fincastle, and out of its territory crea-ted the counties of Kentucky, Washington and Montgomery. The following is the boundary lines of said counties as given in said act, viz:

"That from and after the last day of December next ensuing, the said county of Fincastle shall be divided into three coun-ties: that is to say, all that part thereof which lies to the south and westward of a line beginning on the Ohio at the mouth of the Great Sandy Creek and running up said creek and the main line beginning at the Cumberland Mountain where the line of north or northeasternly branch thereof to the Great Laurel Ridge or Cumberland Mountain thence, south-westardly along the said mountains to the line of North Carolina, shall be one district County called and known by the name of Kentucky: And all of that part of the County of Fincastle included in the line beginning at the Cumberland Mountain where the line of

Kentucky County intersects the North Carolina line to the top of Iron Mountain, thence along the same eastwardly to the source of the South Fork of the Holstein River: thence, westwardly along the highest part of the highlands, ridges and mountains that divide the waters of the Tennessee from those of the Great Kanawha to the most easterly source of the Clinch River: thence, westwardly along the top of the mountains that divide the waters of the Clinch from those of the Great Kanawha and Sandy Creek to the line of Kentucky County, thence along the same to the beginning, shall be one other district County and called and known by the name of Washington, and all the residue of the County of Fincastle, shall be one other distinct County and shall be called and known by the name of Montgomery.

The Justices to meet and hold Court for Kentucky County at Harrodsburg: Washington at Black's fort: for Montgomery at Fort Chiswell."

The Representatives of Fincastle County in the Convention which assembled at Williamsburg, and which adopted the first republican constitution ever adopted in America, were Arthur Campbell and William Russel. Arthur Campbell was born in the valley of Virginia and William Russell in Culpeper County, Virginia, the latter in 1748 and died in Fayette County, Kentucky, July 23rd, 1825. He was a captain at the battle of Point Pleasant, member of the Virginia legislature of 1789, member of the Kentucky legislature from the foundation of the State to 1808, again in 1823, colonel of the Seventh United States Infantry in 1811, and commanded on the frontiers of Indiana, Illinois and Missouri.

Colonel William Christian was the Representative of Fincastle County in the year of 1776, in the House of Delegates.

In the year of 1776 John McComas and Thomas H. Napier with their families came from western Maryland and settled on the New River below the mouth of Walker's Creek, but subsequently removed to the neighborhood of where Pearisburg, Virginia, is now situated, and they, together with the Hall's, built Fort Branch on the land lately owned by Charles D. French, Esq.

Peter's Mountain was named for Peter Wright, an old backwoodsman who about 1776 explored and hunted along the valleys at its northern base, as well as along the valley at the base of East River Mountain, in which latter valley the present city of Bluefield, West Virginia, is located, and this valley is still called Wright's valley, for the same Peter Wright.

John Alderson, senior, born in England, came to New Jersey about 1737 and married Miss Curtis. Mr. Alderson became a Baptist minister, and finally removed to Rockingham County, Virginia. He had a son John, who also became a Baptist minister, and who married Miss Carroll of Rockingham County. John Alderson, Junior, visited the Greenbrier section of country in 1775, and selected a body of land on the Greenbrier river, which he had surveyed, covering the site of the present town of Alderson in Monroe County. He returned to Rockingham, and in 1777 removed to his land on the Greenbrier and built his cabin where the Alderson Hotel now stands. He was a man of great intelligence and indomitable will and energy, and was the first Baptist preacher who carried the Gospel into that region; he organized the Greenbrier Baptist Church in 1781, and through his instrumentality a number of other churches and the Greenbrier Association were organized. His life was a long and useful one, and made an impress on the people in the section in which he lived that will be felt by generations yet unborn.

On the west bank of the Greenbrier River in the now county of Summers, in the year of 1777 lived Colonel James Graham with his family. One night in the early autumn of that year after the family had retired, a knock was heard at the door, and a voice called in broken English "open door" saying at the same time by way of assurance, "Me no Injun." At the time there was in the house only Colonel Graham and his wife, their children, Elizabeth and a young brother occupied an attached cabin off from the main building. Being refused admittance,

the Indians withdrew a short distance and began firing through
the door with their rifles, and finally discovered in the detached cabin the presence of the two children, they fired through
the clapboards and shattered the little boy's leg with a rifle
ball, and then proceeding into the house, they took both children, and started off seemingly well satisfied with their success,
and went into camp a short distance away. The next morning
the little boy being unable to travel they dashed his brains out
against a tree. The little girl, Elizabeth, only about eight years
old was carried by them into captivity, where she remained
about eight years, and was finally ransomed by her father in
1785. She came home and married a man by the name of
Stodghill, and lived to a ripe old age. The name Stodghill
is called by the people of Monroe and Greenbrier Valley, "Stur-
geon."

The Legislature of Virginia in October, 1777, created the
County of Greenbrier, the act to take effect March first, 1778,
which act reads as follows; "That from and after the first
day of March·next ensuing, the said county and parish of Botetourt, shall be divided by a line beginning on the top of the
ridge which divides the eastern from the western waters, where
the line between Augusta and Botetourt crosses the same, and
running, thence the same course continued N. 55 W. to the
Ohio, thence beginning at the said ridge at the said line of
Botetourt and Augusta, running along the top of said ridge,
passing the Sweet Springs to the top of Peter's Mountain,
thence along the said mountain to the line of Montgomery
County, thence along the same mountain to the Kanawha or
New River, thence down the said river to the Ohio."

Colonel William Preston some time previous to the month
of August, 1774, removed from his estate at Greenfield, near
Amsterdam on the James, to Draper's Meadow, the name of
which as before stated, he changed to Smithfield. There came
with him or shortly thereafter, a young man by the name of
Joseph Cloyd, the son of David Cloyd, whose wife and son
John were murdered by the Indians in March 1764, about five

miles west of the present town of Fincastle, Virginia. As stated in a letter from Mrs. Elizabeth Campbell Adams, of Radford, Virginia, to the author, the maiden name of the wife of David Cloyd, was Miss Margaret Campbell. It had been stated by writers, and perhaps believed by his family that Joseph Cloyd settled on Back Creek in what is now the County of Pulaski, Virginia, about the year of 1775. This is believed to be a mistake as to the year, as the declaration of the Fincastle men was made on the 20th day of January, 1775, and Mr. Cloyd would certainly have been at that meeting unless sick or absent from the country, and it is most likely therefore that had Mr. Cloyd been at home or at the residence of Colonel William Preston he would have been among the men who signed that declaration. The absence of his name indicates in the absence of explanation that he did not settle so early as 1775 on Back Creek, as has been stated.

Mr. Cloyd became one of the most highly honored citizens of the county, both in civic and military affairs. He left behind him wealthy, highly honored, and respected descendants. A full sketch of Joseph Cloyd and his civil and military record will be given in the Appendix to be added to this work.

From the date of the building of Fort Chiswell by Colonel William Byrd in 1758 and from 1759 and after, on and along the upper waters of the New River and on the Holstein, settlements were made by the McGavocks, Campbells, McFarlands, Howes, Hoges, and others, but of which little has been or will be said in this work, as being beyond its scope, and beside this, the history of this people has been so fully, clearly and interestingly presented by Mr. Summers in his "His. of South western Virginia and of Washington County," that he has left little, if anything, additional to be related. The chief. reason for mentioning Mr. Joseph Cloyd is, that his history, and that of his family in part, is so closely connected with the history of the Middle New River people that their history would not be complete without that of Mr. Cloyd.

After the battle of Point Pleasant the Virginia government

built Fort Randolph at the mouth of the Great Kanawha, and there established a military post, in command of which was Captain McKee. In the month of May, 1778, a force of some two hundred Indians attacked this fort, but were finally beaten off by the garrison and compelled to withdraw. The Indians proceeded up the Kanawha and Captain McKee being satisfied from the direction taken by them, that their objective point was the Greenbrier settlements, called for volunteers to go immediately to the settlements and warn the settlers of the approach of the Indians. Phillip Hammond and John Pryor at once volunteered, and being rigged out as Indian Scouts, they reached the settlement safely, and their timely notice, no doubt, saved a terrible massacre.

Before passing to the attack on Donnally's Fort attention will be called to the dangerous situation along the border in the year of 1777. Outrages and murders were committed by the Indians upon the white settlers in many places, and the people found it necessary to flee to the forts for safety. Along the middle settlements on New River from Barger's Fort on Tom's Creek to Donnally's Fort on Rader's Run, and Cook's Fort on Indian Creek the settlers were kept huddled in the forts during almost the whole summer. At Barger's Fort Captain John Floyd was in command of the military, Christian Snidow at the Snidow and Lybrook Fort at the mouth of Sinking Creek, Captain Thomas Burke at Hatfield's Fort on Big Stony Creek, Captain Michael Woods at Woods' Fort, Captain John Lucas at Fort Field on Culbertson's bottom. In these Forts or some of them were John Lybrook, John Chapman, Isaac Chapman and others and some of these people were with Captain John Lucas scouting along the New River about Culbertson's bottom, and stationed at Farley's Fort and Fort Field.

Donnally's Fort was situated about ten miles west of the present town of Lewisburg, on Rader's Run. As soon as the intelligence of the approach of the Indians was given to Donnally by the two scouts he had all the neighbors advised of it, and in the course of the night they gathered into the Fort about twenty one men. He also dispatched a messenger to Captain John Stuart at the fort at Lewisburg advising him of the advance of the Indians. Full preparation was made to resist the attack, which was begun the next morning at an early hour. Captain Stuart with Colonel Samuel Lewis went with sixty men to the relief of Donnally and succeeded in entering the fort without loss. During the attack four of the whites were killed, viz: Pritcher before the attack commenced, James Burns and Alexander Ochiltree as they were coming to the house early in the morning and James Graham while in the fort. Seventeen of the Indians lay dead in the yard, and others of their slain were carried off by them. Until the arrival of Stuart and Lewis, there were twenty one men in the fort which was augmented by their force to eighty seven, while the Indian army exceeded two hundred. The Indians failing in the attack withdrew and retreated. While this attack upon Donnally's Fort was being threatened and made, a number of men gathered at Jarrett's and Keeney's Fort, made up in part of men from Captain Joseph Renfroe's company from Bedford County, among them Josiah Meadows who makes a full statement in regard thereto in his declaration for a pension before the County court of Giles County in the year of 1832.

From the Chapman Ms. in posession of the author it appears that Moredock O. McKensey, who came from Culpeper County with John and Richard Chapman and settled at the mouth of Walker's Creek in 1771, had removed in the spring of 1778 to the mouth of Wolf Creek, on New River, and built his cabin below and near the spring on the bottom, a few yards south of the house in which the late Joseph Hare recently resided. McKensey's family consisted of himself, his wife, his sons Isaac and Henley, and his daughters Sallie, Elizabeth, Margaret, Mary Anne, a nursing child and a hired girl—a Miss Estridge, a daughter of Richard Estridge. The people who were beginning settlements had no enclosed boundaries in which to place their stock, and they belled their horses and turned them out into

the woods. Mr. McKensey had done so with his horses, and
on the morning of the day on which the attack was made upon
his family by the Indians, which was in the month of May of
1778, they could not hear the bells, and supposing that the
horses had attempted to go back to Walker's Creek, the place
from which he had recently removed, he took with him his
eldest son, Isaac, then about twenty years of age, and started to
look for the horses. Henley, the next son, was close by the
house, engaged in making hills in which to plant sweet potatoes. Mr. McKensey and his son went up New River and when
they had reached the top of what is known as Big Hill, near
where Pearisburg station on the line of the Norfolk & Western
Railway Company is now situated, they heard the report of
the discharge of a gun in the direction of their home, and they
immediately turned and ran rapidly back, meeting at Wolf
Creek the Estridge girl, who gave them information as to what
had occurred at the house. The Indians lying in wait and
watching, had seen McKensey and his son go away from the
house, and waiting long enough for them to get a sufficient
distance not to interfere with their outrages, began their work
by shooting young Henley dead on the spot. They then rushed
to the house, but Mrs. McKensey and her oldest daughter, Sallie, closed and barred the door. They had no weapons inside
save an axe. One of the Indians pressed against the door until
he got his head and shoulders inside the same, when the daughter, Sallie, with an axe struck him a blow on the shoulder giving
to him a very dangerous wound. In the meantime another one
of the Indians was also pressing against the door, and it yielded and flew open, and then began a scuffle between the Indian
and Sallie, he attempting to take her as his prisoner. She is
said to have been a most beautiful woman, with long flowing
black hair, and it is supposed that the Indian did not desire to
kill her, but to capture her. She was strong and athletic and
succeeded in repeatedly throwing the Indian to the floor, but
he being in nearly a nude condition, she could not hold him
down. In the last struggle she discovered his butcher knife

in the sheathe in his belt and made an attempt to get it, but failing and the Indian discovering this, he drew the knife and stabbed her through the heart, and then killed the mother. The small child, Mary Anne, had been gathered up by the hired girl, Estridge, who had slipped into the shed of the house, and concealed herself in a large trough made for holding soap. The child began to fret and cry and the young woman fearing that this would disclose to the Indians her hiding place, let go the child, and it ran out into the room, and an Indian caught it by its ankles and feet, and dashed out its brains against the door facing. The babe though scalped, was found by the father when he reached the house still alive, and trying to nurse at the breast of its dead mother. The Indians took the two small girls, Elizabeth and Margaret, aged respectively eight and ten years, prisoners, and then ransacked the house, taking a gourd filled with sugar and a large loaf of bread, which had just been baked by the mother, and departed. As soon as the Indians left Miss Estridge came out from her hiding place, and ran up the river to Wolf Creek, where she met Mr. McKensey and his son as hereinbefore related. On this same morning these Indians had killed Philip Kavanah, and captured Francis Denny, a lad of about fifteen or sixteen years. The Indians did not fire McKensey's house for the reason no doubt, that the smoke would attract his attention or that of some of the settlers in the neighborhood, and cause rapid pursuit before they had time to get away with their prisoners and booty. Leaving McKensey's house they dropped down the river a few hundred yards to Perdue's Mill branch, up which they traveled to its source, crossing over the divide to the house of Mathew French at the Boyd place on Wolf Creek. In passing up Perdue's Mill branch the Indians took out their bloody knives and cut the loaf of bread offering a portion thereof to the little girls, who refused to take or eat it, until finally an Indian went to the branch and washed the knife. When they reached the house of French they found it and the premises deserted, he, having learned that the Indians were in the neighborhood,

had taken his family and fled to the McComas-Napier-Hall
Fort, since known as Fort Branch, situated as hereinbefore
described. Mr. French had left home so hastily as to be unable to take but little with him, leaving behind all of his household furniture, his horses cattle and other stock. The Indians
ripped up his feather beds, and scattered the feathers, threw
down his corn cribs, and turned the stock on his corn, killed
a horse and took off his hide, in which they carried away his
table ware, which consisted of a few pewter plates and cups,
and probably some knives and forks which becoming burden-
some to carry, they buried beside a log on East River Mountain.
They did not set fire to French's house for the same reason
that influenced them not to fire McKensey's house. On leaving
French's house they went directly over East River Mountain, into what is now Mercer County and dropped in at the mouth
of East River, and thence down New River by way of the Bluestone and to Paint Creek, Kanawha, the Ohio, and on to their
towns in the neighborhood of Detroit and the Lakes. The two
McKensey girls remained in captivity for a period of eighteen
years, and were not ransomed, and did not return until after
Wayne's victory in 1794. Their father made two journeys for
them, on the first, he succeeded in getting one of them, but had
to make the second journey before he succeeded in getting the
other. Margaret was transferred by the Shawnees to the Delaware tribe. She was adopted by the Indian Chief Koothum-
pum, and her sister Elizabeth in the family of Petasue, commonly called "Snake."

A few years before Margaret McKensey returned home, a
young Indian chief made love to her and vehemently urged
her to consent to marry him, which she peremptorily refused
The young squaws frequently congratulated her on her fine
offer. She at last became so annoyed by the solicitation of the
young chief that she determined to escape to another village
some seventy miles away, to which her foster sister and brother
had removed. Early one morning she secured a very fine horse
and mounted him and pushed off, making the distance that

day. She complained to her foster sister of the treatment she
had received, who replied, "I will defend you with my life."
The young chief, determined not to be defeated in this way, immediately pursued her and reached the village to which she
had fled, the next day in the afternoon. He soon found her
and told her if she did not immediately consent to become his
wife, he would kill her, she refusing, he made a lunge at her
with a long knife, but her sister threw herself between them
and received a slight wound. The girl instantly seized the
knife and wrenching it from his hand, broke the blade and
threw it away. A furious fight ensued between the foster sister and the Indian, the former telling Margaret to hide herself
which she did. The young woman proved too much for the Indian and gave him a sound whipping, thereupon he departed
and was soon afterwards killed in Wayne's battle with the Indians.

Shortly after the return of Margaret and Elizabeth, the former married a Mr. Benjamine Hall, and the latter Mr. Jonas
Clyburn. Mr. Clyburn with his family removed to Chicago
about the time that that city was being first laid out. Mr.
Hall and his wife lived to old age, dying in Mercer County and
are buried near Princeton. They left numerous and highly
respected descendants among them Mr. David Hall, a lawyer
who long practiced his profession in Mercer and adjoining
counties, Mr. Luther Lybrook Chambers, the present judge
of the circuit court of Mercer, McDowell and Monroe counties
and who is the great grandson of the Margaret McKensey captured by the Indians in 1778. Mr. L. A. Dunn an influential
business man of Bluefield is also a great grandson of Margaret
McKensey.

In 1778 Josiah Meadows, herein before referred to, who was
the great great grandfather of Hon. R. G. Meadows of Mercer
County, marched with the expedition of George Rogers Clark
to the Illinois country, and then marched by way of the Falls
of the Ohio to his home in Bedford County, Virginia.

In October of the year of 1778 the Legislature of Virginia

created and erected into the county of Illinois all the northwest territory, being all the territory north of the Ohio, south
of the Great Lakes, and east of the Mississippi. The county
of Illinois continued as a Virginia County until the Deed of
Cession of March, 1784.

Joseph Hare, of North Carolina, and Edward Hale, of Franklin county, Virginia, came into the New River settlements in
1779, and located about the mouth of Wolf Creek. Both Hare
and Hale had been soldiers in the American army. Hare was
with the patriot army at the battle of Moore's Creek Bridge,
now near Fayetteville, North Carolina, fought on the 27th day
of February, 1776. These two men performed important services in the years immediately following their settlement, not
only in the battles with the Indians, but also in the battle of
Whitsell's Mill and Guilford Court House, North Carolina,
about which services more will be said hereafter.

The upper New River valley, in what is now in part Bland,
Wythe, Grayson and Carroll Counties in Virginia as well as
some of the counties on the North Carolina side, were among
the hiding places of the Tories, and they made frequent uprisings and had to be repressed. Some of these uprisings took
place in the years of 1779-80 and were suppressed by bodies of
militia led by Colonel William Campbell, Major Walter Crockett, Major Joseph Cloyd and Colonel Benjamin Cleveland, the
latter of North Carolina. The old court records now in the
office of the Clerk of the County Court of Montgomery County,
Virginia, abound with instances where numerous parties were
summoned before the court on charges of being engaged in
these uprisings, and were required to give bond and good se-
curity to keep the peace and be of good behavior. Should anyone be curious enough to want the names of these people they
can find the same by reference to records referred to.

David Johnston with his family came from the county of
Culpeper, Virginia, in 1778, and settled in the New River val-
ley on the plateau between Big Stony Creek and Little Stony
Creek, about one mile from the river, at the place now known

as the John Phlegar farm in the county of Giles. Johnston's family consisted of himself and wife, two sons, the third son being then absent in the American army, and five daughters, the eldest of the daughters, whose name was Sallie, and who had intermarried with Thomas Marshall, together with her husband, came with the family. David Johnston was the brother-in-law of John and Richard Chapman who then lived at the mouth of Walker's Creek, about two miles from where Johnston settled. The first house built by David Johnston as his new dwelling place, was erected by him in 1778 and is at this writing, 1905, still standing, forming a part of the Phlegar mansion house. A few years after the coming of David Johnston his brother-in-law, Elder James Abbott, a missionary Baptist minister, came. Johnston was, soon after making of his settlement, appointed a constable for Montgomery county. He died in 1786, his wife in 1813, and they were both buried on the Phlegar farm.

Thomas Ingles, a son of the Captain William Ingles, one of the Drapers Meadows settlers, and who was captured and carried away with his mother, by the Indians, in 1755, having returned after thirteen years, and been sent to school at Doctor Thomas Walker's in Albemarle County, Virginia, from which place he went with the army of General Lewis to the battle of Point Pleasant, in which he fought as a lieutenant in a company belonging to Colonel William Christian's regiment of Fincastle men. After the battle young Ingles was in one of the companies left to garrison the fort at Point Pleasant during the winter following the battle. After receiving his discharge from the army in 1775 he returned to Albemarle, and married a Miss Grills. He came back to the New River valley, and in 1778 he located and settled in Wright's Valley, in which the city of Bluefield, West Virginia, is now situated, and about two miles west of said city, at a spring near the mansion house of the late Captain Rufus A. Hale. Here Mr. Ingles remained some two years, but finding himself dangerously near the Indian trail leading from he head of Tug of Sandy southward across East-river Mountain, to the Wolf Creek and Walker's Creek settlements, he determined to seek a place more remote from Indian lines of travel, and thence removed to Burke's Garden to a tract of land owned by his father. He however remained long enough in Wright's Valley to effect in a measure a change of name to "English's", as appears from the early land surveys and grants. His stay in his new home was not long a peaceful one, for in April, 1782, while he and a negro man were engaged at farm work some distance from the house, a large party of Indians captured his wife and children and two negro slaves, and after plundering and firing the house, they left the premises. Mr. Ingles, discovering the smoke from his burning house, approached near enough to see that the trouble was caused by Indians, and that he alone could do nothing, set off in quest of help, crossing the mountains southward, he fortunately met up with a goodly number of men assembled for muster and drill at a settlement in Rich Valley on the north fork of Holstein. A posse of fifteen or twenty men under the leadership of Captain Maxwell, to whose command was added an additional force of five or six men, whom John Hix, a neighbor of Mr. Ingles, had gotten together. This party pursued the Indians and on the fifth day they were discovered in camp in a gap of the Sandy Ridge which divides the waters of the Sandy from the Clinch This gap since that time, known as Maxwell's Gap, is a short distance west of the west end of Abb's Valley, and two or three miles north-northwest of the residences of the late William G. Mustard on the north fork of Clinch River in the county of Tazewell. Captain Maxwell divided his company, he taking a part, and moving around their flank so as to get in their front, while Mr. Ingles remained with the other portion of the company in the rear, and the attack to be made at daylight the next morning. Unfortunately Maxwell, in order to escape detection, bore too far away and was not in position to make the attack at the appointed time. Mr. Ingles after waiting beyond the agreed hour, and seeing the Indians beginning to stir, began the attack. As soon as the first shot was fired, some of the Indians began to tomahawk the prisoners, while others fought and retreated. Mr. Ingles reached his wife just as she had received a terrible blow on the head. They had already tomahawked his little daughter Mary, five years old, and his son William, three years old. The small infant in the arms of the mother was unhurt. In their retreat, the Indians passed close to Captain Maxwell and his party, and firing on them killed Captain Maxwell, who was the only one of the pursuers killed. No dead Indians were found. The little wounded girl died, but the mother recovered. The above statements are taken from the Harman MS., which states that Captain Henry Harman was with this pursuing party.

On September 23, 1779, Mrs. Margaret Pauley and her husband, John Pauley, together with James Pauley, wife and child, Robert Wallace and wife and Brice Miller set out from the Greenbrier section to go to Kentucky. They crossed New River at the Horse Ford near the mouth of Rich Creek and then down New River and up East River, which was the shortest route to Cumberland Gap. Each of the men had his rifle. The women on the horses, on which were packed what household plunder they could carry, were in front, the men in the rear driving the cattle. About noon of the day referred to, and when the party had reached a point on East River about one mile below the mouth of Five Mile Fork thereof, supposed to have been near the upper end of the old farm of Captain William Smith, they were attacked by five Indians and a white man by the name of Morgan, who was in company with the Indians. The first intimation that the party had of the presence of the savages, was the report of the discharge of a gun. The women, Mrs. John and James Pauley, were knocked from their horses by the Indians with their clubs, Wallace and the two children were killed and scalped, and John Pauley though fatally wounded, escaped and succeeded in reaching Wood's Fort on Rich Creek, where he died in a short time. The Indians took Mrs. John and James Pauley prisoners, and on leaving the scene of their atrocities, went up East River to the mouth of the Five Mile Fork, and thence up the same to the head, across the Bluestone and on to the Ohio, and to the Indian towns on the Miami. There the two women and the little boy of Margaret Pauley, born shortly after she reached the Indian towns remained prisoners for about two years. Finally Mrs. James Pauley escaped, and Margaret and her child shortly after this were ransomed. Mrs. Pauley's maiden name was Handley. After the return of Margaret Pauley she married a Mr. Erskine, and by whom she had a daughter who married Hugh Caperton, who became a distinguished man, and who was the father of the late United States Senator Allen T. Caperton, of Monroe County. Adam Caperton, the father of the said Hugh, was killed in a battle with the Indians at Little Mountain, or Estill's defeat, near where Mt. Sterling, Kentucky, is now situated. Captain Estill and six of his men were killed, and seventeen of the Indians were killed. This battle was fought on the 22nd day of March, 1782.

At the date of the attack on the Pauley party in September, 1779, no settlements had been made along the East River, in fact none existed between Wood's Fort on Rich Creek and that of Thomas Ingles in Wright's Valley. The route being traveled by the Pauley party was along the hunters' trail leading from New River up East River by the site of the present city of Bluefield in Mercer County, and across the Bluestone-Clinch divide to the Clinch, down the same and on by way of Powell's River to Cumberland Gap. This was the route usually pursued by emigrants from the Greenbrier-New River section to Kentucky.

John Toney settled at the mouth of East River in the year of 1780, and gave to his place the name of Montreal and later when the line of the Norfolk & Western Railroad was being constructed, the contractors engaged in that part of the work at the mouth of East River, or their employees called it, "Hell's Gate." It is now known as Glenlyn.

In the year of 1780, or 1781 a family by the name of Christain settled on the farm formerly owned by Mr. John L. Woolwine on East River, about two miles above the mouth thereof, and it was this family, or from it that the name "Christian's Ridge," was given to the high ridge land lying north of the place of the settlement.

John Goolman Davidson, an Irishman, born in Dublin, Ireland, a cooper by trade, from which he was generally called and known as "Cooper Davidson," came with his family from that part of the Valley of Virginia now known as Rockbridge County, and with him came Richard Bailey and his family, from the Blackwater section, then in Bedford, now in Franklin County, Virginia, and settled in the year of 1780 at the Beaver Pond Spring, a branch of Bluestone, now in Mercer County. A fort was built which was called and known as the "Davidson-Bailey Fort," the marks of the foundation of which may yet be seen near the residence of Mr. Harvey Bailey just west of the Beaver Pond Creek. Both Davidson and Bailey had considerable families, the latter had eight sons and two daughters. Richard Bailey had been a soldier in the American army. These men as well as their sons and daughters, were a brave and courageous people, and maintained their position on the border at the settlement they had made from the day they came in 1780, until the close of the Indian wars in 1795. Often in battles with the Indians, frequently compelled to flee for their lives, and shut themselves up in their strong quarters, and finally loosing Mr. Davidson, whose tragic and brutal murder by the savages will be hereinafter related. At the time of the settlement at Beaver Pond Spring by Davidson and Bailey, their nearest neighbors, were Captain James Moore in Abb's Valley, some twelve miles away, Mitchell Clay on Clover bottom, about the same distance, a man by the name of Compton on Clear fork of Wolf Creek, about eight miles away, and a man by the name of Wright at a place now called Springville, on the head of the Bluestone about eight miles away.

The American army under Washington, spent the winter of 1779-80 at Morristown New Jersey, not only suffering from severe cold, but even from lack of food. The British General Clinton was determined to capture Charleston, South Carolina,

and to that end toward the close of the year 1779, he embarked
from New York with 7,500 men, leaving Knyphausen in command of the city with a small force, for Washington had sent
the bulk of his troops south, and consequently gave the enemy
little trouble in the northern department. The British expedition reached Charleston near the close of January, 1780. General Benjamin Lincoln was in command of the Continental
troops at Charleston and in the vicinity thereof. On May 5th,
1780, Fort Moultrie was surrendered to the British, and on the
12th of May, General Lincoln surrendered the city of Charleston
and his army numbering 5,000. to be made prisoners of war.
This capitulation on the part of Lincoln left the entire south
virtually at the mercy of the British.

General Horatio Gates had been placed in command of the
American army in the southern department and marched rapidly southward until he reached Camden, South Carolina,
where on the 16th of August he met the British army under
Lords Rawdon and Cornwallis, and a fierce conflict ensued, in
which the American army was decisively defeated. Immediately following organized resistance in the south, American
rule ended. General Gates made his way to Charlotte, North
Carolina, where he was superseded by General Nathaniel
Greene, one of the best officers and fighters in the American
service. The march of the British army northward into North
Carolina not only encouraged the loyalists in the southern part
of the state but they became very much emboldened in the northern and western part of the state as well as in the upper New
River region in Virginia.

 In the latter part of the summer or in the early part of the
autumn of 1780 there was a general tory uprising in Surry
County, North Carolina, which was so formidable in its character as to alarm the friends of the American cause; who not
only appealed to the American patriots in North Carolina, but
in Virginia as well, for help. This was truly the crucial period
in this great conflict, the American cause seeming to be at its
lowest ebb. The western borders were harrassed by the In-

dians. The country north and east of New Jersey was practically in the hands of the British. General Arnold had betrayed the American cause and agreed to surrender West Point to the enemies of America. The great body of the American army had been decisively defeated at Camden. The tories, the friends of the King, were in high glee and everything looked as if the American cause was lost. But a brighter day was near at hand, and the tide of affairs was to turn in favor of the Americans.

Colonel Martin Armstrong, who was in command of the military district in and around Salem, North Carolina, sent his small son, Thomas T. Armstrong, then but little above twelve years of age, with an appeal for help to Major Joseph Cloyd, whose residence was on Back Creek, now in Pulaski County. To avoid suspicion, and to prevent his son from being intercepted, knowing that he had to pass the tory settlements to reach Major Cloyd, he dressed him in a full tory suit, and the manly and brave little fellow carried the message safely to Major Cloyd (this incident was related to the author by Mrs. Colonel Napoleon D. French, the grand-daughter of Colonel Martin Armstrong, and the daughter of Colonel Thomas T. Armstrong, the lad who carried the message.)

Joseph Cloyd was the Major of the Montgomery County militia of which William Preston was the Colonel and Commandant. Cloyd was directed to raise three companies of horsemen forthwith and to proceed to Surry County, North Carolina, and to aid in suppressing the tories.

Among the companies detailed for this service, was one commanded by Captain George Pearis, another by Captain Bryant, but the author has been unable to ascertain the name of the captain who commanded the remaining company. General Jethro Sumner in a letter to General Gates, dated Camp McGoon's Creek, October 4, 1780, says, "That he encloses a copy of letter of Colonel William Preston, of Botetourt, Virginia, dated the 18th day of September, 1780, stating that a body of horsemen is in that section moving against the tories on the

Yadkin." General Sumner seemed not to have been aware of
the presence of the Virginia troops in that neighborhood, except through the letter of Colonel Preston, and a conversation
had by him with Colonel Armstrong.   In his letter General
Sumner refers to the forks of the Yadkin, and to the Shallow
ford thereof, and states that he suspects the latter point to be
the object of the enemy.   This letter also refers to a conversation in which Colonel Armstrong informs him of the approach
of three troops of horsemen from Virginia.   General William
Smallwood, writes to General Gates, (Colonial records in Library of Congress,) from Moravian town, now Salem, under
date of October 16, 1780, and states, "But upon return of my
scouts last evening they informed me that the enemy had attempted to cross the Shallow ford the day before, 14th day of
October, 1780, but they were attacked by Major Cloyd with one
hundred and sixty of the Virginia and Carolina militia, and
that fifteen of the tories were found dead and four wounded.(1)
Our loss one captain killed, and four privates wounded.   (Evidently the captain was Pearis, and he only wounded.)
     Captain Pearis received in this battle a very severe wound in
the shoulder, which disabled him for further military duty.   In
this battle he killed with his own sword, a man by the name of
Burke, his own cousin, from whom he took his sword and this
with his own sword together with his uniform with the bullet
hole in the shoulder thereof, were preserved in the family until
the burning of Princeton, when the same were destroyed together with the house of Mrs. Louisa A. Pearis, where they
had been left for preservation.   These men under Major Cloyd,
were minute or emergency men, and were called out for only
three months service, and returned to their homes about the
first of January, 1781.   Thomas Farley, who was a member of
Captain Pearis' company, in his sworn application made before
the County Court of Giles County in 1832, for a pension, states
his enlistment was with Captain Pearis on the first of October,

<hr>

(1)   The tory army numbered 310 and was commanded by Colonel
Gideon and Captain Hezakiah Wright.—"Draper's Heroes of King's
Mountain, page 483."

1780, and gives the details of the march under Major Cloyd to the Shallow ford of the Yadkin, and of the battle there, and that his captain, Pearis, was wounded in the battle and that he nursed him after he was wounded.

Captain Henry Patton seems to have succeeded Pearis in command of the company which he led to the battle of the Shallow ford of the Yadkin.

General Cornwallis with the British was advancing into the very center of North Carolina, and he had pushed out Major Patrick Ferguson, one of his lieutenants, toward the western mountains of North Carolina, where he could rally and get together the tories of that section. Ferguson had heard of the "Over-Mountain or Backwater men" who occupied the territory on the head waters of the Holstein, Clinch and the Watauga, and he determined to bring them to terms if possible. If they would not go to him and surrender, he would march across the mountain and destroy them. Ferguson then had in his custody a prisoner by the name of Samuel Philips with whom he agreed if he would carry a message from him to Generals Seviers and Shelby, two of the leaders of the Over-Mountain men, he would release him. This message was, "that if they did not desist from their opposition to the British arms, that he would hang their leaders, and lay their county waste with fire and sword." Philips true to his word crossed the mountains, and delivered the message entrusted to him to Shelby at King's Meadows, now Bristol, Virginia. Shelby was not a man to be alarmed by such threats, conscious that the Over-mountain or Back-water men were an equal match for Ferguson's corps. Shelby mounted his horse, and rode rapidly some forty miles to the Nollichucky in search of John Sevier, who was not at home but at Jonesboro, attending the horse races. Shelby pushed on until he found him, and it is said that they went aside, and sat down upon a log and talked over the situation fully, and determined that the better plan was to rally the Over-mountain men both in Virginia and North Carolina, cross the mountains, and destroy Ferguson and his army.

By agreement between Shelby and Sevier, the latter was to rally the men of Washington County, North Carolina, and the former those of Sullivan County, and who was also to communicate and interest Colonel William Campbell, of Washington County, Virginia. Sycamore Ford on the Watauga, about three miles below the present town of Elizabethtown, was agreed upon as the place, and the 25th of September as the time for the rendezvous of these troops. Having succeeded in getting together one thousand men, they assembled as agreed upon at the time and place.

This was the most remarkable gathering of Backwoodsmen that had ever occurred on the western border. Here was a body of men living as it were, beyond the confines of civilization, without law, being a law unto themselves, about to enter into a great campaign, and fight a great battle, not for revenge, plunder or booty, impelled only by their patriotism. No executive authority had commanded them to assemble, they simply obeyed the commands of their local officers. They marched rapidly across the mountains, passing through Gillespie's gap in Blue Ridge, and on to the waters flowing south and eastward; and on the seventh day of October attacked the British forces under Ferguson at King's Mountain, in South Carolina, and won in less than an hour, a most decisive victory, which gave cheer and encouragement to the American cause, and made patriotic hearts throughout the land leap for joy. This was the turning point in the American revolution. These incidents are embodied herein because a part of the men who fought this battle on the American side were Montgomery County men, from the headwaters of the Bluestone and the Clinch. Montgomery County at that time reached westward to the west end of Morris' Knob, some eight miles beyond the present Court House of Tazewell County.

Captain James Moore, from Abb's Valley, the Peery's and others from the upper waters of the Clinch, went with Lieutenant Reece Bowen's company, which belonged to Campbell's Washington County regiment. Moore was a lieutenant in Bowen's company, and when entering into the battle, hearing the British bugle sound charge, directed his men to dismount and give it to them Indian fashion—that is, take trees.

The Americans in this battle captured more than six hundred prisoners, and brought them across the mountains. General Gates, on October 17, 1780, wrote Colonel William Preston to prepare a stockade at Fort Chiswell in which to confine these prisoners, but Colonel Preston replied, "that it was not a safe place; that Montgomery County contained more tories than any other county in Virginia." A full, complete and connected history of the battle of King's Mountain, will be found in Draper's "Heroes of King's Mountain."

On the 17th day of January, 1781, was fought the battle of the Cowpens, in which General Morgan defeated the British under Tarleton, the latter being utterly routed and pursued for twenty miles. The American loss was but seventy-two killed and wounded, while that of the British was more than three hundred, with five hundred prisoners, and an immense amount of supplies. This victory was a crushing one, and caused considerable consternation in the camp of Cornwallis, when the news reached him. Morgan crossed the Broad River with his prisoners, intending to make his way to Virginia; Cornwallis in the meantime started out in pursuit. He was confident of heading off the patriot army at the fords of the Catawba, but reached there two hours after Morgan had crossed. It was late in the afternoon when he reached the river, and he waited until morning to find that the fox had gone. A heavy rain had fallen, and so raised the stream as to prevent the British commander from crossing for several hours, during which Morgan marched rapidly, reached and crossed the Yadkin, where General Greene joined him, and left his troops at Cheraw under the command of General Huger. Greene having learned from Morgan that Cornwallis was in pursuit, he sent orders to Huger to unite with Morgan at Salisbury or Charlotte. General Greene was making for Virginia, and Cornwallis chased him for two hundred miles. The pursuer had been held several hours at the Catawba, but crossing at last he renewed the chase after Morgan, and reached the bank of the Yadkin February 3rd, as the Amercans on the opposite side were forming in line to continue the march. The Yadkin was rising rapidly, but the impatient Cornwallis had to linger until the next day while the Amercans leisurely marched off unmolested. They were joined at Guilford Court House by the troops from the Pedee, but being far inferior to their pursuers in number, they continued their retreat to the Dan, which was already rising, and on the 13th of February they crossed and entered Halifax County, Virginia. When Cornwallis came again in view, he found himself again stopped by high water. This turn of affairs disgusted him, and he wheeled about and marched back to Hillsboro, where he made his headquarters. General Greene rested and · recruited his army, which now aggregated about five thousand men, and he determined to join battle with Cornwallis.

Before proceeding to relate the movements of the military in the New River Valley, the names of some of the settlers who came into the valley in 1780 will be mentioned. William Wilburn and David Hughes from North Carolina, and John and Benjamin White from Amherst County, Virginia, settled on Sugar Run in 1780, and a little later, probably in the autumn of 1781, came William Tracy Sarver, James Rowe and others from North Carolina, who settled in Wolf Creek valley. These men had gone from Culpeper County to the Hawe Patch in North Carolina, where it apears they joined themselves unto the King's men, and in Pyles' defeat on the Haw, on the 25th of February, 1781, James Rowe received from one of Lee's Legion a sabre wound which made him lame the rest of his days. The David Hughes referred to was also a Loyalist, and to escape military service in the American army hid himself in the wilds of the flatwoods about the head of Pipestem Creek, and on the waters of the Bluestone and Guyandotte. A high knob situated about seven miles northeast of Athens in Mercer County, is still called "Dave's Knob," from this man David Hughes, who had a hiding place on the top thereof.

Hughes was a giant in size and strength and on one of his expeditions he caught a cub bear which by its outcries, brought
its mother which fiercely attacked Hughes, seizing him by the
left arm. He succeeded in dispatching the bear by striking it
with his fist in the ribs. It may here be added that the New
River valley received a large number of inhabitants in the years
of 1775-1782 from North Carolina, a large part of whom were
tories, but from whom have descended a large number of highly
honored and respectable people.

Cornwallis' march into upper Carolina had greatly alarmed
the Virginians and General Greene wrote letters to Governor
Jefferson and to the various commanders of detached bodies of
troops in Virginia asking help, and among those to whom he
addressed his urgent appeals were Preston, Sevier, Shelby and
Campbell. Colonel William Preston on February 10, 1781, ordered the militia of Montgomery County to assemble at the
Lead Mines, and on the day appointed three hundred and fifty
men assembled pursuant to the order of their commander. Major Joseph Cloyd, assembled and led the Middle New River
men. It is to be regretted that the names of the men who went
with Preston and Cloyd have not been preserved. One company went from the Middle New River valley, which was commanded by Captain Thomas Shannon, of Walker's Creek, and
one of his lieutenants was Alexander Marrs. A few names only
of the privates who went along have been secured. They were
Matthew French, John French, Edward Hale, Joseph Hare,
Isaac Cole and Thomas Farley.

Preston began his march on the 18th day of February and
reported to General Greene on the 28th day of that month, who
assigned him to the command of General Andrew Pickens. On
his way to report to Pickens he seems to have gotten between
the American and British outposts, and camped for the night
in close proximity to the British without knowing that they
were near him.

On the second day of March, 1781, Lee's Legion and Preston's men had a spirited encounter with Tarleton, which Gen-

eral Greene in a dispatch to General Washington thus notices:
"On the Second, Lieutenant Colonel Lee with a detachment of
riflemen attacked the advance of the British army under Tarleton and killed and wounded thirty of them."

On the sixth of March at Whitsell's (Wetzell's mill), North
Carolina, Williams' men, Pickens and his command, including
Lee's Legion and Preston's Backwoodsmen, met the British
and a severe engagement took place. The Americans were compelled to retreat, and Preston's horse took fright and ran
through a mill pond near the British, threw Preston off and
escaped into the British lines. Colonel Preston, being quite a
fleshy man, found it difficult to keep up with the retreating
army, and Major Cloyd seeing his condition dismounted and
gave Preston his horse. On the eve of going into this battle John
French, son of Matthew, and a member of Captain Shannon's
company, was detailed as one of the guards to the wagon train.
So soon as the firing began at the creek French left the train
without orders—in fact against orders—and went to the fight,
joined therein and shot one of the enemy. The officer in charge
of the wagon train reported him for disobedience of orders, and
demanded that he be court martialed. Major Cloyd remarked
that as French ran not from the fight, but towards it, if they
court martialed him for such a cause, he would never again
draw his sword in behalf of the country.

The Americans continued their retreat to Guilford Court
House, where the main body of Greene's army had assembled
to fight Cornwallis. In the meantime, Colonel William Campbell with about sixty men had joined General Greene, and Preston's Montgomery men were placed under his, Campbell's, command on the extreme left of Greene's army. Colonel Tarleton
says, in his Southern Campaigns pp 241, "That in the battle of
Guilford Court House he held the right of the British army
and that his troops were badly hurt by the Backwoodsmen from
Virginia, that they stood behind a fence until the British Infantry with their bayonets climbed over the same." The Americans were defeated in this battle, and there were some critic-

isms as to the behavior of these Backwoodsmen or militia, and Colonel Preston in a letter to Governor Jefferson, written on the 10th of April, 1781, complaining of this criticism, and the injustice to his men, says, "that part of the men were in one action and all of the men were in two actions." Judge Schenk, in his "North Carolina 1780-81," credits Colonel Martin Armstrong with leading a body of Surry County men in the battle of Guilford Court House.

After the close of this battle the militia returned to their homes, which were then threatened by Indian incursions, their services being badly needed along the frontier to suppress the Indian forays and outrages.

To the battle of Yorktown, fought in October, 1781, went Trigg's Battalion of artillery composed largely of New River Valley men.

The outrages commited by the Indians upon the family of Thomas Ingles in Burke's Garden in April, 1782, greatly alarmed the settlers along the more exposed portions of the border, and they pleaded for protection. The consternation produced along the frontiers from Powell's Valley to New River was so great that the Governor of Virginia directed Colonel William Preston to assemble the field officers of Montgomery and Washington Counties at Lead Mines at once to devise ways and means to protect the settlers from Indian depredations. The meeting of these officers took place on the 6th day of July, 1782. In the meantime Colonel Preston had ordered Major Joseph Cloyd to call out the militia, and to station them at David Doak's Mill. The field officers present at the July meeting from Montgomery County were William Preston, Daniel Trigg, Walter Crockett, John Taylor, Joseph Cloyd and Abraham Trigg; from Washington County, Arthur Campbell, Aaron Lewis, William Edmiston, James Dysart and Major Patrick Lockhart, District Commissioner. The board of officers decided that two hundred men should be drawn out for the defense of the frontiers, to be disposed of into the following districts in Montgomery County, namely, "on New River in the neighborhood of Captain Pearis 30 men, Sugar Run 20, Captain Moore's head of Bluestone 25, head of Clinch 25.   In Washington, at Richlands 20, Castle woods 30, Rye Cove 20, Powell's Valley 30 men. The distances from Captain Pearis' to Sugar Run 10 miles, to Captain Moore's, head of Bluestone 30, to Captain Maxwell's, head of Clinch 16, which is nearest the Washington line, to Richlands 24, to Castlewood's 30, to Rye Cove 28, to Powell's Valley Fort 26 miles, in all 164 miles."

Upon the surrender of Lord Cornwallis at Yorktown, in October, 1781, the war was regarded at an end. Many of the militia men of Virginia and swarms of other people soon thereafter, came over the Alleghanies, seeking homes, and with them for the same purpose, came some of the French- and British soldiers. Vast throngs went to Kentucky. Among those who came in the years of 1782-3-4 and 5, and located in the New River Valley, and who had been soldiers in the American army, were John Peters, Christian Peters, Charles Walker, Isaac Smith and Larkin Stowers, and a little later came Josiah Meadows, Jacob Meadows, James Emmons, Charles Duncan, John Kirk, Peter Dingess and Tollison Shuemate. The Peters, Stowers, Walker, Jacob Meadows and Smith came from Rockingham County, Virginia, Peter Dingess, from Botetourt County, Josiah Meadows from Bedford, James Emmons and Charles Duncan from Stokes County, North Carolina, John and Thos. Kirk, and Tollison Shuemate from Fauquier County, Virginia. Duncan and Emmons had first removed from Fauquier County to Stokes County, North Carolina. John Peters and his brother Christian came in 1783, the former located on the New River on the farm on which Mr. Charles D. French now resides, and the latter settled on Rich Creek, where the village of Peterstown is now situated, and he gave name to that village. Chas. Walker settled on New River, opposite the mouth of Wolf Creek.

Conner, Link and Lugar, who were Hessians—Germans—and who had belonged to the British army, came during one of the years referred to. John Conner was a courier or dispatch bearer for Colonel Tarleton, the British commander on the battlefield of the Cowpens, and had been sent with a message, became intoxicated on the way, failed to deliver the message, was court martialed and sentenced to receive, and did receive one hundred lashes, save one, on his bare back, lived, but fainted under the operation, though he had been heavily dosed with liquor and powder mixed. This whipping caused him to let the hated British do their own fighting thereafter, and thereupon he deserted to the Americans.

Three or four Hessian regiments were surrendered as prisoners of war by Cornwallis at Yorktown, and for safe keeping were sent into the valley of Virginia. Finding there a people who had come from their own country, spoke their own tongue and living in a goodly land, they settled down and became citizens of the country.

The influx of population of the New River Valley, came principally from four directions, viz: the Virginia valley, Piedmont, Virginia, the upper waters of the James and Roanoke Rivers or their tributaries, and from North Carolina. From the valley came the Peters, Walkers, Stowers, Smiths; from the Piedmont, Virginia, the Chapmans, Johnstons, McKensey, Lyttles, Garrisons, Kirks, Emmons, Duncans and Shuemates; from the waters of the James and Roanoke Rivers, the Clays, Baileys, Belchers, Shannons and Whites; from North Carolina, the Harmans, Wilburns, Hughes and Hagers.

It has already been stated that Captain George Pearis settled on the New River, where Pearisburg station on the line of the Norfolk & Western Railway is now situated, in the Spring of 1782. (1) He purchased a tract of land (204 acres) of Captain William Ingles for seventy pounds sterling. It is altogether probable that Mrs. Ingels had observed these lands on her way up New River in November, 1755, after her escape from the Indians, and had given information thereof to her husband, who in 1780 entered and surveyed this 204 acre tract, as well, also,

_____

(1) George Pearis opened the first store in what is now Giles County.

the Chapman I. Johnston home tract, and the tract on which Chas. D. French resides.

It has been noted that Mitchell Clay and family settled on the Bluestone at Clover bottom in the year of 1775, where he opened up a considerable farm. From the date of his settlement to near the autumn of 1783 he had not been molested by the savages, as he seems to have lived off their lines of travel, but his peace was not long to continue.

In the month of August, 1783, after Clay had harvested his crop of small grain, and desiring to get the benefit of the pastures for his cattle off the ground on which his crop had grown, he placed two of his sons, Bartley and Ezekiel, to build a fence around the stacks of grain, while he went out in the search of game. His older sons seem to have been away from home. It was in the afternoon, while these two young men were engaged at their work, and the older daughter with some of the younger girls were at the river washing, that a marauding party of eleven Indians crept up to the edge of the field and shot Bartley dead. The discharge of the gun alarmed the girls at the river, and they started on a run for the house, the pathway leading directly by where Bartley had been killed. An Indian attempted to scalp the young man, and at the same time to capture the older girl Tabitha, who undertook to defend the body of her dead brother, and prevent his being scalped, and in the struggle with the Indian, she reached for his butcher knife, which hung in his belt and missing it, the Indian drew it and stabbed her repeatedly, she however, several times wringing the knife from his hand cast it aside, but he each time recovering it continued cutting her with the knife, and stabbing her until he had literally chopped her to pieces before killing her. The small girls during the melee, had escaped to the house, and the brother Ezekiel, a lad of some sixteen years had been captured by another Indian. The house of Mitchell Clay stood on a high point, or knoll about three hundred yards nearly due west, from the dwelling house now owned and occupied by Mr. Daniel Day. The old chimney, or rather the foundation stones of the chimney of the Clay cabin can still be seen. About the time the attack was made by the Indian, a man by the name of Liggon Blankenship called at Clay's cabin, and when Mrs. Clay discovered her daughter in the struggle with the Indian, begged Blankenship to go and shoot the Indian and save her child, instead thereof he took to his heels and ran to the New River settlements and reported that Clay and all of his family had been killed by the Indians. This cowardly behavior of Blankenship has been handed down from generation to generation and perhaps will be to the end of time. The Indians, after securing the scalp of the young man Bartley, and his sister Tabitha, with their prisoner Ezekiel, left the scene. So soon as Mrs. Clay ascertained that the Indians had departed, she took her children and carried the bodies of the dead ones to the house and placing them on a bed, left the cabin with her children and made her way through the wild woods six miles to the house of Mr. James Bailey (son of Richard, of Beaver Pond) who lived at a place on Brush Creek waters about three fourths of a mile northwest from where New Hope Church now stands, and who had settled there in 1782, and was then Clay's nearest neighbor. Mr. Clay, the father, on his hunting expedition had wounded a deer and followed it until nearly dark, then retraced his steps home, little dreaming of the horrors that had been enacted there in his absence. When he reached the house he soon discovered from the dead bodies of his children and other evidence what had happened, and supposing that all of his family had been killed or were captives, he immediately left the cabin for the New River settlements, following a blind path which led from his place to New River at the mouth of East River. On his way during the night he discovered that the Indians were in his rear, following him, and he left the path in order to evade them. He reached the settlements early in the morning, followed closely by the Indians who stole a number of horses and immediately began their retreat to the Ohio. Information was immediately conveyed to the various neighborhoods, and a party of men under Captain Matthew Farley, among them

Charles Clay, Mitchell, Jr., James Bailey, William Wiley, Edward Hale, Isaac Cole, Joseph Hare, John French and Captain James Moore, went to the Clay cabin and buried the bodies of Bartley and Tabitha. The pursuit then began. The Indians taking the old Indian trail from the Bluestone across Flat Top Mountain, and down the divide between Guyandotte and Coal river waters along the top of Cherry Pound Mountain, where the trail seperated, one branch thereof continuing down the west fork of the Coal River, and the other down the Pond fork of the same. When the whites reached the forks of this path or trail, they discovered that the tracks of the horses, which the Indians had stolen, led down the Pond fork, and not suspecting that some of the Indian party had gone down the west fork, they followed the tracks of the horses. It was late in the evening when they reached a point near the mouth of Pond fork, and discovered smoke from fires started by the Indians where they had camped, and heard the shrill whistle of a fife. The party halted in order to confer as to the best method of attack. They decided to divide their party so as to place a portion of them below the Indians, and to attack at daylight the next morning, and to make this attack from above and below at the same time. The party crept as close up to where the Indians encamped as they thought safe to prevent discovery. All was quiet during the night, but just at the break of day, a large Indian arose from his bed and walked out a short distance, and approaching Edward Hale, by whom he was shot and killed, and thereupon the attack began.

Two of the Indians were killed outright, and one that was wounded attempted to escape to the hill, and in his broken English begged for his life, but Charles Clay, whose brother and sister had just been killed by them, and another brother in captivity, refused him quarter and killed him on the spot. The remaining Indians fled down the river.

Mitchell Clay, Jr., was then quite a boy, and when the attack began one large Indian rushed down toward him. Young Clay had a large rifle gun, much too heavy for a boy of his size to handle, and firing at the Indian he missed him. The Indian wheeled, and attempted to run off, but was killed by another of the party.

The place where this fight occurred is in the now county of Boone, at the head of a little bottom on the Pond fork, on west side thereof, about one-half mile above the junction of the Pond with the West fork of Coal River, and on the farm formerly owned by the late Mr. L. D. Coon, who a few years ago in plowing near the base of the hill where the fight took place, found an Indian hatchet, which he gave to the author, and which he now has in his possession. The spot where this battle was fought is well marked by a large pile of heavy stones, carried by the Indians from the adjacent mountain side, and piled over the bodies of their dead comrades. The white people recovered their horses, but not Ezekiel Clay, who was carried by the hunting party of Indians that went down the West Fork, and with this party the whites failed to come into contact. They took this unfortunate boy to their town at Chillicothe, and burned him at the stake. Both Edward Hale and William Wiley took from the backs of the two dead Indians strips of their hides, which they converted into razor straps and which remained in their families for many years, as souvenirs of the battle.

Mitchell Clay and his family removed to New River, and purchased from the executors of Captain William Ingles a part of the farm which is now owned by J. Raleigh Johnston, Esq., across the river from the Norfolk & Western Railway station at Pearisburg, Virginia, and Clay built his house on very nearly the same spot on which Mr. Johnston's house now stands. This Clay house was removed several years ago to a point on the same farm, about one-half mile north of where it originally stood. It still remains, and in the logs may yet be seen the port holes. A photograph of this house built in 1783, as it now appears will be inserted in the appendix to this work.

Mr. Clay and his wife, whose maiden name was Phoebe Belcher of Bedford, later Franklin County, Virginia, had fourteen children. His sons were Henry, Charles, Mitchell, David, William, Bartley, and Ezekiel; his daughters Tabitha, Rebecca, who married Colonel George Pearis, Patience, who married George Chapman, Sallie, who married Captain John Peters, Obedience, who married John French, Nannie, who married Joseph Hare, Mary, who married William Stewart, and whose descendants, now compose a large part of the population of Wyoming County, West Virginia. Mitchell Clay died on his New River farm in 1812, having sold his Clover bottom tract to Hugh Innes and to his son-in-law, Colonel Pearis. The facts and circumstances connected with this Clay tragedy and the battle fought with the Indians on Coal River is taken from the Clay MSS., written out by Mitchell C. and John Clay, grandsons of the said Mitchell.

In 1783 Captain George Pearis being out on his farm with his rifle and near the lower point of the island just north of his house discovered an Indian standing on the high cliff of rocks opposite the lower point of said island. He fired at and killed the Indian.

In the spring of 1782, a marauding party of Indians made an incursion into Abb's Valley, and attacked the house of James Poague, a brother-in-law of Captain Moore, at night, broke open the door, but finding there were several men in the house (there were three besides Mr. Poague) they did not attempt to enter the house, but after watching it for some time went off; and the next morning killed a young man by the name of Richards, who had been living for some time at Captain Moore's. This incident is related by Kercheval, the Historian of the valley. It seems that this party of Indians on entering the valley divided, a part going to Burke's Garden and attacking Thomas Ingles' family as hereinbefore related, and another part the Maxwell's and others.

James Moore, a son of Captain James, and who was only fourteen years of age, was in September, 1784, captured by three Indians. The boy had been sent for a horse, by his father, to the plantation of Mr. Poague, which was now deserted, as Mr. Poague had left some time before. The boy was taken by the

Indians across the Ohio, and remained a prisoner for about five years, then returned, finding, in fact hearing before he reached home, that his father's family had been destroyed by the Indians. This James Moore was the father of the late William T. Moore, of Abb's Valley, and who lived to about the age of ninety years, one of the most honored and respected citizens of Tazewell County, Virginia. Before his death he erected, largely at his own expense in Abb's Valley, near the place where his grandfather and family were destroyed by the Indians, Moore's Memorial (Methodist) Church.

Many important events transpired during the years of 1784-5. The border land or frontier was rapidly filling up with a restless, energetic people, largely free from governmental restraints, with no other special duties to perform than that of preparing homes, providing food and clothing and fighting savages. These people west of the Alleghanies, on the waters of Wautauga, Holstein and upper New River section, seemingly dissatisfied with the state governments of North Carolina and Virginia, sought what they conceived to be better. The people living in Washington, Sullivan and Greene Counties, North Carolina, set up a new government, created and organized a new state which they named Franklin. The interests of the people living in these counties, as well as on the head waters of the Holstein and upper New River country, were so closely identified, that a scheme was discussed to enlarge the territory of the new state, and to make a great independent Commonwealth. Colonel Arthur Campbell, of Washington County, Virginia, seems to have been at the head of the movement, and in 1785 he proposed the enlargement of the boundaries of the new state as follows, viz: "Beginning at a point at the top of the Alleghany or Appalachian Mountains so as a line drawn due north from thence will reach the banks of the New River, then called Kanawha, at the confluence of the little river, which is about one mile above Ingle's Ferry, down the said river Kanawha to the mouth of Roncevert (or Greenbrier) River, a direct line from thence to the nearest summit of the Laurel Mountain, and along the highest point of the same to the point where it is intersected by the parallel of thirty seven degrees north latitude; west along that latitude to a point where it is met by a meridian line that passes through the lower part of the Rapids of Ohio; south along the meridian to Elk Run, a branch of the Tennessee, down said run to its mouth, and down the Tennessee to the most southwardly part of the bend in said river; a line from thence to that branch of the Mobile, called Donbigbee; down said river Donbigbee to its junction with the Cossawate River, to the mouth of that branch called the High tower, thence south to the top of the Appalachian Mountain at its highest land that divides the stream of the eastern from the western waters; northwardly along the middle of said heights, and the top of the Appalachian Mountains to the beginning."

This new state composed of the three counties mentioned, lived and lasted with John Sevier as its governor four years, and then ceased to further exist; its territory having been finally absorbed or embraced within the limits of the state of Tennessee. This brief mention of the state of Franklin is only made to show that if it had continued its existence with the enlarged territory added as proposed by Colonel Campbell, the counties of Mercer and Tazewell would have been embraced therein.

A raiding party of Indians in 1785 entered the Upper Bluestone and Wolf Creek sections, stole horses and gave great alarm to the settlers.

The general assembly of Virginia in October, 1785, passed an act to take effect May first, 1786, dividing the county of Washington by the creation of the county of Russell; which Act reads as follows: "All that part of said county lying within a line to be run along the Clinch Mountain to the Carolina line, thence with a line to the Cumberland Mountain, and the extent of the county between the Cumberland Mountain, Clinch Mountain and the line of Montgomery County, shall be one distinct county, called and known by the name of Russell. Court to meet at the house of William Robinson in Castlewoods."

In the early morning of July 14, 1786, a band of forty Shaw-

nee Indians attacked the family of Captain James Moore in
Abb's Valley, killed Captain Moore, two of his children, a man
by the name of Simpson, captured Mrs. Moore, and her four remaining children, and a Miss Evans who was living with the
family, plundered, and burned the house, and then made off to
the Ohio with their prisoners and booty. Two men in the harvest field just south of the house, one by the name of Clark, the
other an Irishman, fled and gave the alarm. Clark ran directly
to the Davidson-Bailey Fort at the Beaver Pond spring, the
Irishman to a settlement on upper Bluestone. A messenger
was forthwith dispatched to Major Joseph Cloyd, on Back
Creek, who with a party of men reached the scene of the tragedy the second day after its enactment, but too late to overtake
the Indians. They secured the bodies of the dead and buried
them. They found the body of Captain Moore about two hundred yards north of the house. His body had been horribly mutilated by the savages. It was buried where he fell and it still
reposes there. The spot where the two small children were buried, remained unknown to the Moores until about fifteen years
ago Mr. Oscar B. Moore, the great grandson of Captain James,
while plowing or having plowing done in a field near where the
cabin had stood, turned up the bones of these children and not
far away under the edge of a shelving limestone rock the bones
of a man of very large frame was plowed up, supposed to be
those of the Indian that the horse Yorick killed. The story of
the destruction of Captain Moore and his family, has been giv-
en by several writers, and it is not deemed necessary to repeat
it here in full. The reader for further information is referred
to "Abb's Valley Captives:" Kercheval's His. Val.: Trans Alleghany Pioneers: Summers His. South-west Virginia.

The Federal Convention, which assembled at Philadelphia
on the 17th day of September completed its work, and submitted the same to the states for their action. The Virginia convention convened to consider the ratification or rejection of
this Federal constitution, assembled in the city of Richmond
on the 2nd day of June, 1788. The representatives from the

county of Montgomery, of which the territory of Mercer was then a part, were Walter Crockett and Abraham Trigg. Washington County was represented by Samuel Edmiston and James Montgomery. The opposition to the ratification of the constitution was vigorous, being led by Patrick Henry, while James Madison and Governor Randolph earnestly supported ratification. It was ratified with sundry amendments, recommendations and conditions added, by a vote of 89 to 79, the representatives from west of the Alleghanies voting against ratification. And.thus with perhaps two exceptions, the people living west of the Alleghanies have almost invariably opposed and voted against every constitution presented to them, and the last heard from they were still voting along the same lines. It is true they voted for the ratification of the Underwood constitution of 1869 but this was a matter of self-preservation, to avoid political disabilities, disfranchisement, and negro domination, all of which had practically been incorporated into the constitution, but several of the obnoxious features thereof were by authority of President Grant voted on separately and defeated. But the stronger reason that impelled them to vote for this constitution, was the fear of carpetbag and scalawagism, as well as negro domination.

Captain Henry Harman, who was a German, but born on the Isle of Man, first settled in North Carolina near the Moravian town, Salem, and there married Miss Nancy Wilburn, and from thence removed about the year of 1758 to the New River valley, and settled on Buchanan's bottom, the Major James R. Kent farm. · Some years later Captain Harman settled on Walker's Creek, but soon removed to the north branch thereof, known now as Kimberling Creek (the name believed to have been given from Jacob Kimberline). This farm on which he settled on the Kimberling, and now known as Hollybrook, remained in his family for long years. The last Harman that owned and occupied it was Colonel William N. Harman, a grandson of Captain Henry, a lawyer by profession, and who commanded a battalion of confederate calvery during our civil war. Colonel Harman with his family recently removed to the territory of Oklahoma.

Captain Henry Harman very early in the morning of November 12th, 1788, started out on his usual fall hunt, taking with him two of his sons, George and Matthias, and a man by the name of George Draper.   They had with them their bear dogs and pack horses, with the latter to transport their game. Starting early and traveling the mountain trails by the shortest route, they reached a point on the Tug Fork of the Sandy below the junction of the North and South forks thereof a little more than two miles below said junction on the right bank of the main Tug fork, where they selected their camp, the construction of which was left to the Captain, who desired it arranged to suit his taste. George and Matthias had started to the woods to look for game, while Mr. Draper was looking after the horses.   A short distance from the stopping place George Harman found a camp in which fire was still burning and a pair of leggins, which Captain Harman decided from the odor had been with the Indians, and had formerly belonged to Captain James Moore, who had been killed and his house plundered by the Indians a little more than two years before. Captain Harman satisfied that he was in near proximity to the Indians, and night rapidly approaching, decided to retrace his steps, knowing if he remained he would be attacked, and to get out was safer, and would also enable him to give notice to the settlers; he thereupon called in Matthias, caught up the horses and moved out; he and Mr. Draper in front, the horses next, and George and Matthias to bring up the rear. They had proceeded but short distance, when they were fired upon by the Indians, some six or seven in number. Draper retired at the fire of the first gun, and hid himself in the branches of a fallen tree, a little to the rear of the scene of conflict, so that the Harmans were left alone to contend with at least, if not more than double their own number. The fight was close and bloody, Captain Harman receiving one severe, and other slight wounds from arrows. George had a hand to hand conflict with one of the savages, whom with the help of Matthias, he succeeded in dispatching. Two of the Indians being killed, and two wounded, those still unhurt with the wounded ones, beat a retreat, and the Harmans pursued their way safely homeward. Draper from his hiding place had observed the retreat of the Indians, crept out, hurried into the settlement, and reported the Harmans killed. This brief account of the affair taken from a copy of the "Harman Ms", in posession of the author. A much fuller account of this fight will be found in Bickley's History of Tazewell, and in Summers' History of Southwestern Virginia, to which the reader is referred, and attention is called to the correct date upon which the fight took place, the other publications having the dates wrong by four years. About twenty years ago some gentlemen in McDowell County, West Virginia, (this fight took place in what is now the territory of McDowell County), on a hunting tour over the side of the mountain nearby the battle ground and under a cliff of rock, found the skeleton of a human being, and brought away the skull, and presented the same to Mr. Hiram Christian, of McDowell. It was very peculiarly shapped, and all who saw it pronounced it the skull of an Indian.

Capt. Henry Harman wrote some verses on this battle which are herein inserted, which are as follows:

HARMAN'S BATTLE SONG.

"Come all ye bold heroes whose hearts flow with courage,
   With respect pay attention to a bloody fray
Fought by Captain Harman and valiant sons,
   With the murdering Shawnees they met on the way.

This battle was fought on the twelfth of November,
   Seventeen hundred and eighty and eight,
Where God of his mercy stood by those brave heroes,
   Or they must have yielded to a dismal fate.

Oh! nothing would do this bold Henry Harman
   But down to Tug River without more delay,
With valiant sons and their noble rifles,
   Intending a number of bears for to slay.

They camped on Tug River with pleasing contentment,
   Till the sign of bloodthirsty Shawnees appears,
Then with brave resolution they quickly embark,
   To cross the high mountains and warn the frontiers.

Brave Harman rode foremost with undaunted courage
   Nor left his old trail those heathen to shun;
His firm resolution was to save Bluestone,
   Though he knew by their sign there were near three to one.

The first salutation the Shawnees did give them,
   They saw the smoke rise from behind some old logs;
Brave Harman to fight them then quickly dismounted,
   Saying, "Do you lie there you savage, murdering dogs?"

He says, "My dear sons stand by me with courage,
   And like heroes fight on till you die on the ground;"
Without hesitation they swiftly rushed forward;
   They'd have the great honor of taking their hair.

At first by the host of the Redskins surrounded,
   His well pointed gun made them jump behind trees;
At last all are slain, but two, and they wounded,
   Cherokee in the shoulder, and Wolf in the knees.

Great thanks to Almighty for the strength and the courage,
   By which the brave Harmans triumphed o'er the foe;
Not the women and children, they intended to slaughter,
   But the bloody invaders themselves are laid low.

May their generation on the frontiers be stationed,
   To confound and defeat all their murdering schemes,
And put a flustration to every invasion,
   And drive the Shawnees from Montgomery's fair streams."

In the the early spring of 1789, James Roark and family
lived at a gap of the ridge, dividing the waters of Clinch and
Sandy Rivers, and near the head spring of the Dry fork of
Sandy, and on and near the line dividing the counties of Russell and Mongomery. A raiding party of Indians had come
up the Dry fork of the Sandy, and unexpectedly to them, quite
a snow had fallen and they took shelter or camped under a
large overhanging rock opposite the mouth of Dick's Creek, of
Dry fork. It was while under this rock, waiting for the snow
to disappear, that they discovered William Wheatley, who
lived in Baptist Valley, in search of his lost dog, killed him,
mutulated his body, tore out his bowels, stretched them upon
the bushes, his heart being found in one place, his liver in
another. On a large beech tree near the place where Wheatly
was killed, the Indians cut the figure of a man, which was
plainly visible a few years ago. After the killing of Wheatley,
and the snow had disappeared, they moved up Dry fork and fell

upon the family of Roark, killing his wife and several children and then retired down the Sandy.

In the fall of this same year of 1789, a body of Indians came into the Bluestone and upper Clinch settlements, crossed the East River mountain on to the waters of the Clear fork of Wolf Creek, prowled around for several days to find, as afterwards ascertained, the home of George and Matthias Harman; they supposed they had killed Captain Henry Harman in the fight on the Tug the year before. Late in the evening of the first day of October, 1789, they suddenly appeared at the door of the cabin of Thomas Wiley, on Clear Fork, at what is now known as the "Dill's Place." Mr. Wiley was from home, they took his wife, Virginia, and five children prisoners, plundered the house, and moved off up Cove Creek, where they killed all of Mrs. Wiley's children, crossed the East River mountain by the farm owned by the late Walter McDonald Sanders, down Beaver Pond Creek, by where the town of Graham, Virginia, is now situated, striking Bluestone, and across Flat Top mountain by way of the Pealed Chestnuts, and down the north fork of the Tug fork to the Harman battle ground, (a part of the same Indians that captured Mrs. Wiley, were in the fight with Harman.) On the battlefield they gathered together some of the bones of their comrades who had fallen in the fight, and bemoaned and bewailed their loss, and finally the leader of the party said to Mrs. Wiley, "Here I killed Old Skygusty," the name they had given Captain Harman; Mrs. Wiley replied, "No you didn't for I saw him last week." The Indian, apparently nettled at her reply, said, "You lie, you Virginia Huzza, you lie, for when I shot him I heard him call on his God." Mrs. Wiley was taken to the Indian town at Chillicothe where she remained until the last days of September, 1792, when she escaped; a full history of which will be given later on when we narrate the events occurring in year of 1792. This incident is taken in part from a letter of Mr. Armstrong Wiley and from a report made by Colonel Robert Trigg to the Governor of Virginia which will be found in the Virginia Calendar Papers

A marauding party of Indians entered the Bluestone and upper Clinch settlements, in the year of 1790, which greatly alarmed the settlers, who took prompt measures to repel and punish them.   They committed no other outrage than to steal a large number of horses from the people, which they succeeded in getting away with. At the coming of the Indians in this year of 1790, an event happened in the neighborhood of the Davidson-Bailey Fort, which was deeply impressed upon the minds of those conversant with what is about to be related. John Bailey, son of Richard, the settler, had married a daughter of John Goolman Davidson, the settler, and the buildings at the fort being so crowded, and Mr. Bailey desiring to set out for himself, had on Boyer's Branch, about three-fourths of a mile north-east of the fort, erected him a fairly good one room log house to which he took his young wife, and there in the summer of 1790, was born his first child and eldest son, Jonathan, who was only four days old when the Indians entered the neighborhood. The young mother seized her babe, mounted a horse and rode to the fort, from which she seemed to suffer no injury or inconvenience. If such were to happen in this our day there is at least a probability there would be a funeral or a heavy physician's bill to pay.

Jonathan Bailey long lived, dying in 1770, leaving behind him a numerous progeny of as good people as live in any community.

The General Assembly of Virginia in October, 1789, created the county of Wythe within the following boundaries: All that part of Montgomery which lies south and west of a line beginning in the Henry line at the head of Big Reedy Island, from thence to Wagon ford on Peek Creek, thence to the Clover bottom on Bluestone, thence to the Kanawha line, shall form one distinct county, and to be called and known by the name of Wythe. Court for Wythe to be held at the house of James McGavock." By this same act a part of the western part of the County of Botetourt was added to Montgomery. The western line of Wythe was the same as had been the western line of Mongomery County viz: from the second ford of Holstein above the Royal Oak to the west end of Morriss' Knob and then to the head waters of the Sandy at Roark's gap. And this remained unchanged until the county of Tazewell was created in 1800.

Andrew Davidson, son of John Goolman Davidson had married Rebecca Burke, granddaughter of James Burke, the reputed discoverer of Burke's Garden, and had made his settlement at the head spring of the East River, less than a half mile from what is now the east limits of the city of Bluefield, West Virginia. The spring of 1791 being late, Andrew Davidson having some important business at Smithfield (Draper's Meadows) from which his father and family had removed about ten years before, set off from home in the early part of April leaving at home his wife, his three small children, two girls and boy, and two bound children, orphans, whose names were Bromfield. Mr. Davidson had requested his brother-in law, John Bailey, to look after his family. Shortly after Mr. Davidson's departure, perhaps two or three days, and while Mrs. Davidson was gathering sugar water from sugar maple trees close by the house, there suddenly appeared several Indians, who told her she would have to go with them to their towns beyond the Ohio. There was no alternative although she was in no condition to make such a trip, as she was then rapidly approaching motherhood. Taking such plunder as they could carry, they set fire to the house and with their prisoners departed; the Indians helping along with the children. On the way, near where Logan Court House, West Virginia, now stands, Mrs. Davidson by reason of the exertion and anxiety of mind gave birth to her child. Only two hours relaxation from the march was allowed her and they again pushed on. The little stranger after a day's time, they drowned. On the fateful morning on which Mrs. Davidson and her chidren were captured, John Bailey being at the fort informed his people that he must go over and look after Andrew Davidson's family, whereupon one of his sisters, (he had but two,) told him to get her a horse and that she would go with him, to which he assented and secured the horse for her. They set out on the journey, going up Boyer's Branch to the gap in the ridge, where the livery stable of Mr. J. C. Higgenbothen now stands inside the city limits of Bluefield, and which spot has now been selected for the site of the Federal building shortly to be erected. On reaching this gap Mr. Bailey discovered a heavy smoke from the direction of the Davidson house, and thereupon told his sister to remain on her horse in the gap and watch while he went forward to a piece of ground in the valley, (the hill on which lately stood the Higgenbothen residence, but which hill has been recently removed). He hurriedly returned, reporting the house on fire, and that evidently the Indians had been there and taken the people, as no one could be seen about the house. Mr. Bailey and his sister rode rapidly to the fort, gave the alarm to the neighborhood, and a party gathered as quickly as possible and pursued the Indians, but the leaves being dry the savages had left but few, if any marks, and the party was unable to overtake them. On arriving at the Indian town, the little girls of Mrs. Davidson were tied to trees and shot to death before her eyes. The boy, her son, was given to an old squaw, who in crossing a river with him upset the canoe and the boy was drowned. As to what became of the two bound children, was by the white people never known.

Mrs. Davidson was in captivity from April, 1791, until a date subsequent to Wayne's victory over the United Indian Tribes at Fallen Timbers in August, 1794. Mr. Davidson made the second trip in search of his wife before he found her. He had before his second trip received information through an old Indian which led him across the Canadian border, and stopping at a farm house to obtain a meal, observed a woman passing him as he entered the house, to whom he merely bowed and went in. Shortly the woman came in with a load of wood and laying it down, looked at the stranger for a moment, then turned to her Mistress, (for she had been sold as a servant to a Canadian French farmer), and said, "I know that man;" "Well, who is he?" said the French lady. "It is my husband! Andrew Davidson, I am your wife." Mr. Davidson was not only astounded, but joyfully and more than agreeably surprised, for when he last saw his wife, she was a fine healthy looking woman, her hair as black as a raven's wing, but had now turned to snowy white. Mr. Davidson returned, bringing with him his wife, and they settled at the mouth of Abb's Valley on a farm now owned by A. C. Davidson, Esq. Mr. and Mrs. Davidson raised another family of children, she long lived, and when she died, her remains were removed to and buried in the Burke burying ground at the Horse Shoe farm on New River in the now county of Giles. At the time of the capture of Mrs. Davidson in April, 1791, the place where she was captured was then in that part of Wythe County, which is now Mercer County, West Virginia.

Major Robert Crockett was for a number of years including 1791, and for some years later, the military commandant in Wythe County, and for a good part of the time made his headquarters on the Clinch at Wynn's Fort.

A band of Indians from the Ohio country, came in July, 1792, into the Bluestone and upper Clinch settlements and began their depredations—stealing horses, which they had found to be a profitable business. They stole the horses of the settlers, and ran them over into Canada, where they sold them at remunerative prices.

Major Crockett assembled forty men at the place where stands the residence of the late Captain Thomas Peery. Among the number who obeyed the call of Major Crockett were Joseph Gilbert and Samuel Lusk, the latter a youth of about sixteen years, but with quite an experience as an Indian spy and scout, having made a number of trips with the said Joseph Gilbert, who was a noted Indian scout and hunter.

The late Captain James Shannon of the county of Wyoming, West Virginia, when about ninety three years of age, related to the author, that he rode behind his father on a horse to the assembly ground, and well recollected Joseph Gilbert as an active atheletic young man, and that he also saw Lusk on the same occasion.

Major Crockett moved off with his men to follow the Indians, having no time to prepare provisions for the journey. They took the route down Horse Pen Creek, and to the head of Clear fork, and down to the Tug and on to the mouth of Four Pole, then crossing the dividing ridge between the waters of the Sandy and Guyandotte Rivers. They sent Gilbert and Lusk forward to a Buffalo lick on a creek flowing into the Guyandotte, to secure if possible a supply of game. It appears by the report of Major Crockett, found in the Virginia Calendar Papers, that this was on the twenty fourth day of July that Gilbert and Lusk set out for and reached the lick, where they found and killed a deer and wounded an elk, which they followed, some distance; being unable to overtake it they returned to the lick to get the deer they had killed. On passing along the Buffolo path, near which they had left the deer, Gilbert in front, discovered a stone hanging by pawpaw bark over the path. Gilbert in an instant discerning what it meant called on Lusk to look out. He had scarcely uttered the words, when the Indians fired, a ball from one of their guns penetrating the hand of Lusk, in which he carried his gun, which caused him to drop the same. The Indians immediately began to close in on them, Gilbert putting Lusk behind him, and holding the Indians off by the presentation of his gun. Gilbert and Lusk kept retreating as rapidly as they could with safety. Lusk's wounded hand was bleeding freely, and he became sick from the loss of blood, and begged Gilbert to leave him and get away; this Gilbert refused to do, saying, that he promised his, Lusk's mother, to take care of him. Finally the Indians got close enough to knock Gilbert down with their tomahawks, which they did, and an Indian rushed up to scalp him, when Gilbert shot him dead, but another one of the Indians dispatched Gilbert, and Lusk became a prisoner. The Indians immediately hur-

ried with their prisoner down the creek to Guyandotte, and
then down the river to the mouth of Island Creek, and went
into camp behind a rocky ridge called Hog Back at the present
day. Major Crockett instead of following the tracks of Gilbert
and Lusk to the lick, had turned to the west, and crossed a
ridge onto the right fork of Island Creek, and reached and
camped at a point within two miles of the Indian camp, but
without knowledge of his proximity to them. During the night
Lusk suffered much with his hand until an Indian went off and
brought some roots which he beat up into a pulp, made a poul-
tice, and bound his hand which afforded relief. Early on the
morning of the 25th the Indians took to their canoes, which
they had left at this point on their way to the settlements,
and rapidly descending the river to its mouth crossed the Ohio.
On reaching the northern bank, they placed their canoes in
charge of some of their party and taking Lusk with them
crossed the country.

The Indians had learned some things from their contact with
white men, among them was to wear a hunting shirt, a loose
garment which they fastened around the waist, leaving it open
and loose above the waist. These Indians that had Lusk in
charge had donned the hunting shirt. On the way across the
country, on the evening they crossed the Ohio, and before halting to camp, they passed through some prairie country, and
Lusk observed that they kept now and then stooping down taking something from the ground, and putting inside of their
hunting shirts. When they had reached their camping place,
and had built a fire, they went off and brought a large iron
kettle, put on the fire, and put into it a considerable quantity
of water, and when it began to approach the boiling point, the
Indians gathered around the kettle and began to take something from the inside of their hunting shirts and throw into the
water, and seemed to be in high glee as indicated by their
laughter. Lusk ventured up to see what it meant, and found it
was dry land toads they had gathered on the route and were
putting into the hot boiling water. They were preparing sup-

per, and when they had reduced the water and the toads to the consistency of a good thick mush, they took the kettle from the fire and permitted the mush to cool; they then took wooden spoons, offering one to Lusk, which he refused, and gathered around the kettle and began to eat. Finding that Lusk would not eat with them, one of their number went off and procured some jerked buffalo meat and furnished it to Lusk. The journey was resumed the next morning, and during the day their town of Chillicothe was reached, where Lusk met and made the acquaintance of Mrs. Virginia Wiley, who had been captured on the first day of October, 1789, as herein before related.

Lusk's wounded hand rapidly healed, and the Indians put him to work in their corn fields, and later to aid in building some new cabins for the winter. He appearing to be an expert at what is termed carrying up a corner, while so engaged and notching down a piece of timber, his axe threw off a lage chip of wood, which struck a stout young Indian about Lusk's size and age in the face, which made the young fellow very angry. Believing or pretending to believe, that Lusk had intentionally caused the chip to strike him, he thereupon challenged Lusk for a fight, which challenge Lusk accepted, came down from the house, and gave to his challenger a fearful thrashing. The other Indians stood by and praised Lusk, and made fun at the other fellow, who though whipped, was yet very angry. He went off and secured two large knives, came back offering one to Lusk, and challenged him to mortal combat. The older Indians advised Lusk not to take the knife, but to keep out of his way, and at the same time shake his fist at him, which he did only adding insult to injury; but finally by the interposition of the older heads the matter was adjusted. In September the Indians planned and made ready for their annual fall hunt in the region of the lakes. It was towards the latter part of the month when the hunting party left Chillicothe going north, leaving only the squaws, the children, and an old Indian Chief in charge of the town, and the prisoners Lusk and Mrs. Wiley. Lusk determined to make his escape, and made known his in-

tention to Mrs. Wiley, who declared that she would go with
him. He sought to dissuade her as she could prabably not keep
up with him in traveling, and might very much hinder and em-
barrass him if they would be pursued. Up to the time of the
departure of the hunting party, Lusk had made himself help-
ful to his captors, but expressed himself as delighted with his
new made acquaintances, and expressed a desire to remain with
them, whereby he ingratiated himself fully into their confidence, so much so that they seemed not to have the slightest
doubt of his sincerity. Not so as to Mrs .Wiley, who had frequently shown signs of uneasiness and inclination to go away;
so that when the hunting party was about to depart Mrs. Wiley
was placed in charge of the old Indian Chief with directions to
keep close watch on her.

In the course of events it so happened late one September
evening near the last of the month, and just before the sun was
setting, that the Old Indian Chief, who was lying on the
ground, required Mrs. Wiley to sit down beside him; he drawing the skirts of her dress far enough towards him that he
could lie on the same which he did; turning his face from Mrs.
Wiley, he went to sleep. He had on his belt his scalping
knife, the squaws were busy about their house work, when Lusk
made known to Mrs. Wiley, that he was ready and about to go,
and she determined to go with him, and reaching over the body
of the old Chief she secured his scalping knife, cut that portion of her dress underneath him from the other portion on
her body, and hurrying down to the bank of the Scioto, where
Lusk had a light canoe in readiness, they entered the same and
immediately and as quietly as possible set off swiftly and rapidly down the river for the southern bank of the Ohio, fifty
miles away, Lusk using the pole and Mrs. Wiley the paddle.
They reached the southern bank of the Ohio about daylight the
next morning where they abandoned their canoe, and immediately set out up the Ohio. Lusk believing they would be pursued, and afraid to follow up the Sandy or Guyandotte waters
for fear of either being overtaken, or meeting with some roving

bands of savages, he steadily kept his course up the southern bank of the Ohio to opposite Gallipolis, where a few French people lived, crossed over into the village and found a place of refuge, where he and Mrs. Wiley could hide away until the dan- ger of recapture had passed.

In a few days a pursuing party of Indians reached Gallipo- lis, but failing to find the runaways soon departed. Mr. Lusk determined to take no risks by attempting to return through the Virginia Mountains, and finding some men passing up the Ohio in a push boat bound for Pittsburg, he secured passage with them, leaving Mrs. Wiley, who declined to go in the boat, with her kind protectors in Gallipolis. In a few days after Lusk's departure, Mrs. Wiley made up her mind to endeavor to make her way home by the Kanawha and New Rivers, which she did after many days, and a long tiresome, and dangerous journey, finally reaching her husband's brother and family at Wiley's Falls on New River in the now county of Giles, Vir- ginia.

Lusk made his way to Pittsburg, and from thence to Phila- delphia, where he accidently met Major Joseph Cloyd, of Back Creek, and came home with him some time in October, about one month after his escape from the Indians at Chillicothe.

It was related to the author several years ago by Captain Wil- liam Stowers, of Bland County, Virginia, then a man above the age of eighty years, but very intelligent, that he well remem- bered Mrs. Virginia Wiley, who a number of years after her re- turn from captivity visited his father's house on Clear fork of Wolf Creek near the spot where she was captured, and that her mind was weak, that in fact she had had but little mind since her return from captivity, and that he heard her relate to his father and family the story of her capture, the killing of her children on Cove Creek, her journey to the Indian town, and her escape; and among other things, her conversation with the Indian on the Harman battle field on Tug. A letter from Arm- strong Wiley to the author states that both Mrs. Wiley and her

husband, Thomas Wiley are buried in the Wiley burying
ground at Wiley's Falls in Giles County.

John Goolman Davidson, to whom reference has heretofore
been made, had with his family resided for some time preceding his removal to the Beaver Pond spring with Richard Bailey
in 1780, at Smithfield (Draper's Meadows). While living at
Smithfield, a man by the name of Rice had stolen a hog from
Davidson, for which he was apprehended, convicted and sentenced to receive and did receive on his bare back well laid on
forty lashes, save one. Rice was so enraged at Mr. Davidson,
that he vowed he would have revenge, if he had to bring the Indians upon him. We shall soon see how well Rice kept and performed his vow, and succeeded in having his revenge, although more than ten years had elapsed before the opportunity
was afforded him.

Mr. Davidson having some unfinished business at his former
home in the valley of Virginia, Rockbridge County, among
others, the collection of some eight hundred dollars due him,
determined upon a visit to the valley to close up his business
and get his money. As was not unusual when some one was
going from the frontier into the settlements, it was noised
throughout the neighborhood, that Mr. Davidson was going to
make the journey. In the month of February, 1793, Mr. Davidson set out on horseback, reached his destination safely, settled his business, collected his money, and started on his way
homeward, having with him an extra horse which he was leading. He came over the usual route of travel to Rocky gap, was
seen to pass south of that point by a family residing near the
pathway. The spring of 1793 is said by the old people who
then lived, to have been the earliest ever known by them, the
timber putting forth its leaves the first of March.

Richard Bailey, who has already been spoken of, had given
to his youngest son, whose name was Henry, a small calf, which
had been turned out with the other cattle in the range to make
their living off the young twigs and leaves that had begun to
shoot forth. The calf failing to come up to the fort with the

other cattle on the evening of the eighth day of March, 1793,
Mr. Bailey told his son that it might have gotten mired in some
swampy land down the creek, and that he must get up very
early the next morning, which was on the ninth, and go look
for his calf. The boy rose early, called his bear dogs, and set
off down the Beaver Pond Creek in the direction of where Graham, Virginia, is now situated. Not finding the calf on his
outward trip, he on his return left the Buffalo trail and was
passing up through the swampy bottom land, when his dogs
suddenly raised their bristles as if they were about to engage
in combat with some wild animal; the boy supposing it was
probably a wolf, rushed forward to see the fight, and looking
along the path he saw a body of men and horses, which so
alarmed him, that he fled to the fort and reported what he had
seen. An older brother, Micajah, gathered his rifle and followed
the party far enough, to discover that it was composed of a
body of Indians. He immediately returned to the fort, spread
the alarm, and Major Robert Crockett, then on the head of
Clinch, gathered a party of men, and followed the Indians
whose camp late one evening he discovered on the large island
at the mouth of Island Creek, just across the river from where
now stands Logan Court House, West Virginia.

After carefully reconnoitering the position, Major Crockett
decided to have the men lay on their arms that night, and make
the attack at break of day the next morning. He had observed
that the Indians had hobbled their horses and turned them out
on the island to graze. It may be noted that this island contained originally, about one hundred acres, but after it was
denuded of its timber and put in cultivation, the soil being of a
sandy nature, has by the effect of high tides in the river been
carried away until there remains now but a few acres of what
was the original bottom.

As it is said to have been, on the morning of the 15th of March,
March, Major Crockett had his men up and arranged for the attack by the time it was light enough to see an object. He told his
men that the Indians would be astir early, that while some were

preparing breakfast, one or more would come out to round up
the horses and drive them into camp. His instructions were
for his men to wait for the horse drivers to start them toward
the camp, and to then quietly follow them into camp and make
the attack. Crockett had with him a man by the name of Gid
Wright, who when the advance began, was thrown close to one
of the Indians engaged in driving the horses, and who took a severe Buck Ague as the backwoodsmen term it, (extreme case of
nervousness), and without obeying his orders fired at the Indian missing him, but alarming the camp, so that the whole Indian party took to flight. John Bailey, an active and quick
man on foot, ran close enough as the Indians were leaving to
kill one of them, the rest escaped, leaving their breakfast cooking, which the whites appropriated, and the stolen horses, all
of which were recovered. Among the number of horses captured was one recognized as belonging to Mr. Davidson, and
the one which he had ridden from home, and on which was his
saddle, with one stirrup. a brass one, missing. The party immediately determined that Mr. Davidson had been killed by
this gang, and his horse taken, and after eating their breakfast,
and gathering up the horses they started for their homes and
to search for Mr. Davidson's body. Samuel Lusk was with
Major Crockett's party, and on the return assisted in the
search for the body of Mr. Davidson. So soon as the party
reached the settlement, they sent out men along the path leading through Bailey's gap in East River mountain, and on to
the Laurel fork of Clear fork of Wolf Creek, and through
Rocky Gap, finding on the path on the mountain a hat band
recognized as belonging to Mr. Davidson's hat. On inquiry it
was found, that Mr. Davidson had passed the settlements south
of Rocky gap before noon on the 8th day of March, and it was
discovered at an old waste place at the mouth of Clear fork,
that he had there fed his horses. Further investigation at the
point where the path left the Laurel fork starting up the mountain, evidence appeared of the blade of a hatchet having been
struck into a white oak tree, and that a gun had rested on the

hatchet, and near by on the bark of a beech tree was freshly cut the name of "Rice," and under the root of the tree on the side of the creek, where the water had washed away the earth, the nude body of Mr. Davidson was found, so far advanced in decomposition it could not be removed to his home, and was buried near by where it was found and where it still remains. The statement by some writers that the body was carried to his home and buried is incorrect according to the statements of Mr. Joseph Davidson and Captain John A. Davidson, two of his great grandsons.

Col. Robert Trigg, in his report to the governor, dated on April 10th, 1793, states that Davidson was killed on the 8th day of March of that year, and that there were twelve Indians in the party, who stole a large number of horses and passed through the center of the Bluestone settlement.

Colonel Robert Crockett had reported in October, 1789, to the governor, the capture of Virginia Wiley, and the killing of her four children by the Indians on October 1st of that year.

On October 17th, 1793, Major Robert Crockett and fifty others, among them Joseph Davidson, John Bailey, James Bailey, Reuben Bailey, Richard Bailey, William Smith and John Peery, sent a petition to the governor of Virginia, informing him of the defenceless condition of the border, and asking for assistance, and stating the killing by the Indians of John Davidson on the 8th day of March 1793, and that of Gilbert on the 24th day of July 1792, and the capture of Samuel Lusk at the same time.

The searching party for Mr. Davidson's body found evidences on the ground that satisfied them that Mr. Davidson, had upon being shot from the tree where the blade of the hatchet had been buried, fallen from his horse which took fright and ran out into the brush and vines on the creek bottom, by which one of the brass stirrups had been pulled off. No doubt remains but that Rice and his party got the $800.00 which Mr. Davidson had with him when killed.

Several years after the killing of Mr. Davidson, Captain

William Stowers, then a lad of some fifteen years, while plowing in the bottom where Mr. Davidson was killed, found a brass stirrup which was recognized by the family of Mr. Davidson as one belonging to his saddle, and missing therefrom when his horse and saddle were recovered by Major Crockett and his men on the 15th day of March, 1793.

This Indian incursion was the last made on the waters of Bluestone and the upper Clinch, but the troubles continued for a short while thereafter on the lower Clinch and the Holstein waters as well as along the valley of the Kanawha, where the Indians killed a man by the name of Harriman in the year 1794; he was the last person killed in the valley by Indians.

Davidson and Bailey, the settlers at the Beaver Pond spring in the year of 1780, like all other provident settlers who desired to secure good land, each acquired valuable landed estates, Bailey along the valley of the mountain and around the head of Beaver Pond spring, and Davidson in Wright's Valley, reaching from where the town of Graham is now situated eastward along the valley for three or four miles, including the land on which the city of Bluefield is now located.

So much alarm and consternation was created along the upper Kanawha, and lower New River waters in the early part of the year 1793, by prowling bands of Indians, that the governor of Virginia ordered a company of soldiers to rendezvous at the mouth of Elk on the Kanawha, and to scout through the country to the Ohio.

Captain Hugh Caperton, who lived in Greenbrier County, on the New River, and who was the uncle of the younger Hugh, later of Monroe, was ordered to raise and did raise a company of New River Valley men for the service referred to. Captain Caperton with his men marched to the mouth of Elk, fixing his camp on the right bank of the river at its mouth.

The celebrated Daniel Boone was the commissariat of this company. During the stay of these men on the Kanawha, they guarded the frontier, sending scouting parties to various points along the Ohio and protected the settlers then in the valley, and their homes, by placing one or more men at each house. At this time there were but few settlers in the valley, among them George Clendenin, where Charleston now stands, Leonard Morriss, near where Brownstown now stands, and William Morriss at Kelley's Creek. Clendenin had removed from the Greenbrier section, Leonard and William Morriss from the County of Culpeper, Virginia.

David Johnston, member of Caperton's company, was sent to guard the house of Leonard Morriss. He and Morriss came originally from the same county. Mr. Morriss had a block house for the protection of his family, and some slaves, among them a negro woman, who one day, while Johnston was guarding the house, went outside the stockade to pick up some wood, and was seized by two Indians and carried away. On another occasion, Mrs. Morriss went just outside the gate to milk her cow, the guard accompanying her. He discovered an Indian a little way off in the top of a tree endeavoring to get a view of the fort and its inmates. Mr. Morriss had a small patch of corn in the bottom along the river, which was about ready for cutting, and desiring to look at and to see if anything was troubling it took Johnston, the guard along with him; they agreeing to separate taking different directions so as to get a quick view of the situation and return, and further agreeing that the report of the discharge of a gun should be the signal for them to hasten to the fort. They had not long been out until the report of the discharge of a gun was heard. Johnston reached the fort, and Mrs. Morriss opened for him the gate, which was immediately closed, supposing Mr. Morriss was probably shot, and that the Indians would make a rush for the fort. There being several guns in the fort, Mrs. Morriss said, "Johnston I will load and you shoot." Mr. Morriss soon made his appearance unhurt. Neither he nor Johnston had fired their guns, and after waiting some time they ventured out again, and on going to the place from whence came the report of the discharge of the gun, they found that the Indians had shot a hog there and dressed it. These men of Caperton's company had quite a number of skirmishes with the Indians, but no one was hurt save one man killed, who went across the Kanawha to kill a turkey, whose gobble he had heard. Very soon after crossing the river, the report of the discharge of a gun was heard, and soon thereafter the gobble of the turkey was repeated; whereupon, another of the men remarked that he would get that turkey, and going a considerable distance up the river he crossed, and made his way to the place where he still heard the turkey, and on stealthily creeping up, he discovered the turkey to be an Indian hid in some sprouts that had grown up around a chestnut stump. He killed the Indian and scalped him, but found the Indian had first killed the other man and scalped him.

Captain Caperton and Daniel Boone, his commissariat, had a difficulty, and Boone left the camp, and was absent for some time. Some of the scouting parties met with him at the mouth of the Kanawha, and told him of the necessities of the company and that they needed food, and enquired of him why he had gone off and left them; he replied, "Caperton didn't do to my liken."

The following are the names of the men who belonged to Caperton's company, and were with him on the Kanawha in 1793:

Samuel Henderson	James Keely
Mathias Meadows	George Lake
Isaac Cole	John Conner
John Cooke	John Burton
Edward Farley	Drewry Farley
William Smith	Thomas Cooke
William Lee	Robert Lee
William Graham	Andrew Johnston
James Montgomery	John Garrison
William Stowers	Travis Stowers
Andrew Hatfield	Jonas Hatfield
John Rowe	David Marshall
Francis Farley	Isaac Smith

David Johnston

Henry Massey

David French

Matthew Farley

Felix Williams

James Stuart

James Abbott

Patrick Wilson

John Lewis

Joseph Abbott

Moses Massey

James Graham

David Graham

James Sweeney

Joseph Canterbury

John Scott

—— Noell

Isaiah Calloway ᵔ

William Wilson

George Abbott

On the 20th of August, 1794, General Wayne won his celebrated victory over the Indians, at Fallen Timbers in what is
now Lucas County, Ohio. This defeat completely broke the
Indian power in the Ohio Valley, and a treaty of peace was
soon after made, which gave perfect quiet to all the border settlements, at least south of the Ohio, and perfect peace reigned
supreme for the first time in forty years. No sooner was the
news of Wayne's victory received on the Virginia border, than
the whole country north and west of the settlements, swarmed
with surveyors and land speculators. Nearly if not quite the
whole of the territory south of the Kanawha and the Ohio to
the head waters of Holstein, were entered, surveyed, and carried into grant.

Robert Morris, the patriot and financier of the American
revolution, secured grants for about eight millions of acres of
land. The territory comprised within the now counties of
Mercer, Raleigh, Fayette, McDowell, Wyoming, Boone, Logan,
Mingo, Wayne, Cabell, Lincoln, Kanawha and Putnam were
almost completely shingled over with these large grants, and
frequently they lapped upon each other. Commencing on the
East River Mountain, on the south side, and then again on the
north side, were two grants to Robert Pollard, one for 50,000
and the other for 75,000 acres, then came the grant of 80,000
acres to Samuel M. Hopkins, a grant of 50,000 acres to Robert
Young, 40,000 acres to McLaughlin, 170,000 acres to Moore
and Beckley, 35,500 acres to Robert McCullock, 108,000 acres

to Rutter and Etting, 90,000 acres to Welch ——— 150,000 acres DeWitt Clinton, 50,000 acres to Doctor John Dillon, 480,-000 acres to Robert Morris, 500,000 acres to the same, 150,000 acres to Robert Pollard, 500,000 acres to Wilson Carey Nicholas, 300,000 acres to the same, 320,000 acres to Robert Morris, 57,000 acres to Thomas Wilson, 40,000 acres to George Pickett, and farther down Sandy, Guyandotte and Coal Rivers were large grants to Elijah Wood, Smith and others.

Peace having been restored along the frontier settlements, and no further danger being apprehended from the Indians, there was a great rush of the people, not only from Eastern Virginia and Western North Carolina on to the New River waters, and on to Kentucky, but there was a vast throng of people from the New River Valley, that quickly penetrated the country between the New River settlements and the Ohio, and settled on the Sandy, Guyandotte and Coal River waters, even reaching to the Ohio; among them, the McComas', Chapmans, Lucas', Smiths, Coopers, Napiers, Hunters, Adkins, Acords, Allens, Fryes, Dingess, Lusks, Shannons, Baileys, Jarrells, Egglestons, Fergusons, Marcums, Hatfields, Bromfields, Haldrons, Lamberts, Pauleys, Lawsons, Workmans, Prices, Cookes, Clays, Godbeys, Huffs, McDonalds, Whites, Farleys, Kezees, Perdues, Ballards, Barretts, Toneys, Conleys, Stollings, Stratons, Buchanans, Deskins, and many others, who largely peopled, and left honored descendants throughout the section mentioned.

MANNERS AND CUSTOMS OF THESE BORDER PEOPLE.

When these people left their homes for new ones in the wilderness, they took with them the manners and customs of the people among whom they had lived, and upon their settling down in their adopted abode made such changes in these manners and customs as their new situation, surroundings and necessities required. It often happened that the new emigrant on selecting his proposed future home, found himself very far removed from any one he called neighbor. From whence he removed, he was occasionally honored with a visit of his friends and neighbors, who could come and go without hinderance or fear of molestation. In this wilderness country he must travel with his trusted rifle, even as against wild beast that filled the forest. Later on, after the country had began to settle up, new comers were joyfully received, and the young people on hearing of the approach of the new people coming to the neighborhood, would often go a day's journey in order to meet and welcome them. The young women would make this trip barefoot, with their dresses so short they reached but little below their knees.

A wedding was always a time of high glee. Usually the groom and his friends rode horseback to the house of the bride's father, where there was generally plenty of applejack, and every body would take a drink, even the ministers of that day thought it nothing a_miss for them to take a toddy. At the bride's house and ceremony performed, came the dinner, after which the fiddling and the dancing, the songs and plays among the young folks of "Old Sister Phoebe," would begin:

"I'll put this hat on your head to keep your head warm,
I'll give you a sweet kiss, 'twill do you no harm."

The neighbors soon gathered, chopped logs and erected a house for the young couple. At a log rolling and house raising there was generally a quilting, and at night a dance. It was no easy matter for the young people, who wished to get married to procure the license, for as a rule they lived a long distance from the clerk's office. For many years after the formation of Giles County, it was the habit of Captain John Mc-Claugherty, who was both deputy clerk and deputy sheriff of that county, to go once, and occasionally twice a year down on to the waters of the Coal and Guyandotte, either to collect taxes or to serve process, and he made it a rule to fill his pocket with blank licenses, in order to accommodate the young people, who had always to put off their weddings until the Captain put in his appearance, and when he did, it was soon noised abroad and the young men about to be married hurried to the Captain to get the necessary papers.

There were no schools in that day, and but few boys learned even to read or write. Afterwards, if a school teacher came into the neighborhood and was employed to teach school, he usually boarded around among the families; that is, after settlements had progressed far enough for him to do this. Each family was largely a little independent colony of itself. The father and sons worked with mattock, axe, hoe, and sickle. A loom in every house was a necessity, and almost every woman was a weaver, and wove the linsey-woolsey made from flax cultivated by her own hands, and from the wool of sheep—when they had any. The man tanned or dressed the buck skin, the woman was the tailor and shoemaker, made the deer skin sifters to be used instead of bolting cloths. For the table ware generally wooden trenchers, platters, noggins, and bowls. The cradle of pealed hickory bark or a sugar trough, and plowshares were made of wood, chaff beds if the man had been fortunate enough to raise any small grain, otherwise leaves were substituted. Then there was the hand mill, and the hominy block with a hole burned in the top as a mortar where the pestle was worked. Some times a gritting board was used, and later a pounding mill was invented which was operated by water instead of muscle. For sugar resort was had by tapping the sugar maple trees, and boiling down the water. Salt and iron could not be had in the backwoods, and each family gathered up its furs and peltries, and later ginseng, which were carried out on horses to some coast town, and exchanged for salt and iron. Some, among them Captain James Moore of Abb's Valley, raised considerable number of horses, which they drove to the markets east of the Alleghanies.

It was no common thing at that time, for a man on the New River waters to drive a two year old steer to Fincastle and exchange the same for a bushel of salt, and bring it back on a pack horse. Their horses were usually unshod. Captain William T. Moore, of Abb's Valley, told of a horse that the Indians had taken from his Grandfather, James Moore, but which had been recovered, and which he had plowed, and which lived to the age of thirty five years, and never had a shoe on its foot.

After the backwoodsman had gotten to raising hogs, for at the beginning he could not do so on account of the bears destroying them, he would drive his hogs to market, selling and exchanging them for needed articles at home. The life of these people was a long and dangerous struggle, they had to fell the forests, encounter the forest fires, deep snows and freshets. Swarms of deer flies and midges rendered life a torment in warm weather. Rattlesnakes and copperheads were plentiful, and constant sources of danger and death. For an antidote for the bite of a poisonous serpent bear's oil was freely applied, and some times salt, when they had it. Wolves and bears were inveterate foes of the live stock, and the panther occasionally attacked a man. In the early settlement of the country near the mouth of Wolf Creek in what is now Giles County, the dogs of Mr. Landon Duncan drove a panther up a tree. Mr. Duncan being from home, his wife took his rifle gun and shot and killed the animal; it measured nine feet in length. Every backwoodsman was a hunter, and the forests were filled with deer, turkeys and pigeons, and out of these and the bear, buffalo and elk he made not only his meat, but largely his living. The black and grey squirrels were very numerous, sometimes destroying fields of corn, and at times in immense companies would migrate, and cross mountains and rivers. A race of men unused to war and ever present dangers, would have been helpless before such foes as these wild beasts and the Indians.

People coming from the old world, no matter how thrifty and adventurous, could not hold their own on the frontier. They had to seek protection from the Indians by a bold living wall of American backwoodsmen. These border men were hunters, wood choppers, farmers and soldiers. They built and manned their own forts, did their own fighting in their own way under their own commanders, when they had such, but generally every man was his own commander. There were no regular troops along the frontier, and if the Indians came into the country, each border man had to defend himself, until there was time to arouse the country and gather help to repel the foe. Every man from his childhood was accustomed to the use of the rifle, and even a boy at twelve years was regarded old enough to have a gun, and was soon taught how to use it. He at least could make a good fort soldier. The war was never ending, for even the times of so-called peace were broken by forays and murders. A man might grow from boyhood to middle age on the border, and yet never recall a single year in which some of his neighbors were not killed by the Indians. As the settlements continued to grow they each had their various officers, who in fact exercised but little authority, as they had no way of enforcing orders, and all services rendered were merely voluntary.

When a group of families moved out into the wilderness, for protection they would build for themselves a block house or stockade, a square palisade of upright logs, and looped it with port holes, with a large gate that could be strongly barred in case of necessity. This fort or stockade was generally safe from any attack the savages might make upon it, unless they could take it by surprise. This backwoodsman was generally an American by birth and parentage, and of mixed race, but the dominant strain in their blood was that of the Scotch-Irish, so called. The Irish Presbyterians were themselves already a mixed people, though mainly from Scotch ancestors, who came originally from both lowlands and highlands, for among both were Scotch Saxons and Scotch Celts. From this Scotch-Irish stock, came David Crockett, (1) John Robertson, Andrew Lewis, Andrew Jackson, Samuel Houston, the Prestons, Cummings, Johnstons, Shelbys, Campbells, Grahams, Banes, Gillespies, Georges, McDonalds, McKensey and McComas'.

No great number of them came to America prior to 1730, but

(1). David Crockett is said to have learned the hatter's trade at Christiansburg, Virginia.

by which time they came by multitudes; (2) for the most part,
in two streams; the larger to Philadelphia, the lesser to Charleston, South Carolina. Those from Philadelphia soon made their
way southwest into the valley of Virginia and to the Piedmont
region; while those from Charleston soon pushed their way up
to the mountains. and with those in Virginia became the advanced posts of civilization. They were wholly a different people in manners, customs and temperament from the people of
the tidewater region, in which there was a large admixture of
Germans from Pennsylvania, especially so in the Virginia Valley. Some of this German population came across the Alleghanies, and settled in part, in what is now Montgomery County, and in the eastern portion of what is now Giles County,
among them the Kinsers, Bargers, Highbarges, Shufflebargers,
Hornbargers, Phlegars, Sibolds, Surfaces, Snidows, Straleys,
Boltons, Clyburns, Noslers, Decks. Millers, Honakers, Keisters,
Croys, Worleys and Woolwines. There came also some of the
Scotch-Irish people into the same territory, among them the
McDonalds, Blacks, McKenseys, Johnstons, Christians, Preston,s Craigs, Triggs, McGavocks, Wileys, and Whitakers. (3)
Some Hugenots also came into the territory of what is now
Giles County, among them the Pearis' Hares and DeCamps;
and in the same territory came some Hollanders. among them,
the Lybrooks (Leibroch), Mosers, Walls, Decks and Douthats.
Most of these people brought with them their Bibles, which was
as a usual thing the guide of their lives, and although they at
first had but few, if any ministers among them, yet as a rule
they were religiously inclined, many of them coming from
countries where they had been taught religious principles, but
those coming direct from the old world did not comprehend
what religious freedom and soul liberty meant in its fullest
sense and its fullest extent, until they reached the wilderness
country, where every man could worship God according to the
dictates of his own conscience. They had no church buildings,

(2). Roosevelt's "Winning of the West."
(3). The Willeys and Whittakers came from North Carolina.

but gathered in the groves, "God's first temples" and in dwelling houses to have worship.

Captain James Moore, and also Zechariah Munsey, grand-father of the distinguished William E. Munsey, were christian men and had worship in their families. Munsey was an early Methodist Preacher.

The first preachers that came into the wilderness country, and in fact all who came up to a period long after the close of the American Revolution, were Dissenters, who found perfect freedom in the wilderness from molestation, interruption or arrest. The nearest church of England man to this wilderness country for many long, long years, was located at Fincastle, but so far as known he never ventured across the Alleghanies. Among the first, if not the very first, preachers of the Gospel that ever stood on or reached the banks of the New River were the two who accompanied Lewis' Sandy expedition in 1756. and whose names were Brown and Craig. (4) The first minister to permanently locate in this wilderness section, was the distinguished and learned Presbyterian, Charles Cummings, who came to a place near the present town of Abingdon in 1772. Six years thereafter came Elder Tidence Lane, a Baptist Minister who is believed to have founded the Baptist church at St. Clair's bottom in 1777 or 1778, and who organized two churches on the Holstein waters, one on Buffalo ridge six miles east of Jonesboro, and Cherokee Baptist church four miles east of Jonesboro, both now in Tennessee. In 1773 came Squire Boone from the Yadkin in North Carolina, and whether he was regularly ordained Baptist Minister or not, he at least preached the Gospel. He spent the winter of 1773-4 in Castle's woods, now in Russell County. A little later came James Abbott, a Baptist Minister from Culpeper County, to the New River section. And in 1777 came John Alderson, a Baptist Minister from the Valley of Virginia and located on Greenbrier River, and a little later came a Mr. Johnston, Baptist preacher who subsequently went to the Kanawha Valley, and

(4). They were Presbyterian ministers from the Valley.

then on to Kentucky. Later still came Josiah Osborn, Lewis Alderson and James Ellison, all Baptist Ministers who located in the Greenbrier section.

The early Baptist preachers, in southwest Virginia, were Elders Jonathan Mulkey, Andrew Baker, Edward Kelley, Barnett Reynolds, John Bundridge, ——— Colley, Jesse Senter, and ——— Edwards. In the year of 1788, came the Rev. Francis Asbury, the first Methodist Bishop of America. He reinvigorated the itinerant system, and sent missionaries into wide ranges of country to preach and found new societies. And it is said of him that in 1785 he laid the foundation for the first Methodist College in America, and organized many societies throughout the country. There were practically no church buildings in the wilderness in the days of Bishop Asbury and other early preachers; now the country is dotted over with numerous church buildings of nearly all religious denominations.

Landon Duncan, born in Fauquier County, Virginia, removed from thence to Stokes County, North Carolina, and from there to what is now Giles County, about the close of the 18th century, became a Baptist preacher of the order of New Lights, but in 1818 changed his views, and united with the followers of those who adopted the doctrines taught afterwards by Alexander Campbell. Mr. Duncan was an earnest, faithful preacher during the greater part of his life, which ended about 1867. For many years of his young life he was a school teacher, having among his pupils the late General John B. Floyd, and others who became prominent in their day. Mr. Duncan was for many years, the Commissioner of the Revenue for Giles County.

Except in portions of Greenbrier, Monroe, Montgomery and Tazewell, Presbyterianism had but little footing for many years. Methodism seemed to be well adapted to the soil, and took root quickly, sprang up and grew vigorously. Among some of the early preachers of that denomination was Rev. George Eaken, an Irishman, and most usually called "Father

Eaken;" quaint and peculiar was his style. There was held in
the days of Methodism in its early beginnings in this section,
near the residence of the late Colonel John S. Carr, in what is
now Mercer County, a campmeeting, which Father Eaken attended year by year. Of those who came to the meeting, as
regularly as the meeting was held, were people of the country,
known and designated as "Todds," and so designated on account of their foxey and frolicking disposition, that is they
were drinkers, fighters, gamblers, horse racers and wits generally. These Todds always got happy at campmeeting, and
usually professed to have gotten religion. Father Eaken was
an observant man, and having seen these same people engaged
in drinking and general carousal shortly after the close of the
meeting, he prepared himself for them at the next and while
the meeting was well under way the Todds in a good way
shouting, he suddenly arose, and cried out in a loud voice,
"Would that the good Lord would take a liking to these Todds
just now, for if they ever get to heaven it will be from a campmeeting." The distinguished William G. Brownlow was once
in the County of Tazewell and preached at Bluestone. Among
the early Methodist Ministers who were highly esteemed
in this section of the country were Thomas K. Catlett and Jacob Brillhart. The Methodist had class leaders and exhorters,
among the latter was one Abraham Garretson, who lived on
the East River and whose custom was to go on the Sabbath
into the different neighborhoods in what is now Mercer County and exhort. Garretson had a neighbor by the name of
Blankenship, who though not a christian, yet a constant at-
tendant at his Sunday Exhortations and who always took his
position near the speaker and during the service frequently
said "Amen! Amen!"

On an early Sunday morning in the month of March, Mr.
Blankenship rose early, and went out to feed his cow preparatory to be off to brother Garretson's meeting that day, to be
held at a neighbor's. With Mr. Blankenship to feed his cow went
his dog, which ran a raccoon up a tree, which Mr. Blankenship

captured and took to his house, stripped off its hide, and while
engaged in stretching the same on the side of his cabin there
rode by in the direction of where Mr. Garretson was to hold his
meeting a Mr. Elijah Peters, a Magistrate of the County. Mr.
Blankenship hurried up his work, got his breakfast, took a
shave and put off for the meeting. Mr. Garretson's subject for
the occasion, was the violation of the Sabbath, working on
Sunday; going "coon hunting." Mr. Blankenship squirmed
and twisted as the speaker earnestly told his hearers of these
various Sunday violations till finally Mr. Blankenship being
impressed with the thought that Squire Peters had told Mr.
Garretson that he had been coon hunting on Sunday, determined that he would stand the scourging no longer, and rising
from his seat and addressing the speaker said, "Brother Garretson, who told you I went coon hunting on Sunday?" To
which Garretson replied: "My Lord and Master," whereupon
Mr. Blankenship said in a loud voice: "Well Brother Garretson if Squire Elijah Peters is your Lord and Master, mark my
name off of your book."

Zechariah Munsey was of a family of French extraction,
lived in Giles County, and was a local Methodist Preacher,
and went into various neighborhoods and held meetings. He
was a peculiar, eccentric man with a strange drawling voice,
In the early days, one of his preaching places was at Mechanicsburg, a small hamlet on Walker's Creek. In his congregation at this place were a number of young people who often
became amused at his quaint and peculiar expressions and
were often led into laughter thereby. Mr. Munsey had
frequently reprimanded them, and on one occasion their conduct so disturbed him that it called forth the following utter-
ance from him: "No young gentleman nor young lady properly trained will misbehave at Divine service, and you are in
the habit of doing this, and if the people of Mechanicsburg had
their just dues, they would have been dead and in hell forty
years ago; it's the truth and you know its the truth."

David Munsey, the father of the distinguished William E.

Munsey was a son of Zechariah, and was also a Methodist
Preacher. William E. Munsey spent a part of his young life in
or near that wild, rough section of Giles County known as Dismal. Rough as herein referred to means mountainous and thinly settled. At a campmeeting held at Wabash in the year of
1866 or 1867, William E. Munsey preached on Sunday at 11
o'clock a. m., on the subject of "Hell and the Lost Soul." A
large and attentive audience heard him, among the number,
Captain John A. Pack, who always had a vein of fine humor
and wit. Captain Pack walked up to where was standing a
small group of his acquaintances and friends, and inquired if
they knew why Mr. Munsey had such clear conception of Hell.
Some one inquired why, to which the Captain made answer,
"because he was raised up on Dismal."

Of this Munsey family there were several preachers, a doctor and two or more lawyers. The preachers were Zechariah,
Nathaniel, David, and William E., the lawyers, Thomas J.
Munsey and Thomas J. Munsey, Jr., and Doctor Munsey, a
physician of note, who resides at Pearisburg, Virginia.

Among the most remarkable, eccentric, itinerant, yet local
Methodist preachers that ever lived in the New River Valley,
was Robert Sawyers Sheffey, who was born in the county of
Wythe, Virginia, July 4, 1820, and died in Giles County, Virginia, in 1902. He was a son of Henry Sheffey, of Wythe, and
came into the New River Valley some time in 1859, where he
married for his second wife a Miss Stafford in what is commonly known as Irish settlement, in Giles County, where Mr. Sheffey located. For reasons of his own, he never united with the
Conference, but continued throughout his career as an itinerant, going from place to place, and wheresoever his inclina-
tions led him. He was eccentric beyond description. That
he was a pious devout christian and Godly man was never
doubted. He was a man of wonderful faith in God, and was
usually most eloquent in public prayer. When troubles and
difficulties surrounded him his oft repeated statement was,
"I'll go and talk to the Lord about it." One thing about this

good man which was most remarkable, that his prayers for specific things were not only not in vain, but what he asked the Lord for, he in some way or some how always seemed to receive it. So often were his prayers answered, and his highest hopes and aspirations gratified, that people who knew him well and were disposed to do evil things were frequenly alarmed for fear he would call down vengeance from heaven upon their guilty heads, and many believed that if he should ask the Lord to smite them with pestilence or death it would be done. The eccentricities of this man led numbers of people to express doubts as to his sanity. Some of these expressions reached Mr. Sheffey, and he often publicly repeated what he had heard, and his only comment thereon was, "Would to the Lord they were crazy on the same subject that I am."

Many and interesting are the stories and anecdotes told of this preacher and of his conduct; some of which will here be related, and from which it will appear that while his eccentricities often appear therein, yet the great and strong faith of the man is also exhibited. Twenty-five or more years ago Mr. Sheffey had a regular preaching place on East River in Mercer County, near the residence of Mr. Anderson Tiller, at whose house, when in the neighborhood, he made his stopping place, and where he was always carefully looked after and entertained. It was known that Mr. Sheffey was exceedingly fond of sweet things, and especially of honey. On an occasion, when on a preaching tour, he went to fill his appointment on East River, and became as was usual the guest of his brother, Tiller. Being on a Sunday morning and late in the summer season and while at the breakfast table, Mr. Tiller remarked to Mr. Sheffey that he regretted that he had no honey for him, that his bees had done no good, had not swarmed and that he feared they had frozen out in the winter or that some insect had destroyed them, and that the season was too far spent to have any swarms. Mr. Sheffey arose from the table and went down upon his knees, and told the Lord that the brother's bees had not swarmed, and that there was no honey in the house, and he implored the Lord to have the bees swarm. Scarcely had his petition ceased when the swarms came with such rapidity that Mr. Tiller was unable to procure rapidly enough sufficient gums to save the swarms. The truth of the incident is vouched for by the best people in the neighborhood of where it occurred, and Mrs. James R. White the daughter of Mr. Tiller, and who still lives, and who was at home unmarried at the happening of the incident, vouches for the truthfulness of the story.

At a meeting being held by Mr. Sheffey at Jordan's Chapel, now in Summers County, Dr. Bray, a physician in the neighborhood, together with his wife, was present at Sunday morning service and had with them a nursing infant child, which was taken suddenly ill about the close of the service. The mother became alarmed and grief stricken about the condition of her child, and in her paroxysms she cried out that her child was dying. A large number of people were present and gathered around the mother and child supposed to be dying, when Mr. Sheffey appeared and being informed of the cause of the trouble, said, "Brother, give me the little child," and taking it in his arms he fell upon his knees, and in a most earnest prayer to God asked for the life of the little child and that it might be restored to its mother. Arising from his position on the ground, he handed the child to its father, remarking, "here brother is your little child well and all right;" and so it was.

Mr. Sheffey had a right good vein of humor in his makeup, and he occasionally exercised that faculty to the discomfiture of people. Some thirty years ago, there lived on the upper waters of Brush Creek, a christian gentleman by the name of Robert Karr, a member of the Methodist Church, at whose house Mr. Sheffey was entertained, when on his preaching tours in that neighborhood. He had a protracted service in the neighborhood of Mr. Karr, which had continued some weeks, and which Mr. Karr had not attended, and whose non-attendance Mr. Sheffey had observed, and taking his brother Karr to task about his want of interest in the meeting, enquir-

ed why he did not attend; Mr. Karr replied that he had a good
reason, and being pressed by Mr. Sheffey to give his reason,
he finally said, "Well, I don't just exactly like your way;"
whereupon Mr. Sheffey with a ha! ha! said, "Neither does the
Devil."

On the occasion last mentioned or a similar one, while Mr.
Sheffey was holding a meeting at Mr. Karr's, early one Sunday
morning, a young man rode up to the house and delivered to
Mr. Sheffey a message from his wife that his little son, Eddy,
was very sick, and that the doctors had said he could not live
and for him to come home at once. Mr. Sheffey made no response to the message, but went off a distance to some high
granite boulders on the top of the highest of which he went to
the Lord in prayer, and continued to pray until the time had
arrived for him to meet his congregation at the church. On
reaching the pulpit, he related to his congregation the message
he had received, and then said, "I have talked to the Lord
about this, and Eddy is not going to die." Eddy still lives, a
bright, intelligent, useful and honored citizen.

Mr. Sheffey had wonderful faith in God's providences, his
care for his people in providing for their wants, physical as
well as spiritual. It is told of him that on one occasion he met
a man in the road on a very cold day, and that the man had on
no socks, and that Mr. Sheffey observing this took off his and
gave them to the man. After riding some distance he stopped
at a house to warm his feet, and that the lady of the house said
to him that she had knit for him some nice pairs of socks which
she wished to present him. Another thing may be mentioned
of this man, and that was the tender care of his horse and of
other animals. He could not bear to see them suffer, not even
a bug if turned on its back, and he has been known to dismount from his horse and turn it over. If he found what appeared to him to be a hungry animal or dog, he would give it
his lunch rather than eat it himself. The story is told of him
and another preacher who were out in some wild mountain district, that on leaving the house where they had been entertain-

ed, the woman put a lunch in Mr. Sheffey's saddle-bags telling them that they were not likely to meet with their dinner, that day, and that she had provided a lunch that they might not suffer from hunger. Off the preachers went on along the mountain pathway during the morning hours and until about noon, when Mr. Sheffey's companion who being in front halted, and proposed to eat the lunch. Mr. Sheffey informed him that he had no lunch, that he had just met two very hungry looking dogs to which he had given the lunch.

If there was a man beyond any other that believed that the whiskey traffic was one of the Devil's strongholds it was Mr. Sheffey. He assailed this traffic when opportunity offered and often in public prayed for its overthrow and destruction. He was often appealed to by good people to pray the Lord to remove stillhouses and liquor manufactures. On the upper waters of the Bluestone, many years ago, was a whiskey distillery operated by a man and his son. Mr. Sheffey stopped in the neighborhood at the home of a good Methodist family. The good woman of the house told him of this distillery, and that it was ruining and wrecking the lives of many of the young men in the neighborhood, and requested him to pray for its removal, which he promised to do. The lady inquired "how long will it be before we may expect our prayers to be answered;" "about twelve months," was his reply; and sure enough within the twelve months the distillery was closed up, and the owner and his son in jail on charge of defrauding the government.

On another occasion he was on Wolf Creek, near Rocky gap, when he was informed by the mother of a family with whom he was stopping of the existence of a distillery in the neighborhood that was proving a great evil and requested Mr. Sheffey to pray for its removal. Mr. Sheffey then and there went to the Lord in prayer, and asked Him to destroy the evil, and if necessary send fire from Heaven to burn it up, and that very night an old dry tree near the distillery took fire, fell on the shanty and destroyed the whole thing. The whole neighborhood firmly believed Sheffey's prayer brought down that fire, which rid the neighborhood of the evil.

As has already been stated, Mr. Sheffey went to the Lord about everything he did, even about small things, which sometimes brought him into ridicule by some classes of people, but that did not in the least deter him. He believed that the Lord controlled the actions of animals as well as men, and in verification and illustration thereof the following story is told by a gentlemen living a few miles south of Pearisburg, Virginia. Mr. Sheffey stopped at his house over night, and by Mr. Sheffey's direction his horse was turned on pasture. Mr. Sheffey having an appointment for the next day, and anxious to get off early requested the gentleman to have his horse ready for him. The man went out very early to get the horse which he was unable to do, even summoning help, still the horse would not allow himself to be caught, nor would he be driven into the stable yard or lot. Finally the man gave up the effort to secure the horse, went to the house and informed Mr. Sheffey of the situation, and he went out with the man into the field where the horse was grazing, and requested the man to wait until he told the Lord about it. Down upon his knees he went and told the Lord of the inability of the man to bridle the horse and requested that He put it into the mind of the horse to stand and be bridled, and on rising from his knees he said to the man "you can now bridle the horse," which he immediately did. Many other such things occurred in the history of this man, which for want of space cannot here be related; there is however, just one other incident of his life which will be related, as it shows that he was a man whose religion was pure and undefiled and near akin to that of our blessed Saviour. Mr. Sheffey's hostility and open expression against the liquor traffic and the traffickers, often brought down upon him, not only the curses and imprecations of these people, but once at least, a pounding upon his head. He was preaching in Bland County, and during the service was interrupted by some unthoughted young men under the influence of ardent spirits, which led to their se-

vere censure and arraignment by the preacher, which so offended and enraged them that they took position at the outside of
the church door, and as Mr. Sheffey went out they clubbed and
beat him severely. These people were indicted in the Court of
Bland County, and Mr. Sheffey summoned as a witness for the
Commonwealth. He did not appear, and compulsory process
was taken against him, and on his appearance in Court he endeavored to avoid testifying. The young men were convicted,
when Mr. Sheffey with tears in his eyes, and a prayer on his
lips implored the court to allow them to go unpunished, that
they knew not what they did; that he had forgiven them,
that he had asked the Lord to forgive them, and now
asked the Court to forgive them, which in a measure it
did. Whatever may be said of this peculiar man and his eccentricities, his like will never be seen again. He died in peace
with God and man, and all who knew him revere his memory.

CHAPTER V.

1795-1836.

Marriages, by whom celebrated prior to the passage of Toler-
ation Acts—Real civilization begun—Monroe County created, its boundaries, brief, history of—Formation of Tazewell County, its boundaries, brief history of—Formation
of Giles County, its boundaries, and brief history thereof.

As has already been noticed, the early preachers who came
across the Alleghanies, were Dissenters, and not authorized by
law to celebrate marriages, and therefore all marriages solemn-
ized by these Ministers were by law illegal, but by subsequent
acts of the Legislature such marriages were not only legalized,
but certain acts were passed authorizing a limited number of
these Dissenters to celebrate the rites of matrimony.

After the close of the Indian wars in 1794 the country not
only filled up rapidly, but real civilization began in earnest,

the people built houses, opened farms and roads, elected officers, prepared and carried on civil government without hinderance or molestation.

The people living along the New River to the northeast thereof and north of the Narrows of said river, in what is now Giles County, were inhabitants of Greenbrier County and lived many miles from Lewisburg, their county town. They therefore determined to apply for the creation of a new county, and by an act of the Legislature of Virginia passed January 14th, 1799, the County of Monroe was created out of the territory of Greenbrier, with the following boundaries as set forth in the said Act, viz: "Beginning where the ridge dividing the eastern from the western waters joins Peter's Mountain, and with said eastern ridge to the ridge which divides Howard's and Second Creek, thence with the said ridge westwardly, including the waters of Second Creek to the Wagon road at Robert Knox's, thence with the said creek to Thomas Nichols' Spring branch, thence a straight line to Alderson's ferry landing on Greenbrier River, thence down the said river to the mouth of Muddy Creek, thence crossing the same to the ridge which divides the waters of Muddy Creek and Griffith's run, and with the said ridge to Keeney's Knobs and with said Knobs, including the waters flowing into Greenbrier River to New River, and up the same to where it breaks through Peter's Mountain, thence with said mountain an east course to the beginning."

From Lewis' History of West Virginia the following information is given concerning the organization of said county. "At one mile east of the present town of Union at the house of George King on the 21st day of May, 1799, the first County Court was held. William Hutchinson, James Alexander, Isaac Estill, William Haynes, John Hutchinson, John Gray, John Byrnside, William Graham, James Hanley, and William Vawter holding commissions from the governor of Virginia, composed the members of the first court. John Hutchison was appointed clerk, and John Woodyard Commonwealth's Attorney. Isaac Estill having been by the Governor commissioned as sheriff, entered into bond as such, with James Alexander, William Haynes, and John Byrnside as his bondsmen. John Byrnside was recommended for appointment as surveyor of lands. John Arbuckle was appointed Deputy Sheriff.

The second day of the term was taken up largely in putting the military establishment on a proper footing, whereupon James Graham was recommended for appointment as Colonel for the county; John Hutchinson and John Hanley for Majors; and for Captains, Isaac Estill, John Byrnside, James Jones, Robert Nickel, William Graham, Samuel Clark, Henry McDaniel, and Watt Farley. For Lieutenants, Nimrod Tackett, John Hanley, Jr., George Swope, James Gray, William Maddy, David Graham, Tollison Shumate, and Thomas Wyatt; and for Ensigns, Alexander Dunlap, Charles Keenan, James Young, James Byrnside, James Miller, James Gwin, James Thompson, and John Harvey.

James Graham was recommended for appointment as Coroner, and Thomas Lowe, Robert Dunbar, John Cottrell, William Dison, George Foster, Enos Halstead, and Joshua Lewis were appointed Constables.

On the 19th day of May, 1800, Honorable Archibald Stewart, Judge of the District composed of the counties of Greenbrier, Botetourt, Montgomery, Kanawha, and Monroe held the first court for the county, at Sweet Springs. John Skinner was appointed to prosecute for the Commonwealth, and Samuel Dew to discharge the duties of clerk.

A grand jury was empaneled, composed of William Royal, foreman, Dennis Cochran, John Matthews, Samuel Todd, Hugh Caperton, Joseph Snodgrass, Isaac Snodgrass, William Howell, John Peck, Joseph Cloyd, (the latter two citizens of Giles County,) John Lewis, William Vawter, Jacob Persinger, John Byrnside, and James Byrnside. Two indictments found at the term, parties tried same term and acquitted.

The second term of the court held at the same place on the 18th day of October, 1800, at which Judge Paul Carrington presided.

In 1799, the County Court selected the present site Union, for the County town on twenty-five acres of land the property of James Alexander, and was laid off into lots and streets, and the same was subsequently, to wit: January 1800, established as a town by the General Assembly, and William Haynes, John Gray, John Byrnside, James Hanley, Michael Erskine, John Hutchison, and Isaac Estill constituted trustees thereof."

The territory now embraced in Monroe County was visited by white people as early as 1760. John Alderson and William Morris visited the county about 1777. Christian Peters, an American Soldier, who served in General LaFayette's Corps at Yorktown, came to what is now Peterstown in 1783. In the year of 1770, came the Manns, Cooks, Millers, Alexanders, Nickels, Campbells, Dunsmores, Hokes, Lakes, Calloways, Sweeneys, Haynes, Erkines, Grahams, and Hutchinsons, largely from the Virginia Valley.

The early history of this people is the same substantially as those of the Greenbrier and New River Valleys, which has already been given in this volume.

The military history of the people of Monroe is in a measure written in the chapter devoted to that subject in this volume, as her citizen soldiers served largely with the New River Valley men, with the exception of one company, which was led to the war by Captain Hugh Snidow Tiffany, who fell in the first battle of Manasses. His company belonged to the 27th Virginia Regiment of the Stonewall brigade.

In both civil and military life, Monroe has furnished a number of distinguished men, among them Hugh Caperton, Andrew Beirne, Allen T. Caperton, A. A. Chapman, John Echols, Frank Hereford, John M. Rowan, Judge A. N. Campbell, Rev. J. P. Campbell, and others.

Among her valued citizens, are Campbells, Hansbargers, Swopes, Johnsons, Johnstons, Symns, Clarks, Ballards, Fleshmans, Pecks, Aldersons, Nickels, Rowans, Becketts, McClaughertys, Osborns, Harveys, Pences, Adairs, Packs, Thrashers, Karnes, Spanglers, Shanklins, Vawters, and numerous others.

Its population is steady,industrious, and as little crime is committed in the county of Monroe as any county in the state.

Adam Mann, Jacob Mann, and others as early as the year 1770, built a fort on Indian Creek, some ten miles west from the present town of Union. The Cooks, also built a fort on Indian Creek some three miles from its mouth.

This Mann family was of English origin—from Kent. They came at an early day to America, and that branch of the family, the ancestor of the present New River Valley families of that name was William, who settled in Augusta in 1778. It is a numerous family, some of them attained to prominence in the revolutionary, border and civil wars. From Mann MS. it appears, that two of this family, Thomas and William, were soldiers on the Ohio at fort Randolph shortly after the battle of Point Pleasant, and while there, on the south side of the Kanawha, appeared one Simon Girty, who gave to Thomas and William Mann the sign of distress, and urged them to cross for him as he was pursued by the Indians; yielding to his entreaties, they with others crossed the river in a canoe, and as they approached the shore a party of Indians in hiding fired upon them, killing Thomas Mann, and badly wounding William, who escaped but died in what is now Fayette County, while trying to make his way to Donnally's Fort, in Greenbrier (Mann MS.). Of this family are Isaac T. and Edwin Mann, prominent and successful business men of Mercer County. Mr. James E. Mann of this same family, a most useful, intelligent citizen, and successful financier lived for a number of years in the city of Bluefield, where his widow and children still reside. Mr. Mann died a few years ago, a highly respected and esteemed citizen.

The territory of Tazewell County as it formerly and now exists, has a history much in common with that of the Counties of Monroe, Giles and Mercer. It is not intended in this work to do more than give a general outline history of this county, for to write it in full and that of its people would within itself fill a volume. So far as can be ascertained, with anything like

accuracy, the first white man that put his foot on the soil of
this county, was the man Castle hunting with the Indians in
what is now known as the Castle's wood section, now in Russell
County; and the second white man in the territory referred to
was the hunter Clinche. These two men traversed the Clinch
Valley section prior to 1749 and from the latter the river
Clinch took its name, as hereinbefore related.

The next in order was Doctor Thomas Walker of Albemarle,
and his companions Ambrose Powell and others, who in 1750,
traversed the ridge country, a few miles north of the present
town of Tazewell, passing the site of the present town of Pocahontas, and following the Water Shed dividing the waters of
Bluestone, Sandy, Guyandotte, and Piney, to the New River
near where the town of Hinton, in Summers County, is located.

According to Summers' History So. W. Va., Christopher
Gist, agent for the Ohio Company, on his return from the Kentucky section and the Ohio River, in 1751, came through what is
now the county of Wise, giving name to a river, Gist's, and a
station where he camped, called Gist's Station. (1)   He also
passed along the Water Shed above referred to.

In the year of 1753, James Burke and stepson, Morris Griffith were in what is now known as Burke's Garden, situated in
the south-eastern part of this county. Burke was one of the
Draper's Meadow Settlers, who crossed the Alleghanies in
1748 and made settlement near the present town of Blacksburg
in Montgomery County. His adventurous disposition and love
of the forest led him to the vicinity of the spot called Burke's
Garden, into which, through the gap since known as Hanshue's,
he followed the Elk which he had wounded.

The evidence is not only persuasive, but may be regarded as
conclusive, that Burke removed with his family from Draper's
Meadows into this beautiful land in the year of 1754. He had
cleared out some land, and in the spring of 1755 had planted a
crop of potatoes which were found in the ground unharvested

---

(1). Now, Coburn, in Wise County, Virginia.

by Lewis' men in February, 1756. Colonel Preston in his Journal, describing Burke's Garden says among other things that the soldiers gathered potatoes in the waste plantations; therefore it is certain that in February, 1756, the place was known as Burke's Garden, and that there were potatoes found there in "Waste Plantations." Again it is true, that neither Burke nor his family were at Draper's Meadows on the 8th day of July, 1755, when the settlers were attacked by the Indians, captured or destroyed, as no mention is made of Burke or his family, while all others are accounted for, and we see from Preston's Journal, that Lewis' men met Burke west of New River in Febuary, 1756, hence it appears as most likely and no doubt true, that Burke for fear of the savages left Burke's Garden with his family in the fall of 1755, and the tradition that the Indians followed him to Sharon Springs is no doubt correct. At any rate Burke discovered a magnificent body of most valuable land which was appropriated by other people.

Major Andrew Lewis with about 340 men on his way to the Ohio, in February, 1756, passed through the territory of Tazewell, camping in Burke's Garden, and on the head waters of the Clinch, and from there passed over the eastern and north-ern branches of that stream near by or through the farm owned by the late William G. Mustard, Esq., and thence on to Horsepen Creek of Jacob's Fork of Tug of Sandy. We hear nothing from 1756 to 1766 of any white people in the territory of the county; this is accounted for from the fact that the French and Indian war was occurring during this period, and in fact did not end on the border until the year of 1765, after Johnson's Treaty—the result of Bouquet's expedition into Ohio that year.

It appears from Bickley's History of Tazewell, that two men, Butler and Carr with others from about Carr's or Kerr's Creek in the Rockbridge country, were in this territory about the head waters of the Clinch in 1766, engaged in hunting and trapping, and that all of said hunting party, except Butler and Carr, left on the close of the hunting season.

Butler and Carr erected them a hunter's cabin at the Crab

Orchard, about three or four miles west of the present Court
House of Tazewell. In the spring of 1767 they opened up a
small field and planted a small crop of corn, the seed of which
they obtained from the Cherokee Indians, and a new supply
of ammunition of another company of hunters that came out to
hunt with them.

The territory of Tazewell, very much like that of Kentucky,
was a kind of middle ground between the northern and southern Indian tribes, between whom a war was waging in 1766,
and which was not finally ended until about the beginning of
1774.

As stated by Bickley, in the early summer of 1768, a band of
Cherokee warriors camped near the cabin of Butler and Carr;
they had come to spend the season in hunting around and near
the Lick. Very soon there appeared a large body of Shawnees,
men and women. These had long been open and deadly enemies, and could not long remain near each other on terms of
peace. The Shawnees ordered the Cherokees to evacuate. and
to look for other hunting ground. This order, the latter refused to obey, and took position on the top of Rich Mountain,
which they fortified with rude breastworks. The Shawnees attacked that evening, and continued the battle on the next day;
Butler and Carr furnishing the Cherokees with ammunition.
The Shawnees were forced to retire, retreating to the head of
what is now known as Abb's Valley, and there on the farm
owned by the late Jonathan Smith, erected a rude stone fort,
which stood until a few years ago. The place where they built
this fort is the gateway to the head of the Tug fork of Sandy;
the latter one of the highways when on their way out and return from incursions into the white settlements along the upper waters of the Clinch and the Bluestone. The dead left on
the battlefield were buried in one common grave, and shortly
the Cherokees departed for their homes in the south, leaving
Butler and Carr lords of all they surveyed.

Peace and quiet being restored, Butler and Carr separated,
the latter making settlements on the Clinch about two miles

east of the present county town, while Butler seems to have removed near the Elk Lick. More hunters coming out, and returning with glowing descriptions of the country, induced others desiring to make permanent settlements in this new wilderness country, to emigrate hither.

In the spring of 1771 came Thomas, James and Jerry Witten (1) and John Greenup, the former from the Fredericktown section of Maryland. Thomas settled at the Crab Orchard, purchasing Butler's claim, whatever that was, but there were none to dispute it.

James Witten and John Greenup settled on the Clinch near where Pisgah Church now stands, and Jerry Witten settled on Plum Creek. On the authority of James R. Witten it is stated that a son of this John Greenup became governor of Kentucky.

In this same year of 1771 Absalom Looney, from Looney's Creek in the Virginia Valley, made his way into the section of this county now known as Abb's Valley, where he hunted and trapped for three or four years, having a cave near what is now Moore's Memorial Church, as his hiding place and refuge from the savages and wild beasts.

Looney, on returning to Looney's Creek, met Captain James Moore, and so impressed him by his description of this wonderful valley which he had discovered as to induce Moore to make a journey to see it. The statement that Captain James Moore settled in Abb's Valley in 1772 is incorrect, for more reasons than one. Moore had gone from the valley to the Alamance in North Carolina, to join his countrymen (the Scots), in their struggle against the tyranny of Governor Tyron, and having united with the Regulators, was in the battle of the Alamance fought on the 16th day of May, 1771, in which the Regulators were defeated and scattered by the forces of Governor Tyron. Captain Moore returned to his home on Moore's Creek in the Virginia Valley, now in Rockbridge County, where he remained

(1). The Wittens first halted at a large spring on Walker's Creek, near where the late William B. Allen resided, in what is now Giles County, where they remained for one year before moving to the Clinch.

until 1775, when he raised a company of valley men, and marched at their head, joining General Washington's army then engaged in the seige of Boston. It was at the head of this company of volunteers that he won his title of captain. He and his
men had entered the service for one year, upon the expiration
of which they returned to their homes. Their return was in
1776, and there is no evidence to be found that Captain Moore
visited the territory of Tazewell prior to 1776, but in the fall of
that year he came to spy out the land and prepared for the removal of his family, which took place the next year, together
with the family of his brother-in-law Poague.

Prior to the year of 1776 one Peter Wright, an old hunter,
had traversed the valley known since his day as Wright's Valley, which no doubt led him into the present territory of Tazewell County.

In the year of 1772 Mathias Harman, and his brothers Jacob
and Henry, settled at Carr's on the Clinch, John Craven in the
Cove, Joseph Martin, John Henry, and James King in Thompson's Valley, and John Bradshaw in the valley two miles west
of the present county town. The Harmans came from North
Carolina.

In 1772 William Wynn, John Taylor and Jesse Evans settled
on the upper Clinch waters, and Thomas Marshall, Benjamine
Joslin, James Ogleton, Peter Harman and Samuel Ferguson on
the upper Bluestone, William Butler on the south branch of the
north fork of Clinch above Wynn's, William Webb about three
miles east of the present Court House, Elisha Clary near Butler, John Ridgel on the Clear fork of Wolf Creek, Reece Bowen
at Maiden Spring, David Ward in the Cove, and William Garretson at the foot of Morris' Knob.

Of the people who came in 1772 Thomas Maxwell, Samuel
Ferguson and the Peerys, who were in the battle of the Alamance, came from the Virginia Valley, Reece Bowen from Botetourt, near where Roanoke city now stands. He was from western Maryland, William Garretson from Culpepper county, from

which the Wheatleys came about the same time, settling near the spot where Captain C. A. Fudge now resides.

Thomas, John and William Peery settled where the present town of Tazewell is now located, and John Peery, jr. at the fork of Clinch one and one half miles east of the present county site. In the meantime a number of settlers, among them the Scaggs, Richard Pemberton, Johnson, Roark, and others settled in Baptist Valley, and Thomas Mastin, William Patterson, and John Deskins farther west in the same valley, Richard Oney and Obadiah Paine in what is now known as Deskin's Valley.

Thomas Ingles, son of Captain William Ingles of Draper's Meadows, settled in 1778, in what is now known as Wright's Valley at a spring near the residence of the late Captain Rufus A. Hale, about two miles west of the present city of Bluefield, and a few hundred yards north of the track of the Norfolk & Western Railway. He remained here only about two years, when finding himself too near the Indian trail which led up the Beaver Pond Creek to Bailey's gap in East River Mountain, he removed to Burke's Garden, and occupied a tract of land which had been surveyed by his father, until 1782, when his family was captured, and in part destroyed by the Indians. At this date Ingles and a man by the name of Hicks were the only residents in Burke's Garden.

In the meantime, that is between the date of the commencement of the settlements by the white people within what is now the territory of Tazewell and the breaking up of the Ingles family in 1782, Dunmore's war had broken out, (1774), which in a measure halted emigration into the territory.

In the year of 1773, in September, Daniel Boone and his brother, Squire, with their familes and a number of others, had left the Yadkin in North Carolina and started for Kentucky. The party with Boone had reached Powell's Valley, when needing provisions, Boone's son, with a party, had gone to the house of William Russell, in Castle's woods in search of food, and on its return on the second day after, and before overtaking the main party, were attacked by a band of Indians and destroyed. This caused Boone and his party to halt and retire to the neighborhood of William Russell, in Castle's woods, where a part of his company wintered. Finding, in the spring of 1774, that the Indians were on the war path, and that Governor Dunmoore had ordered the raising of an army to punish the savages; one wing, the northern, he proposed to command, and the other. the southern, to be commanded by Brigadier General Andrew Lewis, who was ordered to rendezvous his troops at Camp Union, now Lewisburg, in Greenbrier County; and that call had been made upon the Fincastle men (this territory was then in Fincastle County,) Captain William Russell gathered the men of his company, and in August marched up the Clinch and down the East River to join his regiment, commanded by Colonel William Christian, then on the New River, and on its way to unite with General Lewis. To Russell's company belonged Reece Bowen and Moses Bowen, who marched with their company to Point Pleasant—Moses Bowen dying on the trip from smallpox.

Daniel Boone was left in command of Russell's Fort, that of Bowen's, and of the Frontier, which he with his men faithfully guarded in the absence of Russell's men.

Roving bands of Indians entered the Castle's woods and Maiden Spring neighborhoods during the absence of Russell and his men. The neighboring women and children had gathered in the forts for protection.

It was the opening of Dunmore's war that led the white people of this and adjacent sections to establish forts and blockhouses for protection. In Tazewell there was a fort erected by the Wynns on Wynn's Branch, at Crab Orchard by Thomas Witten, and one at Maiden Springs by Reece Bowen, and a little later, one at head of Beaver Pond by Bailey's and Davidson's, and later as stated by Bickley, between the years of 1780 and 1794, the Virginia Government occasionally kept a few companies of men along the border, who occupied these forts, and in the absence of such armed bodies of men, sent out by the state, the men within the territory threatened, gathered in these places of refuge. The names of several of these people have been preserved, among them:

James Bailey	Samuel Lusk
John Baily	Robert Lesley
Joseph Belcher	James Martin
Robert Belcher	John Maxwell
Thomas Brewster	James Peery
Edward Burgess	John Pruett
Chrisopher Caffin	Archibald Thompson
James Conley	John Ward
John Crockett	William Ward
John Evans	James Witten
Joseph Gilbert	Michael Wright
Absalom Godfrey	Oliver Wynn
William Hall	Hezekiah Wright
David Lusk	

Robert Trigg was the military commandant while the territory of what is now Tazewell was within the County of Montgomery, and Major Robert Crockett after the territory was erected into the county Wythe.

The Indian depredations began in the territory of what is now the county of Tazewell, in the year of 1776. In the month of May of that year they destroyed John Henry, his wife and six children in Thompson's Valley, and carried one litte boy away a prisoner. In the same year they captured John Evans.

In the year 1779 the family of Jesse Evans was attacked by eight or ten Indians, four of his children were killed, his wife with one child escaping to Major Taylor's.

In the latter part of the summer and early fall of 1780, the British army under Lord Cornwallis was advancing northward through the Carolinas. One division thereof, under Colonel Patrick Ferguson, had reached Piedmont, North Carolina. Ferguson had sent threats t o the Backwater men that if they did not come over and take the oath of allegiance to his Sovereign he would cross into their country and lay it waste with fire and sword. Evan Shelby and John Sevier planned an attack upon Ferguson's troops, calling on Colonel Campbell of Washington County, Virginia, for assistance. Campbell called out the military force of his county, including the company of William Bowen of the Clinch settlements, in which company Reece Bowen, of Maiden Spring and James Moore of Abb's Valley were Lieutenants. Captain William Bowen at the date of the call being sick with fever, the command of the company devolved on Lieutenant Reece Bowen, who led it to the battle of King's Mountain, fought on October 7th, 1780.

At the date of the call for and march of Bowen's company from the Clinch, the western boundary line of Montgomery County reached to Morris' Knob and Roark's Gap, and therefore a part of the men who marched with Bowen from the upper Clinch and Bluestone lived in Montgomery County, and were not within the military district of Colonel Campbell, but within that of Colonel William Preston, of Montgomery. Among the number of those who went from Montgomery territory with Bowen, were James Moore, Samuel Ferguson, Henry Henninger, Thomas Peery, (the Distiller) Thomas Peery (the Blacksmith) William Peery and John Peery, the latter wounded a number of times, but recovering, and one of the Thomas Peerys killed, together with Henry Henninger and Reece Bowen.

No attempt will be made here to describe the march to King's Mountain nor the battle and return home of the men, as the reader is referred to a very full and accurate account thereof given by Draper in his "King's Mountain and its Heroes."

In the month of April, 1782, the family of Thomas Ingles, in Burke's Garden, was attacked by Indians and all who were at the house captured. They were pursued by Thomas Ingles and Captain James Maxwell, and a party of men, who overtook them in a gap of Tug ridge, since known as Maxwell's Gap from the circumstance that Captain Maxwell was there killed.

On the opening of the fight the Indians attempted to kill their prisoners, and succeeded in tomahawking Mrs. Ingles, her little son William, and little daughter Mary, scalping the two latter from which the little boy soon died, the little girl a few days later, but Mrs. Ingles recovered. The Harman Ms. shows that Captain Henry Harman was one of the pursuing party.

Another part of this marauding band at the same time killed and scalped two daughters of Captain John Maxwell, and took nine prisoners, and also killed and scalped near the Clinch two sons of Captain Robert Moffett.

A part of this same band of Indians visited the home of James Poague, a brother-in-law of Captain James Moore, and who had come to Abb's Valley with him in 1777, and had settled and opened up some land on the farm recently known as that of Captain John W. Taylor. These Indians attempted to enter Mr. Poague's house in the night time but finding some three or four men in the house they left without doing any harm to Mr. Poague's family, but the next morning, near Poague's house they killed a young man by the name of Richards, who had been working for Captain Moore.

In 1783 Joseph Ray, living on Indian Creek, with a part of his family, together with a man by the name of Samuel Hughes, who happened at Ray's house at the time, were butchered by the Indians.

Mr. Poague became so much alarmed for fear of the Indians that very shortly after their visit to his house on a night in April, 1872, and hereinbefore referred to, he left the settlement, and went back into civilization, and two years after the occurrence at Poague's viz: in 1784, James, the son of Captain James Moore, was captured on this Taylor farm by Indians, and carried into captivity where he remained about five years.

In the year of 1785 Robert Barnes, born in Ireland, (1) and coming to America about 1782, first halting in the valley of Virginia, then came on to the Cove in what is now Tazewell County, Virginia.

(1)   So stated by Capt. D. B. Baldwin.

From this man Robert Barnes, has descended all the people
of that name now in the Tazewell section, and who are among
the most respectable people to be found there or elsewhere.

On April 11th, 1786, two men one ——Dials and Benjamin
Thomas, were scalped by the Indians on the upper waters of
the Clinch; Dials died in a few hours, Thomas lived several
days.

In 1785 an Act was passed by the General Assembly of Virginia, to take effect 1786, creating the County of Russell out
of the territory of Washington County. The eastern boundary line of Russell to be that of the western line of Montgomery County.

Before describing the destruction of the family of Captain
James Moore in Abb's Valley, reference will be made to the
date of the first coming of Captain Moore to the valley referred to.

William Taylor Moore, who has already been mentioned as
the grandson of Captain Moore, stated to the author that
Looney so accurately described the route from the Virginia
Valley to Abb's Valley that his grandfather had no difficulty
in traversing it, and that he described the route after leaving
the New River to be up a large Creek, (Walker's Creek), to the
mouth of its main north branch, (Kimberling), and thence up
the same to its source, and through a gap, and down to a
stream, to and through another gap through which said
stream passed, and down the same to the mouth of a stream
coming in from the north, (Laurel Creek,) and up the same
and through a low gap of a high mountain to the north, and
thence down the streams flowing west—northwest— to where
the waters flowed over a very high rock, now called Falls Mills,
where he would strike a Buffalo path, following which would
lead him into the valley. (1)

(1). Shortly after Captain Moore's settlement in the Valley a buffalo bull came up to his home with the milch cows, and the Captain
killed the animal.

On July 14th, 1786, Captain James Moore and his family, were attacked by a band of forty Shawnee Indians, and the Captain and a part of his family killed, and part captured and carried away.

In 1788 in the month of August, a man by the name of Pemberton, who lived in Baptist Valley, about five miles from the present County site of Tazewell, was attacked by a party of marauding Indians, but succeeded in beating them off, and making safe retreat to a neighbor's house.

As has already been related, Captain Henry Harman and two of his sons, George and Matthias, on a hunting expedition on Tug had, on the 12th day of November, 1788, a severe battle with seven or eight Indians, part of whom they killed and wounded, the remainder retreated. This fight took place on the bank of the Tug a short distance below the residence of the late Mr. Henry T. Peery. Captain Harman received several wounds from arrows shot into him by the Indians.

In the month of March, 1789, a party of Indians came up the Dry Fork of the Sandy, and about the mouth of Dick's Creek were caught in a snow storm, and took shelter under a large shelving rock opposite the mouth of the above mentioned creek, and while hiding there and sheltering from the storm, William Wheatley of Baptist Valley, in search of a lost dog was killed by these Indians, who mutilated his body in a most horrible manner. They then proceeded to the gap at the head of Dry Fork and destroyed the wife and children of James Roark. They were pursued by the whites but succeeded in making good their escape.

On the night of October the first, 1789, a body of Indians visited the house of Thomas Wiley, at what is now known as the Dill's farm, a little below the mouth of Cove Creek of Clear fork of Wolf Creek, and captured and carried away his wife, Mrs. Virginia Wiley, and her four little children whom they killed on their way up Cove Creek. Mrs. Wiley was car-

ried away a prisoner to their towns where she remained until
September, 1792, escaping with Samuel Lusk.

In the year of 1790 the county of Wythe was created out
of the territory of Montgomery. The western line of Wythe
by the Act of Creation, was the same as between Montgomery
and Russell Counties; that is, from the west side of Morris
Knob to Roark's gap and to the head waters of the Sandy.
The eastern line running from Reed Island Creek to the Kanawha line, passing about one half mile west of the present
town of Princeton, in Mercer County. In April, 1791, the wife
and children of Andrew Davidson, with two bound children
were captured by Indians at their home on the head waters of East River, near the present city of Bluefield, then in
Wythe County. Mrs. Davidson was not recovered by her husband until after Wayne's Victory in August, 1794.

In the same year of 1791, Daniel Harman on a hunting expedition on the upper Clinch waters was killed by Indians.   .

In the month of July, 1792, a band of Indians from the Ohio
section entered the upper Clinch and Bluestone settlements,
and stole horses. Major Robert Crockett, the military commandant of Wythe County, gathered a force of men and followed the marauders. His scouts or spies, Joseph Gilbert and
Samuel Lusk, were sent in advance to a lick on a creek flowing
into the Guyandotte to kill some game for food for the men.
They reached the lick on the 24th day of July, killed a deer and
wounded an Elk, following the latter some distance and failing to over take it they returned to the lick for the deer, and
were suddenly attacked by the Indians, who were in hiding
near by, and Gilbert killed, Lusk wounded and captured. Major Crockett's men failed to overtake them. In September of
the same year, Lusk in company with Mrs. Virginia Wiley,
escaped from the Indian town at Chillicothe, on the Scioto, and
made his way home.

On the 8th day of March, 1793, a body of twelve Indians,
and a white man by the name of Rice, murdered John Goolman
Davidson, usually called John or Cooper Davidson, at the

mouth of a small branch of Laurel Creek of clear fork of Wolf
Creek, and at the southern base of East River Mountain at a
point where the path leaving Laurel passes through Bailey's
Gap. This party was pursued by Major Crockett and a company of men, who overtook them at the Island of the Guyandotte River, where now stands Logan Court House. A skirmish followed in which one Indian was killed, the rest fled leaving their stolen horses and their breakfast, the latter the whites
devoured, and among the recaptured horses was recognized
that of Mr. Davidson, which led on the return of the party to a
search of Mr. Davidson, whose dead nude body they found under the roots of a beech tree on the bank of Laurel Creek.

This Indian incursion was the last ever made into the territory in what is now Tazewell County. The next year, 1794,
General Wayne defeated the United Indian tribes at Fallen
Timbers in Ohio, and this gave peace to the border, along
which had been committed by the savages horrible barbarities
for almost forty years. (1)

With a full establishment of peace and quiet on the border
new people came rapidly into the country, and settlements began throughout the whole Clinch Valley section and on to the
Sandy.

In the winter of 1799 a bill was introduced into the General
Assembly of Virginia, by Mr. Cottrell, the representative from
Russell County, providing for the creation of a new county out
of the territory of Wythe and Russell. The bill of Mr. Cottrell
as stated by Bickley, met with formidable opposition from Mr.
Tazewell, the representative from the county of Norfolk. Mr.
Cottrell inserted in the bill Tazewell as the name of his pro-
posed new county, which not only silenced the member from
Norfolk, but secured his support for the bill.

The following are the boundary lines of the county of Taze-

(1) A family by the name of Sluss was destroyed by Indians near
what is now known as Sharon Springs, but the date and circumstances
are unknown.

well as set forth in the Act of its creation December 19th, 1799 viz: "Beginning on the Kanawha line, which divides Montgomery and Wythe Counties, thence to where said line crosses the top of Brushy Mountain, thence along the top of said mountain to its junction with Garden Mountain, thence along the top of the said mountain to the Clinch Mountain, thence along the top of said mountain to the mouth of Cove Creek, a branch of the Maiden Spring Fork of Clinch River, thence a strait line to Mann's Gap in Kent's Ridge, thence north 45 west to the line which divides Kentucky from that of Virginia, thence along said line to the Kanawha line, and with said line to the place of beginning." On Feb. 3rd, 1835, the Legislature altered the line dividing the Counties of Russell and Tazewell, by running from Mann's gap in Kent's ridge north 45 deg. 45 minutes west the distance of 974 poles. In 1806 a portion of Tazewell was cut off into the county of Giles, and in 1837 another portion of the territory of Tazewell was stricken off into Mercer, and in 1858 the Counties of Buchanan and McDowell were created out of Tazewell territory, and in 1861 Tazewell also lost part of her territory by the formation of Bland county.

The first court held for the county of Tazewell was at the house of Colonel John B. George, in the month of May, 1800. John Ward was elected clerk, and ——— Maxwell made sheriff. The second court was held in June of the same year at the house of Harvey G. Peery, in which month Judge Brockenborough held the first Superior Court of Law. He was succeeded by Judge Peter Johnston.

James Thompson was the first Commonwealth's Attorney for the county.

Bickley in his history of Tazewell, gives the following as the names of the citizens of the county, who were in the battle of the Alamance and in the American Revolution, viz:

At the Alamance	In the Revolution
James Cartmell	Reece Bowen
Samuel Ferguson	Low Bowen
James Moore	Thomas Harrison (2)
William Peery	John Lasley
Thomas Peery	Archer Maloney
John Peery	Neal McGuire
	James Moore
	Solomon Stratton
	Isham Thomlinson

And the following as soldiers in the war of 1812 viz:

William Asbury	Jonathan Peery
Williams Barnes	David Robertson
George Barnheart	Mathew Stevenson
Isaac Bostic	William Smith
James Belcher	Daniel Tabor
Peter Gose	Reece B. Thompson
Col. Henry Bowen	Henry B. Thompson
James Brooks	Charles Vandyke
John Davidson	John Vandyke
Jeremiah Early	Joseph Walls
Pleasant Franklin	Alexander Ward
William Greene	Hugh Wilson
James Higginbotham	William Witten
William Higginbotham	Peter E. Wynne
Isaac King	Samuel Wynne
David Lusk	Israel Young
Capt. Thomas Peery	Nathaniel Young

From 1800, the date of the formation of the county, to the beginning of the year of 1861, this county had within its borders as pure a type of Americanism as any county within the

---

(2). Thomas Harrison came from Birmingham, England, and was the son of a cutler.

Commonwealth. There were few, if any, of what might be deemed foreigners, that is, those who came direct from foreign countries.

In politics this people was so thoroughly democratic that in the two presidential contests, 1828-1832, between Jackson and Clay, the latter in the first contest received in the county but one vote, and the second two votes. This solid democratic wall was shaken but once from 1800 to 1861, and that was in the contest for the State Senate in 1857, between Nathaniel Harrison, Democrat, and Napoleon B. French, Whig, the latter succeeding in reducing the democratic majority largely in this county, which resulted in the defeat of Mr. Harrison in the district.

The bitter fight and exciting contest for Congress in 1848, between Colonel John B. George and Fayette McMullen, both Democrats, in which the latter won by over 2,000 majority, is still remembered among the older people of the county.

The contests for the Circuit Judgeship between George W. Hopkins and Joseph Stras, and again between Samuel V. Fulkerson and Mr. Stras were notable.

The people of this county held but few slaves, the first of these were brought into the county by James Witten, about 1771, and the next by a man by the name of Hicks and Thomas Ingles in about the year of 1780.

When the civil war period approached it found the people of this county as thoroughly united for the south, and the upholding and vindication of its constitutional rights as the people of any county within the Commonwealth. In the election for delegates to the Constitutional Convention of 1861, two of its most distinguished citizens—William P. Cecil and Samuel L. Graham—were elected. Both these men were above the average and imbued with strong convictions in favor of resistance to further Federal aggression, and in favor of Secession if that step was felt to be absolutely necessary for the protection of the rights of the people of Virginia. These gentlemen voted for the Ordinance of Secession, came home, buckled on their armor, and went forth to do battle for their cause and country. The people of this county entered upon the war with zeal and earnestness, organizing and sending to the war above twenty companies. There was as little disloyalty to the south and her cause among the people of Tazewell as in any county in the State, and when the war had ended her people were less annoyed with scalawags and carpetbaggers than the people of any county west of the Alleghanies. After the close of the war and up to the agitation of the State debt question, the people still adhered to Democracy. This debt question divided them, and a large number of the most prominent, respectable and influential people of the county fell in with the Readjuster Movement, which finally landed them in the Republican party; since which time the county has been overwhelmingly Republican.

This county is a little Commonwealth within itself, having within its borders, the most valuable agricultural, grazing and mineral lands to be found in this region of Virginia. Its people are among the most cultivated, lawabiding, and best in the world. Its lawyers among the most distinguished in the State; among the number may be mentioned Honorable Samuel C. Graham, Major R. R. Henry, J. W. Chapman, A. P. Gillespie, Samuel D. May, J. H. Stuart, S. M. B. Couling, H. C. Alderson, J. N. Harman, Barnes Gillespie, E. L. Greever, Thompson Crockett Bowen.

There has been less change in the character of the rural population of this county, than that of most any adjoining county. The building of railroads and the development of mines have had but little apparent effect upon the character of the population. These people are largely the descendants of the Wittens, Moores, Maxwells, Bowens, Barnes, Gillespies, Grahams, Crocketts, Peerys, Georges, Wards, Shannons, Harrisons, Greever, Meeks, Higginbothams, Deskins, Thompsons, Davidsons, Wynns, Cecils, Spotts, Taylors, and Harmans, the most of whom were among the first settlers of the country. Matters connected with the Courts of this county, the names

of the judges and members of the House of Delegates, together
with a list of the military organizations, or at least the names
thereof, that entered the Confederate service will be found in
the appendix to this volume; but before closing it will probably not be out of place to relate an anecdote given to the author by the late Major Rufus Brittain.   Honorable Benjamin
Estill, long the respected, honored judge of the Circuit Court
of Tazewell, was a very grave and dignified gentleman, and was
held in high respect by the bar and people.   In the early years
of his administration, in the trial of a case before him, there
came a witness from lower Sandy country, who for the first
time in his life was at his county town and his county Court
House, and who had never testified as a witness in a court of
justice.   He was illiterate and meanly dressed.   Having given
his evidence and when he was about to leave the stand, the
judge, apparently not impressed with the truthfulness
of his story, leaned forward, and in a very quiet but earnest
manner, said, "Mr. Witness have you told the truth, the whole
truth, and nothing but the truth?"   The witness looking
straight into the face of the Judge replied, "Well, Mr. Jedge, I
think I have and a little the rise."

Prior to the formation of Giles County, in 1806, the people
inhabiting the New River settlements and westward beyond
in Montgomery County, when compelled to attend the court,
had to travel many miles through the wilderness to reach their
county Court House at Christiansburg.   By the creation of
Giles County, out of the territory of the counties of Montgomery, Monroe and Tazewell, the people along the lower New
River settlements, and on the waters of the Bluestone, Guyandotte, and the head waters of the Coal Rivers were brought
nearer to their County Court House.   In January, 1806, the
County of Giles (1.) was created with the following boundary
lines described in the Act, viz: "Beginning at the end of Gauley Mountain on New River where the counties of Greenbrier
and Kanawha intersect; thence, up the river with the Green-

(1)   Named for Hon. Wm. B. Giles.

brier and Montgomery County Line to the upper end of Pine's Plantation; thence, a straight line to the mouth of Rich Creek, thence with the Montgomery and Monroe line to the intersection of Botetourt County line, and with the line of Mongomery and Botetourt to the top of Gap mountain, thence along the top of said mountain to New River, crossing the same to the end of Walker's Creek Mountain, thence along the top of said mountain to the intersection of Wythe County line, thence northwestward with said line to the intersection of Tazewell County line, and with Tazewell and Montgomery County line to the top of Wolf Creek Mountain to a path leading from Round Bottom to Harman's Mill about three miles below the mouth of the Clear fork of Wolf Creek, thence a straight line to the mouth of Militon's Fork, thence a direct line to the head of Crane Creek to the top of Flat Top Mountain, thence a direct line to the three forks of the Guyandotte, thence down said river until it intersects the Kanawha County line, thence with said line to the beginning."

There have been since the creation of the county of Giles four changes in the boundary lines thereof. The line between Giles and Monroe was altered in 1830, by running from a point on Peter's Mountain, opposite the Grey Sulpher Springs, down Rich Creek near Peterstown and to Wiley's Falls, taking from Monroe and adding to Giles this strip of territory. In 1841, by adding a small strip from the county of Mercer by running from Toney's Mill dam to Wiley's Falls. Again in 1851, on the formation of the county of Craig, by cutting off to that county a strip of the territory of Giles and, later in 1858, another strip to Craig; and likewise in 1861, by the formation of Bland County, Giles lost a very considerable strip of her territory.

The territory embraced in the now county of Giles is very mountainous, and of the most rugged character, covering at the period of its formation the New River Valley for a distance of over one hundred miles in length with a mean width of about thirty miles, embracing not only waters which flow into the New River proper, but also the head waters of the Guyandotte, which flows into the Ohio, and the headwaters of the Coal River, which flows into the Kanawha. The names of the streams in the then territory of the county and flowing into New River are as follows: Spruce Run, Sinking Creek, Doe Creek, Big Stony Creek, Little Stony Creek, and Rich Creek on the northeast side of the river, and Walker's Creek, Wolf Creek, East River, Brush Creek, Bluestone, Piney, Big and Little Coal Rivers, and some of the branches of the Guyandotte on the west and northwest side of the river. The mountain ranges—Walker's Mountain, Angel's Rest, Great Flat Top, Guyandotte, Peter's Mountain, East River Mountain, Wolf Creek Mountain, Butt Mountain, Brush Mountain, and Salt Pond Mountain.

Pursuant to the act creating the County of Giles, the first court was held on the 13th day of May, 1806, in a house adjacent to the dwelling house of Captain George Pearis (1) on New River, near where Pearisburg station is now situated. The building in which the first court was held remained standing until two or three years ago, when it was destroyed by fire.

The Governor of the Commonwealth, William H. Cabell, had issued commissions to the following named gentlemen as Justices of the Peace of the new County, viz: George Pearis, Thomas Shannon, Christian Snidow, David French, David Johnston, (2) Edward McDonald, Isaac Chapman, John Kirk, John Peck, Christopher Champ, John Burke, and James Bane. Thomas Shannon and Christian Snidow, the second and third named persons in the commission, administered the oath to George Pearis the first named, and he then administered it to the others. David Johnston produced a commission from the Governor of the Commonwealth as Sheriff of the new county, and qualified as such with Christian Snidow and Isaac Chap-

(1) The first settler where Pearisburg station is now situated and the first merchant in what is now Giles County.

(2). David and Andrew Johnston were the first merchants and opened the first tannery; Dr. John H. Rutter, the first resident physician; W. C. Charlton, first tailor.

man as his sureties, giving bond in the penalty of $7,000, and
James Hoge qualified as his Deputy. David French was elect-
ed clerk, and at his request the court apointed John Mc-
Taylor as his deputy. Captain George Pearis was elected pre-
siding Justice, and also commissioner of the revenue. Philip
Lybrook was appointed county surveyor, and afterwards gave
bond in the penalty of $3,000 with John Lybrook and David
French as his sureties.

Henley Chapman produced a license authorizing him to
practice law in the courts of the Commonwealth, and on his
motion was admitted to practice in the courts of the County.
The second term of the court convened on the 10th day of June,
1806, at which term the first Grand Jury for the county was
impaneled and was composed of the following named gentlemen: William Smith, foreman, Matthew French, John Peters,
Charles Walker, Joseph Hare, Thomas Clyburn, Adam Johnston, William Wilburn, William Brown, John Chapman, William Tracy, David Summers, William Law, John Sartin, Edward Hale and Robert Clendenin.

Two indictments were found by the jury at this term, to
wit: one against Peter Dingess for retailing spiritual liquors,
and one against William Stowers, for entering the whiskey
house of John Toney without leave and making use of his
liquors. George Pearis and John Toney were each granted a
license to keep an Ordinary at their respective houses, they
having given the required bonds. Thomas Lewis, an attorney-
at-law, and who was afterwards, in 1816, near Christianburg,
Va., killed in a duel with McHenry, was admitted to practice
in the courts of the County. The following named persons were
appointed constables for said County, viz: John Hale, Charles
Stuart, Henry Clay, Jacob McPherson, Edward Lewis, Reuben Johnston, Noah Mullet and Delaney Sweeney, and Christian Snidow and Isaac Chapman were recommended to the
governor as being qualified to discharge the duties of the office of Coroner.

It was ordered that the next term of the court be held in

the house to be erected by James Aldridge on one of the public lots.

Captain George Pearis donated fifty three acres of land to the County on which to erect its public buildings, and a town was established on this land, called Pearisburg in honor of Captain Pearis. Andrew Johnston agreeing to survey and lay off the town lots and public square for the consideration of $31.00, was appointed to do so. The first petit jury impaneled in the County consisted of Patrick Napier, John Peters, Joseph Jackson, Isaac Jackson, William Clay, Colby Stowers, William Pepper, Nimrod Smith, Henry Dillion, Charles Clay, Philip Peters, and Larkin Stowers. The second Grand Jury consisted of the following named persons, viz: Thomas Burke, foreman, John Peters Theodore Hilvey, Charles Walker, James French, John Martin, William Caldwell, William Wilburn, Thomas Clyburn, John French, John Sartin, John Lybrook, Thomas Farley, Reuben Johnston, James Johnston, Adam Taylor, and Michael Williams.

On these early records of Giles County appear the names of Chapman, Johnston, Oney, Givens, Price, Farley, Straley, (1.) Hare, Lybrook, Burke, Copley, McKensey, Garrison, Gore, Solesbury, Roberts, Harman, Mustard, McDonald, Fry, French, Miller, Clay, Cooke, Eaton, Munsey, Canterbury, Mullens, Burgess, Maupin, Jones, Hall, Emmons, Little, Spangler, Clyburn, Blankenship, Snodgrass, Atkins, Bogle, Conley, Rowe, Epling, Cecil, Tracy, Sarver, Marrs, King, Smith, Bowling, Hager, Lester, Meadows, Albert, Scott, Ford, White, Bane, Shannon, McClaugherty, Watts, Pearis, Sweeny, Snidow, Toney, Napier, McComas, Burton, and Rowland, the latter named family from Philadelphia, Pa.

Before giving further history of the County notice will be be taken of some interesting matters appearing on the old court record of Fincastle and Montgomery Counties. Among the numerous orders of the County Court ordering parties sus-

---

(1)   David Straley and John Fillinger first blacksmiths.

pected of being Tories to appear in court, and either take the oath or give bond for their good behavior, is an order made upon the petition of numerous citizens praying that the place for the holding of court be removed to Craig's, as it is a "better place for hitching horses."

It must be remembered that the County Courts, for there were no others in this section at that date, constituted practically, the legislative, executive and judicial authority and power of the County, before the itinerant District Judge came along.

On March 3rd, 1778, Benjamin Rogers was appointed a constable in Captain Pearis' company. In June, 1785, David Johnston was appointed a constable. On the 26th of April, 1785, an order was made by the County Court allowing a sum of money to George Pearis for provisions, bacon and Indian meal furnished to two spies, and to the militia in June, 1782. Thomas Shannon and George Pearis were appointed in 1785 to review a road down New River on both sides to the Greenbrier County line, and the same year George Pearis and Snidow and Chapman had ferries established across New River. In 1787, September 8th, Mitchell Clay conveyed one half of the Clover Bottom tract of land to Hugh Innis, of Franklin County. On the 7th of April, 1788, George Pearis conveyed a tract of land on Sugar Run to Joseph Cloyd, and in June of the same year, conveyed a tract on New River to David McComas. June 1st, 1790, Mitchell Clay conveyed to George Pearis the remaining half if the Clover Bottom tract. In 1793 Colonel Christian Snidow erected his dwelling house on the east side of New River, at the Snidow-Chapman Ferry, and Isaac Chapman settled on the opposite side of the river from Col. Snidow, and in 1794, George Chapman erected his dwelling house on the east side of New River, about one mile below Colonel Snidow's, on land now belonging to H. B. Shelton and H. L. Phlegar.

The following extracts are taken from the record of Fincastle County Court. On January 6th, 1773, the Court recommended to His Excellency, the Governor, that he will be pleas-

DWELLING HOUSE OF COL. CHRISTIAN SNIDOW

Built in 1793, opposite Ripplemead, Va.

ed to establish a Court House for the County, at a piece of land commonly called McCaul's Place, near the property of Ross and Co., and the lands of Samuel Crockett, in lieu of the Lead Mines for the several reasons following: "that the said McCaul's Place and Crockett's lies on the Great road that passes through the county and that it is well watered, timbered, and level; that it is much more central than the Mines, and that it is in the neighborhood of a great deal of good land and meadows; that the Lead Mines are near the south line of the County, and there is no spring convenient, very scarce of timber, and in a neighborhood where there is very little pasture, and entirely off the leading road. To which order Arthur Campbell dissented." At March Court, 1773, John Aylett and John Todd qualified to practice law. John Aylett produced a commission appointing him His Majesty's attorney. On the second day of April, 1775, appeared James Clevars agent for General Washington, and being first sworn as the law directs, produced to the court a valuation of the improvements on the lands situated on the lower or south side of the Great Kanawha, containing 10,990 acres, property belonging to General Washington, with a certificate granted by William Russell, Justice of the Peace for this County, and that Stevens, George Aubry, and John Clemonts, being first duly sworn to value the tax improvements, which said valuation of the improvements amounting to 1,100 lbs., 15 sh. 7½ pence, together with the above mentioned certificate is ordered to be recorded according to law.

The following extracts are taken from the records of Montgomery County Court: John French qualified as Lieutenant in the eighty-sixth regiment. John Chapman appointed ensign at March Court, 1778, in Captain Lucas' company. On the eighth day of April, 1778, the following order was entered:. "The court proceeded to vote for a place for the Court House. John Montgomery, Walter Crockett and James McGavock having made the several proposals and the question being put, a majority were of the opinion that it should be at Fort Chis-

well, Mr. McGavock giving the county twenty acres of land on
the hill above the house on 'the north side of the road to within ten poles of the mill, thence down the branch and binding
thereon so as to make the same nearly square, with the use of
the spring in common with himself; also twenty acres of wood
land to begin at the corner near his and extend eastwardly
along the line ninety poles, and then such course and distances
as will include the said twenty acres; likewise the use of any
quarries on the Fort Chiswell tract for building, which lands
and privileges he is to convey to the court for the benefit of the
County in fee simple without any consideration other than the
advantage of having a Court House located on his land; and
a reservation of one half acre lot in said land, such as he shall
choose after the ground for the public buildings is laid off."

At September Court, 1785, John Chapman was appointed
one of the Viewers to view a route for a road from Big Crossing of Walker's Creek by Thomas Shannon's and Sugar Run,
at Taylor's land to Captain Pearis'. At November Court, 1790,
John French was recommended for ensign and John Chapman
for Lieutenant. At the June term, 1804, Isaac Chapman was
recommended as Lieutenant in the eighty-sixth regiment and
John French recommended as Captain in the second Battalion
of the eighty-sixth regiment, and David French a Lieutenant in
the same. At the October Court, 1795, William Dingess was appointed Deputy Surveyor. At the June term, 1801. the following order was entered: "Henley Chapman Gentl., having produced a license under the signature of the Honorable Richard
Parker, Paul Carrington, Jr., and Archibald Stewart permit-
ting him to practice as attorney in the Superior and Inferior
Courts within this Commonwealth, and having taken the oaths
required by law, he was admitted to practice in this court.

Our second war with England, usually called the war of
1812, drew from the population of Giles County a considerable number of men, who served at different periods during
its existence. Among those who served were James Straley,
John Straley, Daniel Straley, Captain John Peters, Julius

FIRST COURT HOUSE BUILDING FOR GILES COUNTY

Erected in 1806.

Walker, Berry Blankenship, James Sarver, John Spangler,
Capt. C. H. A. Walker, William Oney and many others whose
names the author has not been able to secure. Near the close
of the war Andrew Johnston, as Captain, marched with a company of men from Giles County, who were ordered to report
at Norfolk, Virginia. On their way thither, on reaching Liberty, now Bedford City, they received information that a
treaty of peace had been signed and that their services
were not needed, and they were ordered to return to their
homes.

There came into the County of Giles, at quite an early date,
a family by the name of Lucas, who became very notorious on
account of their crimes. There were other families of Lucas'
in the New River Valley, and some in the county of Giles, who
were people of standing and repute, and in no wise related to
this criminal gang generally known as the Randall Lucas Tribe.
Jeremiah Lucas, a son of Randall on May 28th,1814, was hanged in the public square of Pearisburg for the murder of Julius
Walker, committed on the 9th day of the April preceding.
Walker was a soldier of the war of 1812, and during his absence, Lucas became intimate with his, Walker's, wife, and on
his return Lucas determined to kill him, and in order to accomplish his purpose he feigned friendship for him, and invited him home with him, and on their way along the New
River Cliffs not far from the Eggleston Springs, Lucas struck
Walker with a club and continued to beat him over the head
until he supposed him dead and then hid him away, and went
on to Walker's house and stayed that night, and as is not un-
common with a murderer he went back the next morning to
visit the spot where he had left his victim, and found him sitting upright against a tree, unable, however, to move or get
away. Walker begged Lucas to spare his life and told him if
he would not kill him that as soon as he was able to leave the
country he would go and never return, and would say nothing
about Lucas' assault upon him. Lucas was unrelenting-brute-
like and clubbed the unfortunate man to death. So soon as the

murder was discovered, the murderer fled, taking refuge in the great Butt or Salt Pond Mountain. There was snow on the ground at the time and a posse of citizens pursued Lucas and finally ran him down and captured him. His captor was John Marrs, who died only a few years ago in Fayette County, West Virginia. Lucas was promptly indicted in the month following his capture, quickly tried, convicted and sentenced to be hanged on the 28th of the May following. The names of the jurors who tried Lucas are, viz: Joseph Canterbury, John Eaton, Joseph Hare, John Chapman, Isaac McKinsey, Philip Peters, Edward Hale, Isaac French, Thomas Clark, James Emmons, William Tracey, and John, (name not legible.) William Chapman, Deputy for John Chapman, Sheriff of the County, carried the sentence into execution. After his sentence and while awaiting execution the jailor of the county, George Johnston, had confined his prisoner in what they call the dungeon, and on giving him food on one occasion, Lucas, who was a physical giant, struck Johnston over the head with his handcuffs, felling him to the floor, then sprang out and started on a run to escape; Johnston, the jailor, had an old musket loaded with powder and buck shot, which he kept in an adjoining room, and as soon as he could recover himself he seized the musket and ran out into the street; but by this time Lucas had gone more than 150 yards away, when Johnston pulled down on him and wounded him in one of his legs, which brought him to the ground, and the jailor soon had him back in the dungeon.

Michael Montgole and family, in 1821, lived on the end of the Little Mountain, just below the mouth of Wolf Creek, in a small hollow, a few hundred yards west of the late residence of the late Joseph Hare, Esq. Montgole was accused of the murder of his wife, by shooting her with a rifle gun, on June 16th, 1821. He claimed that the shooting was accidental, and insisted upon his innocence. He was arrested and promptly indicted by the Grand Jury of Giles County. Feeling against him was so strong that he was enabled to procure a change of

THOMAS BERRY FARLEY

RIPPLEMEAD, VA.

Born 1795, Died 1903, age 108 years when this photograph was taken.

venue to the Circuit Court of the County of Montgomery, wherein he was tried and convicted in May, 1822, and executed on the 21st of June, 1822. He died protesting his innocence.

Dave Lucas, another son of Randall's, was more than once in the Virginia penitentiary for larceny and other crimes, and finally, in 1841, he murdered John Poff, of Franklin County, Virginia, and being suspected of the murder, he ran away into Botetourt County, where he was arrested and brought back, indicted and on the 13th day of May, 1842, was tried by a jury composed of Robert Farris, Robert Caldwell, Christian Simmonds, Olliver C. Peters, Tobias Miller, Edward Nelson, Reuben Hughes, St. Clair French, Samuel Thompson, Joseph Fanning, Charles Miller, and Hiram Pauley, who found him guilty of murder and on the 16th day of the same month he was sentenced to be hanged. The sentence was carried into execution June 24th, 1842, by Abalsom Fry, deputy for John Peck, Sheriff of the County. Mr. Fry often related the incidents connected with the execution of this man, and among others the funeral sermon preached by Rev. Mr. Harris, a Methodist minister, on the day of execution, and that the text from which he preached was "As the Lord liveth and my soul liveth there is but a step between me and death."

Thomas Berry Farley was the principal witness against Lucas, and upon his testimony he was convicted. Farley was born in 1795, on Gatliff's bottom on New River, in what is now Summers County, West Virginia, and died in Giles County, Virginia, in 1903. He was the grandson of Thomas Farley, who settled on Culbertson's bottom now in Summers County, about the year of 1755.

John, a third son of Randall Lucas also killed a man and was tried for his life; the jury however found him guilty of murder in the second degree and fixed his punishment in the penitentiary at nine years.

The only other execution for murder in Giles County (1)

(1). On March 23rd, 1906, Morris Cremeans is to hang for the murder of one Kidd.

was that of Mahala Mason, a negro woman who was hanged May 14, 1852, for the murder of Sallie, a negro woman the property of W. B. Mason. The murder was committed on the 15th day of January, 1852. The funeral of this colored woman was preached by a negro preacher by the name of Harry Chapman, from the text: "Put thine house in order, for thou must die and not live."

In the early history of Giles County there were some very interesting characters, both wags and wits, among the number one John Conley. On an occasion Mr. Conley was passing over the old County road across Cloyd's Mountain, and meeting Mr. Frank Wysor riding in a two wheeled vehicle, Conley accosted Mr. Wysor, who had a very large nose, saying to him, "Stranger turn your nose to one side until I can get by it." Mr. Wysor did as requested, and after he had passed Mr. Conley in the road, he stopped his horse and called to Conley, saying, "Old man, wouldn't you like to have a drink this morning?" to which Mr. Conley replied he would. Mr. Wysor dismounted from his vehicle, taking a bottle therefrom and placing it on the ground, told Mr. Conley to help himself, and as Mr. Conley stooped down to reach for the bottle Mr. Wysor with his fist struck him on the side of the head, knocking him over the bracing of the road, and when Mr. Conley recovered himself Mr. Wysor was in his vehicle and several hundred yards away.

One Chrispianos Walker, a young man at that time who lived with his father on New River, opposite the mouth of Wolf Creek, had fallen in love with a young lady, a Miss Peters, whose parents lived nearly two miles above Walker's, on the river. They were engaged to be married, but the match was vigorously opposed by the girl's parents, and Walker was forbidden the house and the girl put under watch, but Mr. Walker succeeded through some one in informing his betrothed that at a given time he would be at his father's house, have the necessary papers and the preacher on hand, and for her to attempt to make her escape at the time he had indicated. So, early one morning, the young lady suddenly disappeared from her

home; her absence soon being detected she was pursued by two
of her brothers, but out ran them, reaching Mr. Walker's house;
and springing in at the door almost breathless she cried out to
her lover "now or never." Her intended husband was still in
bed when she reached the door, but he immediately sprang out,
having on but one garment, and the preacher then and there
said the ceremony, at the conclusion of which the brothers appeared, but too late.

About the year of 1829, there appeared in Giles County (2) a
quaint eccentric man, about thirty years of age, by the name
of Norman Roberts, who came from Massachusetts, and many
interesting stories are told of his peculiar doings and sayings.
A gentleman driving a wild cow met Roberts at the forks of a
road, and the cow taking the wrong road, the one on which
Roberts was approaching, called out to Roberts: "head that
cow." Roberts replied, "She is already headed." He then said
to Roberts "Turn that cow," to which Roberts replied "She already has the right side out," and the man then said to Roberts "Speak to that cow," whereupon Roberts said "Goodbye,
cow." Roberts wore long hair, lived in caves, and often hid
himself from his fellowmen. The young girls were afraid of
him, as he pretended to make love to all he met with He died
in Mercer County, West Virginia, about 1854.

A brief history will be given of the general laws, Legislative and Constitutional, bearing upon the subject of suffrage,
which will lead up to the assembling and action of the Virginia people in holding various Constitutional conventions.
Sir George Yeardley, governor of Virginia, arrived in April,
1619, he was the first to summon a General Assembly to be
held by the inhabitants, every free man voting, and which was
to make laws for the government of the country. He issued
his summons in June, and on July 30th, 1619, the first Legislative body that ever sat in America assembled at Jamestown,
the then capital of Virginia. This was a notable event, and

(2). The first newspaper, called "The Southwest," was published
by John Sower, about 1858, and the first picture gallery by Bushong, in
1860.

portended radical changes in the form of government. Popular right in America had entered on life and the long struggle to hold its own. Whatever might be the issue, the fact remains that at least it had been born. Here commenced the question of popular and restricted suffrage which has agitated the body politic from that time to the present. In 1670 suffrage was restricted to free-holders and housekeepers. From the first years of the colony to 1655 all the settlers had a voice in public affairs, first in the daily matters of the Hundreds, and after 1619 in electing Burgesses. In the year 1655 the Burgesses declared that none but, "Housekeepers, whether freeholders, leaseholders or otherwise tenants should be capable to elect Burgesses." In the year of 1656 the ancient usage was restored and all freemen were allowed to vote. In 1670, the first act restricting the suffrage was restored, and this, it seems, was thenceforth the determinate sentiment, with the exception of the year, 1676, when Bacon's Assembly changed it and declared that freemen should again vote. This however, was swept away by the general abrogation of all Bacon's Laws, and the freehold restriction was thus restored, and was in operation when the Virginia convention assembled in 1776. That convention provided in the Constitution which it framed that "the right of suffrage in the election of members for both Houses shall remain as exercised at present;" and this remained the law until the assembling of the convention of 1829-30.

On the 5th day of October, 1829, a convention of delegates from the senatorial districts of the Commonwealth of Virginia began its session in the city of Richmond. James Monroe, Esq., ex-president of the United States, was elected president of the convention, but on account of ill health served only for a short time, being succeeded by Philip P. Barbour.

From the 15th senatorial district, composed of the counties of Montgomery, Giles, Wythe and Grayson, the following gentlemen were elected as delegates to said convention, viz: General Gordon Cloyd, of Montgomery, Henley Chapman, of Giles, John P. Matthews, of Wythe and William Oglesby, of Grayson.

The Constitnion framed by this convention made many radical changes in the organic law of the state, and enlarged or rather extended, the right of suffrage to persons who had not theretofore exercised the same; but it failed to give satisfaction to the people west of the Alleghanies.

The vote in the convention on the adoption of the Constitution as engrossed, and as a whole, was taken thereon on January 14th, 1830, and stood 55 for and forty against. Of the forty votes cast against the adoption of the instrument, twenty were by delegates from west of the Alleghanies, and whose names are as follows, viz: Andrew Beirne, William Smith, Fleming B. Miller, John Baxter, William Naylor, William Donaldson, John B. George, Andrew McMillan, Edward Campbell, William Byars, Gordon Cloyd, Henley Chapman, John P. Matthews, William Oglesby, Edwin S. Duncan, John Laidley, Lewis Summers, Adam See, Alexander Campbell, and E. M. Wilson. The constitution was adopted by the people by a majority if 10,492 votes.

About 1832 and for some years subsequently the incorporation and building of turnpike roads gave great impetus to the trade of the century; among these roads Price's Mountain and Cumberland Gap turnpike, Wythe, Raleigh and Grayson and Giles, Fayette and Kanawha. (1.)

--------○--------

CHAPTER VI.

1837-1861

Formation of Mercer County—Its Boundaries, Etc.—Courts Organized—First Grand Jury empanneled—Popular election—Including election of Members of Secession Convention.

In the election held in the county of Giles in 1836 for dele-

(1) The Va. & Tennessee Railroad extended west of New River about 1856 and the C. & O. Ry. about 1872.

gate for Legislature, Daniel Hale, Esq., of Wolf Creek, was chosen. The people living along the Flat Top Mountain, Bluestone and its upper waters and Brush Creek, partly within the territory of Giles and partly within the territory of Tazewell, finding themselves greatly inconvenienced by the distance they had to travel to their County seat, determined to have a new County, and so petitioned the General Assembly of Virginia. Among the petitioners were Captain George W. Pearis, Colonel Daniel H. Pearis, William White, Cornelius White, Captain William Smith, William H. French, Joseph Davidson, (2) John Davidson ,James Calfee, Isaac Gore, Elijah Bailey, and various others, then living within the territory of the proposed new County. The bill was introduced. passed, and became a law on the 17th day of March, 1837. The act in so far as the boundaries of the new County is concerned is as follows: "Be it enacted by the General Assembly, that all that part of the counties of Giles and Tazewell contained within the following boundary lines, to-wit: Beginning at the mouth of East River, in Giles County, and following the meanders thereof up to Toney's mill dam; thence along the top of said mounain, East River Mountain, (the line from Toney's mill dam to the top of the mountain was evidently omitted in the act); to a point opposite the upper end of the old plantation of Jesse Belcher, deceased, thence a straight line to Peery's mill dam near the mouth of Alp's (Abb's) Valley, thence to a point well known by the name of the Peeled (Pealed) Chestnuts, thence to the top of the Flat Top Mountain, thence along said mountain to New River, thence up and along the various meanderings of the same to the beginning, shall form one distinct and new County, and be called and known by the name of Mercer County, in memory of General Hugh Mercer, who fell at Princeton." The Governor was authorized to appoint eighteen persons as Justices of the Peace for the County, the Justices then

---

(2) Made settlements in Wright's Valley, within what is now the corporate limits of the city of Bluefield, West Virginia, and built what is known as "Davidson's House," in Hick's Addition; was a son of John Goolman Davidson.

in commission residing in that part of Giles and Tazewell Counties, which will be in Mercer County after the commencement of the act were to be of the number to be commissioned for the new County. The following are the names of those who held commissions as Justices of the Peace within the territory of the new County, viz: Captain William Smith, Captain C. H. A. Walker, Elijah Peters, John Davidson, John Brown, Robert Gore, Robert Lilley, Robert Hall.

A court for the County was directed to be held on the second Monday of every month. The following named genlemen were by the act to locate the site of justice for the county, to-wit: Thomas Kirk, of the County of Giles, James Harvey, of the County of Tazewell, Joseph Stratton, of the county of Logan, and Henry B. Hunter, of the County of Greenbrier.

The first meeting of the justices for organization was to be at the residence of James Calfee, (Gladeville about one mile west of Princeton), on the second Monday in April, 1837.

The County by the said act was attached to the same judicial circuit with the County of Giles; the circuit superior Courts of Law and Chancery to be held on the first days of May and October.

Philip Lybrook, of the County of Giles, John H. Vawter, of the County of Monroe, and John B. George, of the County of Tazewell were named as commissioners to run and mark the lines between the Counties of Giles and Tazewell and County of Mercer, and make report to the County Courts of each County. It may here be noted that the line between Wythe and Montgomery crossed the County of Mercer from a point on East River near the present Ingleside station, and running northwest passed a little to the west of the public burying ground at Princeton, crossing Bluestone at the Clover Bottom. The Giles and Tazewell County lines crossed about three miles west of Princeton; the Big Spring at Jarrell's being one of the points on this line, and the mouth of Milton's fork on Bluestone, and head of Crane Creek another.

The County Court met on the second Monday in April and

elected Moses E. Kerr, Clerk, and named Captain William Smith as Sheriff, who was afterwards duly commissioned as such by the Governor of the Commonwealth. Captain Smith named John Jarrell as his Deputy, and he was duly appointed. Robert Hall was appointed Surveyor of the County.

The Commissioners to locate the place on which to erect the public buildings for the County, did so on a plat of land donated by Captain William Smith, and near the Glady fork of Brush Creek, about one mile east of Gladeville, and the same on which the present Court House of Mercer County now stands, The question of the name of the County town was debated, some wishing to call it Banesville for Mr. Howard Bane, one of the Commissioners, but finally as the more appropriate, they called it Princeton, inasmuch as the county was named in memory of General Hugh Mercer, who fell at Princeton, that it was altogether proper to name the County town for the place where General Mercer fell mortally wounded.

The first Circuit Court for the County was held on the 1st day of May, 1837, by Judge James E. Brown, of Wythe, who appointed John M. Cunningham Clerk, and Thomas J. Boyd, Attorney for the Commonwealth.

The first grand jury empanneled for Mercer County was composed of the following named gentlemen: Robert Hall, John Martin, Sr., Christian S. Peters, Green W. Meadows, John Walker, George W. Pearis, James M. Bailey, John Davidson, Archibald Bailey, William Cooper, Richard Runion, Thomas Maxwell, Joseph McKinney, Jr., Joshua L. Mooney, William Ferguson, Achilles Fannon, Philip P. Bailey, Chrispianos Walker, Samuel Bailey, William Garretson, Lewis M. Wilson, Robert B. Davidson and Josiah Ferguson. The following Attorneys were admitted to practice at the first and second terms of the Court: viz: Joseph Stras, Albert G. Pendleton, Thomas J. Boyd, A. A. Chapman, M. Chapman, A. T. Caperton and David Hall.

A list of all the judges, attorneys, clerks, justices of the peace, including names of members of the house of delegates

will be found in the appendix to this work, covering as far as
possible the period from the first organization of civil government within the territory of which Mercer County had formed
a part down to the date of the completing of this work.

Since the date of the act creating the County of Mercer there
has been three changes in its boundary lines. Under an act authorizing it, the line between Mercer and Tazewell from the top
of East River Mountain to Peery's mill dam, was run, throwing
a small strip of the territory of Tazewell into Mercer. In 1841
on its eastern border, by an act of the Legislature, the line
along New River at Wiley's Falls to the Toney mill dam was
changed so as to run from said mill dam a straight line to Wiley's falls; thus cutting off a small strip of territory from Mercer and adding it to Giles County. In 1871 the county of Summers was created, and all that part of the territory of Mercer
County lying east and northeast of a line drawn from Round
Bottom on the west side of New River to Brammer's Gate on
the top of Flat Top Mountain was stricken off to the County
of Summers, leaving to Mercer about 420 square miles.

Some of the men who aided in securing and organizing
the County of Mercer had come over the Alleghenies a few
years after the close of the American Revolution, and some
were the sons and grandsons of men who had come prior to
the Revolution. Those who came during the war for independence were called "Over Mountain or Peace men" for the reason that they were from over the mountains, and Peace men,
because it was supposed that many of them were opposed to
war with Great Britain, but this could not be true of all, because many came before the Revolution began, and a large
number of those who came fought gallantly in several battles;
notably, King's Mountain, Shallow Ford of the Yadkin, Wetzell's Mills, and Guilford Court House.

It is doubtless true that there were Tories in the New River
Valley region, mostly however on the upper waters of the New
River. Colonel Preston, when requested to secure the British
and Tory prisoners captured at the battle of King's Mountain,

in stockades to be built at Fort Chiswell answered, "that he
did not regard the place as secure, as there were more Tories
in Montgomery County than any other county of Virginia."
It is certain that some among the most prominent families of
today in the New River Valley, and upon the Clinch waters
are the descendants of Tory ancestors during the Revolution.
For fear of giving offense or wounding the feelings of the more
sensitive, no names are here mentioned, but no just reason can
be assigned why men of that day may not have well been on
the King's side.   It was at least a question of opinion as to
who was right and who was wrong.

Returning to the organization of Mercer County it will be
noted that the justices met and chose one of their number as
Presiding Justice, and this was what had substantially been
provided by former laws.

Captain William Smith, who was born in the County of
Rockingham, Virginia, in 1774, came to the New River Valley
with his father and family when a small lad. He had often before, as well as after 1837, been honored by his fellowmen. He
was the Presiding Justice of Mercer County for twelve years,
and although not a man of letters, without education in the
common acceptation of the term, only able to write his name
and that mechanically, for he could write nothing else, but his
high sense of honor, coupled with his great native ability and
common sense, commended him to the favor of his fellow citizens, who not only honored him by keeping him in the office of Justice of the Peace and making him the presiding officer of the court for a long term of years, but the court had his
portrait painted, framed and hung over the judicial bench in
the Court House, where it remained until the destruction of
that building on the 1st day of May, 1862.

Captain Smith was several times elected to the House of
Delegates of Virginia as the representative of the County of
Giles, and of Mercer and Giles after the formation of Mercer.
He was a candidate for the Legislature twelve times and was
elected six times.

The first settler at the place where the town of Princeton is situated, was French C. Smith, who was a son of one Ezekiel Smith, who went to Texas in the early thirties, was captured by the Mexicans and kept in confinement for five years. French C. Smith, the son, shortly after his father left the country for Texas, also went there, and became quite a prominent figure in Texas politics, having been the Whig candidate for Governor against General Sam Houston, the Democratic candidate, and by whom Smith was defeated by a large majority.

The first merchant to open a store at Princeton was Theodore Jordan, who was followed by Captain William H. Howe, George W. and Daniel H. Pearis, Ward and Gibbony, Johnston and Pearis, Pack and Vawter, John A. Pack & Co., Scott Emmons & Pearis, Pearis & Mahood, John W. Smith, Brown & Shumate. (1)

The first hotel keepers were James M. Bailey and Charles W. Calfee, who were followed later by George W. and Daniel H. Pearis and J. H. Alvis. Daniel Straley was the first Blacksmith, followed later by George B. Newlee, and later by J. W. Dorsey. The first shoemaker was Isham Brinkley, followed by Crockett Scott, and the first tanners were Thompson & Chapman. The first Court House was built in 1839 by a man by the name of Ledbetter. Mercer County enjoys the distinction of having had more Court Houses than any other county in the state and promises to build still more. The first Court House was so badly erected that it had to be taken down and rebuilt, and this was destroyed when the town of Princeton was burned in 1862. The third, in part built at Concord Church by George Evans, contractor, and abandoned after an expenditure of several thousand dollars; the fourth built in 1874 by Andrew Fillinger was destroyed by fire in 1875, supposed to be the work of an incendiary; the fifth and present one with the additions thereto was built in 1876 by D. W. McClaugherty in part and also later by John C. Darst; and it is now seriously proposed to build the sixth one at Bluefield,

(1) Dr. R. B. McNutt was the first resident physician.

that is, whenever the necessary vote of the people can be had removing the County seat to Bluefield.

For a number of years the Counties of Giles and Mercer sent a delegate to the Legislature. The political parties in the two counties were very closely and equally divided.

The census of 1840, the first taken after the creation of the county of Mercer showed a population of 2,243 people. Many fierce political battles were fought in the two counties. from the year of 1840 to that of 1854. These spirited political contests were usually over two offices, member of the house of Delegates ·and the office of Sheriff.

In the year of 1841 Oscar F. Johnston defeated Captain William Smith for the House of Delegates. In the year of 1842 William H. French defeated Chapman I. Johnston for the House of Delegates.

Before proceeding to relate incidents occurring in later contests, it will here be mentioned that two quite distinguished gentlemen and members of the bar, viz: Albert G. Pendleton and Nathaniel Harrison, over a trifling matter came very near venturing out on the field of honor to settle their differenes; the interposition of mutual friends settled the difficulty, and no blood was shed.

In the year of 1843 the contest for the House of Delegates was between William H. French of Mercer, the Whig candidate and Albert G. Pendleton, of Giles, the Democratic candidate, in which contest French won by eleven votes. At that day there were only two voting places in the county of Mercer, one at Princton and the other at Pipestem. It was customary and usual in those days for the opposing candidates to get together at the Court House on the day of an election and sit in the polling room. The voting then was viva voce, and when an elector cast his vote, the candidate for whom he voted expressed his satisfaction by publicly thanking him. A very amusing little incident as well as a clever trick occurred at Princeton in the election between French and Pendleton, and is deemed worthy of relating here. French, the Whig candidate was at

Princeton on the day of the election sitting in the polling place. Captain George W. Pearis, a very ardent democrat, and known to be the special champion and friend of Colonel Pendleton, lived at Princeton and had charge of Mr. Pendletons interest at that place on the day of election. Only those could vote who had a freehold, and were assessed with some part of the public revenue and had paid the same.

One Samuel Waldron, who lived about 1½ miles southeast of where the city of Bluefield is now located, but who under the law was not a voter, was present at the election at Princeton and expressed to Captain Pearis his desire to vote, and inquired of Captain Pearis whether he, Waldron, was a legal voter. Being informed by Pearis that he did not think he was, but that if he would vote for Pendleton he thought he could arrange the matter for him. Out of the three commissioners conducting the election, two of them were Whigs and known friends of French. Captain Pearis told Waldron to go in and offer his vote, and that when his name was called he, Pearis, would suddenly appear at the Court House door and challenge his vote, and that he had no doubt that the commissioners would promptly decide that he was a legal voter. Waldron appeared before the commissioners and expressed his desire to vote, and the Crier called out "Samuel Waldron, who do you vote for?" Before he could answer Captain Pearis appeared at the door and shouted at the top of his voice, "I challenge that vote, that man is not a voter." From these circumstances French's friends concluded that Waldron wanted to vote for him, and they promptly decided that he was a qualified voter, and being again inquired of as for whom he wished to vote, he replied, "Pendleton," much to the chagrin and disappointment of French and his friends. Another incident occuring at this same election is worth telling as Mr. Pendleton was the butt of the joke this time. Mr. Pendleton very early on the morning of election day on his way to Pipestem voting place, went several miles out of his way to see Mr. John Comer, who lived on Christian's Ridge and after a talk with Comer, was led to believe that he was a friend and would vote for him, so he took him up on his horse behind him and rode to the polling place about ten miles away, and when Comer's name was called by the Crier at the polls, Comer shouted "French."

A few years after this Cornelius White was elected to the House of Delegates from the counties of Mercer and Giles. Mr. White was a plain farmer, without much education, but a man of good native sense. After reaching Richmond and entering the House he introduced a bill of some local nature, touching some local matters connected with roads, and seemed to have taken no further interest in the bill until within a day or two of the close of the session, when he inquired of some friend if he knew anything of his bill and being answered in the negative, Mr. White inquired what he should do about it; his friend told him to call up the bill and ask for unanimous consent to put the bill on its passage. The next morning at the opening of the session. Mr. White addressed the Speaker telling him about the bill and how anxious he was to have it pass and then said "Mr. Speaker, if you will take up that bill and have it passed I promise you that I will show you the frog of my foot to-morrow morning."

In the year of 1847 difficulties growing out of relations between the United States and Mexico brought on war between the two countries. No organized troops went from either of the two Counties of Giles or Mercer, though Col. Daniel H. Pearis, the commandant of the militia of the latter County, sought to obtain a commission as Colonel of the Virginia regiment then being organized for the field, but failed, the commission being given to Colonel John M. Hamptrampeh, and to John Randolph as Lieutenant Colonel, and to Jubal A. Early as Major.

Captain James F. Preston, of Montgomery County, raised in that County a company which was attached to the Virginia Regiment. Many of these men who went with the Virginia Regiment to Mexico, became distinguished soldiers in our late Civil War: viz: Jubal A. Early became a Lieutenant General, Captain James F. Preston became Colonel of the Fourth Virginia Regiment of the Stonewall Brigade, Robert D. Gardner succeeded Preston in command of the Fourth Regiment, Charles A. Ronald also became Colonel of this Regiment, and at one time commanded the Stonewall Brigade, Joel Blackard became Captain of the first company from Giles County, and while such was killed in the battle of Frazier's farm in 1862, W. W. McComas, a prominent physician of Giles County, as Captain led a company of artillery from that County, losing his life in the battle of South Mills, N. C. Judge Robert A. Richardson, at one time a Judge of the Supreme Court of Appeals of Virginia, was a soldier in the Mexican war, and led the first company from Mercer County into the civil War, Andrew J. Grisby, who aided in the organization of the first company of volunteers that left Giles County, was made Major of the 27th Virginia regiment of the Stonewall Brigade, afterwards becoming Colonel of that regiment, and several times in command of the Brigade, was a member of Doniphan's regiment of Missouri Cavalry in the Mexican war. Harvey Wall, who long lived in Mercer County, was a member of Captain Preston's company, as well and Daniel H. Harman, of Boone County, West Virginia, Benjamin Linkous, another member of Preston's company, became a Colonel of a Confederate regiment, and Greenbury Chandler, who was with Preston in Mexico, became a Confederate officer and was slain in the battle of Piedmont Virginia.

Another step forward was to be taken by the Virginia people in the enlargement of the right to vote, and a convention assembled at Richmond on the 14th. day of October, 1850, and framed a constitution which was adopted, whereby the restrictions upon the right of suffrage were practically swept away; excluding only persons of unsound mind, paupers, noncommissioned officers, soldiers, seamen, and marines in the service of the United States, and persons who had been convicted of bribery in an election or of any infamous offense.

The representatives in this convention from the district in which Mercer County was included were Albert G. Pendleton of Giles, Allen T. Caperton and Augustus A. Chapman of Monroe.

The Constitution framed by this convention was adopted as a compromise measure between the east and the west.

In 1850 Lewis Neal defeated John Miller, of Sinking Creek, for the House of Delegates. In 1851 Captain George W. Pearis was elected to the House of Delegates over Alexander Mahood, and in 1852 Reuben Garretson defeated Colonel James M. Bailey. Under the Constitution of 1851 Mercer was accorded a delegate.

The most remarkable and notable contest in the matter of an election, that ever occurred in Mercer County, was over that of a delegate to the Secession Convention. The contest was between two brothers, William H. French and Napoleon B. French. At the time of this election Napoleon B. French was serving as a senator in the Legislature of Virginia from the district of which Mercer County was a part, and was in Richmond at the time of this election. These men were and had for long years been prominent in politics, and were the two best known men not only in the County, but in this particular section of the state. Both brothers had been Whigs all of their lives and up to a short time prior to the beginning of the Civil war, when William H. left the Whig and united with the Democratic party. This action on his part so incensed his old political friends that they determined to get even with him the first opportunity, and when he announced himself a candidate for the convention and made known his views, which tended toward secession, his old political friends who had become his enemies, as well as the political friends of his brother, Napoleon, at once named the latter as the opposing candidate. There was considerable feeling in this contest and some bitterness. At this time a large majority of the people of Mercer County were strongly union in sentiment.

The great political battle between these two brothers was

fought to the finish, and resulted in the election of Napoleon B. French by a majority of more than 300. On the assembling of the convention in February, 1861, Mr. French took his seat therein as the representative of the people of Mercer County.

The next spirited contest was for the Legislature, a battle royal which took place between Captain Robert A. Richardson and Dr. Robert B. McNutt, in May, 1861. Richardson had raised a company of volunteers for the Civil War, of which he had been elected Captain, and consequently had gathered to himself a very large following and was then on the eve of starting off for the war, and the people of the County were very much agitated and excited. Dr. Robert B. McNutt had long lived in the County, was a very eminent physician, had quite a strong relationship, and a host of friends, personal and political. He was defeated by Richardson by a small majority.

The Secession Convention which assembled in Richmond in February, 1861, was composed of the ablest men in the state; they were not only able but patriotic, and weighed well and carefully every step that was taken. A great deal of the time of the convention was taken up in considering the report of the committee on Federal relations. The report of this committee recommended certain amendments to the Constitution of the United States fixing the limits of the slave territory, and the rights of slaveholders to take their slave property into the limits of such territory. There were a great many substitutes offered for this report, and it was evident from the various votes taken on these substitutes that in the beginning the larger number of the members of the convention were opposed to separation from the Union, and on the other hand the majority thereof seems to have been unwilling to see the Federal Government coerce the states which had seceded. At last and when the point was reached and it became evident that the Federal authorities were determined to attempt to coerce the seceding states, it became necessary for the convention to take some decided step. It went into secret session on Tues-

day, the 16th day of April, 1861, and on that day Mr. William
Ballard Preston, of Montgomery County, submitted an ordinance "to repeal the ratification of the Constitution of the
United States by the state of Virginia, and to resume all the
rights and powers granted under said Constitution."

In the afternoon session of that day Mr. Robert Scott, of
Fauquier, offered a substitute for Mr. Preston's ordinance.
This substitute recited that there were still eight slavehold-
ing states within the Union, and some members of the convention favored consultation and co-operation with these states,
and that it was desirable to ascertain the preferences of the
people of the state as to whether or not they desired co-operation with the eight slave states or immediate secession, and to
that end a vote of the people of the state be taken on the 4th
Tuesday in May next thereafter. When a vote on this substitute was called for, Mr. Baldwin of Augusta moved an adjournment, but the convention refused to adjourn by a vote of sixty-
five to seventy- eight, Mr. French, the representative from Mercer, voting for adjournment. After the transaction of some
other business another motion was made to adjourn, which
was carried by a vote of seventy-six to sixty-five, French again
voting for adjournment. On Wednesday, the 17th day of April,
1861, the convention resumed consideration of the ordinance
submitted by Mr. Preston and the substitute offered therefor
by Mr. Scott. The vote was first taken on the substitute which
was lost by sixty-four to seventy-nine, French voting for
the substitute, and casting his vote with John A. Campbell, of
Washington, John J. Jackson of Wood, John F. Lewis of Rockingham, John S. Burdett of Taylor, Jubel A. Early of Franklin, Samuel Price of Greenbrier, Henry L. Gillaspie, of Raleigh, and other members from northwestern Virginia. The
Monroe, Giles and Tazewell delegates voted against the substitute. The substitute being lost, a vote was then taken on
the ordinance proposed by Mr. Preston which was adopted by
a vote of eighty- eight to fifty-five. On this final vote French
voted for the ordinance as did almost all the members from the

southwestern part of the state, while the major part of the members from the northwestern part of the state voted against it.

It is here noted in this connection that the Congress of the United States agreed to and submitted an amendment to the Constituion, which was approved March, 1861, touching the slavery question and known as amendment number "Thirteen," and which was ratified by the Legislature of the restored Government of Virginia at Wheeling, the 13th day of February, 1862. The amendment is in the following words: "No amendment shall be made to the Constitution which will authorize or give to Congress the power to abolish or interfere in any state with the domestic institutions thereof, including that of persons held to labor or service by the laws of the said state."

The convention of Virginia provided for the submission of the ordinance of secession to the people on the 23rd day of May, 1861, for ratification or rejection. It was ratified by a majority of 96,750 out of a total vote of 161,018 votes. The Counties of northwestern Virginia in a vote of 44,000 gave 40,000 majority against the ordinance. The vote in Mercer County on the ordinance was practically unanimous, only seven votes being cast against it. Giles County cast her 1033 votes solidly for the ordinance; electing at the same time Captain William Eggleston to the House of Delegates over Dr. John W. Easly by 234 votes.

As has been seen by reference to the vote of the delegates in the convention from the Counties west of the Alleghenies and north of the Kanawha, as well as the vote of the people of those Counties, that they were intently and earnestly opposed to secession, while all he Counties south of the Kanawha, and particularly those in the New River Valley and southwest Virginia were almost a unit for it. Toward the closing days of the secession convention, a party of gentlemen from several Counties in the state—representative men, catching the spirit of the people at home, which seemed to be in advance of that of the convention, by self appointment met in the city of Richmond with the view and purpose of influencing if possible the action of the convention in favor of immediate secession. What bearing if any the meetings of this self constituted body of men had on the action of the convention can only be conjectured.

Such was the intense feeling and excitement in Richmond, and in fact throughout the Commonwealth, that the representatives in the convention from the northwestern and other parts of the state who opposed the action of the convention and refused to vote for the ordinance, became alarmed for their safety, some leaving and traveling incognito, while others thought it necessary to procure letters of safe conduct from the Governor of the Commonwealth in order to enable them to reach their homes.

The news of the passage of the ordinance of secession, spread throughout the state like unto wild fire in a dry stubble on a windy day. The intelligence was greeted with shouts of applause by the populace, bells were rung, cannons boomed, great gatherings of the people were had, and oratory dispensed without stint.

Virginia had stood for peace, placed herself in the position of mediator between the contending sections. Her appeals on the one side were unheeded, and the threats and demonstrations on the other, did not move her. She did not intend to act in haste, and only decided to leave the Union when the Federal Executive called for seventy-five thousand troops to coerce the Seceded States.

History can scarcely furnish a parallel of the beginning of a revolution so orderly, peaceful, and without blood shed or excesses of any kind, all accomplished in a quiet, Constitutional form and method—Virginia claiming nothing further than to be allowed to depart in peace, uttering as she withdrew from the Union the hope and prayer that war might be averted. Without waiting for the result of the vote on the ordinance, the people went to work with energy to organize and equip the whole military force of the state for defense, not for aggressive war on the Federal Union, but to prevent if possible, the Federal power from crushing the state and overthrowing Constitutional government therein, and to prevent further encroachments upon the rights of the state. Virginia had resumed her original sovereignty, and had withdrawn all the powers and rights that she had delegated to the Federal agent; she had revoked the power of attorney that she had given that Federal agent, and did not propose to withdraw the revocation, but to maintain it by force of arms if necessary; that was all.

The position of the south, and particularly of Virginia, seems not to have been well understood by the great bulk of the northern people, who were led astray by the cry for the Union, and that these people of the south were preparing to establish a government based upon slavery as its chief cornerstone, when in fact our southern people were attempting to escape from a government and power which sought to destroy their Constitional rights. It was not the establishment of a southern Confederacy that our people sought and fought for, but it was to uphold and maintain the integrity and sovereignty of the state, and with no view of making war on the other States of the Union or on the Federal Government.

---o---

CHAPTER VII.

1861-1865.

The organization of Military Companies—The concentration of Armies—The War Begins—Great Union Uprising in Northwestern Virginia—Restored Government of Virginia —Formation of West Virginia—Various battles and engagements—Campaigns of 1861, 1862, 1863, 1864, 1865— The war ends—Peace restored—Reconstruction in Mercer County.

At the period of the organization of military companies referred to above, the whole state of Virginia, in a measure, presented a fair picture of a grand military camp and the people, except those in the northwestern part of the state were aglow with enthusiasm for the defense of Virginia. Enlistments were rapidly going on in all theCounties, cities, towns and villages within the Commonwealth, and the people of the New River Valley Counties were abreast with their sister Counties in this great movement.

The change in public sentiment wrought in the minds of the people in a few short weeks was most remarkable. In the County of Giles Mr. Manilius Chapman, known to lean strongly towards separation from the Federal Union, was in February elected to the convention by a majority of only about twenty votes over Mr. Charles D. Peck, an open and avowed Unionist, and who declared that "he would give up his slaves rather than dissolve the Union." A little more than three short months, the solid vote of Giles County was cast for the ratification of the ordinance of Secession. The same is true of the people of Mercer county, where the Union candidate was elected by a vote of over two to one; yet in the same length of time the sentiment of the people had been so revolutionized, that, save and except seven votes, the County went solidly for secession; this, too, in County whose population was composed almost wholly of white people, there being but few slaves in the county.

The following companies were organized and sent to the war by the County of Giles, viz: Captain James H. French's company of infantry attached to the 7th Virginia regiment; Captain W. W. McComas' company of artillery attached to Sarke's battalion; Captain Andrew Gott's company (1) attached to the 36th Virginia regiment of infantry; Captain Porterfield's company attached to the 36th regiment of Virginia infantry; Captain William Eggleston's company attached to the 24th Virginia regiment of infantry; Captain William H. Payne's company attached to the 27th Virginia battalion of cavalry. To these should be added numbers of Giles County

Note 1.   The officers of Captain Andrew Gott's company I, 36 Va. Infty., were, Capt. Andrew Gott, Lieuts. James K. Shannon, Leander Johnston and Jno. M. Henderson.

men who attached themselves to companies from other counties, and also the Reserve forces composed of those between the ages of sixteen and eighteen years and forty-five and fifty years. (2)

Mercer County organized and sent to the field ten companies as follows, viz: (3). Captain Robert A. Richardson's company attached to the 24th regiment of Virginia infantry; Captain William B. Dorman's company attached to a regiment of the Wise Legion; Captain John A. Pack's company and Captain W. G. Ryan's company, both of which were attached to the 60th regiment of Virginia; Captain Richard B. Foley's Independent company of infantry; Captain John R. Dunlap's company attached to the 23rd Virginia battalion of infantry; Captain William H. French's company attached to the 17th Virginia regiment of cavalry; Captain Napoleon B. French's company of artilery, unattached, and captured at Fort Donnelson, and afterwards divided, part going to the 17th regiment of Virginia cavalry and the remainder thereof to Clark's 30th battalion of Virginia infantry; the companies of Captain Jacob C. Straley and Captain Robert Gore attached to the 17th regiment of Virginia cavalry. The company of Captain William B. Dorman was captured in the battle of Roanoke Island, in 1862, and on the return of the members of said company they separated, some going to Captain Jacob C. Straley's company and some to a company commanded by Captain Thomas Thompson, who was succeeded by Captain James H. Peck, and this company was attached to the 26th Virginia battalion of infantry commanded by Colonel George M. Edgar.

It is not intended here, in fact it is not at all possible, as the information is not at hand, to present a list of the names of the men who composed these various companies, but the rolls of some of the companies from the Counties of Giles and Mer-

(2). A company of Reserves commanded by Capt. Wm. H. Dulaney.

(3). In addition to these ten companies, Mercer County also sent Capt. Alex. Pine's company of Reserves, attached to the 4th Va. Battalion. *See Appendix G.*

cer, as far as they have been obtained, together with the names of the various company, officers will be found in the appendix to this volume.

As has already been stated, when our people entered upon the war it was with brave determination and vigor—not counting the cost. It was to them simply the question of defending Virginia, and Virginia's soil from the threatened invasion of a Northern army; and to preserve our rights and liberties as free people, and for which our ancestors had shed their blood in our contest with Great Britain. It was not a war on the part of our people to preserve or perpetuate slavery, for thousands of our best and bravest soldiers, nor their ancestors had ever owned a slave. We were forced to the choice of which master we should serve—we could not serve both. We regarded our primary allegiance due to the state which, with the other states, had given life and existence to the Federal agent that now proposed to turn upon, crush and destroy its creators. These were the arguments and presentations of the question at that time. For these contentions our people stood ready to surrender their lives, their all, save honor, and fought to the finish, only yielding to overpowering and overwhelming force, but not surrendering an iota of the principles for which they so long, so faithfully and bravely battled. These principles are just as sacred today as they ever were, they were not lost by the results of the war, only the effort to maintain and establish them by the arbitrament of the sword was a failure.

In the months of May, June and the early days of July, 1861, the Federal Government had gathered two great armies in the East under the command of General Winfield Scott; one at Washington and in that vicinity, which during the months referred to had crossed the Potomac into Virginia, the other along the upper Potomac in the vicinity of Martinsburg and Harper's Ferry. The first named army under General McDowell as field commander, the second under General Patterson as commander in the field.

The Confederate Government to oppose these hostile and invading armies, had gathered and mobilized an army at and around Manassas Junction under General G. T. Beauregard; another to oppose General Patterson on the upper Potomac and in the Valley under General Joseph E. Johnston.

During the month of May many of the companies from the New River Valley Counties marched away to their respective places of rendezvous, among them the companies of Captain James H. French, of Giles, and Captain Richardson, of Mercer, which left their respective Counties about the last days of May, 1861, and hastened to Lynchburg, Virginia, their appointed place of rendezvous, and on the first day of June thereafter joined General Beauregard's army, then being concentrated at and around Manassas Junction on the Orange and Alexandria Railroad and about twenty-five miles from the city of Washington. The companies of French (1) and Richardson were assigned to the 24th regiment of Virginia infantry then commanded by Colonel Jubal A. Early. The company of Captain McComas was assigned to duty with the Wise Legion, and did its first service in the Greenbrier-Sewell Mountain country, and was then transferred to the eastern department with the Legion to which it belonged. The other companies as organized, those from Giles as well as those from Mercer, went forward to their respective places of assignment. It is estimated that the County of Giles sent into the Confederate service about eight hundred men, of whom nearly forty per cent. were lost, and that about fifteen hundred men went from the County of Mercer, of whom it is estimated that fully forty per cent were lost. These two Counties had their representatives on every important battlefield in the state of Virginia, West Virginia, Maryland, Pennsylvania, and on some of the fields in Tennessee, Kentucky and North Carolina.

General Beauregard's outposts were at Fairfax Court House, and on the morning of June 1st, 1861, a Federal scouting party entered the town and a skirmish with the Confederates un-

(1) French's company was subsequently and prior to the first battle of Manassas, transferred to the 7th Virginia Regiment.

der Major Ewell took place, in which Captain John Q. Marr, of Fauquier County, was killed.

During the month of June and the early days of July, General Beauregard was actively engaged in the organization of his troops and in preparing them for field service. The regi- regiment and place dunder the command of Colonel Jubal A. 24th Virginia regiments were brigaded with the 7th Louisiana regiment and placed under the command of Colonel Jubal A. Early.

Rumors were afloat in the camps for several days previous to the Federal advance that we would soon be attacked by General McDowell's army.

Soldiers, even at that early stage of the war, seemed to have the peculiar faculty of finding out things that it was difficult to conceive how or where they got their information,—probably a kind of intuition.

In the early days of July our pickets on the outposts were required to be more vigilant, and orders were issued requiring the men not on picket to keep strictly within the camp. One night during this time a picket fired his gun at some object, real or imaginary; nevertheless the long roll sounded to arms. We had the guns but no ammunition, and such confusion was scarcely ever seen, but we survived it—got straightened out, and became much more calm when we found no enemy was approaching.

Orders came to prepare three days rations and to be prepared to march at a moment's notice. Everything transportable was packed and in readiness, the soldier's knapsack was full and heavy, and this together with his musket and forty rounds of cartridges, made a burden too heavy to be borne on a July day and we learned better later on, soon finding out how to reduce our baggage to the minimum. The order to march came on the 17th day of July and we left our camp and proceeded to the high ground overlooking the valley of Bull Run, and Mitchell's, Blackburn's, and McLean's fords, where we remained that night and until about noon on the 18th, when we discovered a cloud of dust rising beyond the stream, which indicated the advance of a body of men, which proved to be the vanguard of the Federal army, which threw itself against General Longstreet's brigade and was repulsed; but soon renewed the attack, when the seventh Virginia regiment was led into the action by Colonel Early, and this attack was repulsed. After a sharp cannonade of two hours or more, the enemy retired and some of our men crossed the stream, picked up hats, guns, blankets, and the enemy's wounded. The loss in the 7th regiment was small, a few slightly wounded, among them Isaac Hare and James H. Gardner, of the Giles company, struck with spent balls. Lieutenant. Colonel Lewis B. Williams was in command of the regiment, Colonel Kemper being absent on detached service, but he joined us the next day We occupied the field that night, next day and until Saturday, when we were relieved and allowed to retire a short distance into a pine thicket to rest and recuperate. The enemy having sufficiently felt of our position and of us to satisfy him that we were there and meant to stay as long as necessary, retired out of the range of our guns, and began the flank movement which culminated in the battle of Sunday afterwards.

On Sunday morning, the 21st, we were lined up along the belt of pines and timber which fringed the southern bank of the stream, where we were subjected to a severe shelling from the enemy's guns posted on the heights beyond. On the day preceding, the companies of Richardson, of Mercer, and Lybrook, of Patrick, were sent to Bacon Race Church to guard the road leading to our position from that direction, and these companies remained in their position throughout Sunday and did not participate in the battle.

About 11 o'clock A. M. of Sunday, July 21st, Colonel Early led his brigade of three regiments, less the two companies above referred to, across Bull Run at McLean's Ford and on to the hills beyond, forming in line of battle and prepared to advance, when he was recalled to take position in the rear of the troops at Mitchell's and Blackburn's ford.

About high noon could be heard distinctly the roar of battle far to the left and to the west. It was fully eight miles away, and Colonel Early receiving an order to march to the field of contention, moved off rapidly, the 13th Mississippi, Colonel Barksdale, having been substituted for the 24th Virginia regiment, which had been placed in position at one of the fords. The movement of Early's brigade for the grater part of the distance was at double quick through a broiling hot sun and many of the men were almost completely exhausted and famished for water. The brigade reached the field of action about three o'clock and twenty minutes, P. M., the time consumed in the movement being about two hours and twenty minutes. In this rapid movement no roads were looked for or traveled, but the command was governed alone by the sound of the firing. On the arrival of this brigade the situation was anything but promising to the Confederates; the Federals were making another, and it was the last, swing around the Confederate left. The brigade of General E. Kirby Smith, which had just preceded that of Early on the field, had passed through a strip of woods, behind which Early's command marched to the left, and into an open field beyond, and near to the Chinn house, which was almost immediately on the left of the brigade. Here the deployment of the brigade began to meet the oncoming foe. The 7th Virginia regiment being in the advance made its deployment quickly, but not without serious loss from the enemy's fire, from which the regiment suffered in killed and wounded within a few minutes forty-seven men, of whom nine were killed and thirty-eight wounded. Colonel Early advanced his regiments promptly against the enemy, who soon left the field in a panic, and were pursued as rapidly and as far as the broken down condition of the men would permit. The Federals continued their retreat to the Potomac, and even beyond, some of them not stopping short of their homes; and thus the first "On to Richmond" was a disastrous failure.

General Johnston had eluded Patterson in the Valley, and with the greater part of his forces had united with General

Beauregard's army in time to win the great victory at Manassas.

The loss in company D, the Giles company, of the 7th regi-
ment was as follows, viz: Killed, Joseph E. Bane, Wounded,
Robert H. Bane, A. L. Fry, Manilius S. Johnston, Charles N.
J. Lee, Henry Lewy, John P. Sublet, and Samuel B. Shannon.

In a few days after this battle, the army moved forward to
Fairfax Court House, picketing along the Alexandria Leesburg
and other roads leading in the direction of Alexandria and
Washington. Late in the fall the main body fell back to Centerville and Bull Run, where it passed the winter. The 7th
Virginia regiment was separated from the 24th Virginia and
7th Louisiana, and added to another brigade which for a while
was commanded by Brigadier General Ewell, later by Brigadier General Longstreet. In March, 1862, a brigade was formed
of the first, 7th, 11th and 17th Virginia regiments, and placed
under the command of Brigadier General Ambrose Powell
Hill.

General Henry A. Wise, in the early summer of 1861, had entered the Valley of the Kanawha with a considerable number
of Confederate troops, among them a considerable number of
New River Valley men, and on the 7th day of July, 1861, had
a successful fight at Scary Creek with the advanced troops of
the Federal General Cox. Subsequently, in fact in a few days,
General Wise being threatened by a force of Federal troops
from the upper Gauley section under the command of General
Rosecrans, was forced to retire towards Lewisburg. About
the middle of August, 1861, General John B. Floyd with a brigade arrived in the vicinity of Lewisburg, and he assumed command of all the Confederate troops operating in that section,
and about the movements of which more will be stated hereinafter.

In all revolutions excesses are committed, and the same was
true of our revolution in 1861. After the retreat of General
Wise's forces from the Kanawha, a plain unlettered farmer of
Mercer County, by the name of Parkinson F. Pennington, who

resided on the waters of Laurel Creek, in August of the year
mentioned, took his team.and wagon loaded with produce, and
went to the Valley of the Kanawha, and purchased goods, salt,
etc., returning to his home, and known to be a strong Union
man in sentiment, and freely expressing his views, made himself quite obnoxious to some of his southern neighbors, and was
arrested without warrant and charged with being a spy.   The
party arresting Pennington was headed by Captain James
Thompson a strong resolute, bold southern man of quick tem-
per, and when aroused became wholly unmanageable.   Pennington's captors started with him to the Court House, and
he on the way becoming very boisterous and insulting incensed
the party that had him in charge, and they halted and put
him to death by the road side, by hanging him by the neck,
with a hickory withe, to a dog-wood tree that stood nearby.
This was a very unfortunate affair for all the parties concerned, and the first act of the kind that had ever taken place in the
County, and greatly shocked the community.   Great regret was
expressed by the people, as the act portended no good to the
parties engaged nor to the southern cause.   The civil authorities were powerless to punish the perpetrators, and the military would not.   After the close of the war, the most of those
engaged in hanging Pennington, except Captain Thompson,had
either been lost in the war or left the country.   Pennington's
father, with a body of eighteen United States soldiers went to
the house of Captain Thompson intending to arrest him, but
Captain Thompson discovering their approach attempted to
escape, but was shot by one of the party and killed.

Notwithstanding the apparent unanimity of sentiment
among the people of Mercer County in favor of Southern rights
and armed resistence to Federal attempt at coercion, there
were quite a number of good men in the County opposed to the
war, and who remained steadfast in their convictions for the
Union throughout the conflict; among them, Colonel Thomas
Little, George Evans, Andrew J. Thompson, John A. McKensey
James Sarver, David Lilley, Sylvester Upton, Augustus W.

Cole, Augustus W. J. Caperton, James Bowling, William C. Honaker, W. J. Comer, Russell G. French, and many others. Some of these men, believing it unsafe to remain in the country, went within the lines of the Federal army, and there remained during the entire period of the war, others remained quietly at their homes, taking no part in the contest. There were a few, glad to say few, who enlisted in the Confederate army and then deserted to the enemy, and some of these became a set of outlaws, thieves and robbers, who respected neither friend nor foe, and made incursions into the country, plundering indiscriminately.

The commands of Generals Wise and Floyd, being sorely pressed by the enemy, the militia brigades of General Alfred Beckley and Augustus A. Chapman were called into service in August, 1861, and sent to Cotton Hill, in Fayette County. A call had been made in the early part of the summer of 1861 for the services of the militia of the County of Mercer, and Colonel Thomas Little, the then commandant thereof, declined, in fact refused to obey the call, and in a public meeting of the citizens held at Princeton he was fearfully denounced, and threatened with personal violence, so much so that he thought it prudent to immediately retire within the Federal lines. The Mercer and Giles regiments of militia, belonged to Chapman's brigade. The Giles regiment was commanded by Colonel James W. English with Samuel E. Lybrook and J. C. Snidow as Majors. The Mercer regiment was commanded by Lieutenant Colonel John S. Carr, with Harman White and W. R. Bailey as Majors. H. W. Straley was the brigade Commissary. The militia brigades were disbanded in the fall of 1861, and later in the same fall the troops of Wise and Floyd were withdrawn from the Gauley and New River section; Wise going to the eastern coast of Virginia and North Carolina, and Floyd with his command, in which was the 36th Virginia regiment of infantry, composed in part of New River men, to Fort Donelson, Tennessee.

During the winter and spring of 1861-2, the 8th Virginia

regiment of cavalry under the command of Colonel Jenifer, occupied the territory of Mercer County, as a corps of observation, with headquarters at Princeton.

Before proceeding further with this narrative, it becomes important and interesting to relate what is transpiring during this period among the people of the northwestern Counties of Virginia, who were so violently opposed to Secession. It is not proposed to discuss the military side of this rather novel situation, but the civil. It is well known and need not here be related, that Federal troops had largely occupied all of the territory of the northwestern counties north of the Kanawha, and mostly that west of the Alleghanies, in what is now the state of West Virginia. As already stated, that in the Secession Convention, which assembled at Richmond in February, 1861, a majority of the members from the northwestern Counties of Virginia were earnestly, conscientiously and violently opposed to Secession and a number of them voted against the ordinance. These men returned to their respective constituences, and public meetings were held in many of the northwestern Counties for the purpose of determining what action should be taken by the people of these Counties. A large meeting of the people was held at Clarksburg on the 22nd of April, 1861, under the auspices of the Honorable John S. Carlisle, the late delegate from that County to the convention. About twelve hundred people attended the meeting, and after reciting in a long preamble the means which had been resorted to by the Secessionists to transfer the state from its allegiance to the Federal Government to the Confederate states without the consent of the people, and reciting many other grievances, recommended to the people of all the counties composing northwestern Virginia, to appoint not less than five delegates from each County to a convention to be held at Wheeling on the 13th day of May following, to consult and determine upon the course of action to be taken by the people of northwestern Virginia in the then fearful emergency. Delegates were accordingly selected from twenty-six counties, viz: Hancock, Brooke, Ohio, Marion, Monongalia, Preston, Wood, Lewis, Ritchie, Harrison, Upshur, Gilmer, Wirt, Jackson, Mason, Wetzel, Pleasants, Barbour, Hampshire, Berkeley, Doddridge, Tyler, Taylor, Roane, Frederick, and Marshall.

The convention met on the 13th day of May, and was organized by the election of John W. Moss as permanent president. After a long and somewhat stormy session, this convention ended its work by recommending that in the event the ordinance of secession should be ratified by the people, the Counties there represented, and all others disposed to co-operate, appoint on the 4th of June, 1861, delegates to a general convention to meet on the 11th day of the same month at such place as should be designated by a committee to be afterwards appointed by the convention.

The convention was composed of about five hundred in number, and from its close to the election which took place on the 23rd of the same month, the country was in a feverish state of excitement. On election day the people voted for the members of the House of Representatives to the Federal Congress from the three districts west of the Alleghanies. In twenty-five Counties, embracing a part of what is now West Virginia, there was a majority of over twenty-four thousand votes against the ordinance of Secession. There was great interest manifested in the coming election for delegates to the convention to be held on the 11th day of June. The County committees appointed persons to hold the election at the various precincts on the 4th of June. There was a very full vote polled, and delegates from twenty-one counties were reported elected, which number was subsequently augmented to thirty-five. The delegates met in Washington Hall, in the city of Wheeling, on the 11th day of June, 1861, and elected Arthur I. Boreman, of Wood County, President of the convention. On the 19th day of June the convention passed an ordinance for the reorganization of the state Government of Virginia; and on the following day elected the following officers: Francis H. Pierpont, of Marion, Governor, Daniel Polsley, of Mason, Lieutenant Governor, and James S.

Wheat of Ohio, Attorney General. The General Assembly met in pursuance of the ordinance of the convention at Wheeling on the 1st day of July. The session was held at the custom house, where the Governor had already established his office, and where the other officers of the Government were subsequently located. On the 9th of July the House on a joint vote elected L. A. Hagans, of Preston, Secretary of the Commonwealth, Samuel Crane, of Randolph, Auditor of Public Accounts, and Campbell Tarr, of Brooke, Treasurer. On the same day John S. Carlisle and Waitman T. Willey were elected Senators to the Federal Congress. The convention was reinforced by the appearance of several members from the Kanawha Valley, which for some time previous thereto had been occupied by the Confederate Military forces. On the 20th of August the convention passed an ordinance providing for the formation of a new state out of a portion of the territory of the state of Virginia,which included the Counties of Logan,Wyoming,Raleigh, Fayette, Nicholas, Webster, Randolph, Tucker, Preston, Monongalia, Marion, Taylor, Barbour, Upshur, Harrison, Lewis, Braxton, Clay, Kanawha, Boone, Wayne, Cabell, Putnam, Mason, Jackson, Roane, Calhoun, Wirt, Gilmer, Ritchie, Wood, Pleasants, Tyler, Doddridge, Wetzel, Marshall, Ohio, Brooke, and Hancock; thirty-nine in all, and the convention was empowered to change the boundaries so as to include the Counties of Greenbrier, Pocahontas, Hampshire, Hardy, Morgan, Jefferson, and Berkeley, or either of them, and also all the Counties contiguous to the boundaries of the proposed state, or to the Counties just named, were to be added if the people thereof by majority of the votes given should express a desire to be included on the same day that the election was held in the other Counties, and should elect delegates to the convention.

Kanawha was proposed as the name for the new state, and the election was to be held on the fourth Thursday of October succeeding. Delegates to the convention were sent from all the foregoing enumerated Counties, except Webster and Berkeley.

The convention met on the 26th day of November. 1861, completed its labors, and adjourned on the 18th day of February, 1862, providing for the submission of its work to the people on the 3rd day of April, 1862, and was accordingly voted upon on that day and adopted by a vote of 18,862 in its favor to 514 against it.

The Legislature of the reorganized Government assembled on the 6th day of May following, and gave its formal assent by the passage of a bill on the 13th of the same month, for the formation and erection of the state of West Virginia, within the jurisdiction of the state of Virginia.

As has already been shown it was at first proposed to call the new state Kanawha, but the convention finally gave it the name of West Virginia.

In the convention which framed this first constitution for the state of West Virginia, Captain Richard M. Cooke, of the County of Wyoming, was admitted as a delegate from Mercer County, by authority, as he claims, of a petition of a few people in the western portion of said County of Mercer. It is uncertain, under this first Constitution, how Mercer County became a constituent part of the state of West Virginia. Research does not disclose that any vote was taken whereby the people of the County elected, authorized or commissioned any person to represent them in the said convention. And it is further certain that no election was held in the County of Mercer by the people thereof upon the question of the ratification or rejection of the said Constitution, and hence it would seem to follow that Mercer County was not legally a part of, or one of the Counties of the state of West Virginia prior to the adoption of the Constitution of 1872.

In the ordinance adopted by the reorganized Government of Virginia, giving consent to the formation of the new state, it was provided; "that the new state should take upon itself a just proportion of the public debt of the Commonwealth of Virginia prior to the 1st day of January, 1861, to be ascertained by charging to it all state expenditures within its limits, and a just proportion of the ordinary expenses of the state Govern-

ment since any part of it was contracted; and deducting therefrom the moneys paid into the treasury of the Commonwealth
from the Counties included within the new state during the
same period." This provision was duly assented to by the new
state, and hence, the principle and basis upon which West Virginia's part, part if any, of the anti-bellum debt of Virginia
is to be ascertained, is fixed and determined.

Francis H. Pierpont had been chosen as Governor of the reorganized government of Virginia, and Arthur I. Boreman as
Governor of West Virginia, whose government went into operation, on the 20th day of June,1863,in accordance with the proclamation of the President of the United States, under an act
of Congress authorizing the admission of the state into the Union.   Upon the admission of the new state, the reorganized
Government of Virginia under Governor Pierpont removed
from Wheeling to Alexandria, Virginia. During the existence
of the reorganized government at Wheeling, the formative period of the new state and afterwards, all kinds of excesses, political, military or otherwise were perpetrated. The Virginia
Government at Richmond claimed and attempted to exercise
jurisdiction over the same territory that the reorganized Government at Wheeling and the new state claimed to exercise,
and this led to the arrest of many citizens by both sides for alleged political offenses, each government charging treason. It
was more dangerous to life, liberty and property to live in the
section refered to than to have been in the army of one or the
the other of the belligerents. A peaceable non-combatant was
liable at any hour night or day to be arrested, carried away
and incarcerated in prison without any charges preferred
against him, and worse than all, he was frequently allowed to
lie in prison and perish without knowing with what offense he
was charged, if any. In partial illustration of this statement
it is stated that one Augustus Pack, of Boone County,an old
man and a non-combatant, who carried on trade between the
lines, was frequently arrested, first by one side and then by the
other, and carried to military prison where he remained some

times for months, and then released upon taking the oath of allegience to the Government that had him a prisoner. General Cox, the Federal commandant in the Kanawha Valley, had had Mr. Pack so frequently before him that he had become very well acquainted with him, and so, as the story goes, on an occasion after Mr. Pack had been arrested by the Federal troops and was being carried to General Cox's headquarters, he was discovered by General Cox approaching his tent under guard, whereupon the General exclaimed, "Here you are again, Pack,"to which he replied,"Well,General,I am an old man and have nothing to do with the war, and try to remain at home a quiet, peaceable citizen, when along comes the Rebels who arrest and carry me within their lines and require me to take the oath of allegiance, and as soon as I return home I am picked up by your men and brought within your lines, and required to take the oath of allegiance, and this process has been going on for several months; the truth is, General, that the foxes have holes and the birds of the air have nests, but as for me I have no where to lay my head."

The Federal army of the Potomac under General George B. McClellan, began in the early spring of 1862 its movement to the Peninsula, and General Johnston's army, which in the last days of March had retired from Centerville behind the Rappahanock, commenced moving by way of Gordonsville and Richmond to the Peninsula. The brigade of General A. P. Hill left Richmond by steamer on the James River on April 10th, and disembarked at King's landing and from thence marched to a point within one or two miles of Yorktown, where and in the vicinity of which, it remained for about twenty days engaged in picketing and drawn out in line of battle in the swamps. The 24th Virginia regiment remained attached to the brigade of General Early.

During the last days of April or the first days of May, at any rate before marching orders were received, the "Wiseacres" were telling us that we were to retire towards Richmond.

The Confederate Soldier was the most remarkable of all the

soldiers that the world has produced, and that in many ways. He could seemingly know more, and in fact did, than the officers in immediate command, and he could know less than any soldier in an army when he wanted it that way—or when so instructed, or when he found it necessary for his convenience or profit, he could forget his name, company, regiment, brigade, division or army commandant; could even forget where he was from or whither he was going. This same soldier could get farther from camp, get more rations, and get back quicker than any other fellow you ever met. When he was marching he could see more, laugh louder, brood less over his troubles, and when he wished, could carry more than any soldier any other army ever produced. He could march barefoot, go farther, complain less, eat nothing, never sleep, and endure more genuine suffering than any soldier that ever marched under the banners of Napoleon. When he reached camp after a long, toilsome march he could start a fire, find water, and go to cooking quicker than the best trained cook in the land. Such were these men who were being trained by the Lees, Johnstons, Longstreet, Jackson, Pickett and the Hills.

Before passing to the description of the retreat of the Confederates from Yorktown, it will be noticed that in the fall of 1861 General Jackson with his division had marched from the lines in front of Washington to the Valley of Virginia; where, the next spring, the most wonderful military campaign in recorded history was conducted and directed by him, in which he defeated three Federal armies in succession, and then in June of that year stole away from his enemies and helped to defeat the fourth one.

In the month of January, 1862, the McComas Battery had gone with the Wise Legion to Norfolk, and was to have been sent from there with the command of General Wise to Roanoke Island, but owing to want of transportation, only a part of the company reached the Island. Those of the company who crossed over to the Island, together with Captain Dorman's

Mercer company, were captured, along with the other Confederate troops thereon.

In the month of March this battery, under the command of its Captain, left Norfolk and went to Elizabeth City, North Carolina, near where, shortly after its arrival, it engaged without loss in an artillery duel with the enemy. A short time thereafter the company marched with the 3rd Georgia regiment of infantry, under the command of Colonel Wright, to the vicinity of South Mills, North Carolina, where on the 19th day of April it was engaged in a severe battle with the enemy, in which its gallant Captain was slain while behaving in the bravest manner. Sergeant James M. Peters, and Privates Oscar Blankenship and William Hern were wounded.

The Federal troops 3,000 strong, with four pieces of artillery, led by General Reno, attacked Colonel Wright's troops, composed of the 3rd Georgia infantry 585 strong, some North Carolina militia, Gillett's company of Southampton cavalry, and McComas' Battery of four guns; the whole Confederate force not exceeding 750 men. The fight lasted for three hours. Mr. D. H. Hill, Jr., in his Military History of North Carolina, in reporting this engagement says: "At last McComas, who had fought his guns manfully, was killed, and Colonel Wright fell back a mile to his supports. General Reno did not attempt to follow, and that night at 10 o'clock left his dead and wounded behind, and made a forced march to his boats."

The Confederates lost 6 killed 19 wounded, the Federals 13 killed and 92 wounded. Captain McComas informed one of his company on the night preceeding this battle that he had orders to return with his company to western Virginia, but that he did not want to go until he had fought at least one battle.

This company, after the capture of Norfolk by the enemy, under the leadership of its First Lieutenant, David A. French, marched to Petersburg. Its subsequent history will be stated later.

In December, 1861, the 60th Virginia regiment of infantry commanded by Colonel William E. Starke, in which were the

Mercer Companies of Pack and Ryan, was ordered and went to South Carolina where it remained under the command of General Robert E. Lee until it returned to Virginia about the last days of April, 1862, and was then attached to the brigade commanded by General Charles W. Field of A. P. Hill's division.

On the evening and night of the 4th of May, 1862, General Johnston quietly withdrew his army from the Yorktown intrenchments and hastened up the Peninsula as rapidly as the condition of the roads would permit. The Federal gunboats were passing up the James and York Rivers with an army corps on transports on the latter, having in view the cutting of General Johnston's line of retreat.

The enemy pressed so hard and closely upon General Johnston's rear that in order to protect his trains he was forced to halt and offer battle. The Divisions of Longstreet and D. H. Hill were covering the retreat, and upon them fell the brunt of the battle which followed. The rear of the army had reached Williamsburg, twelve miles distant from the starting point about daylight on the morning of the 5th, amidst a drizzling rain.

The skirmishing began at early dawn, and grew fiercer as the morning wore away; so that by high noon it had drifted into regular volleys.

The brigade of General A. P. Hill, in which was the 7th Virginia regiment of infantry, passed from the grounds of the Eastern Lunatic Asylum, where it had encamped two hours previous, by William and Mary College to a point near Fort Magruder, and then by a flank movement to the right for a half mile or more, was brought face to face with the enemy, who were in line of battle in a wood, Hill's brigade being in an open field where it received a volley from the enemy which killed and wounded many men. The brigade pushed forward into the wood, getting close up to the enemy, and fired into them a destructive volley, and then charged, driving them rapidly for more than a quarter of a mile, when it met a fresh line of the enemy lying

down behind fallen timber. Here the battle raged for more
than two hours, and until the men had exhausted nearly every
round of ammunition; whereupon General Hill ordered another
charge, and the enemy was driven for some distance through
and beyond this fallen timber. It was now growing dark, the
brigade halted and returned to the position from which it had
started in the charge, and where it remained for an hour or
more after dark, and then resumed its line of march.

The loss sustained in the 7th Virginia regiment was 77, and
in company D., the Giles Company the loss was as follows, viz:
killed, William H. Stafford, wounded, Lieutenant E. M. Stone,
and the following men of the line, Allen M. Bane, Charles Wesley Peck, Andrew J. Thompson, John A. Hale, John W. East,
Isaac Hare, George Knoll, Anderson Meadows, John Meadows,
Demascus Sarver, William I. Wilburn, Edward Z. Yager, and
David E. Johnston, a total of fourteen killed and wounded, being about 25 per cent. of the number carried into action. Tap-
ley P.Mays, of this company, was the color Sergeant of the regiment, and although he escaped unhurt, the flag which he bore
was pierced with 23 balls and the staff severed three times. For
his gallantry in this action Sergeant Mays was awarded a
sword by the Governor of Virginia.

On the evening of the same day General Early led two regiments of his brigade, the 5th North Carolina and 24th Virginia regiments, against a fort held by General Hancock's Federal brigade. While General Early's men fought with great
steadiness and bravery, they were forced to retire with the loss
of 190 men killed, wounded and prisoners. General Early
was among the severely wounded; as was also Colonel William R. Terry and Lieutenant Colonel Peter Hairston. The
killed and wounded in Captain Richardson's Mercer Company
G, 24th Virginia regiment were as follows: Killed, Isaac Alvis, Edward Bailey, John A. Brown, John Easter, and Tobias
Manning, and the wounded were Alexander East, James H.
Mills, lost an arm, Stephen Prillman, Rufus G. Rowland, Gor-
den L. Saunders, lost a leg, and A .J. Whittaker, Robert

Batchelor, Granvil F. Bailey, William Bowling, Jesse Bowling, L. A. Cooper, Jordan Cox, Marshall Foley, John M. N. Flick, Peter Grim, James T. Hopkins, Dennis Johnson, Addison Johnson, Isaac A. Oney, Theaddeus Peters, John M. Smith, Allen Smith, William Stewart and George W. Toney were captured, a total of twenty nine.

As already related, the company of Captain Napoleon B. French, of Mercer, had gone with General Floyd's command to Fort Donelson, where it was engaged in the battle of the 13th day of February, 1862, losing William Oney killed by a shell from one of the enemy's guns, and the whole company with the other troops, except Floyd's brigade and Forrest's cavalry regiment, were surrendered as prisoners of war. Captain French being absent in Virginia, the command of the company had devolved upon Lieutenant John J. Maitland.

Later in the year of 1862, the company of Dorman, captured at Roanoke Island, and that of French, surrendered at Fort Donelson, were exchanged and returned home. The time of their enlistment having expired, they went into other organizations, a portion going to Captain Jacob C. Straley's company of the 17th Virginia Cavalry regiment, another portion to Edgar's battalion of Virginia infantry, and another portion to the 30th battalion of Virginia infantry commanded by Colonel Clark, attached for part of the time to the brigades of Echols or Wharton.

Captain William H. French having been commissioned Colonel of the 17th Virginia regiment of cavalry, was energetically at work during the early spring and early summer months of 1862, in getting together and organizing his regiment, which participated in many of the expeditions and skirmishes along the outposts in Western Virginia up to the date of the advance of the Federal army of General Crook from the Kanawha Valley in May, 1864, when this regiment with others of Jenkins' cavalry brigade and the troops of Colonel William L. Jackson, under Colonel French, were stationed at the narrows of New River in Giles County to guard that point, and to meet the forces of General Crook, should they move by that route, of which full statement will be made hereinafter.

General Johnston's army, after defeating the Federals at Williamsburg and at White House on the York River, retired behind the Chickahominy.

By the middle of May and first of June the army of General McClellan had made its approach very near to Richmond, and had extended its right wing far up in the direction of the Virginia Central Railroad, leaving its left wing across the Chickahominy in front of Richmond. Brigadier General A. P. Hill had been promoted to Major General, and given the command of a Division, which included Field's brigade, to which was attached to the 60th regiment of Virginia infantry.

Upon the promotion of General Hill to the command of a Division, Colonel James L. Kemper, of the 7th Virginia regiment, had been commissioned a Brigadier General, and assigned to the brigade previously commanded by Hill.

For some time previous to and on the night of the 30th day of May, 1862, Kemper's brigade had been in camp at Howard's Grove, a few miles north of Richmond. On the night of the 30th occurred a most remarkable electric storm, accompanied by an exceeding heavy downpour of rain, which continued for many hours during the night, and so flooding our camp that we were compelled to stand on our feet in our tents during the long hours before the coming of daylight. This rainfall had flooded the low lands of the Chickahominy, and caused such a rapid rise in that stream as to carry away or flood the bridges over the same, whereby General Johnston was led to attack the Federal troops then occupying the bank of that stream on the side next to Richmond. The Divisions of Longstreet and D. H. Hill marched at an early hour on the morning of the 31st, encountering on the way to the battlefield streams so swollen as to greatly delay and impede the march. The 7th Virginia regiment with Kemper's brigade belonged to Longstreet's Division. The 24th Virginia regiment to Garland's brigade of Hill's Division. The former mention-

ed Division marched down the White Oak swamp road, the
latter down the Williamsburg road. Hill opened the battle a
little after noon, and while it raged with great fury, the sound
thereof, which was to be the signal for Longstreet's attack,
was not heard by him for some time, on account of the condition of the atmosphere, although he was scarcely two miles
away. Finally, General Hill requested assistance, and Kemper's brigade was sent him. This brigade moved rapidly
through swamps, water and mud until it reached the field of
Hill's contention on the Williamsburg road, when about four
o'clock,P.M.,it advanced in good order against the earthworks
thrown up by the command of the Federal General Casey, and
after a stubborn contest of a little more than half an hour it
charged and carried the works, capturing the enemy's camp
and a number of prisoners. The loss in company D, of the
7th regiment was A. D. Manning, killed; Serjeant Elijah R.
Walker, privates Tarvis Burton, John W. Hight and Joseph
Lewy wounded. The total regimental loss was about 75.

The 24th Virginia regiment was in this battle in the brigade
of General Garland and suffered a loss of one hundred and
seventeen killed and wounded, among them its Major, Richard
L. Maury, who was severely wounded. The Mercer company
loosing G. H. Gore, killed, George P. Belcher, Hugh M. Faulkner, William H. Herndon, George A. Harris and Luther C.
Hale wounded.

On the evening and night of the day after this battle the
troops returned to their former camps, wherein they for the
most part remained until the opening of the "Seven Days Battles."

In the interim between the close of the battle of Seven Pines,
which has just been referred to, and the opening of the "Seven
Days Battles," the 24th Virginia had been detached from Garland's brigade, and attached to that of Kemper, now composed
of the 1st, 7th, 11th, 17th, and 24th Virginia regiments.

General Branch, of North Carolina, with a brigade of North
Carolina troops and some others, was fiercely attacked on the

26th of June near Mechanicsville by a superior force of Federal troops under General Porter, and Branch defeated with serious loss, though after a brave and gallant defense on his part and that of his men. General A. P. Hill going to the support of Branch, and advancing with the remainder of his division, supported by Ripley's brigade, struck the Federals at Beaver Dam, and a bloody engagement followed lasting far into the night of the 26th, without any particular advantage to the Confederates.

General Jackson, with his corps, having arrived from the Valley, joined Hill's left and swinging around the Federal right compelled General Porter to withdraw and retire to Cold Harbor, where he occupied an exceedingly strong position, but from which he was driven with heavy loss on the 27th, as hereinafter related.

The movement of the troops of Hill and Jackson had uncovered the front of General Longstreet's Division on the Mechanicsville Road, and he immediately crossed the Chickahominy and set out in pursuit of the retreating enemy, passing on the route immense piles of bacon, flour, wagons, tents, etc., which the Federals had sought to destroy to prevent them from falling into the hands of the Confederates.

About noon or a little past on the 27th, the head of Longstreet's column reached the New bridge, in the vicinity of Cold Harbor or Gaines' Mill, where it halted and formed a line of battle behind a long range of hills, which hid it from the enemy's view. The enemy occupied a strong position behind a small creek on a range of hills in part fringed with timber. In front of the position of the enemy was a deep ravine, through which flowed a small branch or creek, this ravine he filled with his sharpshooters, and in his rear was a wooded bluff on the side of which was a line of infantry protected by log breastworks. Behind this line was another line of infantry, sheltered by the crest of the hill, and the high ground behind them crowned with artillery. To reach the po-

sition of the enemy, the Confederates must pass over an open
space of some five hundred yards.

Kemper's brigade was in line of battle behind the crest of a
low ridge, and behind the brigades of Wilcox, Pryor, Pickett,
and Featherstone. The battle raged for hours with great fury;
more than once was the charge repeated before the enemy's position was carried. Kemper's brigade was not engaged, though
exposed to the fire of shot and shell, but suffering little loss.
The field had been won, and the day was ours.

In this terrific engagement, as well as that of the day before,
the 60th Virginia regiment was a participant, and suffered severe loss, its Colonel Starke being wounded in the engagement of the 26th, and the two Mercer Companies of Ryan and
Pack losing a considerable number of men in killed and
wounded. Colonel Starke in his report of .the engagement of
the 26th, says: "Our loss here was considerable, Lieutenant S.
Lilley of Company I, Ryan's Company, being killed, Captain
John L. Caynor and Lieutenant P. M. Paxton of Company F,
and Lieutenant S. D. Pack of Company A, being wounded, and
many privates both killed and wounded. On the next day, the
27th, this regiment was again engaged, repelling a cavalry
charge of the enemy, and losing many valuable officers and
men. Colonel Starke, in commending its conduct and that of
its officers refers specially and by name to Lieutenant Colonel
B. H.Jones, Major John C. Summers, Captain John M. Bailey,
and Lieutenants R. A. Hale and George W. Belcher, the three
last named Mercer County men, of Company H, and Lieutenants A. G. P. George, Stephenson, and Lilley, the latter killed
the day before, and adds: "I desire to notice particularly the
good conduct of Lieutenant A. G. P. George, not only through
out all the engagements in which the regiment participated,
but for months past while in charge of Company I,in faithfully
discharging the responsible duties of his position * * * the highest terms of praise apply with equal justice to Lieutenant R. A.
Hale * * * upon whom owing to the wounds or sickness of his

Captain in particular engagements devolved the command of the company."

The enemy having been driven from the field of Gaines' Mill with a loss of 6,837 men, retreated on the night of the 27th across the Chickahominy, followed on the next and two succeeding days to Frazier's Farm, where the divisions of Longstreet and A. P. Hill had with almost the entire Federal army, a more than four hours bloody engagement, without decided results to either army. In this battle the brigade of General Kemper, together with that of General Field, was heavily engaged; the former brigade constituted the extreme right of the general line of battle, and was posted upon the rear edge of a dense body of timber and on the right of and nearly perpendicular to the road leading through Frazier's Farm, with the 17th Virginia regiment, under Colonel Montgomery Corse, occupying the right; the 24th Virginia under Lieutenant Colonel Peter Hairston the left; the 1st Virginia regiment under Major George F. Norton in the center; the 11th Virginia regiment Captain Kirkwood Otey the right center, and the 7th Virginia regiment under Colonel Walter Tazewell Patton the left center. After suffering from a severe shelling for some time, about 5 o'clock P. M., the order to move forward came, and the brigade advanced steadily and in good order, notwithstanding the entangled undergrowth which filled the wood, and the raining of shot and shell from the enemy's guns directly in front of the moving column. Upon striking the enemy's skirmish line, the advance from a quickstep into a double-quick followed, with loud cheers, and by the time the brigade had cleared the wood and reached an open field at the farther side of which stood the enemy in full line of battle behind log breastworks with their batteries beside them and firing rapidly, the continuity of the line was lost and much confusion followed, but the impetuosity of the forward movement was not broken, and the brigade fired rapidly, and throwing itself upon the enemy's infantry and artillery swept them away like chaff before a hurricane.

General Kemper says in his official report of this charge: "A

more impetuous and desperate charge was never made than
that of my small command against the sheltered and greatly
superior forces of the enemy. The ground which they gained
from the enemy is marked by the graves of some of my Veterans, who were buried where they fell; and these graves marked
with the names of the occupants, situated at and near the position of the enemy, show the point at which they dashed at the
strong holds of the retreating foe." Continuing, General Kemper says: "It now became evident that the position sought to
be held by my command was wholly untenable by them, unless
largely and immediately reinforced. The inferior numbers ·
which had alarmed the enemy and driven him from his breastworks and batteries soon became apparent to him, and he at
once proceeded to make use of his advantage. While greatly
superior numbers hung upon our front, considerable bodies
of the enemy were thrown upon both flanks of my command,
which was now in imminent danger of being wholly captured
or destroyed * * * no reinforcements appeared and the dire alternative of withdrawing from the position, although of obvi-
ous and inevitable necessity, was reluctantly submitted to."
Again, says the report: "Among those reported to me as deserving notice for gallantry on the field are Captain Joel
Blackard, Company D, and Lieutenant W. W. Gooding, 7th
Virginia, who were both killed, Sergeant Major Tansill and
Color Sergeant Mays, the latter of Company D, both wounded,
and both of whom had distinguished themselves in the battles
of Williamsburg and Seven Pines, Lieutenant Calfee of Company G, Mercer County, 24th Virginia, who was killed within
a few paces of the enemy's battery."

The Federal General McCall, who was captured in this
battle, says of this charge: "Soon after this a most determined
charge was made on Randall's battery, by a full brigade, advancing in wedge shape without order, but in perfect reckless-
ness; somewhat similar charges had as I have stated, been previously made on Cooper's and Kern's batteries by single regiments without success, they having recoiled before the storm of

canister hurled against them. A like result was anticipated by
Randall's battery, its gallant commander did not doubt his
ability to repel the attack, and his guns did indeed mow down
the andvancing host, but still the gaps were closed and the enemy came in upon a run to the very muzzle of his guns. It was a
perfect torrent of men, and they were in his battery before the
guns could be removed."

General Kemper had ordered his brigade to retire, which it
did, but not in good order, but soon ralied again near the spot
from which it had made the charge. The loss of the brigade was
414, of which 44 were killed, 205 wounded, and 165 missing; of
which the 7th Virginia regiment lost in killed 14, wounded 66,
missing. The 24th Virginia regiment lost 4 killed, 61 wounded and 14 missing. The loss in Company D, 7th Virginia regiment were killed, Captain Joel Blackard, wounded Joseph C.
Shannon, Daniel Bish, Jesse B. Young, David C. Akers, Hugh
J. Wilburn, Tim P. Darr, Francis M. Gordon, George A. Minnich, T. P. Mays, John W. Sarver, Joseph Southron, Ballard
P. Meadows, Lee E. Vass and Joseph Eggleston, and Allen M.
Bane captured; total killed, wounded and missing 16. The loss
in Company G, Mercer Company, 24th Virginia was, killed,
Lieutenant Harvey M. Calfee, wounded Thomas C. Brown, lost
a leg, John Coeburn, A. J. Holstein, Jeff Thomas, lost a leg,
and Lieutenant Benjamin P. Grigsby.

The 60th Virginia regiment, with its brigade and division, had a most distinguished part in this battle. Among other things stated by Colonel Starke in his official report of
this battle, are the following: "On Monday evening the 30th,
June, we were ordered to the support of General Kemper's
brigade then engaged near Frazier's Farm with an overwhelming force of the enemy. The regiment advanced at a double
quick nearly two miles to the brow of the hill where a battery
of eight guns, Randall's Pennsylvania battery, was posted,
which had been taken from the enemy and by them recaptured
before we reached the ground. Delivering a few volleys, the
regiment moved forward, charged the enemy, drove them into

and through the woods for a considerable distance, killing
wounding and taking many of them prisoners, and recapturing
the battery. On reaching the wood, however, the enemy poured
a heavy fire into our line, upon which the command was given
to charge bayonets. This command was obeyed with alacrity,
and very many of the enemy fell before the formidable weapon.
I cannot close this report without noticing the conduct of Privates George R. Taylor of Company E, and Robert A. Christian
of Company I. Private Christian in the bayonet charge of the
30th was assailed by no less than four of the enemy at the
same time. He succeeded in killing three of them with his
own hands, though wounded in several places by bayonet
thrusts, and his brother Eli W. Christian going to his aid dispatched the fourth." Both Robert A. and Eli W. Christian
belonged to Ryan's Mercer company. We again quote from
the report of the Federal General McCall, in which he says:
"It was here my fortune to witness one of the fiercest bayonet
fights that perhaps ever occurred on this continent. Bayonet
wounds, mortal or slight, were given and received. I saw
skulls crushed by the butts of muskets, and every effort made
by either party in his life or death struggle, proving indeed
that here Greek had met Greek." The total loss of the 60th
Virginia regiment in the engagements of the 26th, 27th and
30th day of June was 204. It is regretted that the names in
full of the killed and wounded in the two Mercer companies of
the 60th regiment cannot be given further than already mentioned, and to add to the list of the wounded Washington
Hodges, Rufus McComas and Wesley Dillon, the latter mortally. In the headlong charge of the 60th Virginia regiment on
June 30th, and as it reached the log breastworks of the enemy,
John Hartwell, of Pack's Mercer Company, a man of about six
feet six inches high, raw boned, big footed, clumsy and awk-
ward, caught his foot in getting over the works and fell headlong over and among the enemy, exclaiming as he fell, "Get
out of here, you d——d Yankees, or we will kill the last one of

you." John got out safe and all of the enemy not killed, wounded or captured, took John at his word and ran away.

On the next day, July 1st, the battle of Malvern Hill was fought, but neither Kemper's nor Field's brigades were engaged, though drawn up close to the firing line as supports and subjected to a severe shelling from the enemy's batteries in front and his gunboats in the river. On the night of the first the enemy withdrew from the Confederate front, and retired to a strong position at Harrison's Landing under the cover and protection of his gunboats; and thus ended the second "On to Richmond," and the Confederates returned to the vicinity of Richmond and went into camp.

The McComas Battery, now commanded by Captain David A. French, had been brought from Petersburg to the north of the James and was in position on the Confederate right at the battle of Seven Pines, and during the Seven Days Battles, but was not engaged. After the battle of Malvern Hill it was sent with some infantry down to Turkey Island on the James, and later to a position in front of Harrison's Landing. During the campaign of 1862 in Northern Virginia and Maryland, it remained as part of the forces left to guard the defenses of Richmond.

A few weeks after the close of the battle around Richmond, August 5th, the 60th Virginia regiment was ordered to join General Loring in western Virginia. Captain William H. French, as senior Captain, with several companies of cavalry, also joined General Loring in his Kanawha Valley campaign.

It now becomes necessary at this place to relate some of the incidents occurring in western Virginia. As has been related, in the summer of 1861, the Federal troops had advanced to Kanawha Falls and Gauley Bridge, General Wise retiring to the Big Sewell Mountain and Hawks Nest district of country, and General Floyd marching out from Lewisburg to reinforce him and to oppose the Federal advance. After some severe skirmishing by the troops of Wise with the Federal advance, and some maneuvering on the part of both armies, General Floyd advanced to Cross Lanes, in the county of Nicholas, where, on the 26th day of August, 1862, he had a severe combat with the Federal troos, whom he routed. General Floyd after the battle at. Cross Lanes fell back to Carnifix Ferry on the Gauley and fortified his position, which was fiercely assailed by Federal troops under General Rosecrans on the 10th day of September, but they were finally beaten off, Floyd holding his position until after nightfall and then retreating. In this engagement the Federals outnumbered the Confederates about three to one. These incidents are merely mentioned because some of the companies from the New River Valley were in the commands of Generals Floyd and Wise.

After the withdrawal, in the fall of 1861, of the troops of Generals Floyd and Wise from the Kanawha District, and the disbanding of the militia brigades of Generals Beckley and Chapman, the Federal troops under General Jacob D. Cox advanced and occupied Fayetteville, the County town of Fayette County,and later Beckley, the County town of Raleigh County at which latter place on the 22nd day of April, 1862, Colonel E. P. Scammon reports Colonel Thomas Little and W. J. Comer as having arrived that evening from Princeton, and who gave as far as they knew statements of Confederate forces, etc., and adds, "Colonel Little confirms reports of intended destruction of town and county property." In the last days of April the Federal advance reached Flat Top Mountain and encamped at what is known as the Miller Tanyard, place on the turnpike road about two miles south of the main top of the mountain. At this time the only Confederate troops in the County of Mercer were the small cavalry forces of Colonel Jenifer acting as a mere corps of observation, and the independent company of Captain Richard B. Foley known as "Flat Top Copperheads." Foley was on the extreme outposts next the enemy, and in fact was the eyes and ears for Jenifer's command.

General Cox's command consisted of two brigades of infantry; the first commanded by Colonel E. P. Scammon, made up of the 23rd, 30th and 12th Ohio infantry regiments and Mc-

Mullen's battery; the second brigade under Colonel A. Moor composed of the 28th, 34th and 37th Ohio regiments of infantry and Simmond's battery, also one battalion of Colonel Boler's second Virginia cavalry, and Smith's Ohio cavalry troop, with a train of 250 wagons.

On the last day of April the Federals had thrown forward, under Lieutenant Botsford, some seventy-five men of the 23rd Ohio regiment, who on the night of that day occupied the dwelling house of Henry Clark, which is situated on the west side of the Wythe, Raleigh and Grayson turnpike road, about eight miles from Princeton. Russell G. French acted as guide, as he was thoroughly familiar with the country, his home being in that neighborhood. Foley and his men, who were on the alert and hovering around the enemy's camp, discovering the least movement on their part, determined on an attack on the Federal outpost at Clark's house. Lieutenant Botsford and his men had scouted all day of the 30th of April in search of Foley and his men, but were unable to find them; had even gone to Captain Foley's home and throughout the neighborhood on and along the waters of Camp Creek. They did not see Foley, but he saw them, and when late in the evening tired, and worn by their days tramp, they returned by way of Campbell's Mill and on the turnpike road at Clark's house they determined to camp for the night. Captain Foley immediately dispatched messengers to Confederate headquarters at Princeton advising of the situation, and an attack was determined upon. And so on that night Major Henry Fitzhugh, of Kanawha, with the border Rangers, Captain Everett, Kanawha Rangers, Captain Lewis, Mercer cavalry, Captain W.H. French, Lieutenant Graybeal in command, Tazewell troopers, Captain Thomas Bowen, Bland Rangers, Captain William N. Harman, Grayson cavalry, Captain Boring, Nelson Rangers, Captain Fitzpatrick and Captain R. B. Foley's independent company of infantry, moved out to Clark's house reaching there a short while before daylight on May 1st, and took position near the house, some of the companies not fully up. Mr. Clark was an ardent southern man, and

had been compelled to quit his home to keep out of the way of
the Federals, but his brave and heroic wife with her small son
and daughter remained at home and braved the storm of battle that raged furiously around her for nearly an hour. Mrs.
Clark whose maiden name was Mize, was born and raised in
Patrick County, Virginia, and was a woman of strong natural
sense, and in her undying devotion to the southern people and
their cause, she was excelled by no woman in the south. She
lived to a ripe old age, and died an unrepentant, unrecon-
structed, Confederate. It may well be said of her as Whittier,
the poet, said of Randolph:

> "Too honest and too proud to feign
> A love she never cherished,
> Beyond Virginia's border line
> Her patriotism perished."

At dawn on the 1st day of May the Federals came out of the
house into the yard and fell into line for rollcall, apparently
little suspecting that a lurking foe was so close at hand. The
Confederates, that is Foley's, Harman's, Bowen's and French's
companies now in position, immediately opened fire, the enemy rushing quickly into the house, which is of hewn oak logs
—equal to a block house, a secure fortress against rifle balls.
The house as it then existed, since removed, was only one and
one half stories high and had a rather flat roof covered with
chestnut shingles. The position occupied by a portion of the
Confederates was on high ground above the house, the Federals occupying the second floor of the house and were exposed
to the balls fired by the Confederates into and through the
roof, and it was chiefly from these balls that the Federals suffered loss. It has already been stated that four of the Confederate companies had taken their position before the firing
began, but in point of fact this is not strictly correct. Foley's
company was the only one in proper position, the others
were moving to position and the remaining companies had not
all gotten up. The intention of the Confederates was to surround the house, and compel the surrender of the Federal

CLARK'S HOUSE, Mercer County, W. Va.

Where engagement on May 1st, 1862, was fought between a Confederate force under Major Henry Fitzhugh, of Kanawha, and a portion of the Federal forces of Gen'l Jacob D. Cox, of Ohio,

troops that had taken shelter therein, but the unexpected appearance of the enemy in the yard for rollcall prematurely precipitated the opening of the fight. The soldiers in the house displaced the filling between the logs, and utilized the space for placing their guns therein to fire, their bodies being in a great measure protected by the walls of the house. The Federals boldly and bravely maintained the fight, and just as Major Fitzhugh had given the order to surround and charge the house, the head of a column of Federal reinforcements came in sight and immediately opened fire, advancing rapidly at a double quick, their cavalry at full speed. The Confederates were now greatly outnumbered, they beat a hasty retreat closely followed by the whole of General Cox's forces. The loss on the Confederate side was only eight wounded, viz: Captain R. B. Foley, James H. Fletcher, James Butler, Hugh Farmer, and Alexander Miller, severely, and Greene Bryson, and Montgomery Cox, mortally. Fletcher and Butler belonged to the Mercer Cavalry, Cox to the Tazewell Troopers, Bryson and Farmer to Foley's Company, and Miller to Harman's Bland Company. The Federal loss was 20, one killed and 19 wounded, among the latter, Russell G. French. Colonel R. B. Hayes, of the 23rd Ohio regiment, reporting this engagement to Colonel E. P. Scammon, mentions Mr. French and says: "French will perhaps be crippled for life, probably die; can't he be put in the position of a soldier enlisted or something to get his family the pension land, etc.? What can be done? He was a scout in our uniform on duty at the time of receiving his wound." French lived until recently, having died in Mercer County at the age of about eighty seven years. He was a great sufferer from the wound he received. He lived in Mercer County at the beginning of the war, and was on principle opposed to the war, and became an earnest, zealous, conscientious Union man. During the retreat of the Confederates from Clark's house to Princeton, Cornelius Brown, an independent Confederate volunteer and a Mercer County man, was killed on Camp Creek, near the house formerly owned and occupied by Captain

Thomas J. George. The retreat which was continued through Princeton to Rocky Gap and beyond, was covered by the Bland Rangers, commanded by Captain William H. Harman, and well and gallantly did this devoted body of men and officers perform this service.

As before stated, Colonel Jenifer, whose headquarters when the fight took place, were at Princeton, was in the immediate command of all the forces then operating in Mercer County. He had won fame and reputation as a Lieutenant-Colonel of cavalry at the battle of Ball's Bluff, on the Potomac, in October, 1861, but now he was about to and did commit an act of vandalism almost, if not quite unparalleled in the annals of civilized war, and one which tarnished his fair name, and overshadowed all the glory and laurels won by him at Ball's Bluff. To destroy the homes of non-combatant enemies in time of war is horrible enough! What excuse can be offered for one who destroys the homes of his friends, especially of as devoted and self sacrificing a people as those of Princeton?

Learning, for he was near the fight, that his forces were retreating before the army of General Cox and that the latter would in a few hours occupy the village of Princeton, Colonel Jenifer, without warning or notice, ordered the burning of the village, which was accomplished under his own supervision, whereby old men, women and children were not only deprived of shelter, and of all their worldly goods, but were turned out into the highways in the mud and cold rains to flee wheresoever they might, and to find food and shelter wheresoever they could. Not only did this man Jenifer have burned the houses in the village, including the public buildings, except the jail, but had the church buildings in the western and southern part of the County destroyed, and then fled to Wytheville and advised the burning of that town. In volume 12, part 1, Rebellion Records 450, will be found the official report of Colonel Jenifer to General Heth concerning the burning of this village which is inserted herein and is as follows: "On April 30th it was reported to me at Rocky Gap, that the enemy was advancing on Princeton from the direction of Raleigh. In consequence of this report I ordered out Lieutenant Colonel Fitzhugh with about 120 dismounted cavalry and some 70 or 80 militia to meet the enemy and to detain him if possible until I could remove the few remaining stores from Princeton to Rocky Gap. I also ordered up the forty-fifth, Colonel Peters, to the support of Colonel Fitzhugh, but before this regiment could reach Princeton the enemy had advanced so rapidly that fearing Colonel Peters would be cut off I ordered him back to his camp, and in returning his regiment was ambushed by the enemy and thrown into some confusion. In order to enable me to save stores and property at Princeton, it became necessary to engage the enemy's advance column, which Colonel Fitzhugh, did, inflicting considerable loss on the enemy. The fight was kept up for thirteen hours and for a distance of 22 miles, was well contested by the small force under Colonel Fitzhugh. During the engagement we lost one killed, four or five seriously wounded, and eight or nine slightly wounded. The wounded were all brought off safe from the field; the few who were seriously wounded, were taken to houses near the field. The enemy's loss is supposed to be 35 in killed, wounded and missing. I evacuated Princeton just as the enemy entered it, having first fired the town."

The official report of the engagement at Clark's house on May 1st by Colonel E. P. Scammon, 23rd Ohio regiment is as follows: This morning at daylight the advance guard of Lieutenant Colonel Hays, a company of 23rd regiment under Lieutenant Botsford was surrounded and attacked by about 300 rebels at Camp Creek. Lieutenant Botsford reports one man killed and twenty wounded, all but three or four slightly; six or seven of the enemy killed; wounded not yet known. Six prisoners, three wounded, had been taken, and others being brought in when messenger left. The enemy fled and Lieutenant Colonel Hayes had reached Camp Creek."

The turnpike road leading southward from Princeton to Rocky Gap was literally lined and thronged with soldiers and civilians, the latter mostly of women, children and old men, fleeing from the vanguard of the Federal army which was entering Princeton as the last of these people were passing out. The Federal soldiers did what they could to save the burning buildings, and among these Federal soldiers were two who became Presidents of the United States, viz: R. B. Hayes and William McKinley. The Federals seemed satisfied when they reached Princeton, and did not immediately pursue the retreating Confderates.

By this time the Confederate authorities had become aroused by the gravity of the situation, and the threatened advance of the army of General Cox to the Virginia and Tennessee Railroad, and they took prompt steps to gather a force to repel the invasion.

Brigadier General Henry Heth collected a force at Dublin, consisting of the 36th, 22nd and 45th Virginia regiments of infantry, the 8th Virginia cavalry regiment, dismounted, Chapman's, Otey's and Vawter's Virginia batteries of artillery.

Colonel Gabriel C. Wharton commanding the 51st Virginia régiment of infantry, rendezvoused at Wytheville, and General Humphrey Marshall with the 5th Kentucky infantry under Colonel Andrew J. May, 54th Virginia infantry under Colonel Trigg, 29th Virginia regiment of infantry, Colonel Moore, and a small Virginia battalion of infantry under Major Dunn, a battalion of Kentucky cavalry under Colonel Bradley, and a battery of artillery under Captain Jeffries, at Tazewell Court House, Virginia.

General Cox had sent forward to Pearisburg, Virginia, under Colonel R. B. Hayes, of the 23rd Ohio regiment of infantry, from whence it was driven by a brisk skirmish, by General Heth's forces on the 10th day of May with a loss to the Confederates of two killed and four wounded, among the latter Colonel Patton slightly; the loss to the Federals was two men killed, and five or six wounded, among them, Colonel Hayes slightly.

The Federal advance under Major Comly, of the 23rd Ohio

regiment, reached Pearisburg on May 6th. Major Comly in his report says: "arrived here and took the place completely by surprise. No houses burned—citizens all here. We have captured one Major, one Lieutennat Colonel, and fifteen or twenty other prisoners."

Colonel Hayes with the remainder of his regiment arrived on the evening of the 7th. On the 8th in his report to Colonel Scammon he, among other things in speaking of Pearisburg and its people, says: "this is a lovely spot, a fine, clean village; most beautiful and romantic surrounding country, polite and educated secesh people."

Between the 1st and the 10th days of May, General Cox had advanced with the main body of his forces to French's Mill, now called Oakvale, on East River, eleven miles south of Princeton and seventeen miles from Pearisburg. Having learned of the retreat of Hays' regiment from Pearis- burg and that Heth's forces were pursuing and that his rear was threatened by both Wharton and Marshall, Gen- eral Cox made up his mind to advance no further, but to return to Princeton; however, before doing so and to guard against an attack from Wharton's column moving north to- ward Princeton, he detached on the evening of the 15th and sent westward up the Cumberland Gap and Prices' turnpike road Lieutenant Colonel Lewis Von Blessing, with five com- panies of the 28th, four companies of the 37th and two com- panies of the 34th regiments of Ohio infantry; but Von Bless- ing seems to have returned to his camp, and on the 16th moved up East River again, camping about Mills' that night, and moving toward the cross roads on the morning of the 17th.

General Wharton's regiment camped on the night of the 16th at the Peery-Gibson farm at the southern base of East River Mountain, breaking camp at a very early hour on the morning of the 17th. The men were in light marching order, encumbered with only one wagon containing medical stores, among which was a barrel of whiskey. Wharton's instruc- tions were to press forward to Princeton, this being the point

of concentration for the three Confederate columns advancing
upon General Cox, whose troops or a part of them had had
quite a lively skirmish west of Princeton on the evening of the
16th with the vanguard of Marshall's forces.

On reaching the top of East River Mountain, early on the
morning of the 17th, Colonel Wharton discovered some three
miles away to the east, Colonel Von Blessing's command advancing westward along the turnpike road. Wharton did not
know, could only surmise who these people were. He did not
stop to see; his orders were to go to Princeton, gallant, faithful soldier as he was, he performed his duty; that is, obeyed
his orders. Without halting, but pressing forward, passing
the junction of the road before Von Blessing's column reached that point, and throwing out a rear guard he took the road to
Princeton, Von Blessing following and taking the short route
by the old mill of Calfee and Bailey and into the turnpike near
the present residence of Mr. Estill Bailey; Von Blessing, apparently, in fact evidently, not knowing Wharton was in his
front, or if he did he took it to be a very small force with
which if he overtook, he would have no difficulty in dealing.
Colonel Wharton on reaching Pigeon Roost Hill, found himself in full view of Princeton and only about one mile south
thereof; halting his regiment and reconnoitering, he discovered
that instead of Princeton being in possession of the Confederates under General Marshall, as he had been led to suppose,
that it was occupied by the Federal troops. In the meantime
he had heard the sound of Marshall's guns west of Princeton
on the New Hope road. He at once made disposition of his
troops, placing Major Peter J. Otey, late an honored member
of Congress from Virginia, but who died a short time ago, in
command of three companies of infantry and one piece of artillery under Lieutenant B. Langhorne, and with instuctions
to Major Otey, the next in rank to himself to place a line of
men on the front towards Princeton, and one facing to the rear
with instructions for these lines to furnish support to each other as necessity might require, he took a guide and started to

find General Marshall. At the place where Colonel Wharton
made his formation the road winds around the hill in the form
of nearly a double half circle.

General Cox knowing that his Lieutenant was on the Wythe,
Grayson and Raleigh Turnpike road, and doubtless being advised of Wharton's movements, with whom Von Blessing was
likely to come to blows, sent forward a battalion of infantry to
reenforce Von Blessing. This advance having been discovered,
Major Otey threw forward to meet this force two companies
of infantry, one of them the Grayson company under its fearless and gallant leader Captain William A. Cooper, and one
gun under Lieutenant Langhorne. This small force met the
advance of the Federal battalion and repulsed it, thereby preventing its union with Von Blessing. The situation just then
was critical for both sides. Von Blessing was cut off from his
friends, and Wharton's regiment placed in a position to be attacked both front and rear at the same time. Von Blessing
could not help hearing the sound of the contest between Langhorne's gun, Cooper's men and the Federal's, and no doubt
this caused him to hasten his steps, for he knew of the force he
had been following from the cross roads, and had evidently
made up his mind that they would soon be between two fires
and killed or captured. Overtaking Wharton's medical wagon,
causing Dr. J. M. Estill, the regimental surgeon, and his corps
of assistants to hurriedly seek shelter behind the Confederate
battle line, Von Blesing's men unloaded the barrel of whiskey
heretofore mentioned, and soldier like they soon had out the
head, and imbibing freely they got enough to make them largely forget their tiresome, worn out condition, and soon hurried
on to the field of slaughter and death. Marching by the route
step and at rapid gate, doubtless enthused by the whiskey,
and perhaps also by the thought that they would capture the
Confederates in their front, they approached without discovering Wharton's men in position as above described, and suddenly
meeting a rapid and concentric fire were thrown into utter
confusion and panic. Under orders from Major Otey the Con-

federates charged, and the Federals fled, closely pursued by the exultant Confederates. Major Otey sprang over the fence in the bend of the road, and met face to face a large burly German Federal soldier, armed with a Belgian rifle, which he presented at Otey, the latter firing at the German with his pistol striking the ground about his feet, and railing out at him, saying: "Why are you trying to shoot me when you know that your men are running?" to which the German replied, "Well, Mister, my gun ain't loaded."

Retreating for about one mile on the road over which they had just advanced, and reaching Brush Creek Bridge, they were piloted by some one who knew the country, over a by-path through the farms of Bratton, Straley and others, to a point on the Princeton and Twelve-Mile Fork road, about two miles south of the first named place. Here they were within two miles of the town now occupied by General Cox, and why Colonel Von Blessing did not move immediately into the town is unexplainable, except upon the supposition that General Cox was yet at French's Mill. There can be no sort of question that Colonel Von Blessing and his men were greatly demoralized, consequent upon their being suddenly attacked, in fact surprised. His loss according to his own report, was 18 killed, 56 wounded and 14 captured, while the Confederates lost but one man and he killed by accident, and nine wounded. The total Federal loss around Princeton during the two days of partial engagements, was 23 killed, 69 wounded, and 21 missing. The total loss of the Confederates was three killed, 21 wounded, among them Captain Elliott of Kentucky, mortally and who soon died. Von Blessing on his march from the bridge over Brush Creek, two miles south of Princeton, and in passing through the farm of Mr. H. W. Straley, met him in the road on his horse on his way from the mill, whither he had been to get bread for his family. He took charge of Mr. Straley, as also of his horse, and dismounting him, placed a wounded Federal soldier on the horse.

The fight at Pigeon Roost Hill took place about 10 o'clock on

the morning of the 17th. Colonel Von Blessing, with his badly
scared and demoralized men, did not reach the Princeton and
Twelve Mile Fork road until towards the middle of the afternoon, and although only four miles away he did not reach the
mouth of Twelve Mile Fork at Spangler's, until after dark. He
halted at the mouth of the fork for several hours, and then retraced his steps to the right-hand branch of that fork and up the
same, passing out through the farms of Major Wm. M. Reynolds
and Charles Stinson, and directly across the front of General
Heth's command occupying the Princeton and French's Mill
roads, and on through the Gooch and Grigsby farms to the old
Logan road near Pisgah Church. Before fair dawn on the morning of the 18th they had reached the farm lately owned by T.
K. Lambert, formerly by Captain William A. Cooper, and were
in sight of the Princeton and Red Sulphur roads, whereupon
they discovered a troop of Confederate cavalry passing, which
seemed to give fresh impetus to their fleeing capacity; in fact
thew were so alarmed that they cried out, "Rebel Calvary!
Rebel Cavalry!" and broke into panic and wild confusion,
fled with all speed on and along the old Logan road, throwing
away guns, cartridge boxes, indeed everything that could in
any way impede their making a successful run; which did not
end until they had joined at Spanishburg, nine miles away,
General Cox's column retreating from Princeton. The reader
no doubt has asked himself the question, what became of Mr.
Straley, his horse and the wounded man? So soon as the panic
began at Lambert's farm the wounded man on Straley's horse
dismounted and fled with his comrades. Mr. Straley seized
his horse's bridle and attempted to mount, but his saddle turned and the already affrighted horse became only the more
frightened and simply kicked himself free from the saddle. Mr.
Straley did not stop to gather up the saddle, but mounting the
horse without the saddle, sped rapidly through the woods and
swamps, until he reached home some four miles away.

The Confederate column under General Heth had on the 17th
advanced on and along the French's Mill and Princeton road

to the west side of the Adam Johnston farm and about four
miles from Princeon; having ample time by continuing the
march to have joined battle with General Cox before nightfall,
but for some reason best known to General Heth, he halted his
command at the point indicated until after night. A wagon
and team belonging to General Cox's forces had driven out on
this road in search of some baggage left at a farm house by
the Federals retreating from French's Mill, and a Federal courier was captured, from whom Heth got information which induced him to retire his forces to Big Hill, about two miles north
of French's Mill. Whether the courier was sent specially to
mislead General Heth no one on the Confederate side knew,
but Heth's non-action and retrograde movement enabled General Cox to retreat in safety, and he did so that night, in fact
began his retreat before night, for Marshall's command occupied the village the next morning.

As before stated, Marshall's column advanced on the New
Hope Church road, and did not encounter resistance until it
reached a point about one mile east of New Hope Church, where
it met the Federal skirmishers. The 5th Kentucky regiment under Colonel A. J. May led the advance, and rapidly pushed the
Federal skirmishers back upon their reserve at Princeton.
General Marshall brought forward his battery, planting it on
the high bluff just west of the dwelling house owned by the late
Leander P. Johnston. The Federal battery in opposition to
Marshall's, one parrot gun was posted on the cemetery hill
about one half mile west of Princeton, and was supported by
some companies of the 37th Ohio regiment under Col. Moore.
The pressure from the columns of Marshall and Wharton from
the south and west, and the threatening attitude of Heth's column from the east, caused Gen. Cox to withdraw from Princeton and return to Flat Top. He began his retreat on the evening of the 17th, but all did not get away until in the early
morning of the 18th, when the forces of Marshall occupied the
village of Princeton about sunrise of the same morning. In
the skirmish on the New Hope road between Marshall's forces

and the Federals, the loss of the former was a few men wounded, while the latter had two or three killed and several wounded.

Lieutenant Colonel Lewis Von Blessing the commandant of the Federal force which was defeated by Wharton's Virginia regiment on Pigeon Roost Hill, on the morning of the 17th of May, made to his superior officer his report, in which among other things, he states: "It is difficult to give the force of the enemy against us in the fight of the 17th. They fired all sorts and all Calibers of balls, even with fire balls and hand grenades. The dead of the 37th regiment number 11, so many having been recognized, and 36 severely wounded have been transported to Princeton and left in the hands of the enemy. Seven slightly wounded have been brought back to the regiment, and 18 are still missing from the four companies engaged in the combat. The loss of the 28th regiment is 5 killed and 10 wounded; from the companies of the 34th regiment 2 wounded."

Except a few troops from Kentucky, and from the Virginia border along the Kanawha, Ohio and Sandy waters, the men who fought the battles around Princeton were chiefly New River Valley men. It may here also be noted that a number of companies of New River Valley men served in General Jackson's corps. Pulaski, Wythe and Montgomery Counties furnished three or more companies to the 4th Virginia regiment of the Stonewall brigade, while Monroe furnished one company and the 27th regiment of the same brigade.

Of the numbers Federals and Confederates engaged in this campaign, they were not far from equal, with perhaps a slight preponderance in favor of the Confederates. General Cox certainly out generaled the Confederates, and the military critics will say in reviewing this campaign its management and results, that the Confederates woefully blundered, and that their adversary took advantage of their blunders, escaping when within their grasp. It may be added here that of the fatally wounded on the Confederate side at Clark's house on the 1st of May, Greene Bryson died at the house of William Ferguson,

on Wolf Creek, and Montgomery Cox reached his home in
Wytheville, where he soon expired.

In the little village of Princeton, out of near an hundred
houses, only about nine or ten remained after the burning. The
suffering of the non-combatants, the old men, women and children, who were compelled to abandon their homes, and the
county, and most of whom never returned, are beyond the powers of description.

After the close of the military operation around Princeton
in the spring of 1862 General Heth moved across New River,
and marched upon Lewisburg, then occupied by a Federal force,
with which on the 23rd of May he fought a severe battle in
which his troops were totally defeated with considerable loss.
The Federal forces numbered about 1500, Heth's about 2,000.
The Federal loss was 13 killed, 53 wounded and 7 missing; the
Confederate loss was 38 killed, 70 wounded and 100 captured
together with four pieces of artillery. Among the Confederate
officers captured was Major George M. Edgar. Captain Thomas
W. Thompson, of Mercer County, commanding a company in
Edgar's battalion, was permanently disabled by a severe
wound.

Between the close of this campaign and the advance of General Crook's Federal army in the spring of 1864, no very considerable body of Federal troops entered the county of Mercer.
There were numerous scouting parties and frequent small
skirmishes between small bodies of Federals and Confederates
during this period. There are some things and incidents to be
related which occurred during this period along the border and
in the county of Mercer which are reserved until the proper
date is reached in which these events occurred; and a return
will now be made to the movements of the army of Northern
Virginia, which, as will be recollected, was left in camp in front
of Richmond after the close of the Seven days battles.

About the time of the close of the fighting around Richmond
on the first day of July, 1862, the Federal General Pope making himself troublsome in Northern Virginia, Major General

Jackson with his corps in the latter days of July marched in
the direction of Rapidan, and on the 9th day of August fought
a fierce and bloody battle at Cedar Mountain, in Culpeper
County, with a large part of General Pope's army, in which the
latter was defeated and driven from the field, but that night
and the next day being largely reenforced, and greatly out-
numbering the troops under General Jackson, the latter retreated across the Rapidan to await help from General Lee,
who by this time believing himself and Richmond safe from
any attack from the army of General McClellen at Harrison's
Landing, on August 13th sent forward General Longstreet
with his division, including Kemper's brigade, to the assistance
of General Jackson; and on the 15th himself left for the
Rapidan.

General Lee prepared to strike Pope's left, but that distinguished General took fright and retired behind the Rappahanock, whither General Lee closely followed; and for several
days continual skirmishing and artillery duels were kept up
at the fords along that river, until finally General Jackson had
so far removed to the left and up the river as to allow General
Longstreet to occupy his place on the river front, and so to
speak pulled the bridle off Jackson and turned him loose after
Pope.

General Lee sent General Stuart with a portion of his cavalry to sever Pope's connection with Alexandria and Washington, which he in some measure accomplished, but not fully on
account of the terrific rainfall, and at the same time impelled
General Jackson's corps on the 22nd and 23rd up the Rappahannock to Warrenton Springs; Pope marching up on parallel
lines, but not fully understanding the significance of the movement, rather supposing at the first that Jackson was making
for the Valley.

Jackson still pushing up the river on the 25th with his three
divisions, crossed the upper Rappahanock and bivouaced that
night at Salem, on the Manassas Gap Railroad, General Lee
in the meantime occupying as far as possible Pope's attention

on the Rappahanock with Longstreet's troops. General Jackson continued his movement until he reached the rear of the Federal army, cutting its line of communications and capturing immense stores at Manassas Junction, appropriating so much thereof as he could use and get away with, destroyed the remainder. General Longstreet's corps soon followed, taking the same route pursued by Jackson's corps, and on reaching Thoroughfare Gap on the evening of August 28th found it held by the enemy. Next morning the forward movement began, Kemper's brigade following another, moving through the gap while some other Confederate troops by a flank movement had caused the enemy to withdraw from his strong position in the gap.

As Kemper's men cleared the gap and reached the vicinity of Haymarket, they could distinctly hear the roar of the guns of the enemy and those of Jackson. The pace was quickened as the troops passed on and along the highway in clouds of dust and suffering for water. It was near high noon when Kemper's brigade reached the vivinity of the battlefield, and late that afternoon the roar of the battle on the left told us that Jackson's men with a portion of Longstreet's were hotly engaged. Some skirmishing and artillery firing occurred in the forenoon of the 30th, and then for a while there was a calm; in which both armies were preparing for the fray.

General Kemper was placed in command of a division consisting of Jenkins', Hunton's and his own brigade, the latter commanded by Colonel Montgomery D. Corse of the 17th Virginia regiment.

The battle rolled along the left front of Kemper's brigade with fury, when about three o'clock, P. M., the order came to move forward, which was done at double quick, the men fixing their bayonets as they went. Through a strip of woods and into an open field a little to the south of the Chinn house, brought the brigade almost into the presence of the enemy, but in the direction of a right oblique from them; and in order to face them a left half wheel was made which brought it in full face to the enemy, only a few hundred yards away, standing in line of battle in open ground across a small ridge or elevation beyond the Chinn house, and a little north and west of an old Virginia rail fence, with a five gun battery on top of the elevation in line with its infantry supports.

Kemper's brigade went forward in good order at a quick step, until striking the Chinn house which compelled it to make a left oblique movement creating some confusion, which however was but momentary. Away it dashed at the enemy's line firing as it advanced, reached and crossed the rail fence and on to and over the Federal battery, scattering the canoniers with their infantry support. A short distance beyond the brigade was halted; its supports coming up it was finally withdrawn to a pine thicket in the rear of the ground over which it had fought. After the brigade started on the charge every man was his own General, and there was no earthly power could have stopped it until it had accomplished the object for which it had made the charge, viz, the capture of the Federal guns and defeat of its infantry supports. In this charge the left of the 7th Virginia regiment became somewhat intermingled with the right of the 24th Virginia regiment, so that both regiments are entitled to claim credit for the capture of the guns. The colors of the 7th regiment having fallen, were seized by Lieutenant Colonel Flowerree, who upon the fall of Colonel Patton handed them to Lieutenant Stewart. In addition to the five guns the brigade had captured, a flag from the enemy was also taken, but it had paid dearly in precious lives and blood for its victory. The enemy was beaten and was getting away, but night now upon us prevented successful pursuit. The brigade loss was 33 killed, 240 wounded, and one missing. The 7th Virginia regiment lost 5 killed, and 48 wounded. The 24th Virginia regiment lost 11 killed and 67 wounded. Among the field officers wounded were Colonel Corse commanding the brigade, Colonel Patton, Lieutenant Colonel Flowerree, and Major Swinler, the latter losing a leg, as well also as Adjutant Hugh M. Patton and Sergeant Major

Park of the 7th regiment. Company D, of the 7th regiment, lost the following members: killed, John Q. Martin; wounded Captain R. H. Bane and Lieutenant John W. Mullens, and privates W. H. Carr, John S. Dudley, Elbert S. Eaton, Adam Thompson, William C. Fortner, James H. Fortner, Francis H. Farley, J. Tyler Frazier, John W. Hight, Gordon L. Wilburn, Hugh J. Willburn, William I. Wilburn, James J. Nye, and Washington R. C. Vass, the latter two mortally; Vass dying that night and Nye in a day or two after. Out of about 57 men carried into action only 40 came out unhurt. The loss in officers in the 7th Virginia was 12. The loss in the Giles and Mercer companeis in the 24th regiment was severe. The names of those killed and wounded in the Giles company seems not to have been preserved. A partial list of those killed and wounded in the Mercer company shows that Lieutenant Ballard P. French was slain, and that Captain H. Scott and Private John Coeburn were wounded. In front of Kemper's brigade fell mortally wounded Colonel Fletcher Webster of Massachusetts, the only son of Daniel Webster.

General Lee's skillful tactics compelled the enemy to fight at a disadvantage, and yet it was among the most fiercely contested open field battles of the war, and in scarce no other did the Confederates acquit themselves with more honor. They had beaten an enemy superior to them in numbers and equipment, inflicting upon him heavy loss of men and guns.

With Longstreet's division, Kemper's brigade occupied the field the next day and buried the dead, and cared for the wounded amid a heavy rain storm.

Early on Monday the 1st day of September the division moved across Bull Run and to the vicinity of Chantilly, reaching there at night and in the midst of a pelting rain. On the 3rd it moved to and through Leesburg and to the banks of the Potomac at White's Ford, where it encamped on the night of the 5th. The enemy had taken shelter within his entrenchments in and around Alexandria and Washington, and another "On to Richmond" had come to grief.

At Leesburg all the men who were sick, broken down, barefoot, lame and halt, were allowed to remain, and there were
not a few of them, whose services were so sorely needed beyond
the Potomac a few days later. A little after sunrise on Saturday, the 6th day of September, 1862, Kemper's brigade crossed
the Potomac and made its footprint on the sacred soil of Maryland, my Maryland, and as the men wended their way across
the Potomac, some one remembering Randall's soulstirring and
patriotic poem, began to sing:—

> "The despot's heel is on thy shore,
>   Maryland, my Maryland,
> His torch is on thy temple door,
>   Maryland, my Maryland,
> Avenge the patriotic gore,
> That flecked the streets of Baltimore,
> And be the battle queen of yore,
>   Maryland, my Maryland."

Thousands of voices joined in the song, while a bugler on
the Northern bank took up and made the welkin ring, which
was answered by long and gladsome shouts by the men. Halting that night and camping a few miles out from the river;
reaching the Monocacy River next day where it is spanned by
the Baltimore & Ohio Railroad bridge, where the command
spent two or three days in resting and recuperating. The men
were in light marching order, having learned to burden themselves with as little as possible; a cloth haversack, canteen and
blanket were the sum total of a soldier's luggage at this period
of the war. They had no change of clothing as a rule; a grey
cap, jacket, pants, and colored shirt, made up about all the
clothing he had, and when he thought he would like to have a
clean shirt, he took off the soiled one, went to the water and,
generally without soap, gave it a rubbing, hung it out in the
sun, hunted a shade and waited for the garment to dry sufficiently to put it on again. As for rations, especially on this
campaign, if he could get a little green corn and fresh beef he
counted himself fairly well provided for; enough to march and
fight on. He preferred a pair of shoes if he could get them and
if he could not, he, like many on this campaign, marched bare-

foot, and complained but little if it was light enough for him to see where to place his feet.

Remaining at the Monocacy some three or four days, the command turned its face westward, passing through Frederick, Middletown, and Boonsboro to Hagerstown. It had become the custom for each regiment to have inscribed upon its flag the various battles in which it had been engaged. At that time the 7th Virginia regiment had inscribed on its flag among the names of battles, that of Seven Pines, and as the regiment marched through Frederick a lady among a considerable group catching sight of the words Seven Pines on the flag proposed, "Three cheers for the battle flag of Seven Pines," which were given with a hearty good will, and thereupon the regiment began to sing:—

> Oh! have you heard the joyful news
> Virginia does Old Abe refuse,
>   Hurrah! Hurrah! Hurrah!
> Virginia joins the cotton states,
>   Hurrah! Hurrah! Hurrah!
> The glorious cry each heart elates,
>   We'll live and die for Dixie."

Longstreet's division reached Hagerstown on the 12th and went into camp on the southwest side of the town, where it remained until Sunday, the 14th as hereinafter related. General D. H. Hill's division had been left to guard the passes through South Mountain, while General Jackson had led his troops for the reduction and capture of the Federal garrison at Harper's Ferry. On the march of Kemper's brigade from Frederick through Middletown, it met with few smiles if any, but on the other hand strong exhibitions of Union feeling and sentiment, especially from the females, who seemed intent on saying bad things and in having the last word. The men took it in good part, said funny things to them and sung for them a part of the words of the beautiful southern poem:—(1)

---

(1). The above arrangement of lines is a fac-simile of the original manuscript; and while incorrect, from the standpoint of arrangement, it is followed, as a matter of interest. The song is given line-for-line.

"We are a band of brothers and native to
  The soil,
Fighting for the property we've gained by
  Honest toil,
And when our rights were threatened the
  Cry rose near and far,
Hurrah! for the bonny blue flag that bears
  The single star,

Hurrah! Hurrah! For the southern rights
Hurrah!
Hurrah! for the bonny blue flag that bears
  The single star.

As long as the Union was faithful
  To her trust,
Like friends and like brothers, kind
  Were we and just.
But now when northern treachery
  Attempts our rights to mar,
We hoist on high the bonny flag that
  Bears the single star.

Then here's to our Confederacy—strong are
  We and brave;
Like pátriots of old we fight our heritage
  To save;
And rather than submit to shame, to
  Die we would prefer,
So cheer for the bonnie blue flag that
  Bears the single star."

In Hagerstown more signs of the southern sentiment were visible, even displayed,—for a young girl about fourteen standing on the top of a gate post as the brigade passed, cried out, "Three cheers for Jeff Davis, why may not he be honored?"

On Sunday the 14th about 11 o'clock, A. M., the long roll sounded and the men of Longstreet were quickly in line, and with faces turned eastward marched at a quickstep towards Boonsboro about 14 miles away. The roads were cleared of everything that would in any way delay the march, which was quickened by the continuous roar of guns east of or about Boonsboro Gap, where as was understood General D. H. Hill's division was closely engaged with the main portion of the Federal army, now under the command of General McClellan, who was gradually pressing the Confederates back to the Mountain top. Longstreet's division, except one brigade left by him at Hagerstown, was pressing forward with all speed to the relief

of General Hill's command. It was near 3 o'clock, P. M., when
Kemper's brigade reached the foot of the mountain east of
Boonsboro. Turning to the right at the western base of the
mounain, it was conducted to a point about half way up the
mountain side in the direction of a gap, and thence to the left
into the main gap through which the great highway passes.
While being conducted from this gap up and along an arm of
the mountain to the left, the movement was discovered by a
Federal battery to the right rear, which at once opened fire
throwing shot and shell into the ranks, one of which struck the
head of the leading company of the 7th regiment, killing one
man instantly. To dodge at the sound of a cannon shot, the
whistling or singing of a minnie ball, was altogether natural
with a soldier, no matter how strong and brave he might be and
was no indication of cowardice. Dodging was one of the weak-
nesses of John Meadows, of Company D, 7th regiment. John
would always dodge, but wouldn't run; so on this occasion John
began to dodge, which happened to be observed by John Crawford of the same company, who called out to Meadows, "What
the devil is use of dodging now, the ball has gone by, the first
thing you know you will dodge in the way of a ball." The brigade hastened its steps to the mountain top, on reaching which
it found itself face to face with the enemy.

Before describing the fight which ensued, a statement as to
the situation and relative position of the Confederates at and
near the place occupied by Kemper's brigade is necessary to a
clear understanding of what had and was about to take place.
Colquitt's Georgia brigade was occupying a line on both sides
the turnpike road and perpendicular thereto, and from which
the enemy had been unable to dislodge it. Rode's Alabama
brigade, supported by that of Evans, of South Carolina, held
the extreme Confederate left, and by whom a most gallant and
unqualed struggle had been maintained for several hours, until
the enemy by overpowering force of numbers had about succeeded in crowning the mountain, when Kemper's brigade arrived on the field of contention. General Pickett's brigade,

now commanded by General Garnett, was thrown forward and posted on the left of Colquitt's brigade; and Kemper's brigade across the old road to fill the gap or space between the right of Evans and left of Pickett. These two brigades numbering not more than eight hundred men, and against whom was pitted not less than 5,000 Federals, bravely held their ground until long after nightfall, withdrawing from their position without molestation. The ranks of Kemper's brigade had been greatly depleted by sickness, the battles around Richmond, Second Manassas, and the barefoot, sick, lame men left at Leesburg, and broken down men on the rapid march made from Hagerstown to Boonsboro; so that the five little regiments of his brigade that reached the firing line on the evening of September 14th, 1862, could not have exceeded in the aggregate 500 men rank and file.

The 17th Virginia regiment occupied the right of the brigade, then 11th, 7th, 1st, and 24th regiments in the order named. It was near the hour of 4:30 o'clock, P. M., when the brigade of General Kemper reached the crest of the mountain, and as stated met the enemy face to face, only a short distance away and seemingly intent on crowning the mountain if possible. Here for more than an hour and thirty minutes, the battle raged fiercely, the enemy at some points reaching almost up to the points of the Confederate bayonets. On the southeast side of the county road referred to were the 17th and 11th regiments, and partly in their front was a small field in which was a growing crop of corn, through which, a little after dark, the enemy came up almost to the muzzles of the guns of the regiments referred to, when some one cried out "There they are, men; fire on them!" The fire from the guns of the combatants was so near each other that it appeared to intermingle. It was at or about this time that Major John W. Daniel, Adjutant of the 11th regiment, now United States Senator from Virginia, received a ball in one of his hands. The enemy finding the ground so firmly held against them, a little after dark desisted, leaving the Confederates in possession of this part of the field, from which in about one hour later they very quietly departed, taking with them such of the wounded as were able to be removed without stretchers.

Since the reports can be had of the strength of the Federal troops pitted against Garnett's and Kemper's brigades, on the evening of the 14th of September, it can now be stated that General Hatch's division of 3500 men, reinforced by Christian's brigade of 1500, which was put into the fight, were unable to drive these two small brigades from their position, and this should be glory enough for these men, tired, broken down, footsore, half naked and starved. It is stated upon authority that in this battle the Federals had about 30,000 men, the Confederates about 9,000.

Want of official or other data prevents the statement of losses sustained by Kemper's brigade in this battle, except as to a single company, D, of the 7th Virginia, which company carried 21 men into the battle and lost T. P. Mays and James Cole, killed, and George Knoll and John R. Crawford wounded; a proportionate loss throughout the companies of the brigade would indicate a loss of 28 in the 7th regiment and of 100 in the brigade, and may be set down as not far short of this number. Color Sergeant Mays died with his flag clutched in his hands.

The command passed quietly down to the turnpike and through Boonsboro and the little village of Keedysville, crossing the Antietam and reaching Sharpsburg the morning of the next day, Monday the 15th, about 11 o'clock, A. M. Filing to the left, Kemper's brigade took position behind the range of hills between the road leading from the town to Harper's Ferry and the Antietam, where it remained in the afternoon and night of Monday. Being out of rations, nothing, however, unusual, Sergeant Taylor of D company of the 7th regiment with a detail was sent in quest of the much needed food, which he did not succeed in getting to the regiment when the battle opened on Wednesday, though he had secured a quantity of beef and had it cooking in one of the houses in the town when the

battle began, but did not make delivery to the men until after
night put a stop to the contest.

Nothing of importance transpired during Monday evening
beyond a partial artillery duel and some skirmishing with the
rear guard. The artillery opened early on Tuesday morning,
and as Kemper's brigade with others were shifted from place
to place along the line, it was exposed to the shot from
the enemy's guns across the Antietam. Later in the evening the fire far to the left seemed to increase, which, however,
ceased when night came. On this day and prepared for the
morrow's fray, Kemper could not muster in his brigade but
few more than 400 muskets. The 17th Virginia regiment numbered but 55 officers and men, the 7th regiment 117, the 1st
regiment was less than a half size company, the 24th regiment
not exceeding 150 men and 11th regiment scarcely more than
100 men. On Kemper's left was Drayton's small brigade of
three regiments, one South Carolina and two Georgia. To the
left of Drayton was Garnett's brigade reduced to a mere skeleton, and beyond Garnett, and with its left resting on the turnpike road, was Jenkins' South Carolina brigade, likewise much
depleted.

General D. R. Jones was in command of the division composed of the brigades mentioned, together with General
Toombs' brigade of four small Georgia regiments and a Georgia
battalion, numbering in all, about 600 men, which together
with the other brigades could not have given General Jones an
aggregate of over 2,000 men to defend a line fully a mile in extent, and threatened with a column of quite 15,000 of the enemy.
General Toombs had been sent to defend a bridge over the Antietam, and to prevent the enemy's crossing at that point. He
had with him two small Georgia regiments and some artillery
with which he held the bridge for several hours on the 17th, and
only withdrew after inflicting heavy loss upon his assailants,
and they had found a ford which enabled them to flank his position.

Before daylight on the morning of Wednesday the 17th, the

artillery opened rapidly on the Confederate left, and very soon thereafter the crash of small arms began, and the battle on that part of the field raged with intense fury for hours, and rapidly extended towards the Confederate center and right. Near or a little past noon, the 24th Virginia regiment was detached and sent some eight hundred or a thousand yards to and beyond the Confederate right, to keep watch in the direction of some of the fords of the Antietam. A short while after this regiment was detached, the 7th Virginia under Capt. Philip Ashby was sent to a point from five hundred to six hundred yards to the right of the position it had been occupying in brigade line, leaving General Kemper with three small regiments, 1st, 11th, and 17th Virginia numbering not exceeding two hundred men. Skirmishers from the brigade had been thrown forward a few hundred yards, and had taken shelter behind a stone fence in part and behind a board fence, at the base of the hill occupied by the brigade. Upon the retirement of the regiments of General Toombs from the bridge, the enemy under the command of General Burnside pushed over the creek, and after some delay deployed in line of battle. The creek was not large and contained but little water, and might have been crossed at any point the enemy might have chosen, except at the bridge defended by General Toombs. They seemed anxious to secure the bridge and they did after several hours bloody battle, and the loss of more than 300 men killed and wounded, and this only after they had flanked the position. About three o'clock, P. M., the columns of General Burnside's 9th Federal army corps, covering its front with a cloud of skirmishers, advanced to the attack. The skirmishers were quickly repelled by those of the Confederates lying behind the fences described. The Federal brigade that first came to the relief of their skirmish line, came near sharing a like fate; and this too from the Confederate skirmish line alone supported by a few pieces of artillery. There quickly came however other battle lines to the help of their friends, which by their very momentum, if nothing else, enabled them to bodily rush over the Confederate skirmish line, but few escaping, and crowning the heights. Their seeming victory was short lived, and was soon turned into a signal repulse and defeat. Generl Burnside's long sweeping lines advancing up the hill overlaped the right of Kemper's three little regiments by several hundred yards, brushing them away and capturing McIntosh's South Carolina battery before it had fired a shot. Just then General Toombs with his small brigade that moment arrived from the bridge, threw his men on the Federal flank, and together with Kemper's handful, Drayton's, Garnett's and Jenkins' brigade renewed the fight with vigor with the Federal corps. Doubtless overpowering numbers would have soon won but for the good fortune of the Confederates in this unequal contest; General A. P. Hill's division, which had left Harper's Ferry that morning, having marched 17 miles, reached the field of contention at the opportune moment. Gen. Hill took in the situation at a glance, and threw upon the flank of the enemy's column of attack three of his brigades, Archer's Branch's and Gregg's, and in less than thirty minutes, Burnside's whole corps was in full retreat towards the Antietam.

The 24th Virginia regiment was not engaged, but suffered some loss, however, from the severe shelling to which it was subjected, while the 7th regiment was but slightly engaged, losing some men in killed and wounded. The three small regiments, viz: 1st, 11th and 17th regiments, especially the latter suffered severely in killed and wounded. Company D of the 7th regiment had but 15 men in the action, and lost Isaac Hare, slightly wounded, and John S. Dudley captured on the skirmish line.

General Jones reports the strength of his division in this battle at 2430 men, far too high, and General A. P. Hill reports that he carried into action 2,000 men; making 4430 men, against whom came Burnside's Federal corps of eight brigades of infantry numbering near 15,000 men, with seven batteries of field artillery, besides three companies of cavalry. The loss in Jones' division was 178 killed, 979 wounded, and 272 missing; total 1435. Hill's loss was 63 killed, 283 wounded: total 346. Aggregate loss of Jones' and Hill's divisions 1781; Burnside's loss was 2349. Brigadier General Branch, of Hill's command, was killed and General Gregg wounded. In Jones' division General Toombs was wounded.

In front of Kemper's brigade, and on and over the ground over which it fought, lay 35 men of the 8th Connecticut regiment dead and mortally wounded. The loss in Kemper's brigade was 144. At the close of the contest, the 7th and 24th regiments returned to the brigade, which occupied that night and the next day the same position it had occupied at the beginning of the battle that morning.

The 18th was spent in gathering up and caring for the wounded, burying the dead, Confederate and Federal. That night the Confederates quietly marched away, and crossed to the south side of the Potomac. Kemper's brigade going into bivouac about four miles from the river; a few days thereafter removing to a large spring near Bunker's Hill. Here quite a number of additions were made, not only to the brigade, but to the whole army from the lame, sick, and shoeless men left at Leesburg. The battle of Sharpsburg may be said to have been gratuitous on the part of the Confederates, for they had ample time and opportunity after the fall of Harper's Ferry on Monday morning to have retired to the Virginia side, and there the better prepared to fight a successful battle. During the 15th day of September, General Lee did not have with him at Sharpsburg more than 12,000 men, though by his maneuvering and shifting his men from place to place, he convinced the Federal General that he had a vast army ready for the fight.

The Federal General McClellen in his official report states that he put 87,500 men into the battle of Wednesday; and it is more than doubtful if the Confederate army in this battle exceeded more than 33,000 men. It has been truly said that this was the bloodiest one day's battle of the war; and in none did Southern individuality and self reliance, noted characteristics of the Confederate soldier, shine more brilliantly, or perform a more important part.

After the close of the battle, and on the night of the 18th, the cries of distress of a wounded Connecticut soldier lying in the forty-acre cornfield, were heard by J. M. Norton, a Georgia soldier belonging to Toombs' brigade and he determined to reach and relieve the sufferer, if possible. Taking his canteen filled with water, he crept and crawled to the spot from whence came the cries, and found Mr. B. L. Burr, a badly wounded Federal soldier famishing—dying for water. He supplied him with a canteen of water, and then made his way safely back to his regiment. Subsequently, the following poem written by A. W. Burkhardt, which is here inserted, was suggested by the reading of this incident.

"FROM THE SAME CANTEEN."

On Maryland's soil, by Antietam's clear stream,
There was a clashing of sabres and bayonet-gleam,
And booming of cannon and shrieking of shell,
While the Angel of death plied the engines of Hell.

Two vast armies met there, in stern battle array,
And Antietam ran crimsoned with blood on that day;
While death-dealing bullets were falling like hail,
And the fate of a nation hung poised in the scale.

In far-away homes many loved one shall weep,
On that red gory field many warriors shall sleep;
The mother shall watch, but her waiting is vain,
Her brave soldier boy shall return not again.

The wife, so devoted, so loyal and true,
Has given her loved one a last long adieu;
And now, when the sun shall sink low in the west,
A fatherless babe she will clasp to her breast.

The fair maiden betrothed, and dreaming of bliss,
While on her lips lingers her lover's last kiss,
The fond hope of her heart no more shall behold,
He lies at Antietam, all lifeless and cold.

The bright morning sun will rise in the sky,
And look on the scene with a pitying eye,
And weep for the loved ones, all bleeding and torn,
Sad, wounded, forsaken, and dying forlorn.

Earth quenches it's thirst with the blood of the slain,
While the cyclone of death sweeps over the plain;
And the war Demons dance in the moon's misty light,
And mockingly laugh, as each soul takes its flight.

Oh, bloody Antietam! oh, death dealing day!
When the North and the South met in battle array
On the banks of thy stream—in the gloom of thy shade,
Where widows and orphans by thousands were made.

As line after line, with a firm, steady tread,
O'er the gory field charged over wounded and dead,
Through the smoke of the battle, and its sulphureus breath,
Pressed onward—still on—to the harvest of death.

The "Bridge" is now taken—though fearful the loss,
And Burnside advances his columns across;
As forward and backward the battle tide flows,
A part of the field is abandoned to foes.

As the smoke of the conflict lifts over the scene
Where the day's bloody struggle the hottest has been,
And the red, gory field lies thickest—o'er spread
With the wounded, and mangled, the dying and dead,

'Twas here, lying helpless, at ebb of the tide,
A soldier was left, on the fearful divide,
'Twixt the camps of the foemen where battle raged hot
And the sharp shooter's rifle commanded each spot.

The day's work was done, and the din of the fight
Gave place to the darkness and gloom of the night;
The pickets were ordered strict vigils to keep,
While the weary combatants attempted to sleep.

But alas for the wounded!—deserted, alone,
Their couch the red field, and their pillow a stone!
No "touch of the elbow," no kind "comrade" near
To inspire them with courage, or speak words of cheer.

All bleeding he lay, 'mid the dying and dead,
While the earth echoed back to the sentinels' tread;
And the grief burdened air gave vent to a groan,
As upward it wafted some comrade's last moan.

He thought of his home, of his friends far away,
As through the long night he awaited the day.
At length the sun rose, but to add to his grief,
No kind, friendly hand came to give him relief.

Thus forty long hours, all helpless he lay;
Day gave place to night, and night changed into day!
With his life current ebbing—while weaker each breath,
He sighed but for "Water!"—for water or death.

The thirst of the wounded—not pencil nor pen
Can portray half its horrors; nor language of men;
It's pangs may be felt but no tongue can tell,
'Tis the acme of misery!—quintessence of Hell!

For "Water!"—Oh Water!"—for Water the cry—
While Antietam, her current rolls mockingly by,
There faint and exhausted, in hopeless despair,
He sniffs the foul stench of the war-burdened air!

at a glorious vision his eyes now behold!—
Treasure, more precious than silver, or gold,
He drinks at the fountain!—he bathes in the stream!
He awakens—Alas!—it was only a dream!

But a picket, a "Johnnie in Gray," it is true,
Hear the cry of distress from the "Yankee in Blue,"
And all enmity vanished his soldierly heart
As he quickly resolved kind aid to impart.

But to give the relief, he must creep 'mong the dead
Through the down trodden corn, where the earth was still red,
Full exposed to the sharpshooter's deadly aim,
On his mission of mercy—he went and he came!

Soon the Blue and the Gray, whilom enemies, met;
From the "Johnnie's" canteen, the "Yank's" lips were made wet,
And as kindness and gratitude readily blends,
Two hearts were made happy, two foes became friends;

And the angel of mercy looked down from above
With a pitying eye, while a tear drop of love
Cemented the friendship begun on that day,
Where "Yankee" and "Reb" fought in hostile array.

Of all the brave deeds, on that battlefield done,
None exceed in bravery and kindness that one;
And from that day to this no friends were more true
Than the "Jonnie in Gray" and the "Yankee in Blue."

General McClellan's army began crossing the Potomac east of the Blue Ridge and at Harper's Ferry in the last days of October, which impelled General Lee to move to Culpeper, where he conentrated the major part of his army about the first day of November.

While at Culpeper in the early days of November, Pickett's division was oganized, and composed of the following Virginia regiments, viz:

1st brigade;
Brigadier General James L. Kemper
Regiments: 1st, 3rd, 7th 11th, and 24th Virginia,
2nd brigade:
Brigadier General R. B. Garnett
Regiments: 8th, 18th, 19th, 28th, and 56th Virginia
3rd brigade
Brigadier General Lewis A. Armistead
Regiments: 9th, 14th, 38th, 53rd, and 57th Virginia

4th brigade
Brigadier General Montgomery D. Corse
Regiments: 15th, 17th, 29th, 30th, and 32nd Virginia
And Jenkins' South Carolina brigade. To the division was attached Major James Dearing's battalion of artillery, and Faukey's, Stribling's and Latham's batteries.

In the last days of November the division marched from Culpeper over the Orange plank road to the hills overlooking Fredericksburg, where on the 11th of December it was called to arms to resist the enemy reported as crossing or threatening to cross the Rappahannock. The division stood to arms until early on the morning of the 13th, when it was marched to a position in the Confederate battle line on the right center of Longstreet's corps, where it remained until about 1 o'clock, P. M., when Kemper's and Jenkins' brigades were marched rapidly to the relief of the Confederates holding Mayre's Hill, and who were being sorely pressed. The brigade of Kemper moved forward into the line about dark, taking the place of Cobb's Georgians and Cook's North Carolinians; remaining during the night of the 13th, the day and night of the 14th engaged for most of the time in brisk skirmishing with the enemy, who decamped and crossed the river on the night of the 14th. The loss in the brigade was 46, of which there were four in the 7th regiment, and seven in the 24th regiment. Lewis N. Wiley of company D, of the 7th was wounded. Another "On to Richmond" movement had been scotched.

The enemy gone and the present danger having passed, the troops retired to their respective camping places on the hills, south of Fredericksburg. The winter was severe, the men were without tents, but few blankets and numbers still without shoes, and not one in a dozen with an overcoat, therefore poorly prepared for the winter blasts. Necessity, however, compels man to resort to almost any expedient to make himself comfortable, and the men erected rude wooden shanties out of timber, placing one end in the ground, and slanting the other for-

ward resting on poles held up by forks or against trees, and
the top of the timber or slabs covered with earth to the depth
of several inches. In front they built their fires; some rolling
away the logs that had been burning during the day, made
their bed on the warm ground. Rawhide moccasins were substituted for shoes. The regiments by detachments did picket
duty off the river beyond Hamilton's Crossing, while the cavalry watched the fords of the upper Rappahannock.

During that long, dreary, cold winter while in the bivouac
amid privation and suffering, not exceeded by that of Washington's army at Valley Forge, the men freely discussed the question touching the war, its conduct, prospects for peace, etc. An
ever abiding confidence in the justice of our cause, and the be-
lief in its final triumph, coupled with and backed by invinci-
ble, unconquerable spirits ever ready to brave the storm of
battle, caused the sufferings and hardships to be treated as
trival as compared with the great issue at stake.

On January 20th the men were called from their quarters
and marched up the Rappahannock in the direction of Bank's
Ford, where it was reported that a portion of the Federal army
was threatening to cross. Remaining out one night in the rain,
snow and mud, returned to their camps, seeming to have
marched up that hill for no other purpose than to march down
again.

At an early hour on the morning of Monday, February 16th,
in the midst of snow, sleet and storm, Pickett's division took up
its line of march heading towards Richmond. The march continued to within about eight miles of that city, when a halt
was made and the men rested for a few days, when they again
marched, moving through the city to Chester station, on the
Richmond & Petersburg Railroad. Here the command remained until about the 1st of March, when it removed to a point
about two miles south east of Petersburg, where it remained until March 25th, then was placed aboard a train of cars and proceeded to Weldon, then to Goldsboro, and from thence to Kinston, North Carolina. Here the command did some scouting and

picketing on the roads leading to Newberne. Leaving Kinston
on April 9th it moved by rail by way of Goldsboro to Weldon,
and from thence marched to Suffolk, Virginia, reaching there
on April 12th, and joining the Confederate forces of General
Longstreet, then investing that place. It was from a train
of cars on this journey that Manley Reece, of the Mercer
company of the 24th Virginia regiment was knocked from the
top of the train by an overhead bridge and killed.

The principal object of the investment of the town of Suffolk, seems to have been to keep the enemy closely confined
within his lines immediately in and around that place and the
city of Norfolk, and thus enable the Confederate Commissary
Department to gather all available supplies for the army from
the southeastern counties of Virginia, and to transport them
into the interior for the use of our army. Beyond some severe
skirmishes, nothing very important occurred during our stay
around Suffolk. General Longstreet quietly withdrew his
forces on the night of the 3rd of May, and marched to the vicinity of Chester Station, between Petersburg and Richmond.
On our way from Suffolk to Petersburg we heard of the battle of Chancellorville, the woundeing of General Jackson and
later of his death. The command remained at Chester Station
until about the middle of May, when Pickett's division marched through Richmond to Taylorsville and went into camp,
where it remained and rested until the last of the month or
the 1st day of June, when it marched across the Pamunkey into
King and Queen County, returning in a day or two to its camp
at Taylorsville. On the 2nd day of June the division was again
in motion in the direction of Northern Virginia, and the movement continued until it reached, on the 10th, a point within
about eight miles of Culpeper Court House, where it went into
bivouac. Here had assembled, as was assembling, a large part
of the army of Gen. Lee, including his cavalry corps under its
matchless leader, General J. E. B. Stuart.

The passionate ardor of our people for their country's cause
had brought to the army nearly every man that was able to

perform active military duty in the field, so that but few additions to the ranks could be hoped for. It was the largest number of men, and composed of the best fighting material, that
General Lee had yet, in fact ever led to battle. Most of them
were men well inured to the service, and therefore well prepared to undergo the greatest hardship; and by this time most
of the cowards, of which there were few, had either gotten out
of the army and gone home, or over to the enemy. As General
Lee, at the head of this magnificent body of men, was passing
through Clark County, in the Valley of Virginia, he dined with
Dr. McGuire, and after dinner on mounting his horse and
about to leave, the Doctor remarked to him, that he had never
before felt confidence in the Southern cause, but was now encouraged as he saw the army marching north. To which General Lee quietly said, "Doctor, there marches the finest body of
men that ever tramped upon the earth." This incident was related to the author by Doctor Edwin McGuire of Richmond.
The usual orders to cook rations and prepare to move at a moment's notice were given the men in their bivouac at Culpeper,
and everything was bustle and confusion in preparation to
move.

Before proceeding to relate the movements of the army
Northward it becomes necessary to go back to Western Virginia and state what has been transpiring in that section. After the battle of Sharpsburg and the Confederates had retired
south of the Potomac, General Stuart with a portion of his
cavalry corps made a ride around the Federal army of the Potomac. On reaching his starting point about Cumberland,
Maryland, he ascertained that the Federal General Cox with
about 5,000 men had started for the valley of the Kanawha, to
intercept or cut off General Loring, who was operating in the
said valley with an army composed largely of New River Valley men. Loring being informed of this movement of General
Cox, retired from the Valley of the Kanawha to the New River
section. In Loring's command were a large number of men
from the Counties of Giles, Mercer, Monroe, and Greenbrier.

These men belonged largely to the 36th and 60th Virginia regiments of infantry and to the 23rd, 26th and 30th battalions of infantry, and to William H. French's battalion, afterwards 17th regiment of cavalry. There was also along with General Loring two or more companies of Tazewell County men, one of which was that of Captain D. B. Baldwin, of the 23rd Virginia battalion. On Loring's return from the Valley of the Kanawha, he was relieved by General John Echols, who soon thereafter on account of ill health, was relieved by Major General Samuel Jones. During the winter of 1862-3 the 36th and 60th Virginia regiments with Otey's battery, and for a part of the time other troops, remained at Princeton, while another portion of the troops that had formed a part of Loring's command were stationed at the Narrows of New River, and some wintered in Monroe, and Greenbrier Counties, while the cavalry of Jenkins' brigade in part sent their horses farther south to be wintered, the most of the men remaining on duty on the outposts. Colonel William H. French took his comand to the county of Floyd and adjacent counties, where it remained until towards the opening of the spring of 1863, when it removed to Roanoke County, where the Colonel succeeded in completing the organization of his regiment, which was attached to General Jenkins' brigade of cavalry, and later moved into the lower Valley of Virginia in the early days of June, leading the advance of General Lee's army into Pennsylvania. The cavalry brigade of Jenkins was composed of the 8th, 14th, 16th, 17th, 19th regiments, and the 34th, 36th and 37th battalions of cavalry. The Virginia batteries of Chapman, Bryant, Otey, and Stamp were also a part of the army operating in southwestern and western Virginia, and were in part composed of New River Valley men from the counties of Giles, Monroe, and Mercer. From October, 1862, to the spring of 1863, the southwest Virginia country and western Virginia, from the Tennessee line at Bristol to Staunton in the Valley, was kept in an almost constant state of excitement and alarm, on account of the frequent incursions of Federal raiding parties, and the march of larger bodies of Federal troops into that territory. Small parties of Federal scouts and patrols, even in the cold winter months, penetrated far into the interior, even within the Confederate line of outposts, and the country was filled with Federal spies, who kept their friends along the lines referred to fully posted as to the strength and movements of the Confederates. To some extent this was likewise true of the Confederate scouts, patrols, and spies as to the movements of the Federals. A large part of the territory referred to was, on account of bad roads and swollen streams, almost wholly impracticable for military operation in the winter season. We left the army of Northern Virginia in its bivouac near Culpeper Court House. Pickett's division left its bivouac at the point above mentioned on Monday, the 15th day of June, the head of the column directed toward the Blue Ridge and Snicker's Gap, through which it passed on the 20th, and crossed the Shenandoah at Castleman's ferry. Here it was detained for two or three days as well as at Berryville, for the purpose of remaining in supporting distance of the cavalry operating east of the Ridge. The division marched from Culpeper left in front, that it might by facing into line, meet the enemy at any moment. Gen. Ewell's corps in the advance had routed Milroy at Winchester, and cleared the route for the rapid movement of the other troops following his corps. Longstreet's corps, which included Pickett's division, of which division only three of the brigades were on this march, continued its movement through Martinsburg, by Falling Waters, and on the evening of Wednesday, June the 27th, it crossed the Potomac at Williamsport, and bivouaced a short distance out of the town, on the Maryland side of the river. The morale of the army was never better, officers and men alike were inspired with confidence in their ability to defeat the enemy wherever he might choose to offer battle. And never did an army move into an enemy's country in better fighting trim and spirit. It was doubtless this spirit of over-confidence that lost us the battle of Gettysburg. The men were in splendid condition, everything in firstclass order, no straggling, no desertion, no

destruction of private property, no outrages committed upon
citizens; the orders of the commanding General on this subject
were as a rule, strictly observed.   Here was a grand, magnificent spectacle; a great army of effective men, and every man a
soldier in the true sense of the word, the heroes of victories
on more than a dozen fields; marching through the country of
their enemy unobstructed and unopposed.

The corps of General Longstreet continued its march on the
25th to Hagerstown, where it halted to allow the corps of General A. P. Hill, which had crossed at Shepherdstown, to pass to
the front.   On Saturday, the 27th, the march was continued to
Chambersburg, Pennsylvania, halting on the road on the outer
edge of the town in front of the beautiful residence of Colonel
McClure, where some ladies made their appearance and delivered quite a spicy address or somewhat of a lecture, which was
responded to with "Dixie" by the band of the 7th Virginia regiment.   A few miles beyond the command halted and went into
bivouac on the York road.   During the 28th, 29th and 30th of
June and 1st day of July the division of Pickett was engaged
in the destruction of the track of the Cumberland Valley Railroad.   At near 2 o'clock, A. M., of Thursday, July 2nd, the long
roll sounded and the men were soon under arms and in line,
and moved promptly on the road leading to Gettysburg, the vicinity of which was, after a rapid and tiresome march of some
twenty five miles, reached about 4 o'clock, P. M., and the divi-
sioh went into bivouac about two miles from the town.   The other division of Longstreet's corps had preceded that of Pickett
some hours, and had been in the fight the evening of the day of
Pickett's arrival.   A little before daylight on the morning of
Friday, the 3rd, the division moved from its bivouac, on the
road between Cashtown and Gettysburg, to the right and
along the valley of Willoughby's Run, reaching its battle line
about 7 o'clock, A. M. The usual inspection of arms and ammunition took place.

The brigades of Corse and Jenkins having been left in Virginia, Pickett had but Garnett's, Armistead's and Kemper's

present, consisting of 15 regiments—all Virginians, numbering on that morning about 4500 muskets; the aggregate effective strength, rank and file, was close to 4700, which will be understood as including the General and staff officers. This division was composed of the flower of the Virginian army, many of them mere youths—schoolboys, of which a large number were from the New River Valley counties, viz: Montgomery, Carroll, Pulaski, Floyd, Giles and Mercer. In the division were companies from the counties of Campbell, Bedford, Franklin, Patrick, Henry, Craig, Madison, Culpeper, Orange, Rappahanock, Greene, Albemarle, Nansemond, Norfolk, Cities of Richmond, Lynchburg, Norfolk and Portsmouth. The first brigade was commanded by the gallant and impetuous General James L. Kemper, and was in front during the morning's march, and in battle line held the right, with Garnett's brigade on the left, and Armistead somewhat to the left and rear.

Fencing and other obstructions were cleared away, and the line moved forward a short distance into a field on which was a growing crop of rye. Arms were stacked and instructions given that upon the report of two guns, which were to be signals, the men were to lie flat upon the ground. In front of the division was massed the Confederate artillery, numbering about one hundred and fifty pieces. On the hills beyond and 1400 yards, or a little more, away and in front, were something like an equal number of Federal guns, prepared and ready for the fray. The heat was exceedingly oppressive, and several of the men had sunstroke, and all suffered more or less for water. It was past one o'clock when the report of the two signal guns rang out upon the air, and down upon their faces went the men, and then began and continued for nearly two hours the most terrific and destructive artillery duel that ever occurred on the face of the earth. The atmosphere was broken by the rush and crash of projectiles, solid shot, shrieking, bursting shells. The sun, so brilliant before, was now darkened by smoke and mist enveloping and shadowing the earth, through which came hissing and shrieking firey fuses and messengers of death, sweeping, plunging, cutting, ploughing through the ranks, carrying mutilation, destruction, pain, suffering, and death in every direction. Whithersoever you might look could be seen at almost every moment muskets, swords, haversacks, human flesh and bones flying and dangling in the air or bouncing above the earth, which now trembled as if shaken by an earthquake. It was afterwards stated by the teamsters and cooks, who were two and three miles away, that the sash in the windows of the houses where they were shook and chattered as if caused by a violent wind. Over, behind, in front, in the midst, and through the ranks, poured shot and shell and the fragments thereof, dealing out death on every hand.

The men remained in their places, except those knocked out by shot or shell, and when the firing ceased, at about a quarter past 3 o'clock, and the order came to fall in, the men sprang quickly to their places, ready to move at the word. General Pickett came dashing along calling out, "Up, men, and to your posts; don't forget today that you are from Old Virginia." At the order forward, the three brigades moved up the hill by the batteries and across the open as steadily as troops ever moved under fire. The fresh batteries of the enemy now opened at short range, and from sheltered positions poured a destructive fire into these advancing columns, the Federal batteries on the Round Top enfilading the Confederate line as it advanced. The enemy had covered his front by a heavy line of skirmishers, which withdrew as the Confederates advanced. Hancock's second Federal army corps, about 18,000 strong, held the lines which Pickett's division assailed, and as the line approached the stone wall behind which lay these men of Hancock's, it was met by a most scathing fire, which killed and wounded not less than twenty-five per centum of Pickett's men. Notwithstanding this fire, not stopping, but with a rush they went over Hancock's line:

> "Now they climb the mountain height
> And plant the flag of freedom's right."

In the headlong rush over the Federal line they had captured a large number of guns, and had effected a lodgment which only needed a strong helping hand for a short while and the Federal army would have been cut in twain, and must have rapidly retreated or been destroyed. Pickett's division had made a great and daring charge, but had been repulsed; and what remained had to retire to the point from which the advance began. Here Generals Lee and Pickett rallied and reformed the men to meet what was supposed to be an advance of the enemy. It was while this rally and reformation was taking place that General Pickett complained so bitterly of the treatment of his division in not being properly supported and the fearful loss it had sustained; and which called forth the noble response of the great soul of Lee that "Its all my fault." It was here, at the same time, that a boy by the name of Belcher, from Franklin County, bearing the flag of the 24th Virginia regiment, addressing General Pickett, said, "General, shall we charge them again?" It was also at this moment that General Kemper was being carried by, dreadfully wounded, that Pickett's anguish was so great that he wept, and then it was that General Lee made the statement above, "It's all my fault." Noble words from a noble man!

It may be truthfully said that no commander of a great army so universally and deservedly enjoyed the perfect love, confidence and esteem of his men, and that no General had higher conception of the manliness and valor of his troops, and no body of men that ever tramped on the earth followed its leader with such supreme devotion as the men who followed General Lee; it was akin to that expressed by Ruth for Naomi: "Entreat me not to leave thee or to return from following after thee, for whither thou goest I will go; and where thou lodgest I will lodge; thy people shall be my people, and thy God my God. Where thou diest I will die and there will I be buried." No higher earthly tribute could be paid to a man than that to General Lee by Senator Ben Hill, of Georgia, in which he said: "He was a foe without hate, a friend without treachery, a soldier without cruelty, and a victim without murmuring. He

was a public officer without vices, a private citizen without
wrong, a neighbor without reproach, a Christian without hyp-
ocrisy, and a man without guile. He was a Cæsar without
his ambition, Frederick without his tyranny, Napoleon without
his selfishness, and Washington without his reward. He was
as obedient to authority as a servant, and royal in authority as
a King. He was as gentle as a woman in life, pure and modest
as a virgin in thought, watchful as a Roman Vestal, submissive
to law as Socrates, and grand in battle as Achilles." No
less deserving is the tribute of Mr. Charles Francis Adams,
who said in seaking of General Lee: "He represented and
individualized all that was highest and best in Southern mind
and the Confederate cause,—the loyalty to state, the keen
sense of humor and personal obligation, the slightly archaic,
the almost patriarchal love of dependent family and home.
He was a Virginian of the Virginians. He represents a
type which is gone—hardly less extinct than that of the great
English Noblemen of the feudal times, or the ideal head of the
Scotch clan of a later period; but just as long as men admire
courage, devotion, patriotism, the high sense of duty and personal honor—all, in a word, which go to make up what we
know as character—just so long will that type of a man be
held in affectionate, reverential memory."

Long since the close of our civil strife, numbers of ex-Federal soldiers are beginning to pay just tribute to the gallantry
and devotion of the Confederate soldier. Among the ex-Fed-
erals who have written on the battle of Gettysburg is Mr.
Charles A. Pacta, of Massachusetts, who not long since published an article in a newspaper, containing a description of
the charge of Pickett's division at Gettysburg on July 3rd,
1863, in which he says:

"In all great wars involving the destinies of nations, it is
neither the number of battles, nor the names, nor the loss of
life, that remain fixed in the mind of the masses; but simply
the one decided struggle which either in its immediate or re-

mote sequence closes the conflict. Of the one hundred battles
of the great Napoleon, Waterloo alone lingers in the memory.
The Franco-Prussian war, so fraught with changes to Europe,
presents but one name that will never fade—Sedan. Even in
our own country, how few battles of the Revolution can we
enumerate; but is there a child who does not know that
Bunker's Hill sounded the death knell of English rule in the
land? And now but twenty years since the greatest conflict
of modern times was closed at Appomattox, how few can we
readily recall of the scores of blood-stained battle fields on
which our friends and neighbors fought and fell; but is there
one, old or young, cultured or ignorant, of the North or of the
South, than cannot speak of Gettysburg? But what is Gettysburg, either in its first day's Federal defeat, or its second
day's terrible slaughter around Little Round Top, without
the third day's immortal charge by Pickett and his brave Virginians? In it we have the culmination of the rebellion. It
took long years after to drain all the life-blood from the foe,
but never again did the wave of rebellion rise so gallantly
high, as when it beat upon the crest of Cemetery Ridge. The
storming of the heights of Inkerman, the charge of the noble
Six Hundred, the fearful onslaught of the Guards at Waterloo, the scaling of Lookout Mountain—have all been sung in
story, and perhaps always will be; but they all pale beside
the glory that will ever enshroud the heroes who, with perhaps not literally Cannon to right of them and cannon to left
of them, but with a hundred cannons belching forth death in
front of them, hurled themselves into the center of a great
army, and had victory almost within their grasp.

"To describe this charge, we will go back to the evening of
the 2nd of July, and recall upon what basis the cautious Lee
could undertake so fearful a responsibility. The victorious
Southrons, fresh from their triumphs at Fredericksburg and
Chancellorsville, had entered the North, carrying consternation and dismay to every hamlet, with none to oppose; their
forward march was one of spoil, and it was not until the 1st

of July that they met their old foemen, the Army of the Potomac, in the streets of Gettysburg, and after a fierce conflict drove them back. The second day's conflict was a terrible slaughter, and at its close the Federal army, although holding its position, was to a certain extent disheartened. Many of our best Generals and commanding officers were killed or wounded, scores of regiments and batteries were nearly wiped out, Sickles' line was broken and driven in and its position was held by Longstreet. Little Round Top, the key of the position, was held at a frightful loss of life, and Ewell upon the right had gained a footing upon the ridge. The Rebel army was joyful and expectant of victory.

"The morning of the 3rd of July opened clear and bright, and one hundred thousand men faced each other, awaiting the signal of conflict; but, except the pushing of Ewell from his position, the hours passed on, relieved only by the rumbling of artillery carriages as they were massed by Lee upon Seminary Ridge, and by Meade upon Cemetery Ridge. At 12 o'clock Lee ascended the cupola of the Pennsylvania College, in quiet surveyed the Union lines, and decided to strike for Hancock's center. Meanwhile, Pickett with his three Virginia brigades had arrived from Chambersburg and taken cover in the woods of Seminary Ridge. What Lee's feeling must have been, as he looked at the hundred death-dealing cannon massed on Cemetery Hill, and the fifty thousand men waiting patiently in front and behind them, men whose valor he knew well in many a bitter struggle—and then looked at his handful of brave Virginians, three small, decimated brigades which he was about to hurl into that vortex of death—no one will ever know. The blunder that sent the Light Brigade to death at Balakava was bad enough, but here was five thousand men waiting to seek victory where only the day before ten thousand had lost their lives or their limbs in the same futile endeavor.

"Leaving the college, Lee called a council of his Generals at Longstreet's headquarters, and the plan of attack was formed. It is said that the level-headed Longstreet opposed the plan, and if so it was but in keeping with his remarkable generalship. The attack was to be opened with artillery fire to demoralize and batter the Federal line, and was to be opened by a signal of two shots from the Washington Artillery. At half past one the report of the first gun rang out on the still summer air, followed a minute later by the second, and then came the roar and flash of one hundred and thirty-eight Rebel cannon. Almost immediately one hundred Fedreal guns responded and the battle had begun. Shot and shell tore through the air, crashing through batteries, tearing men and horses to pieces; the very earth seemed to shake and the hills to reel as the terrible thunders re-echoed amongst them. For nearly an hour every conceivable form of ordnance known to modern gunnery hissed and shrieked, whistled and screamed as it went forth on its death mission, till, exhausted by excitement and heat, the gunners slackened their fire and silence reigned again.

"Then Pickett and his brave legions stood up and formed for the death-struggle; three remnants of brigades, consisting of Garnett's brigade—the Eighth, Eighteenth, Nineteenth, Twenty-eighth, Fifty-sixth Virginia; Armistead's brigade—the Ninth, Fourteenth, Thirty-eighth, Fifty-third, Fifty-seventh Virginia; Kemper's brigade—First, Third, Seventh, Eleventh, Twenty-fourth Virginia. Their tattered flags bore the scars of a score of battles, and from their ranks the merciless bullet had already taken two-thirds their number.

"In compact ranks, their front scarcely covering two of Hancock's brigades, with flags waving as if for a gala day, General Pickett saluted Longstreet and asked, "Shall I go forward, sir?" but it was not in Longstreet's heart to send those heroes of so many battles to certain death, and he turned away his head—when Pickett, with that proud impetuous air which had earned him the title of the 'Ney of the Rebel army,' exclaimed: "Sir, I shall lead my division forward!" The orders now rang out, "Attention! Attention!" and the men realizing the end was near, cried out to their comrades: "Good-

bye boys, good-bye!" Suddenly rang on the air the final order
from Pickett himself, and his saber flashed from its scabbard—
"Column forward, guide center!" And the Brigades of Kemper, Garnett and Armistead moved toward Cemetery Ridge
as one man. Soon Pettigrew's division emerged from the
woods and followed in echelon on Pickett's left flank, and
Wilcox with his Alabama division moved out to support his
right flank—in all, about fifteen thousand men. The selection
of these supports shows a lack of judgment which it would
almost seem impossible for Lee to have made. Pettigrew's
division was composed mostly of new troops from North Carolina, and had been terribly used up in the first day's fight and
were in no condition to form part of a forlorn hope. Wilcox's
troops had also received severe punishment in the second
day's engagement in his attack on the Ridge, and should have
been replaced by fresh, well tried brigades. But the movement
had now begun, and Lee with his generals about him watched
anxiously for the result.

"It was nearly a mile to the Union lines, and as they advanced over the open plain the Federal artillery opened again,
plowing great lanes through their solid ranks, but they closed
up to guide center as if upon dress parade; when half way
over Pickett halted his division, amidst a terrible fire of shot
and shell, and changed his direction by an oblique movement,
coolly and beautifully made. But here occurred the greatest
mistake of all. Wilcox paid no attention to this change of
movement, but kept straight on to the front, thus opening a
tremendous gap between the two columns and exposing Pickett's right to all the mishaps that afterward overtook it. To
those who have ever faced artillery fire it is marvellous and
unexplainable how human beings could have advanced under
the terrific fire of a hundred cannon, every inch of air
being ladened with the missiles of death; but in splendid
formation they still came bravely on till within range of the
musketry; then the blue line of Hancock's corps rose and
poured into their rank a murderous fire. With a wild yell

the Rebels pushed on unfalteringly, crossed the Federal line
and laid hands upon eleven cannon. Men fired in each other's
faces; there were bayonet thrusts, cutting with sabres, hand-
to-hand contests, oaths, curses, yells and hurrahs. The second
corps fell back behind the guns to allow the use of grape and
double canister, and as it tore through the Rebel ranks, at
only a few paces distance, the dead and wounded were piled
in ghastly heaps. Still on they came, up to the very muzzles
of the guns; they were blown away from the cannon's mouth,
but yet they did not waver. Pickett had taken the key to the
position and the glad shout of victory was heard; as, the very
impersonation of a soldier, he still forced his troops to the
crest of Cemetery Ridge.

"Kemper and Armistead broke through Hancock's line,
scaled the hill and planted their flag on its crest. Just before
Armistead was shot, he placed his flag upon a captured cannon and cried: "Give them the cold steel, boys," but valor
could do no more, the handful of braves had won immortality,
but could not conquer an army. Pettigrew's weak division
was broken, fleeing and almost annihilated. Wilcox, owing
to his great mistake in separating his column, was easily routed,
and Stannard's Vermonters, thrown into the gap, were creating havoc on Pickett's flank. Pickett seeing his supports gone,
his generals, Kemper, Armistead, and Garnett killed or wounded, every field officer of the three brigades gone, three-fourths
of his men killed or captured, himself untouched, but broken-
hearted, gave the order for retreat, but, band of heroes as they
were, they fled not; but amidst that still continuous, terrible
fire, they slowly, sullenly recrossed the plain—all that was
left of them, but few of five thousand.

"Thus ended the greatest charge known to modern warfare;
made in the most unequal manner against a great army, and
midst the most terrible cannonade known in wars, and yet so
perfect was the discipline, so audacious the valor, that had
this handful of Virginians been properly supported they would
perhaps have rendered the Federal position untenable, and

possibly have established the Southern Confederacy. While other battlefields are upturned by the plough and covered with waving grain, Cemetery Ridge will forever proudly uphold its monuments, telling of glory both to the Blue and the Gray, and our children's children, while standing upon its crest, will rehearse again of Pickett's wonderful charge."

In the article just quoted, injustice is done to Pettigrew's North Carolinians, as it is known that one or more of his brigades, especially that of General Lane, behaved as gallantly and as bravely as any brigade in that charge, and deserve as much credit and praise.

The army remained on the battlefield during the 4th, that night, and early on the morning of the 5th it withdrew through the passes of the mountain, retiring on Hagerstown and Williamsport, where it remained in battle line until the night of the 13th, not being able to cross the Potomac on account of its swollen condition. Longstreet's and Hill's corps passed over the bridge, while Ewell's forded the river at Williamsport; the three corps going into bivouac in the neighborhood of Bunker's Hill, where they remained for several days. Pickett's division on its retirement from the battlefield, and on its march to Winchester, Virginia, had charge of about 4,000 Federal prisoners, captured during the three days engagements at Gettyburg.

The total loss of this division in the battle of the 3rd, was 2888, of which 224 were killed, 1080 wounded, and 1584 captured or missing. The loss in Kemper's brigade was 729. The 7th Virginia regiment lost 67 killed and wounded, and the 24th Virginia lost 128 killed and wounded. The loss of the division in general and field officers was frightful. Brigadier General Garnett was killed, Armistead mortally and Kemper dangerously wounded. Of the whole complement of general and field officers, aggregating about 48, only one, Lieutenant Colonel was left unhurt. The color bearer of the 7th Virginia regiment, with his eight color sergeants and corporals, went down in the battle, either killed or wounded; the colors falling into the hands of the 82nd New York Infantry, commanded by Captain John Darrow. There went into the battle of Company D, 7th Virginia regiment, 31 men, of which 17 were killed and wounded. The killed were, David C. Akers, Jesse Barrett, Daniel Bish, and John P. Sublett; the wounded, Lieutenant Elisha M. Stone, and Elijah R. Walker, Sergeants Thomas S. Taylor and David E. Johnston, the latter severely, Corporal J. B. Young, and privates William C. Fortner, James H. Fortner, leg amputated, John Meadows, and D. L. Sarver; John W. Hight was taken prisoner. No data is at hand as to the names of the killed and wounded in the Giles company of the 24th Virginia, but the names of the Mercer County company in that regiment who were killed or wounded, are as follows, viz: Killed, Charles Burroughs, Squire Cook, James Kinney, Jesse Parsons, B. W. Peck, and J. P. Thomas; wounded, Captain H. Scott, H. French Calfee, mortally, Jordon Cox, Robert A. George, A. J. Holstein, Rufus G. Rowland, James Snead, and Levi Vermillion; total, fourteen.

General Pickett was greatly distressed over the losses in his division, and wrote his report, which contained matter which General Lee thought for the good of the service ought not to be published, and hence returned the report to General Pickett, suggesting the omission of the objectional matter, and in his letter returning said report, says: "You and your men have crowned yourself with glory, but we have the enemy to fight, and must carefully at this critical moment guard against dissensions, which the reflections in your report would create. I will therefore suggest that you destroy both copy and original, substituting one confined to casualties merely. I hope all will yet be well." The report was never published. It is supposed that General Pickett had seriously reflected upon some one touching the disaster which befell his heroic and gallant veterans at Gettysburg, who so bravely and freely had sacrificed their lives upon the altar of their country. Well may it be said of them:

"Spartans at Thermopylae,
Fought and died for liberty,
But no richer legacy
Left posterity."

General A. G. Jenkins' cavalry brigade led the advance of
the army into Pennsylvania, and was at Gettysburg, but there
does not appear any official report showing its losses, if it sustained any.

French's battery remained around the defenses of Richmond
during the Gettysburg campaign.

Notice must now be taken of affairs in Western Virginia.
Major General Samuel Jones was in command of this department, and in whose command were the brigades of Echols,
Williams, Wharton, and McCausland; constituted as follows,
viz: First brigade, General John Echols, 22nd, 45th, Virginia
Regiment; 23rd and 26th Virginia battalions, and Chapman's
Virginia battery. Second Brigade, General John S. Williams,
63rd Virginia regiment, 64th Virginia regiment, 45th Virginia
battalion, 21st Virginia cavalry, Virginia Partisan Rangers,
and Lowry's Virginia battery. Third brgade, General G. C.
Wharton, 50th and 51st Virginia Regiments, 30th Virginia
battalion,and Stamp's Virginia battery. Fourth brigade, General John McCausland, 36th and 60th Virginia regiments, and
Bryn's Virginia Battery; with Jenkins' cavalry brigade, consisting of the 8th, 14th, 16th, 17th and 19th Virginia regiments,
and 34th, 36th, and 37th Virginia battalions of cavalry, together with some unattached troops, viz: Trigg's 54th Virginia regiment, two Virginia companies of Partisan Rangers,
commanded by Captains Philip J. Thurmond and William D.
Thurmond, respectively, and Otey's Virginia battery; numbering in the aggregate about 10,000 men, and guarding the territory and border stretching from Bristol to Staunton. In
the winter of 1862-3, and up to March of the latter year, these
troops were in camp at various points in the district of country mentioned. Wharton at the Narrows, Echols and Williams in Monroe and Greenbrier section, later General Wil-

liams at Saltville, and General McCausland's command at Princeton.

In March General Jones planned quite a formidable expedition into Northwestern Virginia, and the Kanawha Valley, sending a portion of his troops into the Nicholas County section, and northward thereof. A portion of the cavalry of Jenkins was sent from Tazewell through McDowell, and towards the Ohio; and General McCausland to Fayetteville, but the whole affair amounted to but little. In the early part of May the 26th Virginia battalion, under Edgar, defeated at or near Lewisburg a portion of the 2nd West Virginia cavalry regiment. Later the cavalry brigade of Jenkins, except the 8th regiment and Dunn's battalion, was withdrawn from the Western Virginia department, and sent to the Valley of Virginia, preparatory to the march into Pennsylvania. And in July of this same year, 1863, the brigade of Wharton was also sent to the Valley of Virginia. About the middle of July the brigade of McCausland, stationed in Raleigh County, at the crossing of Piney River, was, by a force of the enemy, compelled to abandon its position, and retreat upon Princeton. This force which threatened McCausland was under the immediate command of the Federal Colonel Toland, who had with him the 2nd Virginia cavalry, the 34th regiment of Ohio volunteer infantry, and a detachment of the 1st Virginia cavalry; these troops had left the Kanawha and crossed onto Coal River, and thence to Raleigh Court House, and to the front and flank of McCausland's command which impelled his retreat.

The Federals then returned to Coal River, and marched by way of Wyoming Court House into Tazewell County, capturing at the head of Abb's Valley, Captain Joel E. Stolling and his company, which were re-captured on the next day by a bold charge made by Colonel A. J. May, at the head of his Kentucky cavalry. The Federals marched rapidly upon Wytheville, then virtually unprotected, entering the same on the evening of the 18th, when a sharp, brisk fight occurred between the enemy and about 130 men badly armed, under Majors Boyer and Bosang, and Captain Oliver with the aid of a few of the citizens of the town. The enemy after the loss of Colonel Toland, who was killed, Colonel Powell dangerously wounded and left a prisoner, and having some 75 or 80 men killed, wounded and captured, retired from the town, first setting it on fire. The Confederates lost three killed, seven wounded, and about 75 captured, including some of the citizens of the town. The Confederates endeavored to intercept and capture this raiding party, by sending troops on and along its most probable routes of retreat. Colonel May, with a portion of his 5th Kentucky regiment, together with Captain Henry Bowen, commanding a company of Tazewell County men of the 8th Virginia cavalry, followed closely, having several collisions and smart skirmishing with its rear guard, but unable to force the party to halt and fight. They finally succeeded in eluding the Confederates, by taking unfrequented paths through Crabtree's gap, over East River Mountain by W. H. Witten's farm, Pealed Chestnuts and over the mountain which led them on to the Tug fork of Sandy, where they were virtually free from successful pursuit.

The Federal Brigadier General Averill having set out from Winchester, Virginia, on the 5th day of August, 1863, with a large force of cavalry and mounted infantry, for the purpose of making a raid into the Greenbrier Valley, and of reaching the Virginia and Tennessee Railroad, marched his command across the mountains into Pocahontas County, where he encountered Colonel William L. Jackson with the 19th Virginia Cavalry, whose command he attacked and drove over the mountain toward Warm Springs.

General G. C. Wharton's brigade, which had been so ordered came over by Staunton to the Jackson River country to meet Averill, who rather suddenly turned back, changing his course toward Lewisburg, when on the 26th of August, about one and one-half miles east of the White Sulphur Springs, he rather unexpectedly encountered a Confederate force under the command of Colonel George S. Patton, consisting of the

22nd and 45th regiments of Virginia infantry, the 23rd and
26th battalions of Virginia infantry, the 8th regiment of Virginia cavalry, the 37th battalion of Virginia cavalry and
Chapman's Monroe County battery of four guns. General
Averill had with him the 16th Illinois cavalry, Company C,
14th Pennsylvania cavalry, 3rd West Virginia cavalry, detachment 2nd West Virginia mounted infantry, 3rd West Virginia mounted infantry, 8th West Virginia mounted infantry
and two West Virginia batteries of six guns. The fight continued from early in the morning on the 26th until about noon
of the 27th, when the enemy drew off, blocking the roads behind him and rendering rapid pursuit impossible, and it had
to be abandoned. The Confederate loss was 162; that of the
enemy 218. The 23rd Virginia battalion of infantry lost three
killed and 18 wounded. Mercer County had one company,
Lilley's, in the 23rd battalion, and Tazewell County had one
company in the 8th Virginia cavalry regiment, and Captain
D. B. Baldwin's company in the 23rd battalion.

Colonel Robert C. Trigg's 54th regiment of Virginia infantry
and Colonel James M. French's 63rd Virginia regiment of
infantry, served in the Chickamauga and other subsequent
campaigns in the Southwest under Generals Bragg and Hood.
In these two regiments were a large number of New River
men, and they made records as good and brave soldiers, ac-
quitting themselves with great credit in all the battles in
which they were engaged.

In the early days of November, 1863, General Averill starting out from Beverly with about three thousand men, passed
over into Pocahontas County and attacked Colonel William
L. Jackson's 19th Virginia regiment of cavalry near Mill Point,
and compelled it to retire to Droop Mountain, where it was reinforced by General Echols with the 22nd Virginia Regiment of
infantry, the 23rd Virginia battalion of infantry, a part of the
14th Virginia regiment of cavalry, Lurty's and Chapman's batteries, aggregating about 1900 men. The command of General
Averill consisted of the 3rd Independent company of Ohio

cavalry, 28th Ohio infantry, 2nd, 3rd, and 8th West Virginia mounted infantry ,and the 10th West Virginia regiment of infantry. After a contest of about six hours duration, the Confederate left having been turned, General Echols withdrew from the contest and retired through Lewisburg and Union, crossing Salt Pond mountain. The Confederate loss in this engagement was 275; among the slain being the gallant Major R. A. Bailey of the 22nd regiment, and among the wounded was the brave and daring Captain John K. Thompson of the same regiment. The Federal loss was 119. While General Echols was engaged in the battle of Droop Mountain, a force of about 1,000 men under the Federal Brigadier General A. N. Duffie, was advancing upon the Kanawha road to Lewisburg, and which threatened to cut off or intercept Echol's retreat. The force from the Kanawha left Charleston on the 3rd of November, and entered Lewisburg on the morning of the 7th, a few hours after the command of General Echols had passed that point.

General Duffie on his way from the Kanawha, was joined at Tyree's by Colonel White with two regiments of infantry, and on reaching Lewisburg joined General Averill's forces, bringing their aggregate up to about 5,000 men. The Federals followed the retreating troops of Echols to Second Creek in Monroe County, and then retraced their steps by way of Meadow Bluff, and in the direction of Beverly.

General Averill, seemingly not satisfied with his previous attempts to reach the Virginia and Tennessee Railroad, set out again for that purpose from New Creek on the 8th day of December with about the same command and same number of men that he had with him in the battle of Droop Mountain. This time he struck for Salem, Virginia, by the most obscure and mountainous routes he could find. He reached Salem on the 16th, destroyed some portions of the railroad track and small bridges, burned a considerable quantity of Confederate commissary stores, and retired beyond the mountains with a loss of 119 men. At the time of Averill's advance to Salem,

General Scammon from the Kanawha, had advanced to and occupied Lewisburg, but soon retired.

Wharton's command had marched from about Covington late in 1863 to the Narrows, and from thence by way of Dublin to East Tennessee, where it joined General Longstreet's command; retiring with it to the neighborhood of Bristol, took up winter quarters at Saltville, where it remained until about the 1st of May, 1864, when it moved to the Valley of Virginia.

General McCausland's command, 36th and 60th Virginia regiments, and other troops, including Bryan's battery wintered at the Narrows, while the brigade of Echols spent the winter in Monroe County. The cavalry brigade of Jenkins during the winter was for the most part on outpost duty in connection with the two Thurmond companies. A part, however, of Jenkins' men were in East Tennessee, where on the 13th day of November, 1863, Corn's 8th Virginia cavalry had a spirited engagement with the enemy, in connection with Colonel Giltner's Kentucky cavalry, in which the enemy was defeated with loss; the 8th Virginia regiment losing one killed and three wounded, and capturing the enemy's wagon train and over 300 prisoners. In December, 1863, Colonel Slemp's 64th Virginia regiment, was driven with loss out of Jonesville, Virginia, by the 16th Illinois cavalry. With the closing of these as the principal events the campaign in Western Virginia and in East Tennessee ended for the year of 1863.

General Lee's army of Northern Virginia, on its return from Gettysburg, had encamped, as heretofore stated, at Bunker's Hill, and in that vicinity. On the 9th of July Pickett's division turned over the Federal prisoners, which were captured at Gettysburg, to the command of General Imboden, and reached camp at Bunker's Hill on the 15th, where it remained until the 19th, and then removed to Smithfield, in Jefferson County. On the 20th it marched to Millwood, and thence to Berry's Ferry on picket duty, and from here on the 21st marched through Front Royal to Chester Gap. On the 22nd it marched all night, reaching Gaines' Cross-roads at daylight on the 23rd, and that night bivouaced at Hazel River. On the 24th it passed through Culpeper Court House and went into camp near the Rapidan. On August 4th Longstreet's and Hill's corps crossed to the South side of the Rapidan, and went into camp in the County of Orange.

The Federal General Meade, in command of the Federal army of the Potomac, having advanced his troops into Culpeper County, and thrown his vanguard out to the Rapidan; General Lee made up his mind to strike him by a flank movement, on his right, by way of Madison Court House, and set out with the army of Northern Virginia about the second week in October. The Federal General immediately withdrew north of the Rappahannock, and finally behind Bull Run, whither Lee followed, and then retired to his winter quarters in Orange. The principal fighting on this expedition was by the cavalry. Longstreet's corps, except Pickett's division, had, on the 9th of September, been detached from the army of Northern Virginia and sent to General Bragg, in Tennessee, and therefore was not with General Lee in his advance against General Meade in October. On the return of General Lee's army to its quarters in Orange, Pickett's division was sent to Taylorsville, Virginia, to rest and recuperate. It spent the early part of the winter at this place.

Captain David A. French, with a section of his battery, and other troops under the command of Colonel A. W. Starke, on August 5th, 1863, marched to Blake's farm, near Deep Bottom on James River, where quite a severe engagement took place with Federal gunboats, which were driven off; after which the command marched to Pickett's farm at Turkey Island, where the attack was renewed on the Federal boats. In these engagements, the loss in French's company was three wounded, viz: Boston Bailey, Henley Clyburn, and Eustace Gibson, the latter reported to have been mortally wounded, but he recovered and lived for many years, and became a prominent man in West Virginia politics, having served two terms in Congress from the Huntington district.

General Pickett having been assigned to the command of the department of North Carolina, Kemper's brigade, now commanded by Colonel Joseph Mayo, Jr., (Kemper having been disabled at Gettysburg), on the 8th day of January, 1864, broke camp at Taylorsville, and took up its line of march through Richmond and on to Petersburg, where it was put aboard a railroad train and transported to Goldsboro, North Carolina, where it remained but a few days. On Saturday, the 29th, the brigade marched to Kingston on the Neuse, and thence through bogs, swamps, and mud, crossing the Trent to the vicinity of Newberne, where some Federal prisoners were taken and a gunboat blown up by Lieutenant Wood, of the Confederate Navy. Among the captured prisoners were some 35 of the 2nd Loyal North Carolina regiment, and who had been Confederate soldiers, but had deserted and joined the enemy. They were recognized, sent to Kinston, tried by Court Martial, condemned and hung. About the middle of February, 1864, the brigade moved to Goldsboro, where it remained until the 5th of March, when it was transported by rail to Wilmington, and from that place by steamer to Smithfield, at the mouth of the Cape Fear. The 24th Virginia regiment was sent to garrison Fort Caswell, the remaining regiments were in bivouac near the town of Smithfield. Leaving the latter named place on Friday, March 25th, by steamer, the brigade reached Wilmington on the morning of the 26th, to find the ground covered with snow, which increased in depth as the train carrying the men receded from the coast. The brigade debarked from the cars at Goldsboro, where it went into bivouac, and remained until Friday, April 1st, when it again set off, marching through snow and mud to Tarboro, which was reached on the 3rd; the distance marched being fifty miles in less than three days. On the 10th orders were issued to be ready to move, and on the morning of the 15th the command began its march down the Tar through Greenville, and across to the Roanoke, to the vicinity of Plymouth, which was reached on the evening of the 17th. The Confederate troops engaged in this enterprise were Ransom's and Hoke's North Carolina brigades and Kemper's Virginia brigade, all commanded by Brigadier General Robert F. Hoke. The Federal troops holding the town of Plymouth, consisted of the 16th Connecticut regiment, 2nd Massachusetts heavy artillery, 2nd North Carolina, companies B and E, 12th New York cavalry, companies A and F, 85th New York, 24th New York battery, 101st Pennsylvania, and 103 Pennsylvania; aggregating 2834 men, all under the command of Brigadier General Wessells. The fight opened on the evening of the 17th, and continued until 10 o'clock A. M. on the 20th, when General Wessells surrendered himself and troops to the Confederates as prisoners of war. The Confederate Ram Albemarle came down the Roanoke on the 19th and joined in the attack, greatly aiding in the success of the battle. The Confederates lost about 300 men, Colonel Mercer, of the 21st Georgia of Hoke's brigade, being among the slain. Company D of the 7th Virginia lost A. L. Fry, and John W. East, wounded.

After only a few hours rest, General Hoke, on the evening of the same day on which Plymouth had fallen, turned the head of his column toward Washington on the Pamlico Sound, which point he reached that night, and immediately prepared to take it by assault; when on the next morning it was found that the enemy had evacuated the place and retired upon Newberne, whither General Hoke immediately marched, and made ready to assault that place; from which, however, he was recalled on the 6th day of May with hurry orders to go to the defense of Petersburg, now threatened, and about to be assailed by the Federal General Butler, who had landed at City Point on the James with a large army and was advancing upon the city. General Hoke, at the head of his command, left the front of Newberne on the 6th day of May, 1864, and by a rapid march passed through Petersburg before noon of Thursday, the 12th, a distance of nearly 175 miles by the route traveled. Mr. D. H. Hill, Jr., in his Confederate Military History of North Carolina, on page 248, speaking of this march of General Hoke from Newberne to Petersburg, says: "This march of General Hoke's troops stands at West Point as the most rapid movement of troops on record." These troops of Hoke moved across the Appomattox and out to Swift Creek, and formed in line of battle, and lay upon their arms the night of the 12th. On moving forward on the morning of the 13th, it was found that the enemy had drawn his lines back towards Bermuda Hundreds, and the Confederates were allowed to pursue their way along the turnpike in the direction of Richmond; halting, however, within the defences of Drury's Bluff.

The armies of Lee and Grant were in a death grapple at Spottsylvania, and no help could come from Lee's army, proper, to meet General Butler's menace against Richmond and Petersburg.

General Beauregard had hastened up from the South, with all troops from his military district that could be spared, so that by the 15th he had assembled an army in and around Petersburg and the defenses of Drury's Bluff, aggregating a little more than 13,000 men. Immediately organizing his troops into divisons, he prepared to attack the enemy, who had now drawn his lines closely up to and around the Drury's Bluff defenses. Beauregard's left division, under Major General Robert Ransom, and which was to lead the attack, was composed of Gracie's Alabama brigade, Hoke's North Carolina brigade, commanded by Colonel Lewis, Barton's Virginia brigade by Colonel Fry, and Kemper's Virginia brigade commanded by Colonel Terry. At two o'clock A. M. on Monday, the 16th, the various commands moved to the respective places assigned them. Among the batteries of artillery assigned to and which fought with General Ransom's division, was that of Captain David A. French, commanded in the early morning of that day by Lieutenant Daniel W. Mason. Its losses were as follows, viz: Wounded, Hugh Hurley, William Kelly, Charles E. Pack, D. C. Robinson, and William Woodyard. It may be here noted that this battery under the command of

Captain French, with Armistead's, and some infantry supports, all under the command of Colonel Starke, on the 6th day of May, 1864, had quite a spirited engagement with the enemy's gunboats on the James, driving them off without loss to the Confederates.

Before daylight on the morning of the 16th of May, 1864, Ransom's division of four brigades, 19 regiments, opened the battle on the Confederate left, which was immediately taken up along the whole line, and raged with varying fortune for several hours, but resulted in the defeat of the enemy, and his withdrawal and retirement within his fortified lines at Bermuda Hundreds, with a loss of about 4500, that of the Confederates being 2827. The loss in Kemper's brigade of four regiments, the 3rd Virginia being on detached duty in North Carolina, and did not reunite with the brigade until the 28th of June, was 57 killed, 264 wounded; the loss in the 1st Virginia was 12 killed, 25 wounded; in the 7th regiment 2 killed, 37 wounded; in the 11th regiment, 15 killed, 94 wounded; in the 24th regiment, 28 killed, 108 wounded; among the latter the gallant Lieutenant Colonel Richard L. Maury, seriously, and Major Joseph Hambrick, mortally, the former falling within a few steps of the enemy's line of works. Company D of the 7th lost John W. East and John S. Dudley, wounded; and the Mercer company of the 24th regiment lost James Calloway, F. M. Mullins, Joseph Stovall, and George Smiley killed, and Harvey G. White, and others whose names the author has been unable to secure, wounded.

Kemper's brigade captured four flags, and 458 prisoners, including Brigadier General Heckman, of New Jersey, who was captured by Sergeant Blakey of company F, 7th regiment, General Heckman surrendering his sword and pistols to Colonel C. C. Flowerree, of the 7th regiment. An account of the charge of Kemper's brigade in this battle, the capture of the Federal General Heckman by Sergeant Blakey, and the flag of the 23rd Massachusetts regiment by the 7th Virginia regiment has been written and published by Mr. Tristram Griffith,

of a Massachusetts regiment, and who was a participant in
this battle. He writes as follows: "During the night of the
15th General Beauregard moved Ransom's division from its
position in reserve on the Turnpike, in rear of his center, to
his left, crossed Kingsland Creek by the Old Stage Road and by
daylight of the morning of the 16th had them in a double line
of battle in an open field with their left well overlapping the
right of the Union line. At early dawn in a dense fog that
made it impossible to distinguish friend from foe, Ransom's
division moved forward and by a right half wheel attempted
to crush Butler's right, get possession of the road to his base
of supplies, and destroy his army. The 23rd Alabama battalion and the 41st Alabama regiment deployed as a heavy
line of skirmishers well to the left of the line of advance, and
the 60th Alabama on the left of the first line swung around the
right of the Union line, took the seven companies of the 9th
New Jersey posted on the right of the Old Stage Road in front
and flank, killing and wounding ten officers and 120 men, and
drove them from their position to the rear. The 23rd Alabama
battalion and the 41st Alabama regiment by this time massed
into a strong line of battle, swung to the left, passed down the
road nearly to the Gregory house, Heckman's headquarters,
and halted. The 60th Alabama passed over the few logs
thrown up during the night by the 9th New Jersey, and when
the right touched the Old Stage Road they, too, halted. The
43rd and 59th Alabama on the right of the 60th struck the
Federal line of battle in front of the 23rd and 27th Massachusetts. Before reaching the edge of the woods they became
demoralized, and General Gracie, who commanded them, sent
word to the line in rear for assistance. Kemper's brigade advanced to the help of General Gracie. The 24th and the 11th
Virginia of Kemper's brigade passed over the 43rd and 59th
Alabama, and went into the edge of the woods within a hundred feet of the Federal line, where they lost their organization, and lay down to escape the heavy fire. The 7th and the
1st of Kemper's brigade, on the left of the 24th and 11th Vir-

ginia, passed over about the same ground as did the 23rd
Alabama battalion and 60th Alabama. The right flank of the
1st Virginia struck the two companies of the 9th New Jersey,
who, unconscious that the seven companies of their regiment
on the right of the road had been driven to the rear, and that
their right flank was exposed, were bravely holding their position. Without obeying the order to surrender, and without
sending word to the 23rd Massachusetts, across the little brook
on their left they ran pell-mell down the road into the rear
of the 41st Alabama, where in astonishment they surrendered.
The 1st Virginia passing over the light log work built by the
Jersey men, took a right half wheel through the woods and
brush, crossed the little brook, when their right flank came
unexpectedly among the men of Company G on the right flank
of the 23rd Massachusetts. Captain Raymond, who had just
taken command of the 23rd, Colonel Chambers having been
sent to the rear, mortally wounded, was near the right of the
line. The first intimation he had that our right had been
turned, was when he saw the Confederates among the men
of his company, and heard them calling out, "surrender!" He
instantly gave the order, "Change front to rear on left company," but, in the thick wood and fog and the confusion of
battle the order was not understood. The men broke back as
they saw those on their right go, leaving all but two of their
right flank company in the hands of the enemy. The color
guard and colors kept together and about 150 feet in the rear
of the line came in contact with the left of the 1st Virginia,
who gave them a volley, killing and wound several of the men.
Corporal Charles D. Fernald, carrying the State colors, moved
back toward the old line of battle, and joined a group of the
men of the regiment centered around Lieutenant Wheeler, of
Heckman's staff. Lieutenant Wheeler being just then mortally
wounded and some one calling out "Ralley on the 27th," Fernald
and some others moved in that direction and joined the right
of that regiment. Colonel Lee, of the 27th, had been informed
that there was trouble on the right by several of the men and

officers of the 23rd who ran by him. Doubting the report, he passed to the right of his regiment to investigate, and about twenty feet beyond he found himself surrounded by the advancing enemy, to whom he was obliged to surrender.

"Let us now go back to the advance of Kemper's brigade to the assistance of General Gracie, and follow the course of the 7th Virginia, as this regiment played an important part in the capture of General Heckman, and the State flag of the 23rd Massachusetts. When the 1st Virginia entered the woods, passed up the Old Stage Road over the position vacated by the two companies of the 9th New Jersey, and wheeled to the right toward the right flank of the 23rd Massachusetts, the 7th Virginia advancing on their left, struck a bog that separated the two or three left flank companies from the rest of the regiment, and left them in the rear at the edge of the woods. When Colonel Flowerree was informed of the fact, he sent his Adjutant, John H. Parr, after them to return them to their places in line, while he continued to move forward with his regiment around the Federal right flank. In wheeling to the right and just after crosing the Old Stage Road, this regiment captured General Heckman. The General, taking this advancing regiment for reinforcements, was about to order it to change front, when seeing his mistake, he tried to pass himself off for a rebel officer. Sergeant Blakey, of Company G of the 7th Virginia, could not be fooled, and the General declining to surrender to anyone but a line officer, was marched by Blakey to Colonel Flowerree, to whom General Heckman gave up his sword.

"To go back to John H. Parr and the two or three companies of the 7th Virginia, which he found stuck in the bog at the edge of the woods; he moved them to the left around the bog and led the way through the woods in an effort to overtake his regiment. Mistaking his course, he took a much shorter wheel, which brought him, with his two or three companies, around the left flank of the 1st Virginia, and upon

the right rear of the 27th Massachusetts, just after the
23rd Massachusetts had broken to the rear, and at just
the moment when the 11th Virginia, and detachments forming the 59th Alabama, who were lying down in the edge of
the woods, and who noticing from the Federal line in
their front that the firing had ceased, moved forward and
joined the 1st Virginia, passing over the ground just vacated
by the 23rd Massachusetts, upon the right flank of the 27th
Massachusetts. It was these rebel regiments that Colonel Lee
walked into when he stepped to the right of his regiment to
see if the 23rd Massachusetts had fallen back. When Colonel
Lee had surrendered, Adjutant John H. Parr, of the 7th Virginia, who had led the two or three companies of his regiment
around the Federal right flank, rushed forward and seized the
staff of the State flag of the 23rd Massachusetts, carried by
Corporal Charles G. Fernald."

The morning succeeding the battle, Kemper's brigade, with
other troops, pursued the enemy to Howlett's house on the
James, where there was an unfinished Confederate earthwork.
The 1st and 7th regiments were sent to hold these earthworks.
The enemy's gunboats in the river opened on the works, and
continued the shelling throughout the evening and night. During the shelling Major Howard, of the 1st regiment, and
Sergeant Thomas Fox, of the same regiment, were seriously
wounded. On the next morning, the 18th, Lieutenant John
W. Mullins, of company D of the 7th, in command of the skirmish line, received a wound from which he died on the 22nd
day of the succeeding month.

Withdrawing on the evening of the 18th, the brigade marched to the neighborhood of Manchester, bivouaced for the night,
and next morning marched through Richmond to the station
of the Fredericksburg and Potomac Railroad; placed aboard
flat cars and moved to Milford station, debarked, moved
across the Mattaponi and bivouaced. There were present of
the brigade at Milford, on the morning of the 21st of May,

about 60 men of the 1st Virginia, seven companies of the 11th
Virginia, numbering about 225, and the 7th Virginia, numbering about 250, making an aggregate of 535. About ten o'clock
A. M., there was a call to arms, and report of the approach of
a body of Federal cavalry, supposed to be a mere raiding party,
but, as subsequently developed, was the Federal cavalry division of General Torbett, leading the advance of General
Grant's army from Spottsylvania Court House toward Richmond. After a spirited contest of more than an hour, in which
the Federal cavalry charges were repeatedly repulsed, the
troops under the command of Major George F. Norton, of the
1st regiment, were withdrawn across the river, dismantling
the bridge to such an extent as to prevent immediate and close
pursuit by the enemy. The Confederate loss in this affair was
about 70, mostly captured, being unable to reach the bridge
in advance of the enemy. The loss sustained was mostly in
the 11th regiment; numbers of the men escaping by swim-
ming the river. The brigade continued its movement until it
joined General Lee's army, en route from Spottsylvania to
the North Anna. On reaching Hanover Junction, the command joined the remainder of the brigade, and the other brigades of Pickett's divison. Here too, was Breckenridge's division from the valley, fresh from the victorious field of New
Market.

The division of Pickett, again united, marched with the
army to Cold Harbor, taking position in the battle line on the
left of Hoke's division, which on the 3rd of June, in co-operation with Breckenridge's, bore the brunt of the Federal assault, in which General Grant lost about as many men in
twenty minutes as Hoke and Breckenridge had in their commands.

In this battle of Cold Harbor, Pickett's men had but little or
no part, beyond severe skirmishing, and receiving a heavy
shelling from the enemy. As a matter of fact, General Lee had
succeeded in repulsing the larger part of General Grant's
army with only a small part of his own. It is stated that the

Federal loss in the assault on June 3rd, was 12,737, while the Confederates lost less than 2,000 men.

On the march from Milford station to Hanover junction, John A. Hale, of Company D, 7th regiment, with a comrade from the regiment, broke completely down, and found themselves within the enemy's lines where they remained for two or three days. Hungry and starving, they ventured to a dwelling to obtain food; finding there a Federal soldier on the same errand, they captured him and took him along with them, until they got within the Confederate lines.

In this battle of Cold Harbor, there were in Breckenridge's division a number of New River Valley men, belonging to companies of the 23rd Virginia battalion, 26th Virginia battalion and 30th Virginia battalion. Very considerable losses in killed and wounded was suffered by these commands, but in the absence of official data it cannot be given. Lieutenant James K. Peck, of the 23rd Virginia battalion, and a Giles County man, was killed; and Colonel George Edgar, commanding the 26th battalion, was wounded by a bayonet thrust and captured. Captain James Dunlap, of Monroe, and Lieutenant W. W. George, of Mercer, were also captured.

In a few days after the battle of Cold Harbor, General Breck-enridge, with his division, marched for the Valley of Virginia, to meet the army of General Hunter, now endeavoring to reach Lynchburg. On the 12th of June General Lee detached his 2nd army corps under Lieutenant General Early, and pushed it to Lynchburg. The retreat of Hunter and the operations of Early's command and that of General Breckenridge, will be taken up in relating the campaigns of 1864 in Western Virginia, Southwestern Virginia, in the Valley, and in Maryland.

General Grant, convinced of his inability to enter Richmond on the line he was traveling, on the night of the 12th of June changed his course, moving direct for the James, followed by the Confederates marching on parallel lines. The line of march of Pickett's division, carried it over the old battle ground of Gaines' mill, crossing the Chickahominy over Mc-

Clellan's bridge near Seven Pines, and halting near the battle field of Frazier's farm; on the 15th marched up Darbytown road a short distance and went into bivouac. Daybreak on the morning of the 16th found the division in line and on the march to the James at Caffin's Bluff, where it crossed the river on a pontoon bridge; passing over the battle field of Drury's Bluff on to the Turnpike road; and had reached a point near Walthall Junction, where the head of the column was unexpectedly fired into by the enemy, who had gained possession of the road. The division was quickly formed in battle line, and sending ahead a strong skirmish line, drove the enemy beyond the first line of earthworks, which had that morning been evacuated by the Confederate troops, who had been called to the defense of Petersburg. About four o'clock, P. M., the divison charged along the whole line, retaking the whole outer line erected by General Beauregard's troops before their removal to Petersburg. This assault was not without loss, and brought from General Lee to Major General Anderson, the corps commander, General Longstreet having been severely wounded in the battle of the Wilderness, the following letter:

"General:—I take great pleasure in presenting to you my congratulation upon the conduct of the men of your corps. I believe that they will carry anything they are put against. We tried very hard to stop Pickett's men from capturing the breastworks of the enemy, but couldn't do it. I hope his loss has been small."

The brigade loss was about twenty killed and wounded. In the 7th regiment, Sergeant William Parrott, of Company I, Corporal J. B. Young, of Company D, were severely, and William Davis, of Company C, mortally wounded.

From the 16th day of June, 1864, until the 5th day of March, 1865, Pickett's division occupied the line from Howlett's house, on the James, to Swift Creek and Fort Clifton, on the Appomattox. The minor occurrences within this period, on, along,

within and immediately without, the lines of the division
would fill a volume.

. The enemy's advance on the north side of the James, and
his capture of Fort Harrison, on the morning of September
29th, drew to that side of the river, among other Confederate
troops, four regiments from Pickett's division, including the
24th Virginia regiment, all under the command of Colonel
Montague. An unsuccessful assault was led by General Hoke
against Fort Harrison on the morning of the 30th of September, in which the 24th Virginia suffered severe loss.

The battery of Captain David A. French was also engaged
in this battle at Fort Harrison, and met with the following
loss, viz: Killed, Adam Johnston; wounded, Lieutenant W.
H. Smith, Privates E. W. Charlton, John M. Walker, John
Burton, Joshua Day, Henry Hicks, John Ingrahan, and Erastus W. Peck. This company was engaged in the battle of Fussells' Mills, on the north side of the James, on the 19th of
August, 1864, and its casualties were as follows: Killed,
Henry Stover; wounded, Sergeant John N. Woodram, mortally; H. C. Clyburn, and William J. Sarver. The Federal loss
in and around Fussells' Mill was 2901, out of the 2nd and 10th
army corps.

During the months of July, August ,September and October,
the regiments and brigades of Pickett's division were frequently shifted along the line it was holding, and which has been
described. Frequent combats, in the shape of sharpshooting,
took place, and occasionally the Confederate skirmishers, and
twice in larger body, made sallies against the enemy's rifle
pits, gathering in large numbers of prisoners. On one of these
expeditions they swept the Federal picket line for several
hundred yards, bringing away without loss more than one
hundred prisoners, including the Federal officers in command
of the line. For the most part of the period between June,
1864, and March 5th, 1865, the pickets of the combatants on
this line were on friendly terms; so much so, that the Confed-

erate officers had to require the picket firing to be resumed in order to break up these friendly relations, which had been carried to the extent of regular traffic between the pickets in the way of barter and exchange of newspapers, tobacco, coffee and other articles. In many places along the line the pickets were near enough to each other that they could carry on conversation in any ordinary tone of voice.

The cold winter winds began to be felt in the close of the November days, and the men, in addition to their bomb proofs and mud houses in the earth, began to improve them as far as possible, in view of the approaching cold weather, by building flues or chimneys, and closing up all openings. The men were not only thinly clad, but some, at least, had but little clothing of any kind, and a large number were without shoes; and when the first blasts of winter came numbers could be seen shivering over the small fires they were allowed to kindle. Famine stared them in the face; the ration being from one-eighth to one-fourth of a pound of becan and one pint of unseived corn meal per day, and occasionally a few beans or peas. With empty stomachs, naked bodies, and frozen fingers, these men clutched their guns with an aim so steady and deadly that the men on the other side were exceedingly cautious how they lifted their heads from behind their sheltered places.

This was not altogether the worst part of the situation, for many a good brave Confederate soldier heard in his rear the cries of distrees of a mother, wife, or children at home, whose needs were as great for bread as his. What could he do? What should he do? This, with his own pitiable condition, was enough to break the strongest heart. It was too much for some, who broke away to look after the suffering ones at home. "How could the Government do any better?" was often said. Whatever food it had for the army was mostly in the far-off South, and could not be brought forward, either for lack of transportation or by reason of the enemy having cut or destroyed the lines of communication.

The private soldier received $11.00 per month for his services

—about enough to buy his tobacco. Confederate money had become worthless, and the price of provisions—that is, where any could be found for sale—was beyond the reach of the poor soldier. Flour was selling for $1500.00 per barrel; bacon $20.00 per pound, beef $15.00 a pound, butter at $20.00 a pound; one chicken could be had for $50.00, soda $12.00 per pound, common calico $12.00 per yard; and at the date, January and February, 1865, it took $100.00 in the currency to buy one dollar in gold. But this currency was all we had, good, bad or indifferent—it was use that or nothing—and the soldier had but little of it, and did not have this little long. Some one wrote on the back of $500.00 Confederate note, about, or just after the surrender at Appomattox, the following lines:

"Representing nothing on God's earth now,
  And naught in water below it,
As a pledge of a nation that's dead and gone,
  Keep it, dear captain, and show it.
Show it to those that will lend an ear
  To the tale this paper can tell
Of liberty born, of the patriot's dream,
  Of a storm-cradled nation that fell.

Too poor to possess the precious ore,
  And too much a stranger to borrow,
We issue today our "promise to pay,"
  And hope to redeem on the morrow.
Days roll by, and weeks became years,
  But our coffers were empty still;
Coin was so rare that the treasury quaked
  If a dollar should drop in the till.

But the faith that was in us was strong indeed,
  And our poverty well we discerned,
And these little checks represented the pay
  That our suffering Veterans earned.
We knew it had hardly a value in gold,
  Yet as gold the soldiers received it;
It gazed in our eyes with a promise to pay,
  And each patriot soldier believed it.

But our boys thought little of price or pay,
  Or of bills that were over-due;
We knew if it brought our bread today
  'Twas the best our country could do.
Keep it! It tells all our history over,
  From the birth of the dream to its last;
Modest, and born of the Angel Hope,
  Like our hope of success, it passed."

Notwithstanding all these things, these heroic men, who loved their cause better than life, stood to their posts, and defied the enemy to the last. The enemy, by general orders and circular letters which they managed to send and scatter among the Confederate soldiers, offered all manner of inducements to have them desert their country; but, as a rule, such offers were indignantly spurned. The consecration of the Southern women to the cause for which their husbands, sons, brothers, and sweethearts struggled and suffered, is beyond the power of pen to describe. The hardships of these women were equal to, and often greater than that of the shivering, freezing, starving soldier in the field. They had not only given these men to the cause, but, in fact, themselves, too; for they remained at home and labored in the fields, went to mill, the blacksmith shops, lived on corn bread and sorghum molasses, and gave practicaly every pound of meat, flour and all the vegetables they could raise to the men in the army, whom they encouraged to duty in every possible way. They manufactured largely their own clothing, out of material that they had produced with their own hands; and would have scorned any woman who would wear northern manufactured goods; and the thought, sentiment, and action is well expressed in lines written during the war:

"Now northern goods are out of date,
  And since old Abe's blockade,
We Southern girls can be content,
  With goods that's Southern made;
We send our sweethearts to the war,
  But girls never you mind—
Your soldier lover will not forget
  The girl he left behind.

"And now young man, a word to you:
  If you would win the fair,
Go to the field where honor calls
  And win your lady there;
Remember that our brightest smiles
  Are for the true and brave,
And that our tears are all for those
  Who fill the soldier's grave."

Through this long, cold, dreary winter, Pickett's division—less than five thousand strong—held the line which, in length,

was not less than four miles; being not many beyond one
thousand men to the mile; only a good skirmish line; over
which the enemy, by a bold, determined charge, could at any
time have gone. It is certain that if the Federal line in front
of Pickett's men had been as weak, and held by as few men as
that of Pickett, they would have either been prisoners before
the 1st day of January, 1865, or have been driven into the
James and drowned.

Every effort was being put forth by the Confederate authorities to bring every available man to the field; the men from
the division on detail or detached service were required to
report to their respective regiments, and their places to be
filled with those unable for active field service. This order
gave great concern to many who had been out in good and
easy places. Sergeant Charles T. Loehr in his "History of
the 1st Virginia Regiment," tells of a Mr. Stegar, of Company
D of that regiment, who did not relish his return to his company, and who wrote:

"THE BOMB-PROOF'S LAMENT."

"With all my heart I hate to part,
  For I'm not happy to be free,
And it will surely break my heart
  To send me back to company D.

We had a snug detail together,
  But Uncle Bob has clipped our wings,
And spring will be but gloomy weather
  If doomed to fight Old Grant in spring.

Farewell, and when some sickly fellow
  Shall claim this bomb-proof I resign,
And three miles in the rear discover
  What ease and safety once were mine."

The new year was approaching; it was to bring nothing to
cheer our aching hearts, but much to depress them. No hope
for peace, nor settlement, or relief from our unfortunate situation. The men who were christians prayed earnestly every
day for the return of peace to our distracted country; and in
the dead hour of the night, often could be seen men on their
knees, engaged in earnest appeals to God for our country and

for peace. Finally in the latter part of January, 1865, there was a rift in the dark cloud which overhung our sky, when it was announced that Confederate Commissioners were on their way to meet the Federal President, to attempt to adjust the unhappy differences. This was known throughout the army, and the men gathered in groups with faces all aglow with intense interest, to discuss the grave question. The one unanimous voice was, settle it, if possible on any terms that are fair and honorable. The return of these Commissioners with the report that no settlement could be made other than downright submission, cast a deep and heavy gloom over the faces of the men, who, but a few days before, had been happy in the hope of a peaceful and honorable termination of hostilities. Gloom and despair were plainly depicted on the faces of some of the men, while grim determination was to be seen on the faces of others. The situation is probably better expressed by telling first of an incident that happened with one of the men of the 7th Virginia regiment, and then the action taken by a large part of the soldiers in the way of meetings and resolutions. This man of the 7th regiment seemed very much dejected and downcast, when he heard of the failure of the Commisioners to make an adjustment of our troubles, and one of his comrades inquiring of him as to what was his trouble, he replied: "Well, the Peace Conference is a failure, Lincoln has called for more men, and President Davis says, 'war to the knife'; what shall we do?"

The Federal soldier was as anxious for peace as the Confederate could possibly be. About the time of the return of the Peace Commissioners it is told of a Federal soldier, that, in the presence of one of his officers, he remarked that he was anxious for the war to close and for the return of peace, and that he knew of a plan by which Richmond could be captured, and that would end the war and bring peace. His officer insisted upon his telling what the plan was that he had for the capture of Richmond; that General Grant ought to know of the plan if feasible. The soldier said he felt not only some hesitancy, but a delicacy in stating it, but if the officer insisted he would tell him. Finally, the officer prevailed on the soldier to divulge his plan, which was this: "Swap Generals; bring General Lee over here and put him in command of this army, and he will have Richmond in twenty-four hours."

As already stated, on the return of the Peace Commissioners with their report of the failure to settle matters, meetings of the soldiers were held in many of the companies and regiments throughout the army, to discuss the situation, in which resolutions were adopted expressive of their views. Among the companies which held such meetings was that of Captain David A. French, the minutes of which meeting are as follows:

"Darby Town Road, February 6, 1865.

At a meeting convened in the Stonewall Detachment, Corporal Charles E. Pack was called to the chair, O. F. Jordan appointed secretary, and the following preamble and resolutions were adopted:

Whereas, we believe that the Confederate authorities have taken appropriate measures to bring about an honorable peace to the Confederacy;

And whereas, said measures have failed to bring about this most desirable result, owing to obstinacy and tyrannical disposition of the Federal authorities; in this, that they refuse all offers of peace, and will listen to nothing save an humble submission on the part of the Confederates:

We, the members of the Stonewall Detachment, Captain D. A. French's battery, do resolve: that we will listen to no terms the least degrading to brave men and free men. That come weal or woe, we will now fight it out at the cost of every drop of blood that flows in our veins; that there is no sacrifice too dear, no danger too hazardous, no suffering too great, that we will not endure for our country and cause; and we pledge ourselves anew to stand by our flag and guns while the one waves, and there is room to work the other."

C. E. Pack, Chairman.

O. F. Jordan, Secretary.

During the fall of 1864, and the early part of the winter of that year, the country had reached such a condition that starvation was not only staring the army in the face, threatening its disintegration and disbanding, but the people at home, in many localities, were suffering for the very necessaries of life, and good people among them, some of even the leading men, had reached the conclusion that the contest could not longer be maintained; they, therefore, were for peace on any terms, and if the Confederate authorities were not willing to take immediate steps to that end, that the people would be placed in position to discourage the continuance of the contest by every means within their power.

The Federal authorities, including the commanding officers of their armies, as well as their spies, emmissaries, and scouts, encouraged the peace feeling by holding out all manner of inducements to the people, and to the soldiers in the army; and by secret orders and organizations among our people and soldiers, sought to influence the people to withdraw their support from the armies, and to encourage the soldiers to abandon the cause for which we had fought for nearly four years. Organizations were found to exist in Southwestern and Western Virginia, known by the names of: "Heroes of America," "Red String," and "White String Party," which had regular signs and pass-words. Into these were drawn, as reported, some of the prominent and leading citizens, and had even partly permeated the army, particularly the 22nd and 54th Virginia regiments of infantry. How far they affected these organizations, and how far their influence reached, it is difficult to say; but it alarmed the Confederate authorities and was made the subject of investigation by the Secretary of War, Mr. Seddon. For a full history of this matter with the names disclosed of persons connected therewith, the reader is referred to Rebellion Records, Series IV, Vol. 3, pp. 804-16.

Returning to affairs in Western and Southwestern Virginia, and resuming the narrative of events at the close of 1863, we find that in December of that year, the 16th Virginia cavalry, commanded by Colonel Milton J. Ferguson, spent the latter part of December, and a part of the following two months, in the Valley of the Sandy, penetrating to the Kanawha River, where a detachment of that regiment, in February of 1864, captured a steam boat on which was Brigadier General Scammon, of the Federal army, who was also captured, brought out and sent to Richmond in charge of Lieutenant E. G. Vertigan, his captor.

On January 3rd, 1863, Brigadier General William E. Jones with his cavalry command, in which, at the time, was the 8th Virginia regiment, partly made up of Tazewell and Mercer County men, attacked a Federal force at Jonesville, Virginia, which he defeated, capturing 385 prisoners, killing 10, wounding 45, taking three pieces of artillery and a number of wagons. The 8th Virginia lost Lieutenant A. H. Samuels and four men killed and 7 wounded.

Echols' brigade, with part of Jenkins' cavalry, spent the winter in Monroe and Greenbrier Counties. McCausland's brigade, with the 17th cavalry, wintered at the Narrows and at Princeton; while Wharton's brigade was in East Tennessee and about Saltville.

The enemy in the Kanawha Valley, early in the spring, began to assemble a force of infantry, cavalry, and artillery, under Brigadier General George Crook, for the purpose of an advance towards the Virginia and Tennessee Railroad; and at the same time a large force of the enemy was preparing to march up the Valley of Virginia to Staunton.

Major General Breckenridge, on the 5th of March, 1864, had relieved General Jones, in command of the department of Southwestern Virginia. In the latter part of April and the first days of May, these Federal divisions from the Kanawha, and in the Valley of Virginia, commenced their advance. General Breckenridge was called to the Virginia Valley, drawing to him the brigade of Echols and Wharton. McCausland's brigade had also been ordered to the Valley, but the advance

of General Crook's column held him at Dublin, with Jenkins'
cavalry brigade at Narrows, with Bryan's battery, Ringgold,
and Botetourt artillery, under the command of Brigadier
General Jenkins.

The Federal cavalry leader in Western Virginia, Brigadier
General Averill, with 2479 officers and men, left the Kanawha
River above Charleston on the 1st of May, by way of Logan
and Wyoming Court Houses, to Abb's Valley in Tazewell
County, and from thence on the road to Wytheville, near
which, on the 10th of May, he encountered a Confederate force
under General William E .Jones, and was defeated. In this
battle was the 16th Virginia cavalry regiment in part composed of Tazewell County men. The loss of General Averill
was 100 in killed and wounded, himself among the wounded.
He drew off his troops and passed down Walker's Creek by
Shannon's and to Pepper's ferry, where he crossed New River,
and from thence proceeded to Blacksburg and Christiansburg;
turning northward in an effort to follow General Crook, he
encountered at Gap Mountain, near Newport in Giles County,
Jenkins' cavalry brigade, and part of the troops of Colonel
William L. Jackson, all under the command of Colonel William H. French, of Mercer, by whom he was driven back, and
forced to retreat by a bridle path over the mountains into
Monroe County, where he joined General Crook, who was
closely followed by Jackson's command; Colonel French's
troops returning to the Narrows.

General Crook left the Kanawha River on the second day
of May, with eleven regiments of infantry, a part of two regiments of cavalry, and two battalions of artillery, aggregating
6,155 men. The march was made by way of Fayetteville,
Raleigh Court House, Princeton, Rocky Gap, and Shannon's,
to Cloyd's farm on Back Creek in Pulaski County; where on
the 9th of May he found the command of General Jenkins,
consisting of the 36th, 45th and 60th Virginia regiments and
45th battalion of Virginia infantry, with Bryan's, Ringgold's
and Douthat's Virginia batteries, drawn up in line of battle

to meet him; with an aggregate force, then, and that of Major
Smith, who joined after the retreat began, of less than 3,000
men. The battle was a fierce and bloody one, and lasted for·
several hours, and the men who fought this battle on the
Confederate side were largely from the middle New River
Valley and from the upper Clinch waters; they were from
Tazewell, Wythe, Pulaski ,Bland, Montgomery, Giles, Monroe,
Greenbrier, Fayette, Raleigh, Mercer, Boone, Logan, Putnam,
Cabell, Wayne, and perhaps some from other Southern West
Virginia Counties. General Jenkins was mortally wounded
and his command outflanked and driven from the field, with a
loss of 76 killed, 262 wounded, and 200 missing. The loss was
inconsiderable in comparison with the value of the slain,
among whom were some of the bravest and most daring sold-
iers in the army. Lieutenant Colonel Edwin H. Harman, a
brave young officer of great promise, and Captain Robert R.
Crockett, of the 45th regiment were killed. Lieutenant Colonel
George W. Hammond, Major Jacob N. Taylor, and Captain
Moses McClintic, of the 60th Virginia, were killed, and Captain Rufus A. Hale, S. S. Dews, Lieutenants Larue, Austin,
Bailey, and Stevenson, together with a number of others of the
60th and 36th Virginia were wounded, as was Major Thomas
L. Broun, Post Quartermaster at Dublin, dangerously. (1) In
this battle, in the 60th Virginia regiment, were two companies
of Giles County men, one of which was commanded by that
brave, fearless Irishman, Captain Andrew Gott, now of Mercer County. The men of Tazewell County in the 45th regiment
suffered heavy loss in this battle, losing not only the gallant
Lieutenant Colonel Harman, but numbers of others killed or
wounded, among the latter the brave Captain C. A. Fudge.
Bland County was also represented on this field as above
stated; and her sons distinguished themselves in this fight,

(1). Rev. Mr. Hickman, a Presbyterian minister, was killed on this
field. Judge E. Ward and Hon. William Prince accompanied the Confederate soldiers to this field and were under the enemy's fire. Prince,
while acting as special messenger and courier, had his horse shot under him.

losing many of their best and bravest killed and wounded, among the latter that tall and heroic youth ,the flag bearer of the 45th, Andrew Jackson Stowers. There also fell on this field, near which was once the home of their ancestor, three remote cousins, viz: Lieutenant A. W. Hoge and his Brother M. J. Hoge of the Ringgold Virginia battery, and George D. Pearis of Bryan's Virginia battery.

The Federal loss in this battle, in killed and wounded, was 688. The Confederates under the command of Colonel John McCausland, who succeeded to the command on the wounding of General Jenkins, retreated by way of the railroad bridge to the East bank of New River, and upon the crossing of the Federals at Pepper's ferry, and their advance to Christiansburg, he continued his retreat to the head waters of the Roanoke. General Crook took fright, and fled across Salt Pond mountain into Monroe County.

No braver or better fight was ever put up in an open field by a body of men so largely outnumbered. (1) The coolness and bravery of Colonel McCausland, and the skillful manner in which he conducted the retreat, with the timely arrival of Major Smith's troops on the field, saved the command from capture or destruction. Colonel McCausland was at once, and deservedly so, made a Brigadier General, and placed in command of Jenkins' cavalry brigade.

General Breckenridge hurried down the Valley of Virginia, with the brigades of Echols and Wharton (2) and other troops, to New Market, where, on the 15th day of May, he met a Federal army some 6,500 strong, under General Sigel, and with less than 5,000 men defeated it with a loss of 831; the Confederate loss being 522. Sigel retreated, and Breckenridge, with his division, moved to Hanover Junction and joined General Lee, leaving General Imboden in command in the Valley, who was shortly thereafter superseded by Brigadier General

(1). The Federal General Crook says, in his report, says: "The enemy remained behind their works until battered away by our men."

(2). Mostly New River Valley men.

William E. Jones, who took with him from Southwest Virginia, McCausland's old brigade of infantry, by which his forces were augmented to about 5,000, including, however, some local bodies of militia, with which to meet about 8,500 Federal troops under the command of Major General David Hunter, who had displaced General Sigel.

At Piedmont in the Valley, on the 5th day of June, Hunter's forces atacked the Confederates, and after a severe and bloody battle of more than five hours the Confederates were badly defeated with heavy loss, and compelled to retreat in much disorder, closely followed by the large body of the enemy's cavalry. General Jones was killed on the field, and the loss in his command in killed and wounded was about 500, besides 1,000 men and several guns captured. (1)   In this battle the men from the New River Valley were engaged and suffered fearfully.   While the Confederates were engaged in this contest, Generals Crook and Averill, with 8,000 to 10,000 men, were rapidly aproaching Staunton from Buffalo Gap on the West, opposed by General McCausland with his brigade and that of Colonel William L. Jackson, who on the occupation of Staunton by Hunter's forces, were compelled to retire.   General Imboden assumed command of the Confederates after the fall of General Jones, and retired to Waynesboro.   In this unfortunate engagement the men from Tazewell, Bland, Giles and Mercer Counties were heavily engaged, and it is to be regretted that the names of those who fell, killed or wounded, have not been preserved.   Here fell the brave and manly Colonel William Henry Brown, of Tazewell, at the head of the 45th Virginia regiment.   The cause claimed no nobler sacrifice than this.   He was born in Tazewell County, and had distinguished himself in the many battles in which his regiment had been engaged.   The loss of the enemy in this battle was 500 in killed and wounded.   In the Giles companies in the 36th Virginia regiment, there were, among others, killed in the battle of Piedmont, W. S. Echols, B. Newton Snidow,

---

(1).   The Federal loss was about 500.

Hamilton Hare, G. B. Chandler; wounded, J. C. Stump, John Kerr, John H. Williams; James W. Hale lost an arm. Lieutenant Thomas G. Jarrell, of a Boone County company, a Mercer County man originally, the son of Mr. George Washington Jarrell, was slain in this battle.

The defeat of General Jones' command left the Valley to Staunton, in fact through to and South of the James River, open to the march of General Hunter's army, now numbering near 20,000 effective men. Hunter did not delay, but pushed on toward Lynchburg, with nothing to oppose save McCausland's cavalry command, which fought him closely and manfully all along the route, and so delayed him that it took him more than a week to march over a good road from Staunton to the front of Lynchburg. It is true that he, Hunter, stopped along the route at Lexington and other points to repeat his acts of vandalism; having in the lower Valley caused the properties of some of his relatives to be burned and destroyed; and after the close of the war it is said, he attempted to conciliate them, but they treated him with scorn and contempt as he deserved, for when his relatives, the females, plead with him to spare their homes he turned a deaf ear:

"As well might you plead with the tiger to pause
When his victim lies writhing and clenched in his claws."

It was these acts of General Hunter, contrary as they were to usages of civilized warfare, that caused the burning of Chambersburg, Pennsylvania, in July of that year.

In November, 1863, a straggling camp follower, or marauding Federal soldier entered the home of Mr. David Creigh near Lewisburg, West Virginia, and attempted by force to enter the room of his daughter, when Mr. Creigh interposed and attempted to eject him; he sought the life of Mr. Creigh, who believing himself in great danger killed the man. General Averill in the spring of 1864, on his retreat with Crook from Cloyd's farm, had Mr. Creigh arrested and tried by a drumhead court martial, which sentenced Mr. Creigh to be hanged, ·

which sentence was approved by General Hunter. See Averill's Report, Vol. 37, Part 1, Rebellion Records, p. 145. The wife of General W. H. Smith has beautifully and fully told this story of the martyr Creigh in verse, which is as follows:

"He lived the life of an upright man,
  And the people loved him well;
Many a wayfarer came to his door,
  His sorrow or need to tell.
A pitying heart and an open hand,
  Gave succor ready and free;
For kind and true to his fellowman
  And a Christian was David Creigh.

But o'er his threshold a shadow passed,
  With a step of a ruffian foe;
While in silent words and brutal threats
  A purpose of darkness show;
And a daughter's wild imploring cry
  Called the father to her side—
His hand was nerved by the burning wrong,
  And there the offender died.

The glory of Autumn had gone from earth,
  The winter had passed away,
And the glad springtime was merging fast
  Into summer's ardent ray,
When a good man from his home was torn—
  Days of toilsome travel to see—
And far from his loved a crown was worn,
  And the martyr was David Creigh.

Here where he lived, let the end be told,
  Of a tale of bitter wrong;
Here let our famishing thousands learn,
  To whom vengeance doth belong.
Short grace was given the dying man,
  E'er led to the fatal tree,
And short the grace to our starving hosts,
  Since the murder of David Creigh.

The beast of the desert shields its young,
  With an instinct fierce and wild,
And lives there a man with the heart of a man
  Who would not defend his child?
So woe to those who call evil good—
  That woe shall not come to me—
War hath no record of fouler deed
  Than the murder of David Creigh.

As has already been noted, General Breckenridge with his division had, on the 10th of June, left Richmond to meet Hunter's forces and prevent their passage through the gaps of the Blue Ridge towards Charlottesville and Richmond. General

Breckenridge, finding Hunter's advance directed toward
Lynchburg, instead of Eastward of the ridge, therefore pushed
his division to the defense of that city, reaching there in advance of Hunter's army, and holding the Federals at bay by
severe fighting until the arrival of General Early with a portion of the 2nd corps of the army of Northern Virginia, on
the 18th. Hunter ascertaining that Early had arrived, took
fright and on the night of the 18th beat a hasty retreat by way
of Liberty and Salem, and across the mountains into Western
Virginia. At Hanging Rock, a Gap in the North Mountain,
on the Salem and Sweet Springs turnpike, a portion of Early's
cavalry struck the flank of Hunter's retreating army, capturing
a portion of his train. In this encounter George Kahle, a
brave young soldier from Mercer County, in a hand to hand
conflict with a Federal soldier, was killed, and the latter slain
on the spot by James O. Cassady, who was also a Mercer man.
Hunter's army now sent in disastrous retreat across the mountains to the Kanawha, and the Valley free from the enemy,
General Early directed the head of his column on the 23rd day
of June towards Staunton, which he reached on the 26th.
With Early was his own corps, to which was added Breckenridge's division, in which were the New River Valley men, not
only in the infantry, but as well in the cavalry and artillery.
Crook's retreat from the New River section had left the Confederate lines along the Western and Southwestern Virginia
border free from any considerable body of the enemy, and
events in the East and in the Valley required the presence of
nearly all the forces that had theretofore operated in Virginia Westward of the Alleghanies.

Resuming his march on the 28th General Early, with his
troops, reached and passed through Winchester on July 3rd.
General McCausland, with his brigade of cavalry, attacked
on July 4th, North Mountain depot on the Baltimore & Ohio
Railroad, capturing 200 prisoners. A portion of Early's infantry under General Gordon, having crossed the Potomac on
the 5th, McCausland's cavalry brigade advanced to Shepherds-

town, and on the 6th to the Antietam, in front of Sharpsburg,
and on the 9th advanced to Frederick City, where he had a
skirmish with the enemy. General Early's troops being fully
up on the 9th, he attacked and defeated, after a fierce and
bloody battle, a Federal army of 10,000 men at the Monocacy
under General Lew Wallace. In this bloody engagement General McCausland's cavalry brigade performed prodigies of
valor and suffered severe loss. The Confederate loss was about
700; that of the Federals reported at 1968. In the 17th Virginia cavalry were three companies from Mercer County, commanded by Captains Graybeal, Gore, and Straley, respectively.
This regiment, as already heretofore stated, belonged to Mc-
Causland's brigade and was in the thickest of the fight at the
Monocacy and suffered severe loss, Lieutenant Colonel Tavener of the 17th Virginia being mortally wounded.

Mr. Floyd A. Bolen has furnished to the author an itinerary
of Company A of the 17th regiment, as well as of that regiment
from the earliest organization of said company and regiment,
down to the close of the battle at Monocacy, where Mr. Bolen
was wounded so severely as to disable him from further service in the army. This itinerary is as follows: "Field officers
of the regiment, William H. French, Colonel; W. C. Tavener,
Lieutenant Colonel; Fred Smith, Major; H. B. Barbor, Adjutant; with Doctor Isaiah Bee for a while as regimental Surgeon, but afterwards promoted to brigade Surgeon. Three
companies from Mercer County belonged to this regiment:
Company A, which was the first company of cavalry organized
in Mercer County, had as its first officer William H. French,
Captain; Philip Thompson, Robert Gore and William B.
Crump, Lieutenants. At the reorganization of the company
J. W. Graybeal was elected Captain and LaFayette Gore and
Albert Austin Lieutenants. When Captain William H. French
was promoted to the rank of Colonel, Captain J. W. Graybeal
became Captain of company A and Judson Ellison and W. A.
Reed became Lieutenants, together with Edward McClaugh-

erty, in the place of Ellison resigned. The officers of company
D were Robert Gore, Captain; Erastus Meador, Albert White,
and William R. Carr, Lieutenants. The officers of Company
E were Jacob C. Straley, Captain; William L. Bridges, Kinzie
Rowland, and Ambrose Oney, Lieutenants. Company A was
organized and entered the Confederate service about the 1st
of June, 1861, and remained in the Counties of Mercer and
Giles until about the 1st of the following October, when it
marched with other troops to Guyandotte. This march was
conducted through the Counties of Raleigh, Wyoming, Logan
and Cabell. On the return of the company from this expedition it went into camp on Flat Top mountain on the Miller
farm, where it remained two or three weeks, then marched by
way of Princeton and Jeffersonville into Russell County, going into camp near Lebanon, where it remained two or three
weeks, and then moved over to the Holstein and went into
camp. Here it remained about one month, and then moved
Southwestward through Abingdon, Bristol and into Tennessee
as far as Union Station, and then returned to Mercer County,
going into camp at Princeton, where it spent the winter.
Early in the spring of 1862, the company, in connection with
other troops, met the enemy at Clark's house, on the Flat Top,
in which a severe skirmish ensued, resulting in the repulse of
the Confederates, and in a loss to said company of Cornelius
Brown and G. H. Bryson, killed, and several wounded. The
retreat continued by way of Princeton to Bland Court House,
where the company remained for a few days and then was sent
back to Rocky Gap, and a few days thereafter to the Cross
Roads in Mercer County. A few days after reaching Cross
Roads this company led the advance of Wharton's command
against the enemy at Princeton, and on the 17th of May was
engaged in the battle of Pigeon Roost Hill, with Wharton's
command. These three Mercer companies accompanied General Loring on his march to the Kanawha Valley, in September, 1862. On reaching Charleston this company, with Gore's
Company D and the Bland rangers, were thrown together,

forming a battalion, and placed under the command of Major
Saliers. This battalion was then detached from Loring's
troops and sent through Jackson County, driving the enemy
across the Ohio. Returning from this expedition this battalion
marched through the Kanawha Valley to Blue Sulphur
Springs in Greenbrier, where the 17th regiment was finally
gotten together with the field officers hereinbefore stated.
Shortly after its organization the regiment marched to Salem,
where it spent the winter of 1862-3. About the 1st of May,
1863, the regiment broke camp and boarded the cars for Lynchburg, and from thence to Staunton, where it went into camp
and remained waiting for its horses to be brought forward.
As soon as mounted the regiment marched down the Valley to
Berryville, Virginia, where it joined and became a part of the
cavalry brigade of Jenkins, which led the advance of General Lee's army into Pennsylvania. On this march into
Pennsylvania, at a point northeast of Gettysburg, this
brigade of Jenkins encountered a regiment of the enemy,
capturing 200 or more prisoners and a train of wagons.
On the first day at Gettysburg, after the Federal line had
been broken, Captain Robert Gore, of Company D, distinguished himself by dashing in front of the Federal lines
alone, and capturing 150 of the retreating enemy. After the
first day's fight was over the 17th regiment took charge of and
guarded the 5,000 prisoners captured on that day. On the
retreat from Pennsylvania this brigade of Jenkins had quite a
lively fight with the enemy near Boonesboro, in which Joseph
H. McClaugherty of Company A, was wounded. Jenkins'
brigade of cavalry covered the retreat of General Lee's army
southward after it crossed the Potomac on its way from
Gettysburg, and in the Valley had several skirmishes with
the enemy, without any serious loss. Near Sperryville, in Rappahannock County, a part of the 17th regiment had a skirmish
with a force of the enemy, in which John R. Newkirk and
Jackson Anderson, of Company A, were captured. Shortly
after this the brigade moved back into the Valley and marched

by way of Staunton into the Greenbrier section, where it remained for a short while, when the 17th regiment marched into Abb's Valley, and then remarched to Red Sulphur Springs and subsequently a part of the regiment marched into Mercer County and went into camp near Spanishburg, where it wintered in 1863-4. On the approach of the Federal army from the Kanawha, in the spring of 1864, the whole of Jenkins' brigade took post at the Narrows. While the battle of Cloyd's farm was about to be, or was being fought, this cavalry brigade, now under the command of Colonel William H. French, crossed New River at Snidow's ferry and marched to Gap Mountain, with the view of cutting off General Crook's retreat; failing in this it succeeded in cutting General Averill's command off from that of Crook's, compelling Averill to escape by the mountain paths. Shortly after this General McCausland took command of the brigade, and marched it into the Valley of Virginia, where it skirmished from near Staunton, with Hunter's advance, until it reached Lynchburg. In a skirmish with the enemy near Lynchburg, Jack Hatcher, of Company A, was killed. On Hunter's retreat from Lynchburg, McCausland's brigade followed closely upon his rear, charging into his wagon train at Hanging Rock, capturing a number of prisoners and two pieces of artillery. From here the brigade marched in advance of Early's command to Staunton, and from thence to the Monocacy, where it engaged in that battle, in which Company A of the 17th regiment lost William French, Thomas Thornley, and A. J. Fanning, killed, and several wounded, among them Mr. Bolen. In the same company with Mr. Bolen was John H. Robinson, who is now an eminent dentist of Mercer County, and who was wounded in the batle of Monocacy and captured and removed to Baltimore to the West Building Hospital, from which he escaped and finally made his way through Maryland into Virginia. The thrilling story of the escape of this brave soldier and his sufferings, is worth relating, but the manuscript furnished by him came too late to be inserted at length in this volume; but something further will be said in regard to it in the appendix to this work.

Immediately upon the close of the battle at Monocacy General Early continued his advance on Washington, McCausland with his cavalry leading this advance, and having many severe combats with the enemy's cavalry, driving it before him. The enemy by this time had become thoroughly alarmed for the safety of the Capital, and poured into and around the city large bodies of troops, which induced General Early, on the night of the 12th, to retire toward the upper Potomac, crossing at White's Ford on the morning of the 14th of July, and camping on the Virginia shore. By the 17th, Early's army had reached and crossed the Shenandoah, and went into camp near Castleman's ferry. On the 18th the enemy crossed the Blue Ridge at Snicker's Gap and made a heavy attack on the Confederates, attempting to cross the river at Cool Springs, but were driven back with loss by the divisions of Rodes and Wharton. On the 19th, in a further attempt to cross the river at Berry's ferry, they were defeated with loss by the cavalry brigades of McCausland and Imboden. On the afternoon of the 20th Early again marched, taking the route up the Valley toward Newtown, and during the night Breckenridge's corps, made up of the divisions of Gordon and Wharton, followed by McCausland, marched by way of Millwood and the Valley turnpike to Middletown. The whole army marched to the vicinity of Strasburg and went into camp. On the 24th General Early turned back to meet the pursuing enemy, which he met at Kernstown and quickly defeated; the principal fighting being done by Gordon and Wharton's divisions of Breckenridge's corps. General Early pressed on to Bunker's Hill and Martinsburg.

It was on July 27th that General McCausland started on his raid to Chambersburg, Pennsylvania. He had with him his own and Bradley T. Johnson's brigades, and acting under and in obedience to the orders of Lieutenant General Early, to demand of the citizens of Chambersburg a named sum of money as an indemnity for the wanton burning of private dwelling houses in the Valley of Virginia by the Federal soldiers, and upon refusal to pay the money to burn the town. Reaching the town on the 30th of July, General McCausland made demand for the money, which was refused, and thereupon the buildings were fired. Adjutant A. C. Bailey, of the 8th cavalry, was killed in Chambersburg by some infuriated citizens. McCausland, on his retreat into Virginia, halted at Moorefield, where before daylight on the 6th day of August his command was surprised by that of the Federal General Averill and defeated with a loss of many killed and wounded; three flags, four pieces of artillery, and 400 captured.

From the 10th of August to the 19th day of September, General Early's command marched and counter-marched repeatedly over the territory between Winchester and the Potomac, with scarcely a day passing without a skirmish or small engagement of some kind. No army was better exercised, or inured to more active service.

The Federal General Sheridan, with an army of more than 40,000 men, on September 19th at Winchester, attacked General Early's troops, numbering not exceeding 12,000, and after an all-day close and bloody battle, the enemy's large body of cavalry turned the Confederate left flank, and compelled a rapid retreat of the army of General Early, with a loss to him of 1707 in killed and wounded; more than 2,000 captured, and the loss of five pieces of artillery and nine flags. The loss of the enemy was 5018. Among those killed on the Confederate side was Major General Rodes, and the brave and magnificent Colonel George S. Patton, mortally wounded; while Lieutenant Colonels Edgar and Derrick were captured. The Federals lost General Russel, killed; and Generals Upton, McIntosh and Chapman wounded. Among the New River Valley men, and those of adjacent territory, killed in this battle, were Captain George Bierne Chapman, commanding Chapman's battery; and Clinton Bailey, of the 8th Virginia cavalry, mortally wounded; and among the captured, were Captain Henry Bowen, and Private William H. Thompson, of the 8th cavalry; Captain James B. Peck of Edgar's battalion; Lieutenant John A. Douglass, of the 30th Virginia battalion; Lieutenant J. N. Shanklin of Monroe County, and Captain Andrew Gott, of Mercer, who though wounded, succeeded in escaping a few days after his capture.

General Early retired with his army to Fisher's Hill, where on the 22nd of September he was again attacked and defeated by General Sheridan; and only saved by the firm and brave resistance of a portion of Wharton's division, and some of the artillery brigade which continued the fighting until General Early ordered them to desist. General Early reports his loss in this engagement at 30 killed, 210 wounded, and 995 missing, and 12 pieces of artillery. General Sheridan reports his loss at 528.

Getting his troops together and giving them a few days for rest and recuperation, General Early, on October 1st, again advanced down the Valley to the vicinity of Cedar Creek, skirmishing all the way. An examination of the enemy's position satisfied the Confederate command that a successful attack could be made, although his army did not number above 10,000 men, while that of the enemy was close to 50,000. A more daring enterprise, under the circumstances, with such disparity of numbers, was never conceived or attempted in modern warfare. It was plain that if he did not succeed the chances were that he would loose his whole army. Notwithstanding the difficulties that were presented, as the movement began on the early morning of the 19th day of October, the obstacles which seemed insurmountable disappeared, and by a movement of a part of his troops on the flank of the enemy under the gallant Gordon, and with Wharton's division on the main turnpike, General Early threw his troops with a bold rush upon the enemy, who were largely asleep in their tents, and in an incredibly short space of time the enemy's 8th and 19th army corps were in utter route and confusion, with a large number thereof prisoners, together with many pieces of artillery and camp equipage. By noon the entire infantry force of the enemy had been routed and driven for several miles. Unfortunately, however, General Early halted his men when in the full tide of a most brilliant success, thus giving the enemy time to get themselves together again, which they did, and later turning upon the broken and scattered Confederate battalions, with his immense cavalry corps some 10,000 strong, drove Early's troops from the field with serious loss; although he had succeeded in getting off 1500 Federal prisoners, he lost most of the artillery he had captured and some of his own by the breaking down of the bridge over Cedar Creek. The Confederates retreated to New Market and there went into bivouac. The Confederate loss in this battle, including prisoners, is put down at about 2500; while that of the Federal army is officially reported at 5665. The Confederates lost Major General Ramseur, killed; the Federal General Bidwell was killed, and Generals Wright, Grover, and Ricketts wounded. It is to be regretted that the casualties in Wharton's division, and McCausland's cavalry brigade cannot be given for want of official or other information.

Between August the 10th and November 16th, 1864, General Sheridan had so completely devastated the country in which his army operated, that it was made most manifest that his orders to destroy the Valley, "So that even a crow traversing it would have to carry a haversack," were almost literally complied with; about the only thing which he did not burn, destroy or carry away, being the stone fences. Scarce any such wholesale pillage and wanton destruction ever followed in the wake of any army. To the people the losses amounted to millions of dollars.

From the time of the battle of Cedar Creek, on the 19th day of October, to the 14th day of December, when Early's 2nd corps of the army, under General John B. Gordon, returned to the trenches around Richmond, there was a succession of marches and countermarches by General Early's troops, and many spirited skirmishes, and some pretty severe combats between the cavalry forces of the two armies, one of which was an attack on General McCausland's brigade, on the 12th day of November, near Cedarville, in which the enemy was several times repulsed, but finally drove McCausland back towards Front Royal, with a loss of two pieces of artillery, 10 killed, 60 wounded, and 100 captured. It is stated upon authority, that up to the 15th day of November, General Early's troops had marched since the opening of the campaign on the 13th day of June, 1670 miles, and fought 75 battles and skirmishes. On the 24th day of November McCausland's brigade, with those of Jackson and Imboden, had a sharp contention with Torbett's two divisions of Federal Cavalry at Liberty Mills, northwest of Gordonsville. The troops became very much mixed up with the enemy in the dark night. The enemy's reported loss in this encounter was 258.

General Early established his headquarters at Staunton, while a portion of General Wharton's division went into camp about the 1st of December at Fishersville. This was the end of the Valley campaign of 1864.

Whatever may be said of Early's Valley campaign as to its conduct and final disastrous results, it is certain that no student of military history will withhold from that officer the credit of being a bold, daring, brave soldier and strategist, who with a small army of scarce more than 12,000 of the most heroic men that ever shouldered muskets for the defense of their country, baffled, beat back, defeated, harrassed, and kept employed for more than five months in an open country, and within a radius of not more than 100 miles, an army of quite five times its numbers, inflicting upon it during that period losses almost equal to double its own numbers; and keeping during the period referred to the Federal authorities in a state of nervous tremor for fear that the bold "Captain of the Valley" might swoop down upon the Federal city.

Lieutenant Colonel Vincent A. Witcher, on the 17th day of September, 1864, with his 34th Virginia battalion of cavalry, left Tazewell Court House, and passing by way of Narrows of New River to Lewisburg, was there joined by the companies of the Thurmonds and those of Captain William H. Payne, J. Bumgards and J. W. Amick, raising his effective strength to 523 men, with which he moved northward across the mountains into the counties of Upshur and Lewis, making extensive captures of horses, beef cattle, and 300 prisoners, and destroying large amounts of government stores, and returning without loss. (1)

On October 20th, 1864, Captain William H. Payne, at the head of his command and while marching down Coal River, in Raleigh County, against the enemy, was shot from his horse, falling mortally wounded. His left arm was broken, the ball passing through his body, from which wound he died on the next day. He was a young man of great promise, the son of Mr. Charles H. Payne, of Giles County. Had young Payne lived a month longer he would have become Colonel at the reorganization of his command. He was a man of exemplary habits, well educated, of dauntless courage, and was a strikingly handsome, fine-looking soldier. The officers of his company at the time of his death were Lieutenant John Tabler and Charles R. Price. Major Nounan with a detachment of cavalry, in the month of October, penetrated the enemy's lines, and marched to the Kanawha River, doing some hurt to the enemy, and returned without serious loss.

On the 2nd day of October, 1864, the enemy 2500 strong, including one negro cavalry regiment, under the command of the Federal General Burbridge, attacked Saltville, Virginia, defended by a small force under the command of Generals Echols, Vaughn and Williams; and were after an all-day contest repulsed and forced to retire, with a loss of about 350 men killed and wounded. In the December following, a Federal army about 6,000 strong, under the command of the Federal General

(1) Witcher's command had, in 1863, a severe engagement at the mouth of Beech Creek, now Mingo County, with the 4th West Virginia cavalry, under Col. Hall, in which Hall was killed and Witcher badly wounded.

Stoneman, marched into Southwestern Virginia and was met
by General John C. Breckenridge with some small remnants
and fragments of Confederate commands, numbering less than
1,000 men. For several days frequent combats ensued, mostly
in favor of the Federals, who penetrated the country as far
east as Wytheville, destroying much of the railroad, especially
bridges, and some Government stores in that town and at other
points, also doing some damage to the lead mines. As stated,
the first named Federal force had with it one regiment of negro
cavalry, whose fighting qualities was the boast of the Federal
officers, they even intimating that the negroes were better soldiers than their white men. On the 20th of December a large
Federal force attacked the command of Colonel Robert T.
Preston at the salt works, and after a brisk fight lasting until
night, Colonel Preston, who had only 400 men—mostly old men
—reserves, withdrew his men, and the Federals entered and
took possession, doing considerable damage, after which they,
finding nothing further to destroy, returned to Kentucky and
Tennessee.

General Thomas L. Rosser, with his Virginia cavalry brigade,
and the 8th Virginia cavalry regiment of Payne's brigade, on
the night of—or rather before daylight on the morning of—
the 11th day of January, 1865, attacked a Federal force at
Beverley, West Virginia, capturing, killing and wounding 572,
without loss to his command.

The old brigade of Echols, of Wharton's division, which had
been in quarters near Fishersville in December, on the 18th
day of January left for Dublin Depot, in Southwestern Virginia, and McCausland's brigade marched from east of the Blue
Ridge, by way of Fishersville, en route to winter quarters in
Alleghaney and Greenbrier Counties. By the last days of
February all of the Confederate troops had departed from the
valley, save a small force of cavalry under General Rosser,
and the remnant of Wharton's division, numbering less than
1,000 men, badly clad and poorly fed. A force of 9,987 Federal
Cavalry, with artillery, under the command of General Sheri-

dan, on the 2nd day of March, attacked Early's small force at Waynesboro, completely demolishing it, capturing about 1600 prisoners, many of them citizens and convalescents, who were getting out of the country with General Early's troops. Early escaped to the mountains, finally reached Richmond, was sent to Lynchburg and from there to Southwestern Virginia to take command of the troops in that department.

General Sheridan crossed the Blue Ridge, laid waste the whole country through which he passed, cut the James River canal, destroyed the Central railroad, and made his way down to the north of Richmond about the middle of March, where he was threatened with serious trouble and turned his course to the White House on the Pamunky, finally joining General Grant, at Petersburg, on March 27th.

On March 5th Pickett's division was relieved by that of General Mahone, and marched to within two miles of Chester Station, near the Richmond and Petersburg turnpike, where it went into bivouac amidst a cold rain which continued for two days. On the 8th Pickett had a grand review of his division, after which and on the next day, the 9th, it marched to Manchester, and on the following day, the 10th, through Richmond and halted in the outer line of works near the Brooke road; thence on the left along the line of works to the Nine Mile road, and the following day, the 12th, returned to the position near the Brooke road. On the 14th it marched to near Ashland, where it was halted in line of battle. On the 16th the 15th Virginia regiment of Corse's brigade had a sharp skirmish with Sheridan's cavalry at Ashland. Sheridan switching off towards the Pamunky, the division followed him to that river, built a bridge, but found it useless to attempt to follow the bold riders any farther, and from thence returned to the Nine Mile road. It marched on the 25th to Richmond and took the train for Dunlop's Station, where it rested until the evening of the 29th, when it was ordered to the right of General Lee's army. It marched to and crossed the Appomattox on a pontoon bridge five miles above Petersburg. Here the brigades of

Stuart, Corse, and Terry took the cars for Sutherland's Station, on the Southside railroad, but there not being room on
the train for all, the first and 7th Virginia regiments had to
march, reaching that night Sutherland's Tavern, on Cox's road,
in a drizzling rain. Before daybreak the next morning, the
30th, the march was resumed to Hatcher's Run and to the
extreme right of the line near Five Forks, where the two last
mentioned regiments, with some cavalry, were thrown forward
to drive off some Federal cavalry, which they succeeded in doing,—Hunton's brigade was detached and serving with Bush-
rod Johnson's division. At an early hour on the morning of the
31st the march was again taken up in the direction of Dinwiddie Court House. Finding the Federals in heavy force at
the crossing of Chamberlayne's Creek, engaged with Fitzhugh
Lee's cavalry, Terry's brigade, led by the 3rd Virginia regiment,
effected a crossing at an old mill dam, but with loss to the
leading regiment, it having to wade the creek, which was waist
deep, to dislodge the enemy posted on the opposite side. The
division advanced rapidly in pursuit of the retreating enemy,
who made several stands, and quite brisk fighting occurred.
Within a mile of Dinwiddle Court House the enemy, with two
cavalry divisions, made a bold stand, but were quickly driven
with loss; the Confederate loss was small. General Terry suffered a severe injury by the fall of his horse, which was shot.
The division occupied the field until 1 o'clock, A. M., of the 1st
of April, and was then withdrawn and posted at Five Forks,
where, with the brigades of Ransom and Wallace and the Confederate cavalry, it was fiercely assailed about the middle of
the afternoon by about 26,000 Federal infantry and cavalry.
The Confederates did not number more than 7,000, yet manfully
and bravely stood their ground until almost surrounded, and
finally, about dark, was forced to yield the field with a loss of
more than 3,000 of their number captured, with several pieces
of artillery. No better fight was ever made under the circumstances. In its close it was hand to hand. The day was lost
simply because the Confederates had both flanks turned, were

in fact pushed off the field by weight of numbers. The repeated Federal assaults up to the last were repulsed with great loss to them. The Confederate loss in this battle is put down at between 3,000 and 4,000 prisoners, 13 colors and six guns; and on the Federal side the loss of Warren's 5th infantry corps is put down at 634 in killed and wounded.

The loss of General Grant's army from the 29th day of March to the 9th day of April, the date of Lee's surrender, is officially reported at 15,692, a number equal to about one-half the number of men Lee had when he left Petersburg, and more than equal to the number that had guns in their hands on the day of the surrender.

Company D of the 7th regiment lost in the Five Forks battle 6 men, viz: John R. Crawford, John S. Dudley, A. L. Sumner, and G. C. Mullens, captured, and William D. Peters and John A. Hale, severely wounded. No record is extant, as far as known, of the losses in the Giles and Mercer companies of the 24th Virginia regiment. An incident, however, occurring in the Giles company of the 24th regiment is worthy of note. Late in the afternoon, when Warren's Federal army corps had swung around the Confederate left and attacked Terry's brigade in the rear, three Federal soldiers attacked McCrosky of the Giles company, one of whom he killed, wounded another and escaped, with a wound in his face, from the third. The man he killed with the butt of his gun, braining him, breaking the gun off at the breach. Leaving the field the night of the battle, Pickett's division marched to Ford's depot on the Southside railroad, bivouacing, and joining, the next morning, the divisions of Heth and Wilcox, retreating from Petersburg. The division was now about 2200 strong, having lost more than half its numbers in the battle of the day before. It continued its march, Hunton's brigade in the meantime having united with the division, on the 2nd of April, to Deep Creek, heavily pressed by the enemy's cavalry; especially was this true of the 4th and 5th, having occasionally to halt and form line of battle, and now and then a square, to keep off the pursuers; without food and living on corn shelled from the cob, which was eaten even without parching.

In the early morning of the 6th the division reached Harper's farm, on Sailor's creek, where it encountered a heavy force of Federal cavalry with which it skirmished for several hours, and finally with a furious attack front, flanks and rear, and in a hand to hand contest, it was bodily picked up by the enemy, whose numbers were sufficient to have thrown down their guns and have captured every Confederate on the field and bound him hand and foot with ropes. A portion of the division escaped capture and got off the field with General Pickett and Brigadier General Stuart. Generals Corse, Hunton, and Terry were captured, as was also Lieutenant General Ewell, Major General Custis Lee, and perhaps others. The escaped portion of the division marched to Appomattox under the command of General Pickett; Terry's brigade being commanded by Major W. W. Bentley, of the 24th regiment; that of Corse by Colonel Arthur Herbert; that of Hunton by Major M. P. Spessard. On the 9th General Pickett surrendered 1031 officers and men. The men captured in the battle of Five Forks, as well also as those captured at Sailor's creek, were sent to prison at Point Lookout, Maryland, from whence they were discharged in the June and July following. Those surrendered at Appomattox were paroled and went home. Of McCausland's cavalry brigade there were surrendered at Appomattox 27 officers and men. Wharton's division, or what remained of it after the disaster at Waynesboro, with other troops in Southwestern Virginia, under the command of General Early, were, on learning of General Lee's surrender at Appomattox, disbanded at Christiansburg, Virginia. General Early had been sick for some days previous to the surrender and was riding in an ambulance, and as said, when receiving reliable information of the surrender at Appomattox remarked. prefixing some expletives, "I wish Gabriel would now blow his horn."

During the year of 1864, along the border of Western and

Southwestern Virginia, in Monroe, Mercer and other counties, many outrages were committed by bands of thieves and robbers who roamed over the country, regarding neither friend nor foe, but seeking their own gain and gratifying their own spleen against non-combatants. There lived on Flat Top mountain a staunch Southern man by the name of James Wiley, quietly at home and disturbing no one. He was attacked in his own house by one of the bands referred to, but succeeded in driving them off, being aided by his young son, Milton, and wounding one of the gang. A short time afterwards he and his son were again attacked by another one of these bands and killed. This occurred in the spring of 1862. On another occasion, in 1864, Mr. Albert B. Calfee, with his younger brother, John C. Calfee, and Mr. Elisha Heptinstall, were traveling from the residence of Colonel William H. French, in Mercer County, toward the Court House, and were fired upon by a band of these marauders from ambush, and Heptinstall was killed and John C. Calfee mortally wounded. This occurred on the 8th day of August, 1864. About the same time a party of Confederate outlaws went to the house of Mr. Jacob Harper, in Raleigh County, and took him a prisoner, led him out into the woods and shot him. Harper was a plain, honest, upright, peaceable citizen and harmed no one.

The war was now practically over and no malice existed between those who did the actual fighting in the battle. The question of secession being one left open by the framers of the Federal Constitution, every man had a right to exercise his own opinion in regard thereto, and hence he had a right to fight on the one side or the other as to him might seem right and proper, provided he fought for his convictions. The Confederate soldier fought for a principle as sacred to him as the one for which the Federal soldier battled. Again, this Confederate soldier felt that he had discharged his duty and had nothing to ask forgiveness for and asked none. He had no apologies to offer or make; he had fought manfully the invaders of his soil, who came to kill and destroy. He did not

ask those who fought against him in the war to forget the struggle; let them remember it if they might, but we would not forget it if we could, and could not if we would. We intend to
perpetuate the memories of the conflict, the battles won or lost
we intend shall be remembered to latest generations. Will the
world forget Marathon, Waterloo or Thermopylæ? No more
than it will forget Manassas, Sharpsburg, Chancelorsville,
Gettysburg, the Wilderness or Spottsylvania. The contest was
between Americans, and their deeds of heroism and valor are
the common heritage of the American people. The story is told
of the great and gifted preacher, Henry Ward Beecher, that in
the early part of the year 1862 he visited England and was
invited to make a speech. The crowd was exceedingly boisterous and he was howled and hissed at so that he could not be
heard, but finally a large brawny Englishman, with a broad,
big mouth and stentorian voice, shouted: "You told us you
would whip the Rebels in ninety days and you have not done
it." The crowd becoming quiet for a moment, Mr. Beecher
said: "If you will be quiet for a moment I will tell you why;
when we started out in the war and made the statement that
we would whip them in ninety days, we thought we were fighting Englishmen, but we soon found out that we were fighting
Americans." There will never be in the history of the world
such soldiers as the Confederate—the Confederate Private.
While it is true that the world has furnished few, if any, such
men as Lee, Jackson, Johnston, Beauregard, Stuart, and many
other Confederate Generals that might be mentioned; but it
must not be forgotten that no Generals ever led forth such men
to battle as the Confederate soldier. His like will never be
seen again. Some one has written some lines in regard to the
Confederate private, a few of which are here inserted:

"From every home in the sweet Southland
Went a soldier lad, at his heart's command,
To fight in a cause both true and just,
To conquer or to die, as a hero must.

The hardships of war bravely bore,
And proudly the shabby gray he wore,

T'was the only color on earth for him;
Not hunger or thirst could his spirit dim.

With every battle hope sprang up anew;
He felt that the cause he loved was true,
And surely the God who brave men led
Would help and guide them, living or dead.

Sometimes they won, then hope ran high;
Again they lost, but it would not die,
They were privates only, and theirs to obey;
Nor theirs to command or lead the fray.

But theirs to endure and follow and fight;
To know that the cause they loved was right.
And so to the end they followed and fought,
With love and devotion which could not be bought."

After the surrender at Appomattox arrangements were soon made by the Federal Government to release the Confederate prisoners in its hands, of whom there were many thousands. They began to return home during the months of June and July, and they were pitiable looking objects indeed. Peglegs, stub arms, sunken eyes, emaciated frames, teeth loose and falling out on account of scurvy, with health broken and hope almost gone; returning to the land of their nativity to find it practically a waste place.

Thousands of men on both sides of our great civil conflict perished in military prisons; charges, criminations and recriminations of ill and inhuman treatment of prisoners by both sides were made. It may be here noted, that military prison life is horrible at any time and under any circumstances. A great body of men thrown and huddled together are not only difficult to control and manage under the best system of dicipline that can be adopted, but such masses are always subject to disease in every form. The facts are too plain and manifest to admit of doubt, that the officials of the Federal Government were wholly to blame for all the ills and horrible results that befell these poor prisoners, their own as well as the Confederates, because of, first, the obstacles they placed in the way of a fair exchange, and in the next place by their absolute refusal to exchange at all. That there were isolated cases of bad treatment of Federal prisoners by Confederate prison keepers is

doubtless true, but if so, they were few in number and excep-
tional cases, while on the other hand the keepers of Federal
prisons were cruel and brutal in their treatment of Confederate prisoners, and this with full knowledge on the part of the
Federal authorities. The North was full-handed with provisions and medicines, while the South was impoverished. For
those whom the fortunes of war had placed in their hands, the
South did the very best it could, giving to them the same rations that the soldiers in the field received; while the Federal
authorities in the midst of abundance willfully inflicted
wanton deprivation on the Confederate prisoners. An examination of the reports of the Federal Secretary of War made in
1866, shows that 22,576 Federal prisoners died in Southern
prisons, and that 22,246 Confederate prisoners died in Northern
prisons. The report of the Surgeon General of the United
States shows that in round numbers, the Confederate prisoners in the hands of the Federal authorities numbered 220,-
000, out of which 26,246 died. That out of 270,000 Federal
prisoners held by the South, 22,576 died; more than 12 per cent.
of the Confederate prisoners, and less than 9 per cent. of Federal prisoners died. The urgency of the Northern people at
home, as well as many prominent Federal officers favoring exchange of prisoners, drew from General Grant a letter to General Butler, dated August 18th, 1864, in which he says: "It is
hard on our men held in the Southern prisons not to exchange
them, but it is humanity to those left in the ranks to fight our
battles. Every man released on parole, or otherwise, becomes
an active soldier against us at once, either directly or indirect-
ly. If we commence a system of exchange which liberates all
prisoners taken, we will have to fight on until the whole South
is exterminated. If we hold those caught, they amount to no
more than dead men. At this particular time to release all
Rebel prisoners in the North would insure Sherman's defeat
and would compromise our safety here."

Among the men of Mercer County who perished in Northern
prisons were Robert H. Brian, A. I. Golden, J. H. Godby, H.

F. Hatcher, William Keaton, W. J. Keaton and John W. Nelson. These men died in Camp Chase, Ohio, during the latter part of the war.

———o———

CHAPTER VIII.

1866-1905.

Reconstruction in Mercer County, W. Va.—Constitutional Amendment Disfranchising Confederates.—Registration Law.—County Seat Agitation.—The "Committee of Safety."—The Creation of Summers County.—The Restoration of the Elective Franchise.—Industrial Development.—The Flat Top Coal Field.—Railroad Construction.—The City of Bluefield.

The Confederate soldier, with the close of the war, returned to his country, where he had once had a place he called home, but now—at least in many instances—he found nothing but blackened ruins and utter waste places. As he had been brave and magnanimous in war, and had in good faith laid down his arms, he returned to engage not in war, but in peaceful pursuits, build up and start anew and become a useful citizen of the young Commonwealth. He had no money or property, save perhaps a small piece of land, if he had been fortunate enough to own such before the war. In many instances, an arm or leg had been lost in battle, or his health greatly shattered. He was not the man he was when he entered the army; and many of his nearest—dearest friends, relatives—had perished in the strife. His only trust was in God and his own good right arm, if he was fortunate to have that limb left. On all sides were gloom and despair, to a less braver heart and manlier spirit. He sought no quarrel with anyone, only asked to be free, not disturbed, and he would try and work his way through the remainder of his days as best he might. He neither wanted nor sought revenge for wrongs, real or imaginary. That for which for four years he had struggled and suffered had not been accomplished, and the effort to establish it had failed. Nothing was left him but to live for the future, in the consciousness of having faithfully discharged his duty in the past, and with a fixed determination to do this in the future. The Governor of his state (2), in a letter to the Federal Secretary of War, opposed his return to his country, and a few in his midst desired to rob him of his rights as a citizen of the new Commonwealth. In time of profound peace, unarmed, perhaps with but one leg or one arm, broken in health and in purse he was as much feared as when he carried his musket with forty rounds of cartridges, marching beneath the "Stars and Bars." If he was found with an old, poor, crippled mule or horse, that General Grant had given him at Appomattox, trying to plow and make bread for his starving wife and children, he was robbed of this upon the plea that it was Government property, either Federal or Rebel. It was dig or die and his enemies preferred him to take the latter course.

It is true that at that time he was a citizen of the state with all his rights as such guaranteed to him by the Constitution of the new Commonwealth, with no law in force that in any way deprived him of the privilege of full citizenship; but the devil is always ready to aid the ingenuity of bad men to accomplish bad things, and hence the only way, in a measure, at least, to get rid of the ex-Confederate soldier, was to decitizenize him, and thereby either drive him from the state, or place him in a condition of political vassalage or serfdom. The political machinery was put to work to accomplish the purpose in view by decitizenizing all ex-Confederates, as well also as all who had aided or sympathized with them. This could not be done under the then existing organic law of the state, and a change in this law was necessary to the accomplishment of the object in view; but be it said to the credit of the better class of the then dominant party, they took no part in this crime against liberty, and did not seek to fix manacles on the poor Confederate—it was

(2). Boreman to Staunton Series II. Vol. VIII. Reb. Record p. 533

the other set, generally of the vile and vindictive; when "Prometheus was chained to the rock it was not the proud Eagle, but the miserable Vulture that came down and tore out his vitals." In all great revolutions, like in all the great floods of waters, it is the filth and foul things that rise to the surface and float, while the gold lies at the bottom.

It was late in the fall of 1865 before there was anything like the full restoration of Civil Government in Mercer County. All things in Government were new or novel to the people. They had always known, and their ancestors before them had known for more than a century, nothing but the old Virginia County Court system, with one or more magistrates in each magisterial district in the county, clothed with jurisdiction to try warrants for small claims, and to sit as a Court and administer county affairs. The Circuit Court trying all criminal and civil cases, as well as chancery causes. Now they found magisterial districts no longer in existence; townships created in their stead, with a justice of the peace in each township, and he regarded the biggest man therein, although in some instances he could not write his name and perhaps did not know the way to the mill, with jurisdiction to try cases involving an hundred dollars, with the right to empannel a jury of six men. In lieu of the old County Court, a Board of Supervisors to administer county affairs, and this board, in part, at least, was composed of men who not only could not write their names, but whose honesty was not above par; however, this was only true for a short while, when better men were selected for this position, such as L. D. Martin, Silas T. Reynolds, William C. Honaker, and others.

Judge Nathaniel Harrison, of Monroe County, having been made Circuit Judge very soon after the close of hostilities, appointed Benjamine White, Sheriff, and George Evans, Clerk and Recorder of Mercer County. White had been a violent Secessionist at the commencement of the war, but had changed his views somewhat about the close thereof; while Mr. Evans, being a Northern man by birth, was doubtless a Union man from the beginning. Judge Harrison (1) had been a Confederate, and as late as 1862 had applied for appointment on the staff of Brigadier General Chapman. Thus it will be seen that men who started out on the Southern side, found out their mistake, as they claimed, in the latter part of the war or just about the close, were honored. They started out in the boat and as long as there was fair breeze and it floated well, they were willing to stay, but when adverse winds blew and it was threatened with wreck and disaster, they jumped out, pulled for the shore and left their friends to perish if they must. This was true of more than one man in Mercer County, even extending to those who had volunteered in the army and taken an oath to support the Confederate Government; yet, disregarding their oaths, deserted and went over to the enemy, and this is not all, came back among their neighbors and friends and engaged in pillage in its worst form. These deserters were without honor among their own people and distrusted and despised by those to whom they deserted.

In the fall of 1865 Judge Harrison rode into the town of Princeton; that is, where it once stood, sat on his horse, no one inviting him to stop or alight; he rode seven and one-half miles east to Concord Church on the Red Sulphur turnpike road where he opened and held his court. The ex-Confederates who had been elected at the election that fall were arbitrarily refused permission to qualify, and others who claimed to have adhered to the Union were installed in their stead.

The Legislature met at Wheeling in January, 1866, and in a contest Colonel William H. French, who had been elected to that body was unseated by Colonel Thomas Little, who had not been elected. By a joint resolution of the two Houses, an amendment to the Constitution was proposed, by which, if adopted, all ex-Confederates and their sympathizers would be decitizenized. At the session which provided for the submission of the amendment to the Constitution, which had been pro-

(1). Articles of impeachment were exhibited against him in the Legislature and he was forced to resign the Judgship.

posed in the session of 1865, an Act was passed declaring that no one should be allowed to vote at the next succeeding election, except those who would take a prescribed oath known as the "Test Oath." The amendment referred to is in the following words and figures: "No person who since the 1st day of June, 1861, has given or shall give voluntary aid or assistance to the rebellion against the United States, shall be a citizen of this state, or be allowed to vote at any election held therein, unless he has volunteered in the military or naval service of the United States and has been or shall be honorably discharged therefrom." This was the first instance in the history of a free government, where the Legislature plainly and intentionally subverted the Constitution of a free state, and openly and deliberately violated their oaths and the plain provision of the Constitution, which provided that "The white male citizens of the state shall be entitled to vote at all elections held within the election districts in which they respectively reside." The election at which this amendment to the Constitution was to be voted upon by the people, was held on the 24th day of May, 1866, and was ratified by a vote of 22,224 for, to 15,302 against the same. Only 75 votes were cast in the County of Mercer, of which 61 were for ratification and 14 for rejection, yet the voting population at that time in Mercer County under the Constitution as it then existed, was not less than 1,000. Among those voting against this iniquity in Mercer will be found the names of Colonel Thomas Little, David Lilley, Sylvester Upton, and Russell G. French, the latter classed an ex-Federal soldier.

Truly loyal officers were now elected to the various offices, and finding so few regarded as qualified to discharge the duties of the same, it was found necessary to give two or three offices to one man; in fact in one or more instances it was stated that one or more men held at least five offices each at the same time.

The Legislature of West Virginia not only disfranchised men and kept them from voting, but passed numerous laws preventing attorneys from practicing their profession, people from teaching school, men from sitting on juries, or from prosecut-

ing suits, unless they would take the "Test Oath." These laws
against attorneys who had been engaged as soldiers in the
Confederate army, or had sympathized with those engaged in
armed hostility against the Government of the United States,
brought to the Courts of the state, especially in the Southern
border counties, swarms of ill pests, Northern carpet-bag
lawyers, who without practice where they came from, and perhaps having left their country for their country's good, came
to feast and to fatten on the miseries and sufferings of the
poor, downtrodden, disfranchised, tax ridden Confederate people. The voice of the lawyer of the community, to whom the
people looked for aid and were willing to trust their lives,
property and honor in his hands, was, with few exceptions, refused a hearing in the court room. There were a few attorneys
residents, or who became residents, who were Union men, fair-
minded and just, among them Henry L. Gillispie, James H.
McGinnis, Frank Hereford, J. Speed Thompson, Edwin Sehon,
and Colonel James W. Davis; the latter gentlemen had been a
Colonel in the Confederate army, but had succeeded in persuad-
ing the Legislature that he was a truly repentant rebel, sorry
for his sins, and succeeded in getting that body, by special Act,
to forgive his waywardness and restore to him the privilege of
practicing his profession without taking the attorneys' "Test
Oath."

Shortly after Colonel Davis had been permitted to enter
again upon the practice of the law, he was employed in a
case in the Circuit Court of Mercer County, involving the title
to a horse, which had been taken or stolen from Colonel John S.
Carr during the war. On the other side of the case was the witty
Irish lawyer, J. H. McGinnis, of Raleigh. In course of the argu-
ment of Colonel Davis before the jury he took occasion to say
how good and magnanimous the Legislature had been to him, by
again conferring on him the privilege to earn a living for his
family by the practice of his profession; he followed this by
a bit of his war experience in the battle of Chapmansville, describing the wounds he received by which he lost a finger, and

received a shot in the shoulder and back. The resourceful Mc-
Ginnis, while listening to the Colonel's speech, had composed
some verses which in his reply, and in his inimitable way, he
repeated, much to the discomfiture of the Colonel, but to the
joy of the bystanders; only one of which verses is recollected,
and ran as follows:

> "On the battlefield I long did linger
>   Where guns and cannons they did crack,
> Until by a cruel shot, I lost this finger,
>   And got this hole in my back."

In order to effectuate the purpose of the framers of the Constitutional amendment and disfranchisement law already ad-
verted to, the Legislature enacted what was known as a Registration law, providing for a registration of the voters and
creating a Board of Registration composed of three members
to be appointed by the Governor, and to hold their office at
his will and pleasure. This proved a powerful weapon in the
hands of the party then in power, who evidently intended
thereby to perpetuate themselves therein. It was almost the
equal of the proposed "Force Bill" introduced into Congress
a few years ago, if it had been wielded by wise and conservative heads, and would have kept the then dominant political
party long in power in the state; but like all other engines of
oppression, originated and constructed in Republics for the
destruction of the liberty of the Anglo-Saxon, they became a
boomerang in the hands of those who wielded them, finally
effecting their own destruction. It is said, "Whom the gods
would destroy they first make mad." This was certainly true
of the dominant party in West Virginia at that time, and especially in Mercer County. Their apparent inordinate desire to
punish those who differed with them about the great civil conflict, and the quest of individuals for place and power, led them
to extremes in the Legislature, and the enforcement of proscriptive laws. They very soon began to quarrel among themselves, and the scramble for the public pap, and the crumbs
which fell from the master's table engendered, as it always

does, bad blood. Very soon the better and more conservative
part of the dominant party became disgusted and disposed to
fall in with their neighbors—ex-Confederates—insisting upon
according to them some rights, besides the payment of taxes
and right to die.

As already stated in this work, the County site had in the
year of 1837 been fixed at a place called Princeton, but so soon
as the Judge of the Circuit Court opened and held a term of
court at Concord Church, some of the people in that and other
sections of the county began the agitation of a removal of the
County site from Princeton to Concord Church. Steps were
very soon taken to have the Board of Supervisors order an
election removing the seat of Justice from Princeton to Concord Church; and an election was held, but Concord Church
failing to receive the requisite three-fifths vote, the removalists failed in their scheme. Very soon another election was
held which also failed, but the Board was induced to declare
the result in favor of removal.

Colonel Thomas Little, the Delegate from the County to the
Legislature at its session of 1867, procured the passage of an
Act locating permanently the County site at Princeton, but
at the session of 1868 George Evans, the Representative from
Mercer County, procured the repeal of the Act of 1867; and
so the fight continued both before the people and in the Courts.
Injunctions were obtained first by one and then by the other
party until the question was finally settled as will be hereinafter stated. The litigation over the County Court House
question ended with the disposition of the Bill, prepared by one
Martin H. Holt, an attorney of Raleigh County, which was
known as the celebrated "Bill of Peace," in which appeared the
names of the Board of Supervisors of the County, a corpora-
tion, plaintiff against a large part of the people of the county,
who favored Princeton as the seat of Justice, as defendants.
In this Bill was set forth the various steps, acts, doings and
proceedings from which it was contended that the County site

had been removed from Princeton and located at Concord Church, and also setting forth the Acts of the Legislature touching the same as hereinbefore referred to; and alleging and charging in effect that all of the people of the county who were opposed to Concord Church as the lawful and proper location for the seat of Justice, were a lawless band and disturbers of the quietude of the people and of the public peace, and praying an injunction inhibiting and restraining them from further action looking to the opening of the question. An injunction was granted, but about as quickly dissolved, and as before stated, this was the end of all litigation concerning this troublesome matter.

In January, 1870, a few of the citizens of the little village of Princeton assembled and constituted themselves a Committee of Safety, for the purpose of devising a plan by which the much vexed County site question might be finally settled. After a careful review and consideration of the situation in all its aspects, local, political, and otherwise, it was concluded that the first and best step to take was to have the Legislature of the State, then in session at Wheeling, pass a special Act submitting to the people the question of the location of the seat of justice, to be settled by a majority vote. In order to get such a law passed, it was deemed necessary to send to the seat of government a man who was recognized as belonging to and a leader of the dominant party then in control of the Legislature. The man was found in the person of Mr. Benjamine White, who had been and was still the Sheriff of the county. White was a man of influence and weight in the county with his party, and was fairly well known in the southern part of the state, and a man of fair address, and when aroused was a bold and plausible talker, and could make himself felt in any enterprise or cause he chose to espouse. He was going on public business, but in the interest of Princeton; which neither he nor those in the secret let the public know. Once in Wheeling and the matter being put under way, on account of the irregularity and uncertainty of mails and the long time that it took

letters and papers to reach our section in mid-winter, it was
felt that no intelligence of what was going on at the capitol
was likely to reach Mercer County until the mission of the messenger had been accomplished and the Legislature adjourned;
which would then be too late for any organized opposition to
Mr. White's bill, should anyone wish to oppose so fair a mode
of settlement of our local trouble. As before stated, Mr. White
was going on public business, and it was not to be expected
that he would be compelled to pay his personal expenses, therefore a few persons raised and placed in his hands $100.00 to
meet these expenses. There were no railroads in this immediate section in that day and no public conveyances of any kind,
so Mr. White, in the dead of winter, mounted his horse and
pushed out over the mountains to the Kanawha, where he took
passage on a steamboat to Wheeling by way of the Kanawha
and Ohio Rivers. On his arrival at the capitol and meeting
several of his acquaintances and political friends, and laying
the matter in hand before them, he soon had his bill introduced,
passed and was on his way home before the people of Mercer
County knew what had transpired. The Committee of Safety
was composed of Captain John A. Douglass, Mr. H. W. Straley,
Major C. D. Straley, Mr. Joseph H. Alvis, Mr. William Oliver
and this writer. To insure success perfect secrecy was necessary, and the Committee of Safety made and took a solemn
pledge that nothing which was said or done touching this matter should be divulged by them to anyone; and none were admitted to their counsels, except those who gave the pledge to
each other to keep within their own breasts whatever happened
or was resolved upon. It soon became known where we held
our meetings, at one of which, a slight disagreement or mis-
understanding with our friend Mr. White took place, and he
withdrew and we were afterwards termed by him the "Town
Clique." We were not offended at this, however, as it is well
known that all towns are said to have their "Cliques." At
our first meeting after Mr. White's return from Wheeling,
held at our place of general rendezvous, there was a very seri-

ous difference of opinion between members of the Committee. Mr. White was for calling the Board of Supervisors of the county together at once and having it order a special election on the question of the location of the seat of justice; the other members of the Committee opposed it, and the vote of the majority was the law which governed its actions. Now it might be well to give some of the open reasons which were expressed for not being willing to hold the election under the new law and before the general election, which was to take place in the following October. First, the special law did not authorize a special registration of voters; secondly, we had a board of registration and by law it could only revise the registration lists at certain stated periods before each regular election; third, if we held the special election under this special law with a new registration, and succeeded, the question might again get into court, where it had already been for nearly five years, and in the end we might be defeated; fourth, there was no reason for haste, as the election could be held before another Legislature would assemble and have opportunity to repeal the Act. These, as have been stated, were the open reasons; but beyond these was one which we dare not disclose to any but the truest—the trusted and the tried.

Fully seventy-five per cent. of our people were proscribed and disfranchised by the provisions of our Constitution, and obnoxious laws upon our statute books; and civil and political liberty to our people were worth more than Court Houses, especially as Court Houses were not free to the proscribed; for to that class there were but four things free, viz: Air, water, payment of taxes and death; therefore the passage of the special Act, ostensibly to settle the Court House controversy, meant to those in the secret much more than appeared on the surface; it meant the breaking of the bonds of political slavery and decitizenship, under which our people, probably twenty-five thousand or more in the state, had suffered and groaned for nearly five years. It also meant the again clothing of that part of our people who had been disfranchised, with the right of citizen-

ship and of freemen, and restoring to them that liberty which
had been torn and wrenched from them by a set of political
pirates, most of whom were moved only by the spirit of revenge,
but others by more sordid motives. By this proscriptive legis-
lation honest men and women could not by law collect their
honest debts, if the debtor had been truly loyal to the Union
during the late unhappy strife. Professional men could not
practice their profession for a livelihood; and no man who had
engaged in the war on the Confederate side, or had sympathized and given aid and comfort to the Confederates, could sit
upon a jury or hold office; nor could the poor young woman,
the daughter of a Confederate soldier, teach school without
subscribing to the "Test Oath." While these laws were pretty
rigidly enforced for a period of nearly five years, the time was
rapidly approaching when they would become a thing of the
past. As has already been stated, the law provided for the
appointment by the Governor of a Board of Registration, consisting of three members, removable at his pleasure. This
board possessed powers somewhat akin to that exercised by
the Spanish Inquisition; they had power to send for persons
and papers—a right to say who should vote and who should
not—by a mere stroke of the pen (that is, such of them as could
write), either to place a man's name on the list or strike it off
at their pleasure, and in this they were protected by law, being
exempt from civil suits or criminal prosecution for any derelic-
tion or violation of law connected with the registration of
voters, or any other outrages they chose to perpetrate touching
the qualification of electors or the right to vote.

The men composing the County Board of Registration of
Mercer County for a good part of the period referred to, were
in most part honest men and desired to do right as far as the
law allowed them. It was not so much the fault of the men
who composed the Board in the latter days of the life of the
law, as it was the law and the District registrars, who were not
always the cleanest birds that could be found, for it was an
open secret that any man who would promise to vote the

Republican ticket, or for any particular candidate, perhaps for the registrar himself, could have his name enrolled as a voter without taking the oath prescribed by law for all voters, or to procure the registration of a voter by deceiving the registrar that the party registered would vote for him, when it was understood he was to vote for another.

In this connection it may be mentioned that the court records of the county had been kept at Concord Church until the fall of 1869, when at a meeting of the Board of Supervisors, Mr. Benjamine White, who was then sheriff and lived at Princeton, made a motion before the Board to remove the records to Princeton for safe keeping, alleging that a threat had been made to destroy them, and in support of his charges produced the affidavits of one or more persons tending to show the truth of his charges. Mr. White's strong and boisterous speech and serious charges alarmed two of the members of the Board of Supervisors, and they actually gathered their hats and left the place, leaving three members only of the Board present, who voted for the motion and the records were immediately removed by wagons procured by Mr. White. The feverish excitement aroused over this removal of the records engendered bad blood, and nearly approached open collision. The fact, though not apparent to the public, was that the people in the interest of Princeton had made a bargain with Mr. George Evans, who, for a certain consideration, would aid in removing the records and abandon his fight for Concord Church as the County site, and espouse the cause of the people in the interest of Princeton; how well this bargain was carried out and the manner of its carrying out, will be fully hereinafter stated.

As hereinbefore stated, the County Board of Registration exercised the right of revision of the list of voters, and the right to strike off the name of any person they chose, and thus deprive him of the right to vote at the succeeding election; and woe to the man that was suspected of disloyalty, not to his country, but to the Republican party, for when the County Board met and it suspected, or some one reported, that a given

man was not loyal in the sense above stated, a summons was
issued requiring the suspect to appear and prove his loyalty;
no charges preferred, none proved, but the party summoned
must come prepared to prove his innocence—that is, that he
was truly loyal to the Republican party and had always voted
and still intended to vote with that party—but if he did not
show up right on this he was adjudged not a legal or qualified
voter. Very few instances of this kind occurred in Mercer
County, but one such at least occurred in an adjoining county,
in which a gentleman of the legal profession, being under suspicion of disloyalty, was summoned before the County Board
of Registration to show and prove that he was true to the grand
old party; appearing before the Board, inquiring what it wanted, and being told he must prove his loyalty, he thereupon became very indignant, using some very rash, opprobrious epi-
thets toward the Board and some of its members for their base-
ness, meanness and ignorance. When he had finished his speech,
one of the members of the Board raised his spectacles upon his
brow and lifting his eyes said: "Well, sir, I am like the apostle
of old, I thank God I am what I am," to which the legal gentleman retorted: "Yes, and you are thankful for d—d small
favors."

This registration scheme was wholly political and one against
liberty; a plot to disfranchise honest, law-abiding people and
to perpetuate the dominant party in power in the state, and
well it succeeded for five years, but they pressed their advantage too far and the conservative element in their party finally
revolted, and the plan that had been devised to ostracise their
neighbors became a useful weapon in the hands of liberty-
loving freemen for the political overthrow and destruction of
the inventors, and resulted in hurling from power the party
which had, as it supposed, firmly intrenched itself behind its
registration disfranchising scheme, which it had theretofore
regarded as impregnable. This registration law, together with
the manner of its execution, became so offensive to the good
people of the state and smelled so badly, that it was said that

"The man in the moon was compelled to hold his nose when he passed over"; and by the close of the fourth and fifth years of its life, no one scarcely dared to do it reverence, or to publicly attempt to justify it. It was doomed and must go, and it was only a question of a short time when it would go; the law itself was bad enough, but its abuses were ten fold worse.

Quite a digression has been made from the consideration of the special law passed to settle the County site question, to let in the explanation of the operation and effect of this registration law; for this very law played an important part, not only in the settlement of the local question, but influenced greatly the political results in the county and state at the general election held in October, 1870.

The Committee of Safety on the part of the Princeton people could no longer have Mr. White in its counsels, and was compelled to go its way alone without the aid of this gentleman and his friendly advice. It was finally determined not to have a special election under the special statute until the new registration could take place in the September following, but the plan was to get control of the Registration Board, not only to have such board friendly, but also favorable to a fair non-partisan registration, and this was a question of grave consideration, for the appointing power of this board was the Governor and he was an extreme, staunch Republican, who could be depended upon to appoint men that he at least believed would do what his party wanted done. This Committee could have no influence with the Governor, and therefore began to cast about as to how they might get control of this registration board, without raising a suspicion that it was engaged in some political intrigue against the Republican party. Mr. George Evans was a Republican of the Republicans, and no man could question his fealty to his party or his zeal for its success; he was a warm personal friend and admirer of the then Governor Stevenson, who was a candidate that spring for re-nomination and for re-election that fall, and as the Republican convention was to be held in the city of Parkersburg, it was not thought likely that any delegate except Mr. Evans would go to the convention and that he would not probably go without it was urged upon him and his expenses paid.

The Circuit Court for the county was to be held at Concord Church in May, which was a short time prior to the meeting of the Republican convention at Parkersburg. The Safety Committee, supposing that the Republicans of the county would hold their convention at the Circuit Court in May and appoint their delegates to their state convention, a plan was hit upon to make known to Mr. Evans that it would be a good thing for the interest of Princeton, he having in the meantime changed his base from the support of Concord Church to that of Princeton, for him to keep in favor with the Governor, and to do this it would be well for him to go as the only delegate from the county of Mercer, and that if he would undertake to manage to hold his county convention during the court and have himself appointed a delegate, and to be sure to appoint men other than himself, none of whom would go, that the committee would undertake to furnish the money to pay his expenses. The bargain was struck, the court came on, the Republicans held their meeting and Mr. Evans, among others, was appointed a delegate to the convention. The committee started out to raise the money, and among the men they came across and asked to contribute five dollars was Honorable Frank Hereford, Democratic nominee for Congress; who inquired what was wanted with the money, and the answer came, "Never mind about that; you will be informed this fall, after the election." Mr. Evans went to the convention; Governor Stevenson was re-nominated, but his election was another question.

For a number of years the people living in the lower district of Mercer County, on and along the New River, and the people of Greenbrier and Monroe Counties occupying the territory adjacent to the New River, near the mouth of Greenbrier, favored the formation of a new county, and the Committee of Safety conceived the idea that this was the favored time to encourage the people to ask the Legislature to create the new county and to vote for a candidate who would be in favor of the project and would push it through the Legislature; and while this committee advised the people to secure the right man, it wanted to see and know that the man was right, not only on the new county question, and therefore on the County site question, but that he would pledge himself to use his best endeavors to secure the repeal of all proscriptive and obnoxious laws. Arrangements for a secret meeting were made between the representatives of Princeton and those in favor of the new county, and it was agreed that Sylvester Upton, a staunch Union man, a conservative Republican, but in every sense an honorable and upright gentleman, should be supported by the combination for the House of Delegates, and he was accordingly named as the candidate. Against Mr. Upton, the Concord Church people nominated or placed in the field Mr. Keaton. In this same combine Mr. George Evans was to be supported for Clerk and Recorder, David Lilley for Sheriff, L. M. Stinson for County Surveyor, and J. Speed Thompson for Prosecuting Attorney.

The support for Mr. George Evans for Clerk and Recorder was the consummation of the arrangement entered into at the time he abandoned the interest of Concord Church and agreed to stand for Princeton; and this was to be in full settlement and discharge of any obligation to him by reason of the previous arrangement for his abandonment of the interest of those favoring Concord Church. Before all the plans could be fully carried out some arrangement had to be made to control the Board of Registration; and in some way, if possible, nonpartisan men, or at least the majority of such must be secured on this board, or there would not be the ghost of a chance for success. The board at this time consisted of L. M. Thomas, Silas T. Reynolds and Mr. Cox. Mr. Reynolds was a high-toned gentleman and liberal in his views, and while he would faithfully execute the law, he would not pervert it; the two others were narrow-minded partisans, and whose chief aim was party success.

The war had now been over for five years and many young
men had attained their majority, and they were almost universally against the party in power. It was hoped that by the
aid of these voters and that of the liberal, conservative element
of the Republican party, and with a non-partisan board of
registration, to be able to overthrow and defeat the radical
wing of that party; not only carry the county ticket, composed
in part of liberal Republicans, but to also carry the Court
House question for Princeton, and the measure in favor of the
new county. But this dreaded Registration Board, like
"Banquo's Ghost," would not down; it was concluded, however,
that down it must go, at all hazards. The committee knowing
that its friends, Mr. Evans and L. M. Thomas, President of the
Board, were close friends politically and otherwise, it was
therefore thought possible for the sake of the local question
that Mr. Evans could control Thomas, but he tried and failed,
and the committee was again perplexed. While brooding over
this apparent ill-luck, with nothing but what seemed a dark
and dismal future, a little incident happened which opened the
way of escape from the apparent difficulties.

Mr. Thomas came to Princeton, and as he was quite fond of
his drink and Mr. Joe Alvis had a little good liquor to give a
man for his first drink, after which he always said he would
then give him the bad and he could not tell the difference—
furnished Thomas what he required along that line, after which
he became exceedingly liberal, and took a tilt at what he de-
nominated the "Cussed Registration Law," saying there was no
reason to have such laws, and that the time had come for every
body to register and vote. It is very doubtful whether Thomas
meant what he said, for it was believed that he meant just the
reverse, and that his talk was only a ruse to deceive the people
as to his real intentions, and to cover up some dark thing that
he had in view to aid the Republican party. Thomas had by
this declaration in favor of liberalism furnished all the cause
necessary for his removal as a member of the Board, for it was
only necessary for a whisper of this declaration to reach the

ears of the Governor's best friend to accomplish his removal. No sooner had he uttered the declaration, than the Committee of Safety had a man getting up affidavits embracing Thomas' statements; these were furnished to Mr. Evans, to whom it was made known that if Thomas carried out his declaration it would destroy the Republican party in Mercer County; and as no one wished to see Mr. Thomas disgraced by being removed from office, it was deemed wise that Mr. Evans should pay a visit to Mr. Thomas, and show him the affidavits and ask him to place his resignation in his hands to be sent to the Governor. Mr. Evans made the visit and returned with the resignation of Mr. Thomas.

This was in the last days of July, or in the first days of August and time was becoming most precious, as the committee had determined to ask the Board of Supervisors to order a special election under the special Act, upon the question of the location of the County site and had planned to have this election take place within a period of less than ten days next preceding the day on which the state election would be held; the object of this being to prevent the Board of Registration from striking off the names of voters, who had been registered to vote on the local question, and thus allow them to vote at the state election; the law forbidding the striking off of the names from the registration books within ten days of any general election. The Committee being satisfied that there was a better showing for a fairer and fuller registration than could be had on state election, and it requiring thirty days' notice under the special Act before the people could vote on the local question, it was determined that this thirty days should expire within less than ten days of the state election, and thereby the people would have the benefit of the full registration in the state election.

As soon as Thomas' resignation was made known to the committee, the question as to who should be his successor arose. Various names were suggested, and finally that of Mr. Andrew J. Davis, and he was found agreeable to Mr. Evans, because he

had always been classed as a Republican, had held office as
such, and no one belonging to that party doubted his being a
Republican, although in fact he was a staunch Democrat. To
carry out this plan and have Mr. Davis appointed was also a
matter of delicacy and required secrecy; for the mails could
not be trusted, none of the committee dare afford to go before
the Governor on such a matter, it was therefore finally concluded that Mr. Evans was the only man that could or should
be trusted with such an important mission. A sufficient fund
was quietly raised, and Mr. Evans set off for the capitol, and
succeeded in having Mr. Davis appointed as President of the
Board of Registration. The secret of the appointment of Mr.
Davis was so well kept by the committee, Mr. Evans, and the
people at the Governor's office, that every one was surprised
when Mr. Davis at the next meeting of the Board took his seat
as a member thereof. Mr. Davis and Mr. Reynolds, a majority
of this board, were known as friends of the Princeton interest
in the local fight. The board appointed its District Registrars
composed of liberal men; and the Board of Supervisors met and
ordered the election on the Court House question, and the
fight opened with spirit and energy all along the line.

So far, the plans of the committee had worked well and were
successful, but in their zeal to succeed they came near committing a serious bunder, which if they had, would have defeated
the settlement of the vexed question. The District Registrars
seemed to forget that they had any other duty than to get out,
hunt up, and register all the male citizens of the county over
the age of twenty-one years. This proceeding at once became
known, and so loud was it noised abroad that it was heard in
the gubernatorial office at Charleston, and gave alarm and
great concern to the Governor and his friends. About the time
the District Registrars had completed their list of voters, the
September term of the Circuit Court of Mercer County began its session at Concord Church; the Honorable Joseph M.
McWhorter, of the Greenbrier Circuit, presiding. There was a
great throng of people at the court to hear Honorable Frank

Hereford, Democratic nominee for Congress, make a speech. There happened to be also present on the occasion Major Cyrus Newlin, a Republican lawyer from Union, who also addressed the people on the political issues of the day.   Newlin was a carpet-bagger of the lower sort and extremely partisan, and his abuse of the Democratic party, particularly of the Southern people, aroused such intense feeling and indignation towards him that it became necessary for his friends to take care of him, in order to prevent personal violence.   The fact is, a crowd gathered that night with a rope, prepared to hang him, and but for the wise counsel of Colonel William H. French and others, who interposed, it would have been accomplished.   On the Court day on which this public speaking took place, it was discovered by the people in the interest of Concord Church, as well as the Republicans, that the registration had been indiscriminate, and that in returning the books to the County Board, the one containing the names of persons registered in Plymouth District, the district in which Concord Church is situate, had been misplaced, and it was suspected by the Concord people that there was some trickery about it; and they became aroused to such a pitch of feeling and excitement as to forget everything else except the local question, which not only absorbed their whole attention and interest, but some of them were willing to sacrifice their political interests and put in jeopardy the chances of shaking off their civil and political shackles; and therefore, in order to wreak vengeance on those opposing them on the local question, they imparted to Major Newlin what they supposed to be the plan for registering every person, with the view to the overthrow of the Republican party.

No sooner had Major Newlin caught on to the supposed scheme than he wrote a letter to the Governor, containing the startling news, that eleven hundred rebels had been registered in Mercer County, all of whom would vote the Democratic ticket; and strange, yet true, it seems that this letter received the approval and endorsement of Judge McWhorter.   When this letter reached Charleston it, of course, very naturally,

aroused the fears of the Governor and his Republican friends
for the safety of the party; and in order to ascertain more fully
the situation the Governor dispatched one A. F. Gibbons, armed
with blank commissions to be filled if he, Gibbons, thought
proper to do so, with the names of a new Board of Registration. This letter had gone and was in the hands of the Governor before the committee discovered that the same had been
written, and by this time it was too late to counteract the effect
thereof at the capitol; in fact, Mr. Gibbons had arrived in the
county before anyone was aware that he had been sent, or what
steps the Governor proposed to take. The committee was confronted by a new, formidable and serious danger; hitherto it
had been equal to every emergency as it had arisen, but the
question now was, would it be equal to this? Up to this time
every movement of the committee's adversaries had been met
and thwarted; being always on the alert, and through information derived from its spies it was kept well advised, and before
the blow was struck a counter one was given, and the arm of
the adversary fell palsied at his side.

The reader must not suppose that these things were idle
dreams—they were stern realities—actual occurrences; and no
question more certainly and effectually divided our people than
did this local question. The war between the states had not
more thoroughly estranged the people of the North and South,
than this question had the people of the two sections of our
county. Military lines were never better connected and more
securely guarded and watched with greater vigilance, than
were the lines between these contending factions; and both
money and brains were at work on both sides, and the struggle
throughout resembled that of two great armies on the battlefield maneuvering for positions and preparing to join in deadly
struggle.

Mr. Gibbons had scarcely more than reached Concord Church,
than the information thereof was brought to the Committee
of Safety. A meeting was called and the situation discussed
and the conclusion reached to watch Gibbon's actions and

await developments, which would doubtless show up in a few hours; and the committee was not mistaken in its conclusion, for Mr. Gibbons by some word or action had given offense to the Concord people, and he left there in high dudgeon and came to Princeton. Now was the time for action, and the committee determined that Mr. Gibbons must be met with open arms and be fully assured that Governor Stevenson's interests should not suffer in the hands of the people who were espousing the cause of Princeton on the local question. To this end large numbers of the people visited Mr. Gibbons, and assured him of their strong friendship for Governor Stevenson, and of their intention to vote for the Governor if the registration books were not blotched by erasure, and that the Governor had all to gain and nothing to lose by allowing the names then on the books to remain untouched. Mr. Gibbons heard these assurances with seeming delight and satisfaction, and his faith in the truth of these statements was strengthened from day to day by the action of and conversations had with our people; at length the adversaries of Princeton, seeing that its people had probably won Gibbons over to its side, and that he was a little too credulous, whispered in his ear that he was being deceived, that the names of too many prominent ex-Confederates were on the registration list for the strong professions of these people to be true; so Mr. Gibbons became a little wary and somewhat alarmed, stating that he thought the names of the more prominent ex-Confederates should be erased from the lists. The committee was reluctantly forced to yield and compromise by the elimination of about two hundred names from the list of voters; yet enough remained to accomplish their purposes, for they knew that while the people had pledged themselves to stand by and vote for Governor Stevenson they had made no further pledges and Mr. Gibbons had not asked or demanded more.

The opponents of Princeton were not without resources, and while these events were transpiring at Princeton they were not idle; for they formulated a plan which they supposed would prevent the people from holding the special election on the local question; and that plan was to get an injunction, prohibiting and enjoining the election officers from opening the polls, holding the election and declaring the result; and with this view, a bill was prepared by Attorney Newlin and entrusted to Attorney J. M. Killey to be taken to Charleston by him and to be presented to a Circuit Judge for an injunction, and if refused, then to be presented to Judge James H. Brown of the Court of Appeals. Mr. Killey had scarcely gotten away from Concord Church before the news of his leaving and that of his mission reached the Committee; whereupon it determined that this last effort of the removalists must be headed off and defeated. It was now only ten days until the election was to be held on the local question. Mr. Killey started on Wednesday, and a messenger was selected and directed to follow Killey, and he started on Thursday morning; however, before starting, Mr. Gibbons requested a little time to write some letters to be sent to the Governor and other friends in Charleston by the Princeton messenger, who took the letters and put off to Charleston, reaching there in less than two days, being only twenty-three and one-half hours in the saddle, and reaching there two hours ahead of Killey, although the latter had twenty-four hours the start and had traveled twelve miles of the distance by steamer. Hurrying to the Governor's office, the Princeton messenger found no one there but Mr. Blackburn B. Dovener, now the Honorable Blackburn B. Dovener, member of Congress from the Wheeling district, private secretary to the Governor, to whom the letters of which he was the bearer were delivered, the Governor being absent in the northern part of the state, leaving Mr. Dovener in charge of his office.

The messenger made known to Mr. Dovener that it was necessary that he should see Judge Brown, and requested him to accompany and introduce him to the Judge, which he did. After stating to the Judge his mission and the character of the bill which would likely be presented to him for action, the Judge promised the messenger that if such bill was presented that he should have opportunity to be heard. Mr. Killey presented his bill to Circuit Judge Hoge, at Winfield, who refused the injunction, and on Mr. Killey's return to Charleston, and on presentation of his bill to Judge Brown the injunction was also refused by him. The Princeton messenger at once started for home, reaching there on the Thursday evening preceding the Saturday on which the election was to be held; and which passed off quietly, a full vote was polled, and the County Court House question was settled in favor of Princeton by a majority of over four hundred. The state election followed on the Tuesday week thereafter, and resulted in the election of the whole Democratic county ticket by an average majority of about three hundred, and a majority of nearly five hundred for Mr. Hereford for Congress; electing Mr. Upton to the House of Delegates; and George Evans Clerk and Recorder over Mr. Green Meador—this was in fulfillment of the agreement of the Princeton interest with Mr. Evans. The county authorities immediately went to work and had erected on the old Court House foundation at Princeton a new building which was completed in 1875. This building was destroyed by fire, but another building was erected immediately thereafter.

Mr. Upton, the Representative from Mercer County, on the assembling of the Legislature in January, 1871, immediately introduced his bill for the creation of a new county out of the territory hereinafter described; and on the 27th day of February, 1871, the bill was passed creating the county of Summers out of parts of the counties of Mercer, Monroe, Greenbrier and Fayette, within the following described boundary, to-wit:

"Beginning at the mouth of Round Bottom Branch, on New River, in Monroe County, thence crossing said river and running N. 47½ W. 5430 poles through the county of Mercer to a point known as Brammer's Gate, on the line dividing the counties of Mercer and Raleigh; thence with said county line in an easterly direction to New River; thence with a line between the counties of Raleigh and Greenbrier, down New River to the line of Fayette County; thence with a line dividing Raleigh

and Fayette Counties, down said river to a station opposite
Goddard's House; thence leaving the line of Raleigh County,
crossing New River and passing through said Goddard's house,
N. 67½ E. 3280 poles through said county of Fayette, to a
station on Wallow Hole Mountain, in Greenbrier County;
thence S. 55 E. 3140 poles to a station east of Keeney's Knob
in Monroe County; thence S. 9 E. 1320 poles to a station near
Greenbrier River, and running thence S. 32 W. 7740 poles to
the beginning."

The period between the close of the civil war and the settlement of the question of the location of the seat of justice of
Mercer County, and the complete removal of all civil and political disabilities, under which our people had been laboring for
a period of nearly seven years, was one of turmoil, trouble and
unrest. Business in Mercer County during this time was largely at a standstill, no one knew what to do, many suits had been
brought against the ex-Confederates for alleged wrongs and
injuries done or committed during the civil war, and they, the
ex-Conferedates, had little show in the courts, which had been
organized, as a rule, in the interest of the dominant party and
for oppression. The men who sat upon the juries of the county
were the political enemies of the ex-Confederates and of the
people who had espoused the Southern cause. No man who had
served in the Confederate army or sympathized with the South,
regarded his life, liberty, property or cause, whatever it might
be, as safe in the hands of the Courts and Juries as they were
then organized and existed. Hundreds of people who had
owned valuable property before the beginning of the war and
lived in opulence, were by its results reduced almost to beg-
gary, and they had a long, hard struggle to earn even a livelihood. The expenses of government—the taxes—had grown
to such enormous proportions that the people had great difficulty in paying the same. The levies of taxes for local purposes
were often outrageous, on account of the character and
amounts of the claims and demands for which they were levied;

and after the levies had been placed in the hands of the collecting officers they were often squandered and never accounted for. In the great struggle over the Court House question, a large amount of the public funds were squandered, stolen or wasted. A jail had been erected at Concord Church and the walls for a Court House had been about half way built, and the expenditures in this regard amounted to thousands of dollars, which was an entire loss to the taxpayers of the county. But, notwithstanding all these drawbacks, the people labored, toiled and struggled on in the hope of a better day coming, and it came at last when we had better government and lower taxes, and the end largely of all the difficulties growing out of the civil war and the questions therein involved.

The Board of Supervisors had power to lay and disburse the county levies, and to make all contracts touching county affairs. After the removal of the records and books from Concord Church to Princeton, the Board of Supervisors consisted of L. D. Martin, William C. Honaker, Silas T. Reynolds, Thomas Reed, and, for part of the time, Washington Lilley.

Mention has already been made of Mr. George Evans, who was of Welsh extraction or descent, and who came from Wilkesbarre, Pennsylvania. He was a man of fair education, good sense, and, although often roundly abused, was yet a very clever man, but in the days in which he ruled was a power among the Republicans, and ruled them generally with a rod of iron. He held as many as four or five offices at one and the same time, and did pretty generally as he pleased touching the control and management of county affairs, civil and political.

After the Board of Supervisors had adjourned its meetings from Concord Church to Princeton, a proposition was made to it by Mr. Evans to sell to the county a small farm which he owned in the valley of East River Mountain as a place on which to keep the paupers of the county. Mr. Evans was, in his political manipulation, always shrewd enough to control one man on each of the Board of Supervisors and Registration;

this man was always a friend of Mr. Evans'—his middle man
or fifth wheel—and by and through whom he was generally able
to carry out any measure he desired, or that he knew was to
his interest or that of his party. The Board of Supervisors
was generally divided politically, two Democrats and three
Republicans, but Mr. Evans could not always rely upon his
political friends to save his pet measures, but when necessary,
he was sometimes compelled to call on the other side, and with
the aid of his man carry his point. Mr. Evans' proposition to
sell his farm to the county met with disfavor, not only from
the two members who were in the Princeton interest, but especially from the two men who were friends of the Concord interest, the two latter being exceedingly hostile to Mr. Evans on
account of his desertion of their interests in the Court House
controversy and his espousal of the interest of Princeton;
therefore, when his proposition was submitted to the Board,
not only the two men from the Concord section voted against
it, but also the two men from the Princeton section, leaving
only Mr. Thomas Reed, the friend of Mr. Evans, to vote for his
proposition. No sooner was the measure defeated than Mr.
Reed made a motion that the Board adjourn to meet at Concord
Church on the next day, and his motion was promptly carried
by his own and the votes of the two Concord men, who were
highly elated at the prospects of the Board again holding its
sessions at Concord Church, which would probably result in
taking the records to that place, and that the Courts would
again be held there. Mr. Reed, with the two men that had voted
with him, mounted their horses and took the road toward
Concord Church, stopping, however, over night with Colonel
William H. French, by whom they were very highly entertained
and cared for, and who was greatly delighted with their action in adjourning the meeting of the Board to the place above
named. The Board met the next morning at Concord Church
with the two members from the Princeton section absent. Mr.
Evans' proposition was again submitted and unanimously carried, but before the Board adjourned the two members from

the Princeton section arrived, and thereupon Mr. Reed moved that the Board adjourn to meet at Princeton; the two members from Concord voting in the negative, but Mr. Reed voting with the Princeton men, the motion was carried. This incident is related here to show that this Court House controversy entered into every public and private transaction of whatever character.

The Legislature at its session of 1870 repealed the "Suitors Test Oath," and amended the oath of teachers and attorneys, and at the same session proposed an amendment to the Constitution commonly known and designated as the "Flick Amendment," which provided that: "The male citizens of the state shall be entitled to vote at all elections held within the election district in which they respectively reside; but no person who is a minor, or of unsound mind, or a pauper, or who has been convicted of treason, felony, or bribery in any election, or who has not been a resident of the state for one year, and of the county in which he offers to vote for thirty days next preceding his offer, shall be permitted to vote while such disability continued." It will be seen that this amendment was intended, and in fact did, recitizenize and reenfranchise those who had been decitizenized and disfranchised by the amendment to the Constitution of May 24, 1866. The session of 1871 adopted the amendment, and provided by law for its submission to the people, and it was adopted by a large majority, on the fourth Thursday in April, 1871. This, however, did not satisfy the people of West Virginia, for they had determined to remodel the Constitution, or, rather, have a new one; and on the 23rd day of February, 1871, an Act was passed to take the sense of the people upon the call of a convention and for organizing the same, and providing for an election on that question to be held throughout the state on the fourth Thursday of August, 1871, and which election resulted in a majority of votes being cast for the call. The same Act provided that in the event of a majority of the vote being cast in favor of the convention, that the Governor should make proclamation accordingly, and on the

fourth Thursday of October, 1871, that delegates to the said
convention should be elected. There were to be elected two
delegates from each senatorial district and one from each
county and delegate district. From the Mercer County senatorial district, Honorable Evermont Ward, of Cabell County,
and Doctor Isaiah Bee, of Mercer County, were chosen over
Honorable Mitchell Cook, of Wyoming County, and Mr.
Harvey Scott, of Cabell County; and from the county
of Mercer Elder James Calfee, a minister of the church
of the Disciples, was chosen over Colonel William H. French.
The members elected to this convention assembled at Charleston on the third Tuesday of January, 1872, and elected Honorable Samuel Price, of Greenbrier County, President. The
convention sat from the 16th day of January to the 9th day of
the following April, and having finished its work, adopted a
schedule submitting the Constitution framed by it to the people to be voted on, on the fourth Thursday of August, 1872,
and the same was ratified by the people by a majority of over
4,000.

At the August election, 1872, Captain William L. Bridges, a
Democrat, was elected to the House of Delegates from Mercer
County, over Jno. H. Peck; and a full set of Democratic county
officers were also elected, but Mr. George Evans, a candidate
for re-election for Clerk of the Courts received but thirty votes;
and this was his last appearance in the arena of politics in
Mercer County. Honorable Evermont Ward was elected Cir-
cuit Judge, over C. W. Smith, Ira J. McGinnis, Henry L. Gilles-
pie, and I. S. Samuel; David E. Johnston was elected prosecut-
ing attorney, over R. C. McClaugherty, J. Speed Thompson, and
Alonzo Gooch; R. B. Foley was elected Clerk of the Circuit
Court, over E. H. Peck and J. C. Straley; Benjamine G. Mc-
Nutt was elected Clerk of the County Court, over John H.
Robinson.

The people who had espoused the cause of Princeton in the
Court House controversy were anxious to remove, as far as
possible, the chagrin and disappointment of the people who had

striven to have the County site located at Concord Church; they induced Captain Bridges to introduce and have passed a Bill establishing a branch of the State Normal School at Concord Church (now Athens), and which is today a most flourishing institution of learning, and of which Captain James H. French was the principal for nearly twenty years.

The political shackles that had been forged by the extreme Republicans—radicals—and placed upon the ex-Confederates and tightly held for more than five years, had been snapped asunder and cast away, and the Confederate people with the Union Democrats took charge of the ship of state and guided her course safely for more than a quarter of a century, and only lost control when the state became flooded with criminal negroes. For a full twenty-five years or more the conservative Democratic people governed the state, during which time there was made more rapid material development than in any other period of her existence, before or since. (1) The whole policy of the state, and her wise laws and administration thereof, during the years referred to, were dictated and controlled largely by the old Confederate soldiers. It was through this influence that the Constitution of 1872 was framed and adopted, and into which was incorporated the provision that no person on either side of the war should be held ,civilly or criminally, liable for acts done according to the usages of civilized warfare.

————————o————————

In the year of 1750, Doctor Thomas Walker and his party, on his return from his second visit to the Cumberland Gap and Kentucky section of country, passed by the site of what is now the city of Pocahontas, Virginia, discovering the outcrop of the great coal beds of the Flat Top region; consisting of some thirteen measures of coal, one of which is known as the Poca-

(1). George W. Anderson began, about 1876, the publication of the Princeton Journal, the first newspaper published in Mercer County.

hontas or No. 3, and which is over ten feet thick. The next
we hear about this coal field is in the report of Prof. Rogers,
State Geologist of Virginia, who visited this section between
the years of 1836 and 1840, and made an extensive examination and a report of this coal formation; however, this report
seems to have excited no particular attention. General Gabriel
C. Wharton of Montgomery County, Virginia, who commanded
during the late civil war a body of Confederate troops and
marched at their head across the Flat Top Mountain, observed
this coal formation, and was impressed with its commercial
value. He having been elected, in 1871, to the Legislature of
Virginia from the County of Montgomery, obtained on the 7th
of March, 1872, a charter for the incorporation of "The New
River Railroad, Mining and Manufacturing Company," with
John B. Radford, John T. Cowan, James Cloyd, James A.
Walker, William T. Yancey, William Mahone, Charles W.
Stratham, Joseph H. Chumley, A. H. Flanagan, Philip W.
Strother, John C. Snidow, Joseph H. Hoge, William Eggleston,
G. C. Wharton, William Adair, James A. Harvey, A. A. Chap-
man, Robert W. Hughes, A. N. Johnston, Elbert Fowler, David
E. Johnston, John A. Douglass, William H. French, R. B. Mc-
Nutt, James M. Bailey and A. Gooch, as incorporators. This
charter was a very liberal one and gave to the company upon
its organization the right and power to construct, maintain
and operate a railroad from New River Depot in Pulaski
County, Virginia, on the line of the Atlantic, Mississippi, and
Ohio Railroad, to such a point as might be agreed upon at or
near the head of Camp Creek in the County of Mercer and
State of West Virginia, with ample provision for the building
of branch roads in Mercer and other counties; the capital
stock not to exceed $2,000,000.00. The first meeting of the
incorporators was held at Pearisburg, and Dr. John B. Radford was elected President and Elbert Fowler Secretary. Various committees were appointed, among them Captain Richard
B. Roane, who was authorized and directed to visit the coal
fields and to secure grants and subscriptions in lands or money.

In part at least, through Captain Roane, Colonel Thomas Graham, of Philadelphia, became interested in the scheme, and finally with some of his friends succeeded in getting control of a majority of the stock of said company, and immediately went to work to secure all the coal land in what is now known as the Pocahontas region, and to push the building of the railroad into that field.

In 1875 experimental lines were run from New River Depot down the New River to Hinton on the Chesapeake & Ohio road. Shortly thereafter Colonel Graham succeeded in securing the Virginia State convicts and placed them on the line and commenced the construction of a narrow gauge railroad. In the year of 1881 Mr. F. J. Kimball, President of Norfolk & Western Railroad Company, met with Major Jed Hotchkiss, of Staunton, Virginia, and in a conversation insisted that his road must have coal. Major Hotchkiss pointed out to Mr. Kimball the Flat Top Field and its accessibility to his road and the wonderful value of the coal, which led Mr. Kimball to join Hotchkiss in a visit to the section. The coal and mineral leases and contracts taken by Captain Roane, together with those subsequently taken by John Graham, Jr., and Dr. James O'Keiffee were in the names of J. D. Sergeant and others, or rather for their benefit.

Some time prior to February, 1881, the mortgage on the Atlantic, Mississippi & Ohio Railroad had been foreclosed, and the road purchased by a Philadelphia syndicate, who changed the name to Norfolk & Western Railroad Company, which very shortly thereafter became the owner of the New River Railroad, Mining and Manufacturing Company's charter, and on the 3rd day of August, 1881, the Norfolk & Western Railroad Company commenced the construction of its New River Branch. In the meantime a charter had been obtained from the state of West Virginia incorporating the New River Railroad in West Virginia, and also a charter for the East River Railroad, in West Virginia.

On the 9th day of May, 1882, the New River Railroad Company of Virginia, the New River Railroad Company of West Virginia, and the East River Railroad Company were merged and consolidated. The work on this line of road was rapidly pushed, so that on the 21st day of May, 1883, the same was completed to Pocahontas, Virginia, the terminal point, and the first shipments of coal were made in the June following. The Messrs. Graham, Sergeant and others, in the meantime, had secured by option and purchase and had gotten together some 50,000 acres of valuable coal properties in the Pocahontas field.

For ten years or more prior to 1882, Messrs. H. W. Straley, C. D. Straley, John A. Douglass, James D. Johnston, and this writer, had been securing coal properties along the north side of the Bluestone River in the Flat Top region, and from the Virginia and West Virginia state line eastward, had gotten control of some 20,000 acres. In the year of 1881, these lands of Straley and others were, through Echols, Bell and Catlett, of Staunton, Virginia, and Honorable Frank Hereford, of Union, optioned to Samuel Coit of Hartford, Connecticut; which options were finally taken by George M. Bartholomew and Samuel Coit, the land was surveyed, paid for and conveyed to said Bartholomew and David E. Johnston, trustees, and subsequently sold to E. W. Clark, of Philadelphia, and his associates, for $105,000.00. The name given to the company by the parties who held these lands prior to the sale to Mr. Clark, was first, Bluestone-Flat Top Coal Company, and afterwards Flat Top Coal Company, but subsequently Mr. Clark and his associates organized several joint stock companies, dividing up these lands and conveying portions thereof to each of said companies. Among the companies organized, were Bluestone Coal Company, Crane Creek Coal Company, Indian Ridge Coal Company, Widemouth Coal Company, Flat Top Coal Company, and Rich Creek Coal Company. While these companies were being organized, Mr. Clark and his associates, together with some other persons, organized the Trans-Flat Top Land Association, for the purpose of acquiring coal lands north and west of the Flat Top Mountain, which association acquired a large territory of lands in the Counties of McDowell, Wyoming, Raleigh, Boone and Logan, including the Maitland survey, called 500,000 acres, the Dillon survey of 50,000 acres, and a large number of small tracts within these surveys held under junior grants. The holdings of the several joint stock companies above named, together with those of the Trans-Flat Top Association, aggregated 232,483 acres. On the first day of April, 1887, the Flat Top Coal Land Trust, which afterwards changed its name to Flat Top Coal Land Association, was organized by Edward W. Clark, Sidney F. Tyler, Everett Gray, Robert B. Minturn, Henderson M. Bell, Edward Denniston and Mahlon Sands, the objects and purposes of which were the purchase and acquisition of mineral and other lands and interests in real estate in the states of Virginia, West Virginia, and North Carolina, and for the development, improvement and sale of the same, and the leasing thereof for the purpose of cutting and the carrying away of the timber, of coal mining for coal and coking purposes, for the purpose of mining iron ore, and the manufacturing of iron, or for any other purposes. The capital of the association was to consist of $40,000.00, with the right to increase the same to $10,000,000.00, and the stock to be divided into two classes, preferred and common shares, of equal amounts. These articles of association constituted E. W. Clark, S. F. Tyler, and H. M. Bell trustees, to whom was conveyed all of the aforesaid lands.

Mr. Samuel A. Crozer of Upland, Pennsylvania, entered early into this coal field on the Elkhorn Creek, and purchased a body of several thousand acres, which he immediately proceeded to open up and develop. The major part of his holdings lie largely on and along the Ohio extension of the Norfolk & Western Railroad. These lands held by Clark, Tyler and Bell have been recently sold and conveyed to The Pocahontas Coal & Coke Company.

It has already been stated that the first coal shipped from this field was in June, 1883, and, as shown by the statistics, the whole output of coal for the first year, 1883, was 55,522 tons, and of coke 23,762 tons. A large number of collieries have been opened and are in operation in Mercer County, and there are a number of others opening up in the Widemouth Valley. The following are among the collieries in the County of Mercer, viz:

Mill Creek Coal & Coke Co.   Caswell Creek Coal & Coke Co.
Booth-Bowen Coal & Coke Co.   Buckeye Coal & Coke Co.
Goodwill Coal & Coke Co.   Louisville Coal & Coke Co.
Coaldale Coal & Coke Co.   Klondike Coal & Coke Co.

The total output from these coal mines for the year of 1904 was 1,274,070 tons of coal, and of coke 190,132 tons.

These coal operations are carried on in the northeast portion of Tazewell County, Virginia, the northwest portion of Mercer, and largely over the southern portion of McDowell County.

When the railroad entered this region in May, 1883, there were no cities, towns or villages. There are now in this field and in the immediate vicinity, the city of Bluefield, in Mercer County, with a population of nearly 11,000; the city of Pocahontas, in Tazewell County, with a population of about 5,000, and the towns of Graham, Coopers, Bramwell, Ada and Oakvale. From the wildest, most rugged and romantic country to be found in the mountains of Virginia, or West Virginia, this has become the most rushing and thriving business center, with a population of perhaps 50,000, whereas, before the coming of the railroad and the developments referred to, the population was comparatively small. Many little thriving villages and towns have sprung up in different portions of the county, mostly, however, along the lines of railroad, and in the mining district. Athens, formerly Concord Church, a few years ago but a very small village, is now quite a thriving town; and Princeton, the county town, is now putting on city airs on account of the prospective building of the Deepwater Railroad.

The people of the county are generally prosperous farmers, and have within the past few years greatly improved their farms, erected a better class of dwelling houses, and there has been a general advance and improvement along the whole line. The city of Bluefield has had a marvelous growth.. In 1888 it was a mere flag station on the farm of John B. Higginbotham; incorporated as a town in December, 1889, with Judge Joseph M. Sanders as its first Mayor. The city has four banks, viz: First National, Flat Top National, Commercial, and State Bank, with an aggregate capital of over $250,000.00, with a line of deposits of over $1,000,000.00; four hotels; four wholesale grocery houses, water works, electric light plant, electric railway line. It has two Methodist churches (white), two Methodist churches (colored), two Baptist churches (white) and two colored Baptist churches, one church of the Disciples, one Lutheran, one Presbyterian and one Catholic. It also has a large high school building, costing about $20,000.00, accommodating nearly 800 school children; a large Institute for the colored people, which was built on state account, and is supported by state appropriations; and also a large opera house.

The city is built on the watershed between the head branch of East River and the waters of the Bluestone, in the extreme southwestern portion of Mercer County, and is about 2557 feet above tide, in a high and healthful location, and bids fair in a few years to have a population of more than double what it has at present. Mercer County has, including the railroad yard at Bluefield, about 195.03 miles of trackage in the county, of which 74.3 miles are within the city of Bluefield.

The taxable values in the county for the year of 1880 were $676,009.00 and in the year of 1905 $4,103,563.00.

APPENDIXES.

———o———

THE COURTS, JUDGES, MAGISTRATES, ATTORNEYS, ETC.

Deeming it of interest to the reader, a brief history of the organization of Courts of Justice for the states of Virginia and West Virginia, taken from the statutes and codes of said states is here inserted. (See Compilation in Code 1849.)

An Act was passed in Virginia, in 1784, for the establishment of courts of Assize (Hen-State Vol. II, p. 422), but it never went into operation; it was first suspended, and then repealed (Id. Vol. 12, pp. 45, 267, 497). It was succeeded by the Act establishing District Courts of law (Id. p. 532, Ch. 39, p. 644, Ch. 1, p. 730, Ch. 67). These District Courts, after being in operation about twenty years, were abolished in 1809, under the Acts establishing a Superior Court of law in each county (1807-8, p. 5, Ch. 3; p. 10, Ch. 14; 1809, p. 9, Ch. 6). The several acts concerning Superior Courts of law were reduced into one by the Act of 1819 (1st Rev. Code, p. 227, Ch. 69). In 1777 an Act passed establishing a high court of Chancery for the state (Hen-Stat., Vol. 9, p. 389, Ch. 15). When first established it consisted of three judges, but the number was reduced to one by the Act of 1788 (Id. Vol. 12, p. 767). The jurisdiction of this court extended over the whole state until 1802, when the state was divided into three districts, and a Superior Court of Chancery established for each district (1801-2, p. 12, Ch. 14). The places of holding these courts were Richmond, Williamsburg and Staunton. In 1812 the Staunton district was divided into four districts; the judge, previously assigned to the Staunton district was to hold courts for these, to-wit: At Staunton and Wythe Court House, and a new judge was to hold court for the two others, to-wit: at Winchester and Clarksburg (1811-12, p. 19, Ch. 15). In 1814 the Richmond and Williamsburg districts were divided into four districts; the judge previously assigned to the Richmond district was to hold courts for two of these, to-wit: at Richmond and Lynchburg, and the judge previously assigned to the Williamsburg district was to hold court for the other two, to-wit: at Williamsburg and Fredericksburg (1813-14, p. 44, Ch. 16). Under a subsequent Act of the same year, the judge of the Staunton and Wythe district was, for certain counties, to hold a court at Greenbrier Court House (1813-14, p. 81, Ch. 33). The Acts concerning the Superior Court of Chancery were reduced into one by the Act of 1818 (1st Rev. Code, p. 196, Ch. 66). The Superior Courts of law held by fifteen judges, and the Superior Courts of Chancery held by four judges, were abolished by the Act of the 16th day of April, 1831, which divided the state into 20 circuits, held by that number of judges, and established a Circuit Superior Court of Law and Chancery for each county and in certain corporations (1830-1, p. 42, Ch. 11). Thus it will be seen that it was about thirty-five years from the date of the establishment of courts of Chancery in Virginia before one of such courts were authorized to be held west of the Alleghanies; therefore our people, having occasion to resort to a Court of Conscience to have their grievances settled, had to travel many miles towards the rising sun to find a law doctor, authorized to administer relief. As stated, the itinerant Circuit Court system was not adopted until April, 1831, before that time the courts were held by the judges of the District and General court, who by allotment were assigned to the various districts as they then existed.

The following judges of the districts and General courts and of the Circuit courts held terms of court in the territory now embraced in the counties of Montgomery, Giles, Tazewell, Monroe, and Mercer from 1809 to the present:

JUDGES OF THE GENERAL COURT.

Hon. John Coalter.   Hon. Allen Taylor.
Hon. Paul Carington.   Hon. Peter Johnston.
Hon. Archibald Stewart.   Hon. James Allen.
Hon. William Brockenborough. Hon. John J. Allen.

CIRCUIT JUDGES.

Benjamine Estill.   John J. Allen.
Edward Johnston.   James E. Brown.
George W. Hopkins.   Andrew S. Fulton.
Samuel G. Fulkerson.   John A. Campbell.
John W. Johnston.   Edward B. Bailey.
Robert M. Hudson.   .... Tipton.
Alexander Mahood.   Evermont Ward.
John H. Fulton.   Randall M. Brown.
D. W. Bolen.   Samuel W. Williams.
R. C. Jackson.   Henry E. Blair.
W. J. Henson.

VIRGINIA CHANCELLORS.

George Wythe.   Creed Taylor.
William Wirt.   Henry St. George Tucker.

COUNTY COURT JUDGES FOR GILES COUNTY.

P. W. Strother.   George W. Easley.
A. N. Heiflin.   Martin Williams.
Bernard Mason.

COUNTY COURT JUDGES FOR TAZEWELL COUNTY.

James P. Kelley.   Sterling F. Watts.
Samuel C. Graham.   S. M. B. Couling.
J. H. Stuart.

THE FOLLOWING are the names of the Circuit judges who have presided over the Circuit Court of Mercer County since its organization, viz:

Honorable James E. Brown, Wytheville, Virginia.
Honorable Edward B. Bailey, Fayetteville, Virginia.

Honorable Evermont Ward, Logan, Virginia and West Va.
Honorable Nathanial Harrison, Union, West Virginia
Honorable Henry L. Gillaspie, Beckley, West Virginia.
Honorable David E. Johnston, Princeton, West Virginia.
Honorable Robert C. McClaugherty, Princeton, West Va.
Honorable Joseph M. Sanders, Bluefield, West Virginia.
Honorable Luther L. Chambers, Welch, West Virginia.

THE FOLLOWING is a list of the names of the justices of the peace for the counties of Fincastle and Montgomery, serving on the courts of these counties from 1773 to 1805:

Arthur Campbell.
Daniel Trigg.
John Henderson.
Adam Dean.
Joseph Gray.
William Christian.
Andrew Lewis.
Daniel Howe.
James Charlton.
James McGavock.
James Thompson.
Andrew Boyd.
James Byrn.
John Preston.
James Craig.
James McCorkle.
Christian Snidow.
William Ward.
Walter Crockett.
John Adams.
James Robertson.
John T. Sawyers.
Robert Moffett.
John Taylor.

John Kent.
Henry Patton.
John Hough.
Flower Swift.
Thomas Goodson.
Joseph Cloyd.
George Rutlege.
William Love.
James Taylor.
Anthony Bledsoe.
Jonathan Isan.
George Pearis.
James Reaburn.
James Newell.
John Taylor.
William Russell.
James P. Preston.
William Davis.
James Woods.
Thomas Shannon.
James Barnett.
William Preston.
David French.

THE FOLLOWING is a list of the names of the sheriffs of Fincastle and Montgomery counties from 1773 to 1806:

William Ingles.	John Montgomery.
Walter Crockett.	Andrew Lewis.
James McCorkle.	Charles Taylor.
Daniel Trigg.	Joseph Cloyd.
James Barnett.	Henry Patton.

THE FOLLOWING are the names of the gentlemen who represented this New River district of country in the various constitutional conventions of Virginia, viz:

1776, Arthur Campbell and William Russell, representing Fincastle County.

1788, the convention assembled to consider the ratification or rejection of the Federal constitution, viz: Walter Crockett and Abraham Trigg, from Montgomery County.

1829-30, Gordon Cloyd, Henley Chapman, George P. Matthews and William Oglesby.

1850-51, Albert G. Pendleton, Allen T. Caperton and A. A. Chapman.

SECESSION CONVENTION OF 1861.

Giles County—Manilius Chapman.

Monroe County—Allen T. Caperton and John Echols.

Mercer County—Napoleon B. French.

Tazewell County—William P. Cecil and Samuel L. Graham.

VIRGINIA CONSTITUTIONAL CONVENTION OF 1869.

Giles and Pulaski Counties—Eustace Gibson.

Tazewell and Bland Counties—James M. French.

VIRGINIA CONSTITUTIONAL CONVENTION OF 1901-2.

Giles and Pulaski Counties—Joseph C. Wysor.

Tazewell County—Albert Pendleton Gillespie.

MEMBERS OF THE HOUSE OF REPRESENTATIVES of the United States, representing the territory in the now counties of Montgomery, Giles, Tazewell, Monroe and Mercer, from 1789 to the creation and organization of the state of West Virginia, June 20th, 1863, and also the names of those who have been members of Congress from the 9th Congressional District of Virginia since 1863:

1789-1863.	1863-1905.
Andrew Moore.	Daniel Hoge, 1865-7.
Hugh Caperton.	James K. Gibson, 1869-71.
Robert Craig.	William Terry, 1871-73.
A. A. Chapman.	Rees T. Bowen, 1873-75.
Fayette McMullen.	William Terry, 1875-77.
Francis Preston.	A. L. Pridemore, 1877-79.
John Floyd.	J. B. Richmond, 1879-81.
William McComas.	Abram Fulkerson, 1881-83.
William B. Preston.	Henry Bowen, 1883-85.
W. R. Staples.	C. F. Trigg, 1885-87.
Abram Trigg.	Henry Bowen, 1887-89.
Robert B. Craig.	John A. Buckhannan, 1889-93.
Andrew Bierne.	James W. Marshall, 1893-95.
Henry A. Edmundson.	James A. Walker, 1895-99.
	W. F. Rhea, 1899-1903.
	C. T. Slemp, 1903-1905.

STATE SENATORS from the district comprising in part Montgomery, Giles, Monroe, Mercer and Tazewell counties from 1773-1863:

William Christian.	William Thomas.
John Preston.	William H. French.
James Hoge.	J. W. M. Witten.
Andrew Bierne.	William Russell.
Manilius Chapman.	John Chapman.
Charles H. Greaver.	Joseph Draper.
A. A. Chapman.	Allen T. Caperton.
William Fleming.	William B. Preston.
James Preston.	Napoleon B. French.
Henley Chapman.	

THE FOLLOWING is a list of the names of the gentlemen who represented Montgomery County in the General Assembly of Virginia from 1785 to 1806, inclusive:

1785-6—Robert Sayers and John Breckenridge.

1788—Daniel Trigg and Joseph Cloyd.

1793—Andrew Lewis and John Preston.

1795-6—James Craig and James Barnett.

1797-8—John Ingles and James Taylor.

1800—Daniel Howe and James Craig.

1804—John Ingles and John Gardner.

1805—John Ingles and Andrew Lewis.

GILES COUNTY, being created in 1806, and being entitled to two representatives, the following named gentlemen were elected as her representatives:

1807-8-9-10—Andrew Johnston and Thomas Shannon.

1811—Andrew Johnston and Hugh Caperton, Sr.

1812—John Chapman, Jr., and Christian Snidow.

1813-14—David Johnston and John Chapman, Jr.

1815-16-17—Andrew Johnston and William Smith.

1818-19—John Peters, Jr., and John Kirk, Sr.

1820-21-22—David Johnston and Christian Snidow.

1823-24—William H. Snidow and William Smith.

1825—Charles King and William Smith.

1826—William H. Snidow and Charles King.

1827—William H. Snidow and William Smith.

1828—William H. Snidow and Charles King .

1829—Samuel Pack and George N. Pearis.

1830—Samuel Pack and Charles King.

UNDER THE CONSTITUTION of 1829-30 Giles County was entitled to one delegate only, and the following named gentlemen were elected to the assembly from that county, to-wit:

1831—William Smith.

1832—William H. Snidow.

1833-34—Morton P. Emmons.

1835—Reuben F. Watts.

1836-37—Daniel Hale.

MERCER COUNTY, created in 1837, and attached to the delegate district of Giles and Mercer, elected the following representatives to the assembly, to-wit:

1838—William Smith.
1839—Manilius Chapman.
1840—Charles King.
1841—Oscar F. Johnson.
1842-3—William H. French.
1844—Albert G. Pendleton.
1845—William H. French.

1846—Madison Allen.
1847—Cornelius White.
1848—Lewis Neal.
1849—Elijah Bailey.
1850—Albert G. Pendleton.
1851—George W. Pearis.

REPRESENTATIVES from Giles County after adoption of the Constitution of 1850-1:

1852-5—Thomas Shannon.
1855-7—A. G. Pendleton.
1857-9—Madison Allen.
1859-61—Samuel Lucas.
1861-3—William Eggleston.
1863-5—Absolom Fry.
1866-8—A. G. Pendleton.

1869-71—F. W. Mahood.
1871-3—J. C. Snidow.
1873-5—P. W. Strother.
1875-7—S. E. Lybrook.
1877-9—James D. Johnston.
1879-81—C. J. Mathews.
1881-3—S. E. Lybrook.

REPRESENTATIVES from Pulaski and Giles:

1883-5—J. H. Darst.
1885-7—J. E. Moore.
1887-9—H. B. Howe.
1889-91—S. E. Lybrook.

1891-3—J. R. Caddall.
1893-7—James W. Williams.
1897-9—D. C. Pollard.
1899-01—J. R. Stafford.

REPRESENTATIVES from Bland and Giles:

1901-3—George T. Bird.   1905—Martin Williams.

UNDER THE CONSTITUTION of 1851 Mercer County was entitled to a delegate of her own, and under that Constitution elections were held every two years, and the following are the names of the gentlemen who represented Mercer County after the adoption of this Constitution, viz:

1851-52—Reuben Garretson.
1853-54—James M. Bailey.

1855-56—William M. Meador.
1857-59—James M. Bailey.

1860-61—Napoleon B. French.   1865—Alexander Mahood; elect
1862-64—Robert A. Richardson.   ed, but did not serve.

WEST VIRGINIA CONSTITUTIONAL CONVENTIONS, 1863-1872.

Captain Richard M. Cook, of Wyoming County, claimed to
have represented Mercer County in the West Virginia Constitutional convention of 1863, but no evidence can be adduced
that he was ever legally elected as such representative, or had
any legal authority to sit in that body as the representative of
the people of Mercer County.

In the convention of 1872 the Senatorial district delegates
were Doctor Isaiah Bee, of Mercer, and Honorable Evermont
Ward, of Cabell; and Elder James Calfee represented the
County of Mercer.

UNITED STATES SENATORS from West Virginia from 1863 to
the present:

Peter C. Van Winkle, Parkerburg; December 7th, 1863, March
    4th, 1869.

Waitman P. Willey, Morgantown; December 7th, 1863, to
    March 4th, 1871.

Arthur I. Boreman, Parkersburg; March 4th, 1869, to March,
    1875.

Henry G. Davis, Piedmont; March 4th, 1871, to March 4th,
    1883.

Allen T. Caperton, Union; March 4th, 1875, to death July 26th,
    1876.

Samuel Price, Lewisburg; appointed August 26th, 1876; De-
    cember 4th, 1876, to January 30th, 1877.

Frank Hereford, Union; January 31st, 1877, to March 3rd,
    1881.

Johnson N. Camden, Parkersburg; March 4th, 1881, to March
    3rd, 1887.

John E. Kenna, Charleston; March 4th, 1883, to March 3rd,
    1895.   (Died in 1893.)

Charles J. Faulkner, Martinsburg; March 4th, 1887, to March 3rd, 1893.

Johnson N. Camden ,Parkersburg; March 4th, 1893, to March 3rd, 1895.   (Unexpired term of John E. Kenna.)

Charles J. Faulkner, Martinsburg; March 4th, 1893, to March 3rd, 1899.

Stephen B. Elkins, Elkins; March 4th, 1895, to March 3rd, 1901.

N. B. Scott, Wheeling; March 4th, 1899, to March 3rd, 1905.

Stephen B. Elkins, Elkins; March 4th, 1901, to March 3rd, 1907.

N. B. Scott, elected January, 1905, for a term of six years.

CONGRESSIONAL ELECTIONS, 1864-1904, in the 3rd and 5th Districts of West Virginia, which districts embrace Mercer County:

1864—K. V. Whaley, Rep., over John M. Phelps, Dem., by 1236 majority.

1866—Daniel Polsley, Rep., over John H. Oley, Dem., by 1471 majority.

1868—John S. Witcher, Rep., over Charles P. T. Moore, Dem., by 1409 majority.

1870—Frank Hereford, Dem., over John S. Witcher, Rep., by 1493 majority.

1872—Frank Hereford, Dem., over J. B. Walker, Rep., by 8884 majority.

1874—Frank Hereford, Dem., over John S. Witcher, Rep., by 5779 majority.

1876—Frank Hereford, Dem., over Benj. T. Redmond, Rep., by 17,573 majority.

1878—John E. Kenna, Dem., over Henry S. Walker, Gr. B., by 2827 majority.

1880—John E. Kenna, Dem., over Henry S. Walker, Gr. B., by 5310 majority.

1882—John E. Kenna, Dem., over E. L. Buttrick, Rep., by 4465 majority.

1883-4—C. P. Snyder, Dem., over James H. Brown, Rep., by 1230 majority.

1884—C. P. Snyder, Dem., over James W. Davis, Rep., by 2119 majority.

1886—C. P. Snyder, Dem., over James H. Brown, Rep., by 815 majority.

1888—John D. Alderson, Dem., over J. H. McGinnis, Rep., by 1293 majority.

1890—John D. Alderson, Dem., over Theophilus Gaines, Rep., by 5014 majority.

1892—John D. Alderson, Dem., over Edgar P. Rucker, Rep., by 1946 majority.

1894—James H. Huling, Rep., over John D. Alderson, Dem., by 4018 majority.

1896—Charles P. Dorr, Rep., over E. W. Wilson, Dem., by 3631 majority.

1898—David E. Johnston, Dem., over William S. Edwards, Rep., by 765 majority.

1900—Joseph H. Gaines, Rep., over David E. Johnston, Dem., by 6570 majority.

1902—James A. Hughes, Rep., over David E. Johnston, Dem., by 4750 majority.

1904—James A. Hughes, Rep., over Simon Altizer, Dem., by 6317 majority.

STATE SENATORS from the senatorial district composed of Mercer and other counties from 1863:

Robert Hager.	David E. Johnston.
William Workman.	Wayne Ferguson.
Mitchell Cook.	Jerome C. Shelton.
Thomas B. Kline.	John W. McCreery.
I. E. McDonald.	John B. Floyd.
W. E. Wilkenson.	William M. Mahood.
Ira J. McGinnis.	John A. Sheppard.
Joel E. Stollings.	W. H. H. Cook.
C. V. White.	James F. Beavers.
Clark W. May.	W. W. Whyte.

THE FOLLOWING are the names of the representatives of Mercer County in the House of Delegates of West Virginia, from 1863 to 1905, inclusive:

1863-7—Thomas Little.
1868—Regular and extra session, George Evans.
1869—William M. French.
1870—George Evans.
1871—Sylvester Upton.
1872—William L. Bridges.
1872-3—Isaac J. Ellison.
1875—William M. Reynolds.
1877—William B. Davidson.
1879—Carroll Clark.
1881-3—Isaiah Bee.
1885—A. C. Davidson.
1887—William M. Reynolds.
1889—R. G. Meador.
1891-93—H. M. Shumate.
1895—J. C. Pack.
1897—James A. White.
1899—Isaiah Bee.
1901—James Hearn.
1903—D. P. Crockett and Thomas Reed.
1905—E. S. Baker and James Hearn.

THE FOLLOWING is a list of the attorneys-at-law admitted to practice in the Circuit Court of Mercer County:

Henley Chapman.
Thomas J. Boyd.
David Hall.
Sterling F. Watts.
William P. Cecil.
A. A. Chapman.
John J. Wade.
Henry L. Gillespie.
Hugh S. Tiffany.
James H. McGinnis.
William A. Monroe.
J. Speed Thompson.
David E. Johnston.
C. A. Sperry.
R. C. McClaugherty.
Alonzo Gooch.
James H. French.
J. W. Hale.
Wirt A. French.
Charles R. McNutt.
Albert G. Pendleton.
Nathaniel Harrison.
James H. Ferguson.
John A. Kelley.
Alexander Mahood.
Samuel Price.
John Echols.
James W. English.
W. G. Ryan.
Cyrus Newlon.
John Phelps.
J. M. Killey.
Samuel C. Graham.
S. S. Dinwiddie.
M. M. Lowry.
James M. French.

Martin Williams.
D. W. McClaugherty.
George E. Floyd.
Edgar Rucker.
A. J. May.
S. M. B. Couling.
Thomas L. Henritzie.
Benjamine F. Keller.
Thomas Bruce.
Allen T. Caperton.
Joseph Stras.
Evermont Ward.
James P. Kelley.
Manilius Chapman.
James D. Johnston.
Robert A. Richardson.
Wade D. Strother.
Frank Hereford.
A. G. Tebbetts.
James W. Davis.
F. W. Mahood.
James B. Peck.
H. C. Alderson.
W. W. Adams.
Thomas J. Munsey.
Samuel W. Williams.
John W. McCreery.
W. W. McClaugherty.
S. D. May.
John Osborne.
Robert L. French.
James L. Hamill.
Joseph S. Clark.
A. W. Reynolds.
A. C. Davidson.
M. T. Browning.

George Evans.
E. T. Mahood.
Charles W. Smith.
James W. St. Clair.
W. L. Taylor.
J. R. Fishburne.
James E. Brown.
H. A. Ritz.
Joseph S. French.
Z. W. Crockett.
H. W. Straley, Jr.
Hugh G. Woods.
B. W. Pendleton.
Jesse D. Daniel.
John M. Anderson.
James S. Browning.
R. R. Henry.
I. C. Herndon.
B. Haden Penn.
Martin H. Holt.
John R. Pendleton.
Frank M. Peters.
J. Frank Maynard.
Jas. French Strother.
D. M. Easley.
George Crockett.
Jas. A. Strother.
William M. Mahood.
John M. McGrath.
A. M. Sutton.
J. W. Hicks.
Wyndham Stokes.
A. P. Gillespie.
J. W. Heptinstall.
Claude Holland.
John Nininger.

(ATTORNEYS OF MERCER COUNTY—Cont'd.).

Okey Johnson.

E. W. Hale.

P. W. Strother.

Bernard McClaugherty.

J. W. Chapman.

G. J. Holbrook.

Joseph M. Sanders.

Cyrus Martin.

John R. Dillard.

D. H. Johnston.

Norman S. Allen.

THE FOLLOWING is a list of persons who have held the office of sheriff of Mercer County from 1837 to the present time:

1837—William Smith was appointed by the Governor of Virginia.

1838—William Smith.

1839—John Davidson.

1840—John Davidson.

1841-2—John Brown.

1843—Robert Gore.

1844-6—Elijah Peters.

1847-8—H. A. Walker.

1849-50—Cornelius White.

1851—Robert Hall.

1852-3—Benjamine McNutt.

1854—Ralph Hale.

1856—Ralph Hale.

1858-60—John A. Pack.

1860-64—John A. Pack.

1866-70—Benjamine White.

1870-1—John T. Smith.

1872-6—George L. Karnes.

1876-80—John S. Carr.

1880-4—Jos. H. McClaugherty.

1884-8—George L. Karnes.

1888-92—James A. White.

1892-96—R. C. Dangerfield.

1896-1900—J. E. T. Sentz.

1904—L. B. Farley.

David Lilley elected sheriff in 1870, but declined to qualify and John T. Smith was appointed in his place.

SURVEYORS OF MERCER COUNTY.

Robert Hall.

Andrew White.

W. J. Comer.

George W. Caldwell.

Edward H. French.

L. M. Stinson.

John Bailey.

JUDGES OF THE CRIMINAL COURT OF MERCER COUNTY.

Hon. James M. French.

Hon. John M. McGrath.

Hon. Charles W. Smith.

Hon. Hugh H. Woods.

THE FOLLOWING is a list of the names of the Clerks of the County Court of Mercer County from 1837 to the present time:

1837—Moses E. Kerr served seven years.

1844—Charles W. Calfee served seven years.

1851—William F. Heptinstall served for one year.

1852-65—Charles W. Calfee.

1865—George Evans, recorder and clerk of Circuit Court.

1870-71—Joseph H. Alvis, Recorder and Clerk.

1872—George Evans, Recorder and Clerk.

1873-9—Benjamine G. McNutt, Recorder and Clerk.

1879-85—C. R. McNutt.

1885-91—Samuel P. Pearis.

1891-7—William H. H. Witten.

1897-1903—A. J. Hearn.

1903—Estill Bailey, elected for six years.

THE FOLLOWING is a list of the names of the Clerks of the Circuit Court for Mercer County from 1837 to the present time:

1837-43—James M. Cunningham.

1843-55—Alexander Mahood.

1855-59—Joseph H. Alvis.

1859-65—William A. Mahood.

1865-69—George Evans.

1869-70—Joseph H. Alvis.

1871-3—George Evans.

1873-9—R. B. Foley.

1879-85—F. A. Bolin.

1885-96—R. C. Christie.

1896-1902—W. B. Honaker.

1902—W. B. Honaker.

THE FOLLOWING is a list of the names of Justices of the Peace for Mercer County from 1837 to 1904:

1837—Moses E. Kerr.

1837—William Smith.

1837—Josiah Meador.

1837—Robert Lilley.

1837—John Davidson.

1840—Henry Brooks.

1840—James Shrewsbury.

1850—William Smith.

1850—George W. Pearis.

1850—N. B. French.

1850—Elijah Peters.

1854—James Brammer.

1854—H. W. Straley.

1854—William M. French.

1854—John S. Carr.

1854—Ralph Hale.

(MERCER COUNTY OFFICERS—Cont'd.).

1855—Cornelius White.
1865—A. W. Cole.
1865—A. W. J. Caperton.
1865—James Bowling.
1865—Joel Sloane.
1866—Russell G. French.
1866—R. Hambrick.
1866—Joel Sloane.
1866—A. W. J. Caperton.
1866—William Meadows.
1867—A. W. Cole.
1867—James Bowling.
1867—A. W. J. Caperton.
1868—Lorenzo D. Little.
1869—A. J. Davis.
1870—William C. Honaker.
1871—John J. Hetherington.
1872—Henry Davidson.
1872—Zachariah Fellers.
1872—A. J. Davis.
1872—A. W. J. Caperton.
1872—Eli Bailey.
1872—Lorenzo D. Martin.
1872—Lewis Lilley.
1872—David B. Pendleton.
1872—A. G. Stovell.
1872—Andrew White.
1872—William A. Wiley.
1877—William Meador.
1877—Henry Davidson.
1881—Elijah Bailey.
1881—Joshua Day.
1881—Henry Davidson.
1881—Harmon White.
1881—Henry Higginbotham.

1881—Leonidas Goodwyn.
1881—A. I. Godfrey.
1881—Lewis Lilley.
1881—John L. Johnston.
1881—L. D. Martin.
1881—T. J. Monroe.
1882—J. F. Holroyd.
1882—N. B. French.
1883—Gaston P. Walker.
1884—John L. Johnston.
1884—John S. Carr.
1884—Lewis Lilley.
1885—George W. Belcher.
1885—H. F. Gore.
1885—Elijah Bailey.
1885—Leftwich Bailey.
1885—James F. Holroyd.
1885—John L. Johnston.
1886—A. J. Young.
1887—A. W. Read.
1888—A. W. Read.
1888—L. C. Shrewsberry.
1888—R. C. Dangerfield.
1889—Z. T. Rodgers.
1889—W. F. Steele.
1889—George Burch.
1889—John T. Carr.
1889—William A. Cooper.
1889—A. I. Godfrey.
1889—H. F. Gore.
1889—L. L. Hearn.
1889—Lewis Lilley.
1890—D. E. Burgess.
1890—M. W. Franklin.
1890—James H. Bare.

1891—W. J. Clark.
1892—Willoughby Miller.
1894—H. G. Thorn.
1894—A. I. Godfrey.
1894—J .A. Chambers.
1894—David French.
1895—G. C. Bailey.
1895—William J. Clark.
1895—H. E. Thomas.
1895—John L. Biggs.
1896—Davis Thorn.
1896—T. C. Comer.
1896—W. J. Rumburg.
1896—L. L. Hearn.
1896—E. T. Oliver.
1897—C. S. Hedrick.
1897—F. J. Brown.
1897—G. C. Bailey.
1897—David French.
1897—Allen C. Wiley.
1899—C. W. Gore.
1900—C. W. Gore.
1900—James H. Brinkley.

1900—F. J. Brown.
1900—T. C. Hubbard.
1900—W. S. Harless.
1900—E. T. Oliver.
1900—Davis Thorn.
1903—Joshua Day.
1903—J. A. Chambers.
1903—Allen C. Wiley.
1903—George O. Tavor.
1903—J. D. Burkholder.
1903—John T. Carr.
1903—W. T. Eperly.
1903—W. A. Henderson.
1903—R. A. Glendy.
1903—J. M. Anderson .
1904—E. P. Godby.
1904—W. S. Harless.
1904—James A. Lilley.
1904—J. A. Chambers.
1904—C. W. Gore.
1904—George P. Danewood.
1904—............ Burk.

---o---

APPENDIX B.

COUNTIES IN VIRGINIA AND WEST VIRGINIA FORMED OUT OF THE TERRITORY OF AUGUSTA AND FREDERICK, AND HOW OR FOR WHOM NAMED.

Prior to 1738 all that part of Virginia lying west of the Blue Ridge was included in the County of Orange, but in the fall session of that year this territory was divided into the counties of Frederick and Augusta. It may be of interest to the reader to present a list of the various sub-divisions of the territory referred to into counties, with the dates of formation and from whence the names of the counties were derived:

Hampshire, 1754, from Hampshire, England.

Botetourt, 1770, from Governor Botetourt.

Berkeley, 1772, from Governor Berkeley.

Dunmore, 1772, from Governor Dunmore, but name changed to Shenandoah in 1777.

Fincastle, 1772, from English country home of Governor Botetourt.

Montgomery, 1776, from General James Montgomery.

Washington, 1776, from General George Washington.

Kentucky, 1776, from Indian name, "Dark and Bloody Ground."

Fincastle, abolished in 1776.

Ohio, 1776, from Ohio River.

Monongalia, 1776, from Indian name.

Youghiogeny, 1776, from Indian name. This county was abolished when line between Virginia and Pennsylvania was settled.

Shenandoah, 1772, name Indian, from River Sherando, formerly Dunmore County; name changed in 1777.

Greenbrier, 1777, from many Greenbriers along the river.

Rockbridge, 1778, from Natural Bridge.

Rockingham, 1778, from English name.

Harrison, 1778, from Governor Benjamin Harrison, of Virginia.

Illinois, 1779, from Illinois Indians; this county passed from Virginia by her cession of the Northwest Territory.

Hardy, 1786, from Samuel Hardy, a member of Congress.

Russell, 1786, from General William Russell.

Randolph, 1787, from Edmund Randolph.

Pendleton, 1788, from Edmund Pendleton.

Kanawha, 1789, from Indian Tribe, Canawhays.

Wythe, 1790, from Judge George Wythe.

Bath, 1791, from English name.

Lee, 1792, from Governor Henry Lee, of Virginia.

Grayson, 1793, from William Grayson, a member of Congress.

Brooke, 1797, from Governor Robert Brooke.

Monroe, 1799, from Governor James Monroe.

Tazewell, 1799, from Mr. Tazewell, member House of Delegates from Norfolk County.

Wood, 1799, from Governor James Wood.

Jefferson, 1801, from Thomas Jefferson.

Mason, 1804, from Stevens Thompson Mason.

Giles, 1806, from Governor William B. Giles.

Cabell, 1809, from Governor William H. Cabell.

Scott, 1814, from General Winfield Scott.

Tyler, 1814, from Governor John Tyler.

Lewis, 1816, from Colonel Charles Lewis.

Preston, 1818, from Governor James P. Preston.

Nicholas, 1818, from Governor Wilson C. Nicholas.

Morgan, 1820, from General Daniel Morgan.

Pocahontas, 1821, from the Indian Princess.

Alleghaney, 1822, from name of Mountain.

Logan, 1824, from Mingo chief.

Page, 1831, from Governor John Page.

Fayette, 1831, from General LaFayette.

Floyd, 1831, from Governor John Floyd.

Smyth, 1831, from General Alexander Smyth.

Jackson, 1831, from President Andrew Jackson.

Marshall, 1835, from Chief Justice John Marshall.

Braxton, 1836, from Carter Braxton.

Clarke, 1836, from General George Rodgers Clarke.

Warren, 1836, from General Warren.

Mercer, 1837, from General Hugh Mercer.

Roanoke, 1838, from Indian name "Much Wampum."

Pulaski, 1839, from Count Pulaski.

Carroll, 1842, from Charles Carroll, of Carrollton.

Marion, 1842, from General Francis Marion.

Wayne, 1842, from General Anthony Wayne.

Ritchie, 1843, from Thomas Ritchie.

Gilmer, 1843, from Governor Thomas W. Gilmer.

Barbour, 1843, from Governor James Barbour.

(COUNTIES—WHEN FORMED, ETC.).

Taylor, 1844, from John Taylor, of Caroline.

Doddridge, 1845, from Philip Doddridge.

Wetzel, 1846, from Lewis Wetzel.

Highland, 1846, named from the High land.

Boone, 1847, from Daniel Boone.

Wirt, 1848, from William Wirt.

Hancock, 1848, from John Hancock.

Putnam, 1848, from Israel Putnam.

Wyoming, 1848, from Wyoming Indian Tribe.

Raleigh, 1850, from Sir Walter Raleigh.

Upshur, 1850, from Abel P. Upshur.

Craig, 1851, from Robert Craig, member of Congress from
    Montgomery County.

Pleasants, 1851, from Governor James Pleasants.

Calhoun, 1855, from John C. Calhoun.

Wise, 1855, from Governor Henry A. Wise.

Roane, 1856, from Judge Spencer Roane.

Clay, 1856, from Henry Clay.

Tucker, 1856, from Henry St. George Tucker.

McDowell, 1858, from Governor James McDowell.

Buchanan, 1858, from President James Buchanan.

Webster, 1860, from Daniel Webster.

Bland, 1861, from Theodoric Bland.

Mineral, 1866, from mineral deposits found in that territory.

Grant, 1866, from General U. S. Grant.

Lincoln, 1867, from President Abraham Lincoln.

Summers, 1871, from Judge Lewis Summers.

Dickenson, 1880, from Mr. Dickenson of that county.

Mingo, 1895, from Indian tribe of that name.

BIOGRAPHICAL.

THE BAILEY FAMILY.

Richard Bailey the elder, was a soldier in the American army during the war of the Revolution, and his residence was on the Black water, in that portion of Bedford County, Virginia, which subsequently became a part of Franklin County. Richard Bailey married Miss Annie Belcher, and their family consisted of ten children, eight sons and two daughters. The sons were John, James, Eli, Micajah, Archibald, Reuben, Richard, and Henry. Mr. Bailey came with his family to the Beaver Pond spring in the year of 1780, and together with John G. Davidson, built the block-house or fort near that spring which was afterwards known as the "Davidson-Bailey Fort." Aside from Mr. Davidson and his family, Mr. Bailey's neighbors were Captain James Moore, in Abb's Valley, some ten miles away; Mitchell Clay, on the Bluestone at the Clover Bottom, about twelve miles away; Joshua Day, at the mouth of Laurel Fork of Wolf Creek, about fifteen miles away; Hickman Compton, on Clear Fork of Wolf Creek, eight miles away, and Gideon Wright, at the head of the South Fork of Bluestone, twelve miles away. The sons of Richard Bailey, especially the elder ones, were great Indian scouts and fighters, and were splendid specimens of physical strength and manhood and of great personal courage.

John Bailey, the eldest son, married Nancy Davidson, the daughter of John G. Davidson, and, in 1789, he built a log house on the south side of Bowyer's branch, on the farm now owned by Thompson Calfee—this building is still standing at this writing—and in which Mr. Jonathan Bailey, their oldest son, was born in 1790, and when he was but four days old an Indian incursion into the neighborhood caused Mr. Bailey to take his wife and child on horseback to the fort at the Beaver Pond.

Henry Bailey, the youngest son of Richard the elder, married a Miss Peters, daughter of John Peters, of New River. Among the sons of Henry were John P., Elijah, Colonel James M., Philip P., and Major William R. Bailey. John P. Bailey went to Texas in the forties. Elijah was quite a prominent citizen in his day, having been a member of the House of Delegates of Virginia from the Counties of Giles and Mercer, and was afterward sheriff of Mercer County and long a Justice of the Peace of said county. Colonel James M. also represented Mercer County in the House of Delegates, and was a colonel of militia; and William R. was likewise a major in the Mercer militia.

Nancy, one of the daughters of Henry, married Charles W. Calfee, who was long the Clerk of the Mercer County Court. Elizabeth first married William Ferguson and subsequently the Rev. Carroll Clark. Jane married Wilson D. Calfee, and Polly first married James Bailey, and, after his death, married John Bailey; she was a woman of strong good sense and intellect.

From the elder Richard Bailey, the first settler, descended all the numerous families by that name, now scattered over several of the counties of West Virginia, particularly Mercer, McDowell, Wyoming, and Logan, and in Tazewell County, Virginia.

Robert H. Bailey, a great grandson of the elder Richard, has been prominent in county affairs. Estill Bailey, another great grandson, is now the Clerk of the County Court of Mercer County. Many of this family are prominent citizens of adjacent counties; among them may be mentioned Theodore F. Bailey, of Wyoming. Nearly all who bore that name, during our great civil strife, were gallant and brave soldiers.

THE BANE FAMILY OF NEW RIVER VALLEY.

This family is of Scottish origin. The founder thereof in America—at least of those of the name who came across the

Alleghanies—was James Bane, who came, in 1688, to New Castle, Delaware. He had left his country because of political ostracism, and sought shelter in the land soon destined to be free. He bought valuable lands of William Penn in what was then, or had been, Pennsylvania.

James, one of the descendants of the first named James, came into the Virginia Valley about 1748, and there married, in 1751, Rebecca McDonald, a granddaughter of Bryan and Mary Combs McDonald, of New Castle, Delaware. It would seem most probable—as some of the McDonalds were settled between 1738 and 1744 in Beverly's Manor, near to where the present city of Staunton, Virginia, is situated—that he married his wife, Rebecca, in that neighborhood, and thence removed to the Roanoke section near where Salem now stands, about 1763, where he remained until a flood in the Roanoke River drove him to and beyond the summit of the Alleghanies, into what is now Montgomery County. He came, probably, about 1775—at any rate he had frequently to take shelter from the Indians in Barger's Fort, on Tom's Creek. His son, James, married Bettie, the daughter of John Haven, of Plum Creek, in Montgomery, about 1776, and from thence he removed to Walker's Creek in 1793. He had a large family of children, viz: 12; Mary married John Henderson, Howard married Miss Hickman, and a daughter of Howard married Colonel Erastus G. Harman, of Bluestone; Colonel James married Mary Henderson December 31st, 1801; Annie married .... Wilson, Sara married John Carr, Rebecca married .... Burke, John married Mary Chapman, Jesse married Jane Carr, Edward and Joseph died unmarried, Elizabeth married William Carr, William Haven married Sallie Snidow.

Colonel James Bane and his wife, Mary Henderson Bane, had the following children: Sallie, who never married; Elizabeth married Tobias Miller; Maria married Madison Allen, John H. married Nancy Shannon, Jane S. married John Crockett Graham, William married Jane Grayson, Nancy married Thomas Jefferson Higginbotham, and Samuel married Lucy

B. Baker. A daughter of William Bane married John D. Snidow, and Mr. William Bane Snidow, a prominent lawyer of Pearisburg, Virginia, is their son. All of this family of Banes, who were in the war 1861-5, were good soldiers; a number of them were killed and wounded. Joseph Edward Bane was killed in the first battle of Manassas, and Major John T. Bane was a distinguished soldier in Hood's Texas Brigade. Of this family have come some of the very best citizens of Giles and surrounding counties. Donald Bane succeeded Malcolm III as King of Scotland between the years 1093-1153.

THE BELCHER FAMILY.

Isham Belcher married a Miss Hodges, in Franklin County, Virginia, and came to what is now Mercer County, then Wythe, in 1796, and settled on what is known as the Waldron farm, about two miles Southeast of the present city of Bluefield. He was a nephew of Phœbe Clay, the wife of Mitchell Clay, the elder. Isham Belcher and wife had a family of thirteen children, eleven sons and two daughters; the sons were Obediah, Isham, Jesse, Asa, Henry D., John, Micajah, Jonathan, Moses, James, and Robert D. From Isham Belcher, the elder, descended all the people of that name scattered over a number of the counties of Southern West Virginia. Captain George W. Belcher, a grandson of the elder Isham, Alexander Belcher and many of that name and blood were bold, courageous Confederate soldiers in our civil war.

THE FAMILY OF BLACK, OF MONTGOMERY.

The Rev. Dr. Samuel Black, a minister in the Presbyterian Church—of Scotch extraction—was born in 1700; educated in Edinburg, Scotland, and licensed to preach at Glasgow; came to America in 1735, and first located at and had charge of the church in Brandywine Manor in Chester County, Pennsylvania. Later he removed to Albemarle County, Virginia, where he was

pastor of Joy and Mountain Plains Churches for the remainder
of his long and useful life.

His sons, John and William, came across the Alleghanies
and settled nearby where the town of Blacksburg, in Montgomery County, is now situated. The year of their coming
seems not definitely known, but it was during the border Indian
wars. John had married Miss Jane Alexander, who, with an
infant son, he brought with him into the wilderness, where
with the aid of a servant he erected a dwelling house which was
shortly thereafter burned by the Indians, he and his family
escaping to the woods and finally to Augusta, where he left his
family until he could erect another dwelling, which he turned
into a fort for protection against the Savages. He served in
the American army during our war for Indpendence, under
General William Campbell, and was with him at the time of
the treaty with the Indians, at Long Island, Tennessee. Two
of his sons were in the war of 1812, and one of them, Matthew,
died in the service. Five of his sons went to the state of Ohio,
where their descendants now live. His daughter, Susan, who
married Stephen McDonald, went to Missouri; Mary, another
daughter, married Walter Crockett, and they went to the
Pacific coast; while the son, Alexander, remained at Blacksburg. John Black lived to the age of ninety-four years; his
wife, Jane Alexander, was of the family of that name, some of
whom settled in the county of Monroe.

William Black gave the land on which the town of Blacksburg, Virginia, now stands, and which was incorporated by the
General Assembly of Virginia, in the year of 1798. By this act
George Rutledge, John Black, James P. Preston, Edward Rutledge, William Black and John Preston were made trustees.
William Black removed to the county of Albemarle in the year
of 1800.

THE BARNES FAMILY.

Robert Barnes, born in Ireland in 1765, first settled in Mary-

land, removed to Rockbridge County, Virginia, and from there
to the Clinch River section, now in Tazewell County, Virginia.
He married Grace Brown, and they had two sons: William
Barnes, born 1790, and John Barnes, born 1793. William
Barnes married Levicie Ward. John Barnes married Lilly
Heldieth as his first wife, and as his second Eliza Allen.

The names of the children of William Barnes are as follows:
Robert, married Ella Gibson; Clinton, married Sarah Gilles-
pie; Oscar F., married Mary Gillespie; John, married Margaret
Smith; Mary, married William T. Moore; Nancy, married James
Harrison; Amanda, married Moses Higginbotham; Rebecca,
died unmarried; Sallie W., married Captain D. B. Baldwin;
Eliza, married A. J. Copenhaver.

John Barnes had one son, William, who died unmarried, in
the Confederate army.

John Ward, who married Nancy Bowen, was the father of
Levicie, who married William Barnes; and the children of the
said John Ward and Nancy Bowen are as follows: Levicie,
married Wliliam Barnes; Jane, married Robert Gillespie;
Rebecca, married William Crawford; Lilly, married John Hill;
Nancy, married Mr. Hargrave; Henry, married Sallie Wilson;
Reece, married Levicie Richardson; Rufus, married Elizabeth
Wilson; David and John, unmarried.

THE BOWENS, OF TAZEWELL.

This family is of Welch extraction, and the immediate ancestors of those that came hither were, long prior to the American Revolution, located and settled about Fredericktown, in
western Maryland. Restive in disposition and fond of adven-
ture, like all of their blood, they sought, fairly early after the
first white settlements were made in the Valley of Virginia,
to look for homes in that direction. How early, or the exact
date, that Reece Bowen, the progenitor of the Tazewell family
of that name, came into the Virginia Valley from his western
Maryland home, cannot be named with certainty; doubtless he

came as early as 1765, for it is known that for a few years prior
to 1772, when he located at Maiden Spring, he was living on
the Roanoke River, close by where the city of Roanoke is now
situated. In the Valley of Virginia, where Harrisonburg is *Margaret*
now situated, then in Augusta County, he married Miss Louisa
Smith, who proved to him not only a loving and faithful wife,
but a great helpmeet in his border life. She was evidently a
woman of more than ordinary intelligence and cultivation for
one of her day and opportunity. She was a small, neat and
trim woman, weighing only about one hundred pounds, while
her husband was a giant in size and strength. It is told as a
fact that she could step into her husband's hand and that he
could stand and extend his arm, holding her at right angle to
his body.

Prize fighting was quite common in the early days of the settlements, by which men tested their manhood and prowess.
The man who could demolish all who chose to undertake him
was the champion, and wore the belt until some man flogged
him, and then he had to surrender it. At some period after
Reece Bowen had settled on the Roanoke, and after the first
child came into the home, Mrs. Bowen desiring to pay a visit to
her people in the Valley, she and her babe and husband set out
on horse-back along the narrow bridle way that then led
through the valley, and on the way they met a man clad in the
usual garb of the day—that is, buck-skin trousers, moccasins,
and hunting shirt, or wampus. The stranger inquired of Mr.
Bowen his name, which he gave him; proposed a fight for the
belt, stating that he understood that he, Bowen, now wore or
had the belt. Bowen tried to beg off, stating that he was taking his wife and child, the latter then in his arms, to her people.
The man would take no excuse; finally Mrs. Bowen said to her
husband: "Reece, give me the child and get down and slap
that man's jaws." Mr. Bowen alighted from his horse, took the
man by the lapel of his hunting shirt, gave him a few quick,
heavy jerks, when the man called out to let him go, he had
enough.

It is also related of Mr. Bowen, that in a later prize fight, at Maiden Spring, with a celebrated prize fighter who had, with his seconds, come from South Carolina to fight Bowen, and when he reached Bowen's home and made known to him his business, he, Mr. Bowen, did what he could in an honorable way to excuse himself from engaging in a fight; but the man was persistent and Bowen concluded to accommodate him and sent for his seconds—a Mr. Smith and a Mr. Clendenin. The fight took place and the gentleman from South Carolina came off second best.

Just when Reece Bowen first saw the territory of what is now Tazewell County cannot be definitely stated. Whether he was one of the large hunting party organized of men from the Virginia Valley, North Carolina and New River, which rendezvoused at Ingles' ferry in June, 1769, and hunted on the waters of the Holstein, Powell's River, Clinch, and in Kentucky, is not known; his name does not appear among the number, but the writer, "Haywood's Civil and Political History of Tennessee," does not profess to give all the names of the party. Nevertheless it is highly probable that Bowen was along, or he may have gone out with the party the next year, or he may have met with the Witten's, and others, on their way out in 1771, and joined them. He seems not to have made his settlement at Maiden Spring until the year of 1772. He went with Captain William Russell's company to the battle of Point Pleasant, in 1774, leaving home in August of that year, and leaving Daniel Boone in command of that part of the frontier. As already stated in this volume, Boone had been forced to give up his journey to Kentucky in September, 1773, on account of the breaking out of the Indian war, and had spent the winter of 1773-4 in the neighborhood of Captain William Russell, near Castleswoods.

Captain Russell's company belonged to Colonel William Christian's Fincastle regiment, the greater part of which did not participate in the battle of Point Pleasant, being in the rear in charge of the pack horses carrying provisions for the

army; but Shelby's and Russell's companies went forward with
the main body and took an active part in the conflict. Moses
Bowen, a relative of Reece, was with Russell's company, but
died on the journey, from smallpox.

From 1774 to 1781, when Reece Bowen marched away to the
battle of King's Mountain, the border on and along the Clinch
was harassed by bands of marauding Indians, and in many of
the skirmishes and troubles Reece Bowen took a hand. During the period from the date of Bowen's settlement at Maiden
Spring until his death, to procure salt, iron, and other necessary materials he had to travel across the mountains to Salisbury, North Carolina, carrying them on a packhorse, and would
be absent for weeks, leaving his wife and children alone. His
trips, however, were always made in winter, when there was no
danger from the Indians. He left rifle guns and bear dogs at
home, and with these his wife felt safe from danger, for she
was a good shot with a rifle, often exceeding the men in ordinary rifle practice. Mr. Bowen had selected a lovely country
for his home, and around and adjacent thereto, prior to the
fall of 1780, had surveyed and secured several thousand acres
of that valuable land, of which his descendants today hold
about twelve square miles.

When it was known that Lord Cornwallis' army was marching northward through the Carolinas, and that Colonel Ferguson, who commanded the left wing of his army, had sent a
threat to the "Over Mountain Men" that if they did not cross
the mountains and take the oath of allegiance to the King,
that he would cross over and destroy with fire and sword, Evan
Shelby, John Sevier, and William Campbell determined to
checkmate Colonel Ferguson by crossing the mountains and
destroying him and his army. Colonel Campbell commanded
the Washington County military force, and William Bowen a
company that belonged to Campbell's command, though a part
of his company lived on the Montgomery County side of the
line. In this company Reece Bowen was a first lieutenant, his
son John a private, and James Moore a junior lieutenant.

When the order came for Bowen's company to join the regiment it found its captain, William Bowen, sick of a fever, and this situation devolved the command of the company upon Lieutenant Reece Bowen, who led it into the battle of King's Mountain, and there, together with several of his men, was killed and buried on the field. His remains were never removed, for the reason that when opportunity was offered for their removal the spot in which he was buried could not be identified. Campbell's regiment lost in this battle 35 killed and wounded; among the killed, other than Lieutenant Reece Bowen, were Captain William Edmondson, Robert Edmondson, Andrew Edmondson, and Henry Henninger, and among the wounded, Charles Kilgore and John Peery, the two latter and Henninger from the Upper Clinch waters.

Reece Bowen has in Tazewell County many highly respected, prominent and influential descendants, among them Mr. Reece Bowen, Colonel Thomas P. Bowen and Captain Henry Bowen, all brave and distinguished Confederate soldiers; the latter, Captain Henry, being frequently honored by his people as a member of the Legislature of Virginia, and a Representative in Congress. The present Mr. Reece Bowen married Miss Mary Crockett, of Wythe; Colonel Thomas P., Miss Augusta Stuart, of Greenbrier, and Captain Henry, Miss Louisa Gillespie, of Tazewell.

THE BURKE FAMILY.

The Burke family of the New River Valley were among the early settlers west of the Alleghanies, having descended from James Burke, who came with the Draper's Meadow settlers in 1748. James Burke was the discoverer of that most magnificent body of land now in Tazewell County, Virginia, known as Burke's Garden (but called by the Indians "Great Swamp"). It is said that he discovered this lovely spot in 1753 and removed thither in 1754, and in the fall of 1755 was driven away by the Indians. He had a family, and among his sons was

Captain Thomas Burke, who became a very prominent man in the Indian border wars, and commanded a company of troops, which was at one time stationed at Hatfield's fort, on Big Stony creek. One of his daughters, Mary, married Colonel Christian Snidow, another, Rebecca, married Andrew Davidson. He had a son, William, who at one time was the owner of the Red Sulphur Springs property, in Monroe County, and several of his family emigrated to the west at an early date. The Horse Shoe property in Giles County, granted to James Wood, subsequently became the property of Captain Thomas Burke, and finally that of Colonel William H. Snidow, his grandson.

THE CALFEE FAMILY.

This family is of German origin, came out of Pennsylvania into the Valley of Virginia and settled in the County of Shenandoah, and from thence came, shortly after the close of the American revolution, to what was then Montgomery, now Pulaski County. The earliest of the Mercer County Calfees was James, who came to that county about 1829, and settled at Gladeville, one mile west of the present village of Princeton. He subsequently moved to Harman Branch, and later to Clover Bottom, on the Bluestone. He had five sons and five daughters. His sons were Charles W., who married Miss Nancy Bailey; Andrew J., who married Mrs. Brown; Davis, William, French; the daughters, Polly, Jane, Betsey, Virginia, and Cynthia, none of whom ever married.

Charles W. Calfee and his wife, Nancy Bailey Calfee, had six sons and two daughters; the sons, Albert B., William McHenry, George, Harvey M., John C., and William D. The daughters, Virginia, who married Dr. John H. Robinson, and Fannie, who married John Boggess. Charles W. Calfee was long clerk of Mercer County Court. Mr. Davis Calfee was a farmer, and lived for many years at New Hope Church, where he died in about 1879; he was a large man, weighing about 450 pounds.

A short time after James Calfee settled in Mercer County, came Samuel T., Wilson D., and James Calfee, Jr.; the latter a minister in the church of the Disciples, a man of fine character and good ability, representing the County of Mercer in the Constitutional convention of 1872.

Mr. Wilson D. Calfee and his wife, Jane Bailey Calfee, had a considerable family of children; the sons are, Augustus B. Calfee, Robert M. Calfee, R. Kohler Calfee, and Luther Calfee. Mr. H. Sayers Calfee, a brave Confederate soldier, is a son of Mr. Samuel T. Calfee, and Mr. Thompson Calfee, who resides near Bluefield, is a son of Elder James Calfee; a daughter of James Calfee married Alexander W. Bailey; another daughter married Captain William A. Cooper.

THE CAPERTONS.

Partly from the manuscript of this family, furnished the author by the late Mr. John Caperton, of Louisville, Kentucky, it is learned that it was one among the early settlers of the New River Valley, and was originally from the South of Scotland, near Melrose, where they were called Claperton; dropping the l they became Caperton; that they afterwards emigrated to Wales, and that John Caperton was the first, and probably the only one of the name, who came to America. He had three sons: Adam, Hugh, and William, and from these three sons descended the Capertons of Monroe County, West Virginia; the Capertons of the New River in Giles County, Virginia, and Mercer County, West Virginia; and the Capertons of Richmond, Kentucky, and of Mississippi.

Adam was the progenitor of the Monroe Capertons; Hugh of the New River Capertons, and William of the Kentucky and Mississippi Capertons. Hugh Caperton, the son of Adam, was born in Monroe County; was taken to Kentucky when an infant, where his father, Adam, in March, 1782, was killed at Mt. Sterling, by the Indians, in the battle known as Estill's Defeat, when his son, Hugh, was only two years old. Hugh returned to Virginia when twelve years of age, and in part was brought up by his uncle, Hugh, of New River. He lived in his native county until his death, which occurred in 1847. He was a self taught man, and represented his county in the State Legislature several years, one session in Congress (1816), was a member of the Board of Public Works of Virginia for many years and until his death. He amassed a large fortune for that day, his property being worth at his death $600,000.00. He stood guard against the Indians when only twelve years old. He married Miss Jane Erskine, and had a family of nine children. His son, Allen T., became a most prominent man, serving often in the Legislature of Virginia, both in the House of Delegates and in the Senate, and in the Constitutional convention of 1850-1; in the Confederate Congress, and was serving as United States Senator from West Virginia at the time of his death. Mr. Allen T. Caperton married Harriet Echols, of Virginia, the sister of General John Echols.

John Caperton, another son of Hugh of Monroe, was a prominent citizen of Louisville, Kentucky, and died recently at a very advanced age.

Hugh, the progenitor of the New River Capertons, was a man of much distinction, having served in the Indian wars as a Captain of a company, in 1793, at the mouth of the Elk River, on the Kanawha; he served in the Legislature of Virginia much over one hundred years ago.

William Caperton, the progenitor of the Kentucky and Mississippi branch of the family, as an orator was without a rival. It is said that Henry Clay spoke of him as a very eloquent man. George and John Caperton, brothers of Hugh, settled in Northern Alabama, where their descendants still reside.

THE CHAPMANS.

The Chapmans (1) were English people, and some of those

_____

(1). It appears that the first place of settlement of this family, after leaving England, was in the state of Connecticut.

who emigrated to this country came from Connecticut to
Charles County, Maryland, long prior to the American Revolution. After the settlement in Maryland, and before the beginning of the Revolution, some of them came to Culpeper County,
Virginia, and settled. Among those who came was Isaac Chapman, who married, in Culpeper County, Miss Sara Cole, by
whom he had three sons and one daughter. The sons were
Isaac, John, and Richard, the daughter, Jemima. Isaac went
South, and finally located in Alabama, where his descendants
still reside. His grandson, Honorable Reuben Chapman, was
a member of Congress from Alabama in 1841. John married
Sallie Abbott and Richard married Margaret Abbott, daughters
of Richard Abbott of Culpeper County, Virginia; the daughter,
Jemima, married Moredock O. McKensey, (1) a Scotsman from
the city of Glasgow, Scotland. Richard Abbott having died,
his widow married a man by the name of Tracey, by whom she
had two children, Bettie, who married James Rowe, and a son,
William Tracey, the ancestor of the Traceys of Wolf Creek of
New River Valley.

In November, 1768, John Chapman, Richard Chapman, and
Moredock O. McKensey removed from Culpeper County to the
Shenandoah, in the Valley of Virginia, and from thence, in
1771, came to the New River Valley and settled at the mouth
of Walker's creek, where John Chapman had two dwelling
houses destroyed by the Indians; his family being forced to flee
to the Snidow fort for protection. In the spring of 1778 Mc-
Kensey removed to the mouth of Wolf Creek, where his family,
in May of that year, was attacked by the Indians, and a portion
of them killed and another portion carried into captivity.
Some years afterward, time not definitely known, Richard
Chapman removed from Walker's Creek to Wolf Creek.

The children of John Chapman were Isaac, who married
Elian Johnston; George, who married Patience Clay; John,
who married Miss Napier; Henley, who married Mary Alex-

---

(1). McKensey died on Five Mile Fork of East River, in the year
1805.

ander; Sallie, who married, first, Jacob Miller of Franklin County, Virginia, and by whom she had a daughter and three sons: Jacob, who married Mrs. Polly Harman; John, who married Sallie Peck; Tobias, who married Elizabeth Bane; Barbara, who married Morton P. Emmons. After the death of the elder Jacob Miller, his widow, Sallie, married David Johnston, and they had the following children: Oscar F., who married Elizabeth French; Chapman I., who married Elian C. Snidow; Olivia, who married William M. Gillaspie, of Tazewell County, Virginia; Louisa A., who married Colonel Daniel H. Pearis, of Mercer, and Sallie C., who died unmarried.

Jemima Chapman married Charles Hall and had the following children: Benjamin, who went to Cook County, Illinois, at an early date, and Chloe, who married John Brian.

Annie Chapman, who married John Lybrook, had a numerous family, of whom was Philip Lybrook, the father of the present Major Samuel E. Lybrook, a great grandson of Philip, the settler.

Isaac Chapman and his wife, Elian Johnston Chapman, had the following children: John, a lawyer of distinction and often a representative of Giles County in the Senate and House of Delegates, who married Ann Freel; Doctor David Johnston Chapman, who married Sallie Pepper; William Chapman, who married Nancy McDonald; Rachael, who married John Snidow; Priscilla, who married Doctor Thomas Fowler; Polly, who married John Bane; Nancy, who married Joseph McDonald; Sallie, who married William Kyle, and Rebecca, who married Samuel P. Pearis.

John Chapman, the son of Isaac, had one daughter, Adeline, who married Colonel William H. Snidow, by whom she had three children, viz: John C., who married Anne Hoge; James P., who married Fannie Hale; Annie, who married Dr. Harvey G. Johnston.

Doctor David J. Chapman had the following children, viz: John, drowned in his youth; William, who married Miss Mather; James, who went west many years ago; David J., Jr., who now lives in Giles County and is unmarried, and who is the only Chapman in Giles County; Annie, who married Colonel James W. English; Jennie, who married Major Samuel E. Lybrook, and Malinda, who married Samuel S. Dinwiddie.

William Chapman, who married Nancy McDonald, had the following children: Isaac E., who married Eliza Gillespie; John, who went to Texas and was drowned; Louisa, who married Rev. Mr. Chanceleum; and Keziah, who married Isaac Chapman Fowler.

John Snidow and Rachael, his wife, had the following children: Christian, who married Sylistine Goodrich; they had no children; James H., who married Elvina Lucas and had the following children: John D., William R., Cornelia, who married Eugene Angel, and some daughters who are not married; David J. L., who married Malinda Pepper, but left no children; Elizabeth, who married John Tiffany, and had the following children: Captain Hugh S., killed in the first battle of Manasses; Charles C., who lives in Kansas, and Elizabeth, who married Andrew B. Symns; Mary B., who married John S. Peck, and had the following children: James P., killed in the battle of Cold Harbor in 1864; Hugh T., who lives in the State of Maryland; Chapman I., who lives in Giles County; John, who died a few years ago; Annie, who married John P. Peck; Elizabeth, who married Harvey Snidow, and Eliza, who married .... Williams.

Elian Chapman Snidow, who married Chapman I. Johnston, had the following children: David Andrew, John Raleigh, Sarah Ellen, who married Honorable William A. French; Annie C., who married Charles D. French; Rachael S., who is now dead, and who first married .... Daugherty, and secondly Joseph Alvis. Ellen J. Snidow, daughter of John and Rachael Chapman Snidow, is unmarried.

Samuel P. Pearis and Rebecca Chapman Pearis, his wife, had three children: Dr. Robert A., who married Amanda Fowler; Dr. Charles W., who married Electra Pearis; and Rebecca, who married Honorable Frank Hereford.

The children of Joseph McDonald and Nancy Chapman Mc-
Donald, his wife, were W. W. McDonald, of Logan; John C.
McDonald, Isaac E. McDonald, Lewis McDonald, Floyd Mc-
Donald; Sallie, who married John Sanders; Nancy, who mar-
ried Lewis McDonald; Elizabeth, who married John Anderson;
John C., Isaac E. and Floyd, who died unmarried.

Dr. Thomas Fowler and wife had the following children:
Thomas, Isaac C., Allen, Elbert; Mary, who married Captain
James D. Johnston; and Amanda, who married Dr. Robert A.
Pearis.

Henley Chapman and his wife, Mary Alexander Chapman,
had two sons and three daughters. The sons were General
Augustus A. Chapman, who married Mary R. Bierne, and
Manilius, who married Susan Bierne; the daughters, Araminta
D., married Captain Guy D. French; Elvina married Colonel
Albert G. Pendleton, and Isabella married Major William P.
Cecil.

John Chapman, son of the settler, and brother to Isaac,
George, and Henley, married Miss Napier; was killed by a
horse, and his widow and children removed to Cabell County
about the year of 1800, where his descendants now reside.
Captain John Chapman, who was a son of Andrew Johnston
Chapman, son of the above John, was a distinguished Con-
federate soldier, and died only a few years ago at his home in
Lincoln County, West Virginia.

Colonel Albert G. Pendleton and his wife, Elvina Chapman
Pendleton, had three children: Nannie, who married Judge
Philip W. Strother; Sallie, who married Van B. Taliaferro,
and Alberta, who married Samuel Crockett.

Major William P. Cecil and his wife Isabella Chapman Cecil,
had one child, Mary, who married Charles Painter.

Captain Guy D. French and wife, Araminta Chapman
French, had four sons: Henley C., who married Harriet Easley; Captain David A., who married, first Miss Williams, second Miss Jennie C. Easley; William A., who married Nellie
Johnston; Charles D., who married Annie C. Johnston; they

had daughters Sarah M., who first married Dr. W. W. Mc-
Comas, second, Captain F. G. Thrasher; Mary, who married
William B. Mason; Fannie, who married J. H. D. Smoot, and
Susan, who married Dr. R. T. Ellett.

John Chapman, son of Richard, married Jemima, a daughter
of the Elder David Johnston, and they had a daughter who
married William Wilburn, of Sugar Run; and James H. Wilburn, whose photograph appears opposite this page, is a grand
son of the said John Chapman, and a great grandson of the
first William Wilburn, who came in 1780 to what is now Giles
County, Virginia.

James W. Chapman, a grandson of John, of Wolf Creek, is
the only descendant of John Chapman bearing that name who
now resides in this section of the country; the remaining members of the Richard Chapman family went at an early date to
the Big Sandy and Eastern Kentucky region, some of them
removing to the State of Ohio. Some of the descendants of
Richard Chapman still reside in the counties of Lincoln, Logan,
Mingo, and Wayne, West Virginia.

The Elder John Chapman, and his son, Isaac, were soldiers
during the Indian wars on the border, and were stationed during the years of 1774 to 1779 in Snidow's, Hatfield's, and
Barger's forts.

The family of George Chapman, who married Patience Clay,
consisted of three daughters and two sons. Sallie Chapman
married Hugh Jordan, Elizabeth Chapman married Joseph
Peck, and Lucretia Chapman married William McClure; the
sons, Isaac and Archer, went to the state of Ohio at an early
day. Opposite page 396 is presented the photograph of the
dwelling house built by George Chapman, in 1794, on the East
Bank of New River, near Ripplemeade, Virginia, and which
house still stands and is on land now the property of Mr. Harvey Phlegar and Mr. H. B. Shelton.

J. H. WILBURN

Grandson of the Settler.

THE CHRISTIAN FAMILY.

This family came from the Isle of Man, and as early as 1732 Gilbert Christian, with his family, removed from Pennsylvania, where they lived in 1726, to a point near where Staunton, Virginia, now stands, and on a creek to which they gave their name. The family of Gilbert Christian, which consisted of himself, wife, three sons, John, Robert, William, and a daughter, Mary, became near neighbors of the celebrated Lewis family.

Captain Israel Christian settled in the Valley in 1740, where he married Miss Elizabeth Starke; removing later to what is now Botetourt County, he gave the land for the town of Fincastle, and still later he came across the Alleghanies, and settled on the New River, near Ingles' ferry. The town of Christiansburg was named from him. His son, Colonel William, was born near Staunton, in 1743; he married Anne, a sister of Patrick Henry. He was long a prominent figure on the border; representing the New River Valley district in the State Senate in 1781; was the Colonel and Commandant of the Fincastle troops, and led a regiment from that county to the battle of Point Pleasant, in October, 1774. Only two companies of his regiment participated in the battle; the remainder, with Colonel Christian, were in charge of the supplies for the army of General Lewis. Colonel Christian, with a few men, in pursuing a marauding band of Indians across the Ohio, was, on the 9th day of April, 1786, killed on the spot whereon now stands Jeffersonville, Indiana.

A part of the same Christian family from near Staunton, in the Valley, settled on East River, in what is now Mercer County, in 1780. Some of these people served with great distinction on the Confederate side in our civil war.

THE CECIL FAMILY.

The Cecils crossed over to England with William the Norman; and the family in the United States is said to be of the Lord Baltimore stock (Calverts), descendants of Sir William

Cecil, of England (Lord Burleigh). Samuel W. Cecil and his two brothers came to America in 1700, and settled in Maryland.

Samuel W. married Rebecca White in Maryland, about 1750, and removed to the New River Valley in what is now Pulaski County in about 1760. He died in 1785 and his wife in 1815. They left a family of seven sons and three daughters. The sons, William, born in 1752, married Nancy Witten, and settled in Tazewell; Thomas, born in 1755, married Nancy Grayson, and went to Ohio; James married Miss Wysor; Benjamin married Priscilla Baylor and went to Kentucky; Zechariah married Miss Mitchell, and went to Kentucky; Samuel married Mary Ingram, and went to Missouri; Rebecca married James Witten, of Tazewell; Malinda married Samuel Mitchell; Eleanor married Thomas Witten, of Tazewell.

Zechariah Cecil, son of Samuel W., married Julia Howe, daughter of Major Daniel Howe, from whom Daniel R. Cecil, of Giles County, Virginia, descends, and who married Ardelia Pearis, granddaughter of Colonel George Pearis, a soldier of the American Revolution, and first settler where Pearisburg station, N. & W. Ry. Co., is now situated.

THE CLAY FAMILY.

The Clays of Virginia and Kentucky, the descendants of their English ancestry by that name, emigrated to America and settled in Virginia prior to the American Revolution. One brother, the father of Henry Clay, of Kentucky, a Baptist minister, settled in the Slashes of Hanover; one, the ancestor of General Greene Clay, settled in Powhatan, and was the ancestor of General Oden G. Clay of Campbell County, Virginia. The one who settled in Franklin County was the ancestor of the elder Mitchell Clay, who came from Franklin to the Clover Bottom on the Bluestone, in 1775.

Mitchell Clay married in Franklin County, Virginia, in the year of 1760, Phœbe Belcher. In April, 1774, there was granted

DWELLING HOUSE OF GEORGE CHAPMAN

Near Ripplemead, Va., built in 1794.

by Dunmore, the Royal Governor of Virginia, to Mitchell Clay, assignee of Lieutenant John Draper, 800 acres of land on Bluestone Creek, Clover Bottoms, then Fincastle County, Virginia, now Mercer County. By the terms of this grant Clay was required to take possesion of this land within three years, clear so much per year, and render so much ground rent to the King of Great Britain. A copy of this grant is on file in the Clerk's office of Mercer County Court. In payment for this tract of land, Clay gave Draper a negro woman and her children, executing to him therefor a bill of sale. Many years afterward, and after the death of Mitchell Clay, which occurred in 1812, this trade gave rise to two interesting law suits; one, by the negro woman and her children against Draper or his representatives for their freedom, which they succeeded in establishing; and thereupon the representatives of Draper sued the executors of Clay and their sureties, recovering a large decree against them, resulting in the bankrupting of Captain William Smith and the estate of Colonel George N. Pearis, sureties of the executors of Clay.

Mitchell Clay and his wife had fourteen children, seven sons and seven daughters. The sons were Mitchell, Henry, Charles, William, David, Bartley, and Ezekiel, the latter captured and Bartley killed by the Indians on Bluestone, in 1783. The daughters were Rebecca, who married Colonel George Pearis; Patience, who married George Chapman; Sallie, who married Captain John Peters, a soldier of the war of 1812; Obedience, who married John French, a soldier of the American Revolution; Nannie, who married Joseph Hare, also a soldier of the American Revolution; Mary, who married William Stewart, and Tabitha, who was killed by the Indians on Bluestone, in 1783.

From Rebecca, who married Colonel George Pearis, descended the family of Pearis of the New River Valley. From George Chapman and wife descended a numerous progeny, of whom Sallie married Hugh Jordan, of Giles County. From Mrs. Peters descended a large part of the family of that name now

living in the New River Valley. From Mrs. French descended
a numerous posterity, and among her descendants is Colonél
James M. French, a distinguished lawyer and one of the bravest soldiers that drew his sword for Virginia in our civil war.
Mrs. Hare left no living descendants. Mrs. Stewart left a large
number of descendants, many of whom are among the most
respectable and prominent citizens of the county of Wyoming
and adjacent territory.

After the destruction, in part, of the family of Mitchell Clay,
on Bluestone, he removed to New River, purchased a farm
which is now owned in part by Mr. J. Raleigh Johnston, opposite Pearisburg station on N. & W. Ry. Co.'s railway line, and
upon which he erected a dwelling house in 1783, which is still
standing, a photograph of which will be seen opposite this
page.

THE CLOYD FAMILY.

This family were Protestant Irish people, and some of that
name were in the seige of Londondary in 1689. Some portion
of the family emigrated to America, long prior to the Revolution, and settled in Pennsylvania, where David Cloyd married
Margaret Campbell, and from thence removed to James River,
in the now county of Botetourt, where, in March, 1764, Mrs.
Cloyd and her son John were killed by the Indians; Joseph,
another son, on the day of the killing of his mother and brother,
was working in the field, and the Indians, by a ruse, succeeded
in getting between him and the house. Perceiving that they
were Indians that had attacked the house, he ran to a neighbor
for aid, hastening back only to find that his mother had been
tomahawked and his brother killed.

Joseph Cloyd in about 1774 or 1775, when quite a young man,
came with Colonel William Preston to the Draper's Meadows
settlement. He subsequently married Miss Mary Gordon, and
it is said, at her request, built a brick church near where Dublin,
Virginia, is now situated, being the first church building erected

MITCHELL CLAY HOUSE

Built in the Fall of 1783.

west of the Alleghany mountains. Mary, a sister of Joseph Cloyd, married James McGavock. The children of Joseph Cloyd were David, Gordon and Thomas. David married Sarah McGavock, Gordon married Betsie McGavock, and Thomas married Mary McGavock. Joseph Cloyd, the elder, became possessed of a very large and valuable estate on Back Creek, now in Pulaski County, a portion of which is now owned and possessed by his great-grandson, David Cloyd. Joseph Cloyd was a soldier in the American army during the Revolution, and Major of the Montgomery County militia. In the year of 1780 there was a great tory uprising in the northern counties of North Carolina, consequent upon the advance of the British army into that state in October of that year. Major Cloyd raised three companies of horsemen, among them one commanded by Captain George Pearis, and marched to the Shallow Ford of the Yadkin, being joined on his way by some North Carolina companies, raising his force to 160 men. On the 14th day of October he fought a severe battle with the Tories at the Shallow Ford, in which he defeated them with a loss on their part of 15 killed, and four found wounded and left on the field; on the American side Captain Pearis and four privates were wounded.

General Greene was retreating before the British army and was hard pressed, and not only called on the Governor of Virginia for aid, but wrote letters to Colonels William Preston, William Campbell, Evan Shelby, and John Sevier for help. On the 10th day of February, 1781, Colonel William Preston ordered the assembling of the militia of Montgomery County at the Lead Mines, and on the 18th day of February he marched with Major Joseph Cloyd, at the head of 350 horsemen, and joined General Greene near Hillsboro, North Carolina, and was ordered to report to General Pickens, then in command of General Greene's left wing, operating on the Haw and Deep Rivers. Preston marched to join General Pickens, but lost his way and camped the night preceding his joining Pickens between the outposts of the two armies, almost within musket range of the

British pickets. On the 2nd day of March a part of Preston's men were engaged with Lee's cavalry in a brisk skirmish with the British outposts, in which the British came off second best, losing about thirty killed and wounded, the Americans losing but few men. On the 5th of March Preston proceeded across the country to Wetzell's (Whitsell's) Mills, where on the 6th a severe battle was fought with a portion of the British army commanded by Lord Cornwallis, the Americans being commanded by Generals Pickens and Williams. In this battle Preston's men took a prominent part and fought bravely and gallantly, but were finally forced to yield the field to the British. Near the close of the engagement Colonel Preston's horse took fright and ran with him into and across a mill pond in the very face of the British. He finally threw Colonel Preston, who made his escape into the American lines just as the retreat began, and being a very heavy, fleshy man, was unable to keep up with the retreating army, whereupon Major Joseph Cloyd dismounted and gave him his horse. Colonel Preston being injured by the fall from his horse, his troops were placed under the command of Colonel William Campbell. The retreat continued until the forces engaged at Wetzell's Mills had reached Guilford Court House, where on the 15th of March the battle between General Greene's army and that of Lord Cornwallis was fought, resulting in the defeat of the Americans. In the battle of Guilford Court House Preston's men, under Colonel William Campbell, occupied the extreme left, which was assailed by the British infantry and cavalry under Colonel Tarleton, who in his book entitled "Southern Campaigns, 1780-81," says: "That the backwoodsmen stood their ground until the British infantry pushed them off the field, and that the greatest injury done to the British in that battle was by the Virginia backwoodsmen."

On receiving information at the Davidson-Bailey fort of the massacre of Captain James Moore and his family, in Abb's Valley, by the Indians, on July 14th, 1786, a messenger was at once dispatched to Major Cloyd, who immediately gathered a body of men and marched to the Valley, reaching there, however, two days after the Indians had departed with their booty and prisoners, and too late to overtake them .

Major Joseph Cloyd was a representative from Montgomery County in the Legislature of Virginia in the year of 1788, and his son, General Gordon Cloyd, was a member of the Constitutional convention of Virginia, 1829-30; and his grandsons, Major Joseph Cloyd and Mr. James M. Cloyd, were prominent citizens of Pulaski County.

THE DAVIDSON FAMILY.

John Goolman Davidson, born in Dublin, Ireland, a cooper by trade, came to America about 1755, and settled in Beverly Manor, in what was then Augusta County. Subsequently he removed with his family to the Draper-Meadow's settlement, and from thence in the year of 1780, he removed and located at the head of Beaver Pond Creek, in what was then Montgomery County, Virginia, now Mercer County, West Virginia. During the same year he was joined by Richard Bailey and family, and they erected a block house, or fort, a short distance below the head of Beaver Pond Springs. From John Goolman Davidson has descended all of the people of that name now in this and the adjoining counties. A portion of the city of Bluefield is built on lands formerly the property of Mr. Davidson. His descendants, or quite a number of them, have been prominent in civil affairs in the counties of Mercer and Tazewell. Honorable A. C. Davidson (1), of Mercer County, is a great great grandson of John Goolman Davidson.

THE EMMONS FAMILY.

James Emmons (2), the ancestor of the New River and Giles County family of that name, was an American soldier, as shown

(1). Died December 19, 1905.
(2). This family is reputed to be of Sweedish origin.

by his declaration for a pension made in 1832. He enlisted in
the County of Fauquier, and served under General Daniel
Morgan in his Southern campaign; was in the battle of the
Cowpens, and in many skirmishes in the Carolinas. In 1781
he substituted for his brother William and went in his place
to Yorktown, was in that battle and after its close guarded
the British prisoners who were there taken, to Winchester,
Virginia. At the close of the war he removed with his family,
and with Charles Duncan and others, to Stokes County, North
Carolina, and from thence to the New River Valley about 1795,
where his son, Morton P. Emmons, intermarried with Barbara
Miller, the daughter of Jacob and his wife, Sallie Chapman
Miller. All of the people of the New River Valley of the name
of Emmons descended from James Emmons. Morton R., who
resides in Bluefield, West Virginia, is a great-grandson of the
said James, as well also as Morton Emmons, of Atlanta,
Georgia.

THE FRENCHES.

The ancestors of this family lived in Scotland, thence removed to Wales, and from thence, long prior to the American
Revolution, came across the Atlantic and settled in the Northern Neck of Virginia—Westmoreland County, within the grant
to Lord Fairfax. It was in Westmoreland, about 1735, that
John French married a lady of Welsh extraction. Among the
children born to them was a son, Matthew, in 1737. Settlers
were pressing across the Blue Ridge and on to the south branch
of the Potomac, and on and along the Big and Little Cacapon.
As information came back from these people of the wonderland
they had found, others became interested and made up their
minds to go; among them John French and his family, in about
1750, made their way up the Rappahannock and over to the
south branch of the Potomac, locating at a place since well
known as French's Neck, a beautiful and valuable body of land
on the south branch of the river mentioned. John lived but a

short while after reaching his new home, and his widow shortly after his death married Captain Cresap. The district in which John French settled soon became the County of Hampshire. There were several sons in the family other than Matthew, among them William and James, and a daughter Esther, who married John Locke.

Matthew and his step-father soon had differences of such a nature as to lead to their estrangement and separation; Matthew, who had not yet attained his majority, sold out his interest in his father's estate to his stepfather, Captain Cresap, and went back over the mountains to Culpeper, where he married an Irish girl whose name was Sallie Payne. In 1775 Matthew, with his wife and seven children, four sons and three daughters, crossed the Alleghanies into the New River Valley, and settled at what is now known or called the Boyd place, on Wolf Creek, in Giles County, then Fincastle. The names of the sons of Matthew were John, Isaac, James, and David; the latter, the youngest child, was born in Culpeper in 1772; the daughters were Martha, Mary and Annie. John, the son of Matthew, married Obedience Clay in January, 1787; Isaac married Elizabeth Stowers for his first wife; his second was a Mrs. Fillinger; James married Susan Hughes, a half sister to the elder William Wilburn; his second wife was Margaret Day; David married Mary Dingess.

Martha, the daughter of Matthew, married Jacob Straley; Mary married Isaac Hatfield; Annie married General Elisha McComas.

The following are the names of the children of John French and his wife Obedience Clay French, viz: William, Ezekiel, Charles C., James, George P., John, St. Clair, Hugh and Austin, and the daughters, Annie, Sallie, Orrie, Obedience, Nancy and Rebecca.

Isaac French and his wife, Elizabeth Stowers French, had the following named children, viz: Sallie, Elizabeth, Docey, and Isaac.

The children of James French, by his first marriage, were

three sons, Isaac, Reuben, and Andrew; and five daughters, Mary, who married Daniel Straley; Sallie, who married William Hare; Elizabeth, who married James Rowland; Isaac married Sallie Straley; Reuben married Miss Meadows, and Andrew L. married Miss Day; and by the second marriage James had two daughters, Esther Locke, who married Kinzie Rowland, and Martha, who married William Milan.

The names of the children of David French and his wife, Mary Dingess French, are as follows, viz: Guy D., who married Araminta D. Chapman; Napoleon B., who married Jane Armstrong; Dr. David M., who married Miss Smoot, of Alexandria, Virginia; Rufus A., William H., and James H., who died unmarried; the daughters, Cynthia, who married Judge David McComas; Harriet, who married Samuel Pack; Minerva, who married Colonel Thomas J. Boyd.

Matthew French died on Wolf Creek, in Giles County, in 1814. Mrs. Sallie Fletcher, a grand daughter of Matthew French, and 95 years old in 1892, gave to the author in writing a personal description of Matthew French and his wife, whom she well recollected, being a married woman and about seventeen years old at the date of the death of her grandfather. Mrs. Fletcher says: "Matthew French was a small, spare made man, light hair and blue eyes; his wife was a very large woman, quite fleshy, fair complexion, light hair and blue eyes."

Matthew French and his eldest son, John, were American soldiers in our war for independence, and served in Colonel William Preston's battalion of Montgomery County militia, of which Joseph Cloyd was Major, and Thomas Shannon the Captain of the company to which the Frenches were attached. They were with their company in the battle of Wetzell's Mills, March 6th, 1781, and again at Guilford Court House, on the 15th of the same month.

The names of the children of Guy D. French and his wife, Araminta D., are as follows, viz: Henley C., who married Miss Harriet Easley (both now dead); Mary, who married William B. Mason (both now dead); Fannie, who married

HON. Wm. A. FRENCH

Great grandson of Matthew French.

J. H. D. Smoot (the latter dead) ; Sarah, who first married Dr. W. W. McComas (killed in battle of South Mills), and secondly married Captain F. G. Thrasher; Susan, who married Dr. R. T. Ellett (the latter dead).

Captain David A. French first married Miss Williams, for his second wife Jennie C. Easley; William A. married Sarah E. Johnston; Charles D. married Annie C. Johnston. Opposite this page is the photograph of Hon. William A. French, a great grandson of Matthew the Settler. William A. died in April, 1902.

The descendants of Matthew French are scattered far and wide over the South and West. Among them were many brilliant men and women; the men have been magistrates, sheriffs, clerks, lawyers, judges, statesmen and soldiers. David McComas, one of the descendants of Matthew French, was an eminent jurist; William McComas, another, was a member of Congress from 1833 to 1837; Dr. W. W. McComas was a distinguished physician and gallant Confederate soldier; Colonel James Milton French, now of Arizona, served his country with devotion and honor both in military and civil life.

THE GILLESPIES, OF TAZEWELL COUNTY.

These people are the descendants of Scottish ancestors who came to America prior to our war for independence, and settled first in Pennsylvania, and then removed to western North Carolina, from whence they traveled westward over the mountains into what is now the State of Tennessee, from which came the immediate progenitors of the family to the Clinch Valley section, about 1794. The Gillespies were quite a distinguished people in Scotland, especially in the affairs of church; the Rev. Thomas Gillespie, a Presbyterian minister of Scotland, is mentioned as being prominent in the affairs of his church in 1752.

Gillespies' Gap is a well known pass in the Blue Ridge, in North Carolina; and Haywood, in his Civil and Political History of Tennessee, at pp. 196-7, mentions a Captain Gillespie

as serving under Colonel John Sevier in 1779 in the Indian
wars in that state, mentioning an incident in connection with
this Captain Gillespie, which shows him to have been a man of
great personal courage, firmness and magnanimity. It appears
from information furnished the author by the Honorable Albert
P. Gillespie, of Tazewell, that two brothers, James and Thomas
Gillespie, came from the Cumberland country in Tennessee,
about 1794, and that James settled near Chatham Hill, in what
is now Smyth County, and that some of his descendants still
reside in that section, and some are residents of the County of
Tazewell. Thomas Gillespie is the ancestor of the larger part
of the family of that name in Tazewell County, and he left the
following sons: John, Rees, B., Henry, William and Robert;
and daughters, one married James Harrison, and another married a Mr. Thompson.

William M. Gillespie, son of the preceding William, married
Olivia Johnston, of Giles County (he and his wife are both
now dead), and they had the following children, viz: David J.,
who married Elizabeth Sanders; Joseph S., who married Mary
Higginbotham; Albert P., who married Nannie Higginbotham;
and daughters, Sarah, who married Clinton Barnes; Margaret,
who married Colonel Joseph Harrison; Mary, who married
Oscar Barnes, and Ella, who married Dr. J. L. Painter. The
daughter of Thomas Gillespie, who married James Harrison,
was the mother of Colonel Joseph Harrison, now living near
Tazewell, Virginia.

THE HALES OF THE NEW RIVER VALLEY.

This family is of English origin, descendants of the Hales
of Kent. The first American emigrant of the name coming in
1632, bore the coat of arms of the Kentish Hales—three broad
arrows, feather white on a red field. The traditional story in
the family of these New River Hales is, that the family was
quite numerous in Massachusetts and Connecticut, and that
some time prior to the beginning of our war for independence

DR. JAMES W. HALE

Great Grandson of Capt. Edward Hale, the Settler.

there were in one family of this name seven brothers, all of whom joined the American army; a part of them served through the war under General Washington in and around Boston, in the Jerseys and in Pennsylvania; that one of the older brothers, who had a family, drifted south to Virginia some years prior to the beginning of the Revolution, and located in what is now Franklin County, Virginia; that this settler had a son Edward, who served in the American army in the early period of the Revolution, and later, in 1779, came across the Alleghanies into the New River Valley, and later married a Miss Patsy Perdue and settled on Wolf Creek. Edward Hale was born about 1750, was a man of rather small stature, fair complexion and blue eyes, was a man of information and intelligence, and became a prominent figure on the border in his day, engaging in the Indian wars, fights and skirmishes. He was with the party under Captain Matthew Farley, that followed the Indians in the summer of 1783, after their attack on Mitchell Clay's family, on the Bluestone at Clover bottom, and was in the skirmish had with a part of these Indians on Pond Fork of Little Coal river, in which he killed an Indian at the first fire. From the back of this Indian, killed by Edward Hale, William Wiley, who was in the party of pursuers, took a strip of the Indian's hide, which he gave to Hale and was used by him and a number of his family for many years as a razor strop. Opposite this page is the photograph of Dr. James W. Hale, a descendant of the Captain Edward Hale above mentioned.

Edward Hale marched with Captain Shannon's company to North Carolina, in February, 1781, and was in the engagement at Wetzell's Mills, on the 6th day of March, and at Guilford Court House on the 15th day of the same month. In 1785 Edward Hale married Miss Patsy Perdue, a daughter of Uriah Perdue, then recently removed from what is now Franklin County, Virginia. Mrs. Hale was a sister of the wife of the elder Joseh Hare. The names of the children of Edward Hale and his wife are as follows, viz: Thomas, Isaiah, Charles, Jesse, Isaac, Daniel, Elias and William; and the daughters,

Mary and Phœbe. Thomas married Miss Lucas, Isaiah married Margaret Lucas, Isaac married Miss Lucas, Jesse married Margaret Watts, Daniel married Elizabeth Watts, Elias married Nancy Peters, William married Miss Williams; Mary married John Williams, and they moved to the state of Missouri, and Phœbe married John McClaugherty, son of James.

Thomas Hale had sons, Charles, Edward, Lorenzo D., Green, Thomas, and Ralph; daughters, Priscilla, who married William H. French; Martha, who married, first, David F. Alvis, second William Shannon; Rhoda, who never married.

Isaac had one son, Daniel P.; daughters, Eliza, who married Captain James F. Hare; Martha, who married Russell G. French; Miriam, who married Isaac H. Day; Mary, who married Charles E. Hale; Sarah, who married, first, Rufus Brown, second, Luke Wells; Daniel P., married Martha Shumate.

Daniel had sons, Thomas, Charles E., John A., and Daniel F., and daughters, Elizabeth, who married William Shumate; Paulina, who married C. W. Tolley; Linney, who married R. G. Rowland; Cornelia, who married William Brown.

Charles had sons, John D., William H., and Isaac (the latter died young); daughters, Hulda, who married Andrew Fillinger; Martha, who married John Walker.

Isaiah had sons, Erastus (who died young), Luther C., who married Miss Alice Peck; the daughters, Charlotte married William Moser, Louisa married Jacob Snidow, Juliana married Wolf Crotching, Virginia married James Kinzie, Wilmoth married Andrew J. Hare. Isaiah Hale married a second wife, Mrs. Sallie Lybrook, whose maiden name was Hall; they had daughters, Lizzie, who married George Spangler; Sallie L., who married J. Harvey Dunn, and the son, Luther C., above mentioned.

Jesse had sons, Hamilton J. (died during the civil war), Edward C., who lives in Giles County; daughters, Julia, who married .... Pettyjohn; Martha, who died unmarried; Mary, who married David French; Eglentine, who married Henry W. Broderick (both dead); Newtonia, who married Erastus W. Charleton.

For want of correct and sufficient information the names of the children of William Hale and his sister, Mrs. Williams (both of whom died in Missouri) cannot be given in this work.

The children of Elias Hale and his wife, Nancy Peters Hale, are as follows, viz: John E., who married Miss Moore; Charles A., who married Miss Bailey; Captain Rufus A., who married Julia Bailey; Comrad married ....; daughters, Mary, who married Calvin Harry; Ardelia, who married John T. Carr; Julia, who died unmarried.

Edward Hale died about 1820, and his descendants are among the most valued citizens of the country; they have occupied prominent and important positions in the civil and military affairs of the district of country in which they have lived. They have been farmers, physicians, lawyers, merchants, magistrates, members of the Legislature and judges. As soldiers they have always been the equals of any that the country has sent forth; they fought, bled and died on nearly every important battlefield of our civil war. Dr. James W. Hale—formerly a distinguished physician—now an able lawyer, residing at Princeton, West Virginia, was a valiant Confederate soldier in the Civil war, losing an arm at the battle of Piedmont, Virginia, June 5th, 1864. He is a great-grandson of Edward Hale. Edward McClaugherty, another great-grandson of Edward Hale, was a lieutenant in Company A, 17th Virginia regiment of cavalry, and died in the service. Honorable Robert C. McClaugherty, also a great-grandson of Edward Hale, is a prominent lawyer residing at Bluefield, West Virginia. He served four years as Prosecuting Attorney of Mercer County, and eight years as Judge of the 9th Judicial Circuit of West Virginia. The late Captain Rufus A. Hale, of Mercer County, was one of the bravest men in his regiment, serving throughout the war 1861-5 with distinction, and was more than once commended by his superior officers for his gallantry and good conduct on the battlefield. Charles A. Hale, a brother of Captain Rufus A., was a highly reputable citizen, made a good record and name as a valiant soldier of the 8th Virginia regiment of cavalry.

James Perdue, who died in Mercer County in 1900, at the age
of one hundred and one years, was a relative of Captain Edward
Hale.

JOSEPH HARE, THE HUGUENOT.

The ancestors of Joseph Hare left France in the days of the
fearful religious persecution, and sought refuge for a short
time in the Barbadoes, from which, about 1710, they came to
South Carolina, where the family remained a number of years,
and thence traveled northward until it reached the southern
border of the State of North Carolina, not far from the present
city of Fayetteville. The breaking out of the American Revolution found in this family eight boys and three girls, all born
in South Carolina, among them Joseph, who was born in 1749.
The great tory or Loyalist uprising in the spring of 1776, in
the neighborhood of Fayetteville, North Carolina, under the
leadership of General McDonald, brought the patriot forces of
that section together under Colonel Richard Caswell, to whose
command Joseph Hare had attached himself. Colonel Caswell,
learning that this body of Loyalists, 1500 strong, was preparing
to march to Wilmington and would on their route have to cross
Moore's Creek bridge, repaired thither with his troops. and
prepared for action, which took place on February 27th, 1776,
resulting in the complete overthrow and defeat of the Loyalists
army, and the killing and capturing of a large number, including their commander.

After the term of service of Joseph Hare had expired he
came, in the year of 1779, to the New River Valley, and finally
settled on Wolf Creek, in what is now the County of Giles. He
became a very distinguished Indian fighter, spy and scout, and
was in many of the skirmishes along the border, between 1779
and 1794, among them the skirmish with the Indians on Pond
Fork of Little Coal river in the summer or early fall of 1783,
in which several of the Indians were slain. The Indians killed
in this action were a part of the band that had a few days previ-

DR. JOS. H. HARE

Great Grandson of Joseph Hare, the Settler.

ously attacked the family of Mitchell Clay, at Clover bottom, on the Bluestone, killing a son and daughter of Clay, and carrying away as a prisoner his young son Ezekiel. Joseph Hare was a member of Captain Thomas Shannon's company, with which he marched to the state of North Carolina in February, 1781, and with his company participated in the action of Wetzell's Mills on the 6th day of March, and on the 15th of the same month in the battle of Guilford Court House. In April, 1789, he married Nannie Clay, a daughter of Mitchell Clay and his wife, Phœbe Belcher Clay, by whom he had two children, who, together with the mother, died young. He then married Phœbe Perdue, a daughter of Uriah Perdue, then lately removed from the County of Franklin. This Perdue family was of French extraction, and possessed of all the eccentricities, peculiarities and nervousness of their French ancestry. Joseph Hare had by his second marriage but one child, a son, William H., who married Sallie French, a daughter of James French and his wife Susan Hughes French.

William H. Hare and his wife had the following named children: Joseph, who married Julia A. Duncan; Andrew J., who married Wilmoth Hale; James F., who married Eliza Hale; Isaac, who first married Miss Rowland, second, Miss Kirk; William H., who married Miss Lambert; John D., who died unmarried; and daughters, Phœbe, who married Rev. Elisha G. Duncan; Susannah, who married James W. Rowland, and Sallie, who married William P. Shumate. The elder Joseph Hare died in 1855, at the age of one hundred and five years.

Dr. Joseph H. Hare, a prominent physician of the city of Bluefield, is a great-grandson of the elder Joseph Hare, and his photograph will be seen on the page facing this. The descendants of Joseph Hare were bold and determined soldiers, among them Captain James F. Hare led a company in the 36th Virginia regiment of infantry. Hamilton, a son of the younger Joseph Hare, and a brother of Dr. Joseph H. Hare, was killed in the battle of Piedmont, Virginia, June 5th, 1864.

THE HOGES.

In addition to other sources of information, we gather from "Foot's Sketches of Virginia," and from a pamphlet entitled "Historical and Genealogical of the Cumberland Valley, Pa.," by William H. Egle, M. D., M. A., the following particulars in regard to the early history of the Hoge family.

William Hoge, the first representative of this family, distinguished in church and state, came to America in 1682; was the son of James Hoge, of Scotland, who lived in Musselburg, near Glasgow. On board the Caladonia, the vessel that brought him over, there was a family named Hume, consisting of father, mother, and daughter; they were Presbyterians, leaving Scotland to avoid persecution. The Humes were from Paisley, Scotland, and the father was a Knight and a Baron; both father and mother died during the voyage to America, leaving their daughter, Barbara, in charge of young William Hoge, who placed her with her relations, the Johnstons, in the city of New York, whilst he decided to make his home at Perth Amboy, New Jersey, on land owned by a Scotch company, at the head of which was Governor Berkeley, and of which he was a member. Subsequently William Hoge returned to New York, married the girl Barbara Hume, who had been his protege, and from this rather romantic marriage a long line of distinguished men and women have written their names on history's page. After the birth of their first son, John, William and his young wife made their home for some time in Chester County, Pennsylvania, and John, when grown, married Miss .... Bowen, a Welch woman, and settled about nine miles west of Harrisburg and laid out the little village of Hogestown. From this marriage sprang a long line of descendants who have fitly adorned the history of Pennsylvania, Ohio, and other western states, many of our country's most distinguished men being numbered among them, but the line is too long to trace these descendants, but rather of the father and remainder of the children, all of whom came to Virginia about the time John was establishing the little village of Hogestown.

The children that came with William Hoge to Virginia, in 1735, were as follows: Solomon, James, William, Alexander, George, Zebulon, and Nancy, making their home about three miles from Winchester, in Frederick County. In the old grave-yard of old Opequon Church—the deed for the land on which the church stands was made by William Hoge on February 14th, 1745—is buried William Hoge and Barbara, his wife, and many of their descendants. The first Pastor of this church was Rev. John Hoge, grandson of William, and son of John, his eldest son, who had remained in Pennsylvania. Solomon married a Quakeress and was the progenitor of that vast family of Hoges in Loudon and other lower Valley and Piedmont counties. Alexander was a member of the Constitutional Convention of Virginia that adopted the Federal Constitution, and was a member of the first Congress.

James, the third son, of the descendants of whom this narrative will especially treat, and who has been said by one in writing of him, to be a "man eminent for his clear understanding, devout fear of God, and the love of the Gospel of Christ," was married twice; the name of the first wife was Agnes, the second Mary, their maiden names unknown; the records of Frederick County show that he and his wife Agnes join in a deed in 1748, and that he and his wife Mary in a deed in 1758. He and his wives are buried in old Opequon graveyard, he having died June 2nd, 1795. His first wife, Agnes, gave him two sons, John and James, and a daughter, who was the mother of General Robert Evans, founder of Evansville, Indiana, and of Mattie Evans, one of the captives of Abb's Valley. John, the eldest son, becoming dissatisfied with his father's marriage, left home and was never definitely heard from afterward, though he was supposed to have been killed in Braddock's defeat on the Monongahela.

The younger brother, James, left home a few years afterwards to search for his brother John, but after reaching what is now Pulaski County, Virginia, gave up the search, and stopped with a new found friend, Major Joseph Howe, a gentleman of English descent, who had several years previous found a home in the then mountain wilds. After staying with him a short while young James Hoge married his daughter, Elizabeth, in 1763, and they made their home near the father-in-law, and this is the old southwestern Virginia Hoge homestead, now owned by the late Governor James Hoge Tyler, a great-grandson of the founder. James Hoge was born January 12th, 1742, and died April 5th, 1812, seventeen years after the death of his father, and is buried in the old Hoge burying ground. James Hoge and Elizabeth Howe Hoge, his wife, had five sons and six daughters: Joseph, John, Agnes, Martha, General James, Sarah, Elizabeth, Mary, Daniel, and William; of the sons General James was a man of most marked characteristics, and attained very eminent distinction. He was a distinguished officer in the war of 1812; served his county and district in the Senate and House of Delegates several terms; was five times Presidential Elector for his district on the Democratic ticket. He was born July 23rd, 1783, and died July 28th, 1861; is buried by the side of his wife, Eleanor Howe Hoge, in the old Howe burying ground. His wife was his first cousin.

Joseph Hoge, the eldest brother, removed to Tennessee, and left a large number of descendants in that and other states. John and William both lived and died in Pulaski, Virginia, and are numerously represented in that and adjoining counties. Daniel lived and died in Wise County, Virginia; he has descendants in southwest Virginia and some in the South; his sons were James, Stafford and Dr. John H.

To briefly revert to the elder James Hoge, grandfather of General James and son of William Hoge and Barbara Hume, will state that by his second marriage there was several sons and perhaps daughters; the names of three of the sons were, Solomon, Edward and Moses, the latter a distinguished minister, was president of Hampden Sidney College and professor in Union Theological Seminary. He died in 1820, July 5th; is buried in the church yard of the Third Presbyterian Church, Philadelphia. He was the grandfather of the eminent Divine,

Rev. Moses D. Hoge, of Richmond, Virginia, whose reputation is worldwide, and of the late William J. Hoge, D. D. Their father was Rev. Samuel Davies Hoge, who was brother to Rev. James Hoge, D. D,. late of Columbus, Ohio, and Rev. John Blair Hoge, father of Judge John Blair Hoge, of West Virginia.

THE HOWES.

There are difficulties in the way of tracing back this family to its English origin. Tradition has to be largely relied upon, and this, as presented by different branches of the family, differs as to the first of the family that crossed the Atlantic, and as to the place of first settlement. One statement is that a Joseph How, belonging to a family of that name long domiciled in the state of Massachusetts, enlisted and served as a soldier in the French and Indian war, in which he was supposed to have been lost, but was afterwards found in the New River Valley, where later he added the letter "e" to the name, the original spelling of the name being How, afterwards Howe. How much of this statement is correct cannot be determined. The author has chosen to follow copies of the "Howe MSS.," furnished him by Honorable J. Hoge Tyler, late Governor of Virginia, who is a direct descendant of the Joseph Howe, a sketch of whose family here follows:

The Howe family, not unlike the Hoge family, with which it is so nearly related, also commences with a little romantic episode in the lives of the first American representatives. Joseph Howe, an English gentleman, first cousin of Lord Howe and General Wayne of Revolutionary fame, came to America in 1737. On board the vessel that brought him over was a beautiful and captivating girl by the name of Eleanor Dunbar; the two young people fell in love with each other on the voyage and married soon after landing and settled near Boston, Mass., from which point they drifted southward and finally settled in the rugged regions of southwestern Virginia when the country was quite a trackless wilderness. They made their home on Back Creek, as nearly as can be established, in 1757 or 1758, and this old homestead, the scene of many pleasant revelries and charming reunions, is still in possession of one of the representatives of the family, Mrs. Agnes Howe DeJarnette, a great-granddaughter of its founder. Joseph Howe had three sons, Joseph, John and Daniel; of Joseph there is nothing known, he having left home in early life; John seems to have left no family.

Daniel was an officer in the Revolutionary war, was a man of strong mind and high character. He married Nancy Haven and had three sons, Joseph H., John Dunbar, and William H.; and seven daughters, Ruth, Julia, Eleanor, Elizabeth, Lucretia, Nancy and Luemma. Joseph married Margaret Feely; John D. married Sarah Sheppard; William married Mary Fisher; Ruth married Thomas Kirk, and removed to Missouri; Julia married Zecharia Cecil; Eleanor married General James Hoge; Elizabeth married Colonel George Neeley Pearis; Lucretia married Colonel William Thomas; Nancy married Honorable Harvey Deskins, and Luemma married Dr. Jackson.

The children of Joseph Howe and Margaret Feely were Eleanor, who married Reuben Sawers; Lucretia, who married Colonel William J. Jordan; Eliza, who married ...... Wassam; Brown, who married William G. Farris; Ollie, who married D. P. Watson; Sue, who never married.

The children of John Dunbar Howe and Sarah, his wife, are as follows: Margaret, who married George Shannon; Susan, who married J. M. Thomas; Eliza Jane, who married Charles J. Matthews; Ellen Mary, who married J. G. Kent; John T., who married Sallie DeJarnette; Samuel S., who died a prisoner of war at Point Lookout; Haven B., who married Kate Cloyd; Willie, who died in infancy, and Agnes, who married Captain E. G. DeJarnette and lived at the old place.

The children of William H. Howe and Mary Fisher Howe are: Belle, who married Dr. Charles Pepper; Lizzie, who married W. W. Minor; William G., who married Alice Brown, Augusta, who married Dr. Hufford; Sallie, who married Mr.

Harmon; Alice, who married Charles Bumgardner; Ellie, who is unmarried. A daughter of Thomas Kirk and Ruth, his wife, married a Mr. Peery.

The children of Julia Howe, who married Zecharia Cecil, are: Russell, Giles, Daniel R., Zecharia and Nancy. The children of Eleanor, who married General James Hoge, are: Daniel, James, Joseph H., William; and Eliza, who married George Tyler, of Caroline, the father of Governor J. Hoge Tyler. The names of the children of Elizabeth, who married Colonel George N. Pearis, are as follows: George W. Pearis, Daniel H. Pearis, Nancy, who married Archer Edgar; Rebecca, who married George D. Hoge; Ardelia, who married Daniel R. Cecil; and Elizabeth, who married Benjamine White. The children of Lucretia, who married William Thomas, were Giles, William, Mary Anne and Julia. Nancy, who married Harvey Deskins, had no children. The children of Luemma, who married Dr. Jackson, are: Mollie, Sue, and Luemma.

John Howe, son of the first Joseph and his wife Eleanor Dunbar Howe, was an active business man, engaged largely in the acquisition of wild land by survey and grant in the early years of the settlements along the tributaries of New River, in what is now Giles County, Virginia, and Mercer County, West Virginia. He made a survey and obtained a grant for a tract of four hundred acres of land on Brush Creek, near where the village of Princeton is now located.

Major Daniel Howe, an officer in our war for independence, was often on detached service in search of Tories. The story is told that one John Haven, of Plum Creek, was suspected of being a Tory, and that Major Howe was sent on more than one occasion to arrest Haven, but was unable to do so, and that finally a pretty, blackeyed daughter of Haven, whose name was Nancy, caught the Major and she became his wife, as already stated.

THE JOHNSTONS.

In the 13th century, says Lieutenant Charles Johnston in his history of this family, "There lived in the mountainous district of Annandale, Dumbriesshire, Scotland, just north of Firth of Solway, a small but hardy clan of borderers, whose chief was called John. They were doubtless of Saxon origin, and up to this time were little known. Their clanbadge was the Red Hawthorne. As the clan grew stronger their Chieftain became ambitious to take his place among the chiefs of the larger clans. Their motto was: "Viva ut vivas." A little after the middle of the 13th century the chief of the clan applied to the Earl of Annandale, who was the grandfather of Robert Bruce, to purchase a tract of land near the center of the district; the deal was consummated, and it thereupon became necessary to give name to the tract in question; Bruce, in the charter, called it Jonistoun (or Johnstoun), and this chieftain, now Lord Jonistoun, was called Sir John de Jonistoun. His clan was thereafter known as Jonistown, or Johnistouns, the name now being spelled Johnstone or Johnston. Some writers have fallen into the error that the name is synonymous with Johnson, but a glance at the derivation of the names easily discloses the error; Johnson is derived from and means the son of John, while Johnston signifies John's Town; the one shows locality, the other indicates descent.

"The Johnstons were a prolific clan as well as hardy, and in the next two centuries after adopting the name, they became strong enough to excite the jealousy of their neighbors, the much stronger clan of Maxwell of Nithsdale, and many a bloody fight took place before the Johnstons established their supremacy at the battle of Dyfe-Sands, in 1593, in which the Maxwells were completely routed, leaving their chief, Lord John Maxwell, dead on the field. At this time the chief of the Johnstons was Sir James, who was succeeded by his son James, who was created Lord Johnston in 1633; both were of the Peerage and served in the English House of Lords. The Johnstons and Scotts, it seems, were near neighbors in Scotland.

Sir Walter Scott, in his "Fair Maid of Perth," gives considerable prominence to the Johnston clan, and adds some verses which run as follows:

> Within the bounds of Annandale
> The gentle Johnstons ride,
> They have been here a thousand years
> And a thousand more they'll bide.

The seat of the Johnston clan was at Lockerby, near the center of the district of Annandale."

After the fall of Londondery, and religious persecution continuing in their country, a large number of the Johnstons migrated to Ireland, settling in County Antrim and near Eniskillen, in County Fermanagh, mostly in the latter county. As early as 1700 several of these Fermanagh Johnstons came to America, locating in Piedmont, Virginia, along the base of the Blue Ridge, in what is now the Counties of Culpeper and Rappahannock, then probably Essex County.

James Johnston, of Fermanagh, had two sons, James and David, the latter born about 1726. The father having died and the estate under the laws belonging to the older brother, James, the younger son David, seeing nothing favorable to his remaining in Ireland, at the age of about ten years, viz: about 1736 or 1737 sought an opportunity to join his kinsfolk in America and succeeded in hiring himself to a ship captain as a cabin boy, and finally landed at Norfolk, Virginia, and made his way across the country to his relations on the waters of the Rappahannock. He became the ancestor of the New River Johnstons. When about twenty-five years of age (1751), he fell in love with and married a pretty Irish girl by the name of Nannie (or Annie) Abbott, a daughter of Richard Abbott of Culpeper, and selected his home on Hazel River, near old Gourd Vine Church, in that county.

John Chapman and his brother Richard, had also married daughters of Richard Abbott. Moredock O. McKensey, from Glasgow, Scotland, had married Jemima, the only sister of the Chapmans. In November, 1768, the Chapmans and Mc-

Kensey sold out their holdings in Culpeper, and crossed the Blue Ridge and settled on the Shenandoah, where they remained until the year of 1771, when they removed to the New River Valley, locating at the mouth of Walker's Creek, in the then County of Botetourt, now Giles. The peculiar spelling of McKensey's name will be noted; the author examined the record of deeds in the clerk's office of the County Court of Culpeper County, finding a deed made by Mr. McKensey and wife in November, 1768, conveying a tract of land on Burgess's River, to which deed the name of McKensey is spelled "Moredock O. McKensey." Burgess's river has disappeared from all the maps, if it ever had a place thereon, and diligent inquiry of the Culpeper people failed to disclose its locality; it is believed, however, that the name has been changed to "Hedges' River."

In September, 1758, Hennings' Virginia Statutes, the House of Burgesses made an appropriation to pay David Johnston, of Culpeper, a sum of money for food furnished by him to friendly Indians. David Johnston remained in Culpeper until 1778, and then came across the Alleghanies, settling on the plateau or territory between Big Stoney Creek and Little Stoney Creek at what is now known as the John Phleger farm, where he died in 1786, his wife in 1813, and they are both buried on this farm. The house which he built in 1778 is still standing and forms a part of the residence of the late John Phleger, and is no doubt the oldest structure in the County of Giles. David Johnston and his wife, Nannie, or Annie, Abbott Johnston, had eight children, three sons and five daughters, all born in Culpeper, the eldest, Sallie, had married Thomas Marshall before the family left Culpeper.

James Johnston, the eldest son of David, had visited the New River Valley in 1775, no doubt on a visit to the Chapmans and McKensey, and on his return to Culpeper, and in January, 1776, he enlisted in a volunteer company commanded by Captain George Slaughter, which company was attached to the 8th regiment of Virginia infantry commanded by Colonel Muhlenberg. James Johnston served two years in the Ameri-

can army; his first service or a part thereof was in South
Carolina and Georgia; his command then marched north and
was under the immediate command of General Washington.
James was in the battles of Brandywine and Germantown,
marched through the Jerseys, and spent the winter at Valley
Forge.

David Johnston and Nannie Abbott Johnston had the following children: James, who married Miss Copley; Sallie,
who married Thomas Marshall; Elian, who married Isaac Chapman; Jemima, who married John Chapman, of Wolf Creek;
Virginia, who married Isaac McKensey; David, born in 1768,
married Mrs. Sallie Chapman Miller, the widow of Jacob
Miller; Andrew, born in 1770, married Jane Henderson of
Montgomery County; Annie, the youngest daughter, married
George Fry, Jr.

This George Fry, Jr., was a son of George Fry who married
the widow of the elder David Johnston, the Settler. Captain
George W. Caldwell, of Mercer, is the grandson of Annie Johnston Fry, and the great grandson of the elder David Johnston.
James Johnston and his wife, ... Copley, had several
children; sons, Reuben and David. The family, except David,
went to Indiana about the time of its admission into the Union.
David married a Miss Peck, of Botetourt County, and resided
on Sinking Creek, where his descendants still live. Thomas
Marshall and his wife, Sallie Johnston Marshall, who settled
near the present dwelling house of George L. Snidow, Esq., in
Giles County, had four sons and two daughters; the sons:
John, David, James and Thomas; the daughters, Nancy and
Aggie. The family of Thomas Marshall removed at an early
date to Powell's Valley, Virginia.

John Chapman, of Wolf Creek, the son of Richard and
Jemima Johnston Chapman, had quite a numerous family;
one grandson, J. W. Chapman, residing on Wolf Creek, in
Bland County, is the only one of that family now bearing that
name that lives in this country. John Chapman and wife had
a daughter who married William Wilburn, of Sugar Run, and

Boston and John Howard Wilburn are her sons. The late John Chapman Wilburn was also a grandson of the said John Chapman.

Isaac McKensey and family went to Kentucky quite a hundred years ago. George Fry and his wife, Annie Johnston Fry, had a number of children, among them two sons, David and James, who went to Cabell County, Virginia, as early as 1820, and their descendants live in Cabell and Wayne, some of whom were men of prominence, among them Chapman Fry, grandson of James, was long Clerk of the County Court of Wayne; William, another grandson, is a lawyer and now the Prosecuting Attorney of Wayne County; Johnston Fry, a son of James, was for many years Deputy Sheriff of Wayne County. Some members of this family settled in Boone and Logan Counties, and their descendants still live there.

Sallie, a daughter of George Fry, Jr., and Annie Johnston Fry, married David Croy; another daughter of George and Annie Fry, Eliza, married John Caldwell, who resided for many years in Mercer County, where he and his wife both died and are buried. They left a number of children, among them Captain George W. Caldwell, who was a faithful and brave Confederate soldier, and was for a number of years surveyor of Mercer County.

The children of Isaac and Elian Johnston Chapman and who they married, will be seen by reference to the biographical sketch of the Chapmans.

David Johnston and his wife, Mrs. Sallie Chapman Miller Johnston, had two sons and three daughters; the sons: Oscar Fitzalan Johnston, was born June, 1807, married Elizabeth French, daughter of Isaac and Sallie Straley French; had three children, David E., who married Sarah E. Pearis; Sallie V. (1), who married, first, Jesse N. Simmons, second, George O'Rayburn; Oscar H., who died in 1879, unmarried. Chapman Isaac Johnston, born January, 1809, died December, 1891, married Elian Chapman Snidow, daughter of John and Rachel Chap-

(1). Died December 2d, 1905.

man Snidow; they had sons, David Andrew, who married Fannie Shumate; J. Raleigh, who married Nona Peck; Sarah Ellen, who married William Augustus French; Annie Chapman, who married Charles Dingess French; Rachel Snidow, who married, first, ... Daugherty, second, Joseph H. Alvis. Olivia Johnston married William M. Gillespie of Tazewell County; had three sons, David Johnston, who married Elizabeth Saunders, Joseph Stras, who married Mary Higginbotham; Albert Pendleton, who married Nannie Higginbotham; the daughters, Sarah, who married Clinton Barnes; Margaret, who married Colonel Joseph Harrison; Louisa, who married Captain Henry Bowen; Mary, who married Oscar Barnes; Barbara, who married George W. Gillespie; Ella, who married Dr. J. L. Painter. Louisa Adeline Johnston married Colonel Daniel H. Pearis; they had three children, two daughters and one son: Virginia, who died in 1860, unmarried; George Daniel, who when little above the age of sixteen years, joined Bryan's Virginia battery and was killed in the battle of Cloyd's farm, May 9th, 1864; and Sarah E., who married David E. Johnston. Sallie Chapman Johnston died unmarried.

Colonel Andrew Johnston and his wife, Jane Henderson Johnston, had five children; three sons and two daughters: James D., a lawyer of great prominence, married Mary A. Fowler, daughter of Dr. Thomas Fowler and his wife, Priscilla Chapman Fowler. Andrew Henderson Johnston married Mary McDaniel, and they had two children, Walter McDaniel, who married Annie Hays; Jennie, who married Honorable Thomas H. Dennis. Dr. Harvey Green Johnston married, first, Annie Snidow, by whom he had four children; secondly, he married Mrs. Mary Fowler Halsey, by whom he had four children. Mary Johnston married James M. Carper; they had two sons and three daughters. Eliza Jane Johnston married James Hoge, of Montgomery County; they had a large family of children.

The children of James D. Johnston and his wife, Mary Fowler Johnston, were: Roberta, who married Dr. John,

Izard; Allene, who died unmarried; Sydney F. (now dead), who married Miss Hattie Carey; Mamie, who married Mason Jamison, and James D., a brilliant young lawyer of Roanoke Virginia.

The children of Dr. Harvey Green Johnston are: Dr. William A., who married Mrs. Dennis; Carrie, who married Mr. J. E. Triplett; Jennie, who married Mr. William Black; Loula, who married Mr. B. E. Bransford; Fowler, who died young; Harvey, Vivian and Ada are unmarried.

Annie Hoge, daughter of James Hoge and Eliza Jane Johnston Hoge, married Major John Chapman Snidow; had two sons and two daughters; the sons, William and Walter; daughters, Florence, who married John T. S. Hoge; Annie C., who married John W. Williams, who was clerk of the Virginia House of Delegates. The sons of James Hoge and Eliza Jane Johnston Hoge are Dr. Robert, James, Joseph, Rev. B. Lacey and Tyler, and a daughter, Jane Nellie.

The descendants of the Settler David Johnston, or many of them, together with the descendants of the Settlers John and Richard Chapman, have not only been prominent and influential people in both civil and military affairs in the New River Valley, but even in other sections of the country. In every Constitutional convention held in Virginia, except those of 1776, and the "Black and Tan," of 1869, this Johnston-Chapman blood has had representatives. Henley Chapman was in the convention of 1829-30; his son, General Augustus A. Chapman, was a member of the convention of 1850-1; his son, Mannilius, a member of the Secession convention of 1861; a great-grandson of David Johnston and John Chapman was a member of the late Constitutional convention of Virginia in the person of Honorable Albert Pendleton Gillespie, of Tazewell. The second David Johnston, Andrew Johnston, Isaac Chapman, and his son, John, were frequently in the Legislature of Virginia; and later, Oscar F. Johnston, Augustus A. Chapman, and Manilius Chapman were members of the Virginia Legislature. A grandson and great-grandson of the Settler, John

Chapman, together with a great nephew, were members of the House of Representatives of the United States, in the persons of General A. A. Chapman, David E. Johnston, and Honorable Reuben Chapman, the latter of Alabama. Two great grandsons of the elder David Johnston and John Chapman have been Circuit Judges in West Virginia, and one of them, Honorable Joseph M. Sanders, has recently been elevated to the bench of the Supreme Court of Appeals of West Virginia. Honorable James French Strother, a great-great-grandson of John Chapman, is now a judge in West Virginia. Major Samuel E. Lybrook and William A. French, great-grandsons of John Chapman, represented Giles County in the Legislature of Virginia; and Samuel Lucas, a great grandson of the elder David Johnston, was also a member of the Virginia Legislature.

About the year of 1800 there came to what is now Giles County and settled in what is known as the Irish settlement, an influx of the Johnstons from Fermanagh County, Ireland. Adam Johnston married in Ireland Elizabeth Stafford, of County Tyrone. Adam and his wife, Elizabeth Stafford Johnston, had a numerous family, among them, John, Adam, James, Edward and others. John, James and Edward had large families, who with their descendants mostly reside in Giles County. Adam is the ancestor of the larger part of the Mercer County Johnstons. Edward, usually called "Squire Neddy," was clerk of Giles County Court for several years. Some of the descendants of John and James Johnston reside in Mercer County, among them Dr. Charles A. Johnston, George S. Strader, and the family of Jacob L. Peters. Among these Scotch-Irish settlers who came about 1800 were the Eatons, Staffords, Egglestons and others.

THE KIRKS.

John Kirk, the ancestor of this family, came from Scotland, and had located, several years prior to the beginning of the American Revolution, in Piedmont, Virginia. John, the son

of this emigrant, came to the New River Valley at an early
date, as shown by his written application, made in 1832, for
a pension for military services rendered as an American soldier
in the Revolution; he was born in the County of Fauquier,
October 10th, 1754. He had a son, Thomas, who was also an
American soldier, and had received, in one of the battles of the
war of 1812, a severe wound in the hand. The Kirks, Duncans and Emmonses were neighbors in Fauquier.

The John Kirk who came to Middle New River married
Elizabeth O'Brien, and his son Thomas married Ruth Howe, a
daughter of Major Daniel Howe. John Kirk enlisted in the
spring of 1776, in the company of Captain John Chilton, of
Fauquier County, which company was attached to the 3rd Virginia regiment of infantry commanded by Colonel Hugh Mercer, of which Thomas Marshall, father of Chief Justice John
Marshall, was the Major. This regiment, after its organization, marched to Alexandria, Virginia, then to Williamsburg,
and from there to New York and was posted on Long Island.
Colonel Mercer, having been promoted to Brigadier General
and put in command of a brigade consisting of the 3rd, 7th,
11th, and 15th Virginia regiments, Colonel Weeden was placed
in command of the 3rd regiment, Thomas Marshall becoming
Lieutenant Colonel, and Captain Leak Major. In the battle
of Long Island, in August, 1776, Major Leak was killed and
Captain Lee was promoted to Major. The brigade of Mercer
marched to White Plains, then into New Jersey and on to
Pennsylvania, camping on the banks of the Delaware, from
whence on the evening of Christmas, 1776, the army crossed the
Delaware through floating ice, and surprised the Hessians at
Trenton, New Jersey, capturing more than 1,000 prisoners,
who were safely brought away. The army rested in the vicinity of the Delaware, where it was confronted by the British
army, which, on the night of the ...... day of January, 1777,
it eluded and by a circuitous route attacked a British force at
Princeton, which it defeated. The brigade to which John Kirk
belonged opened this battle; its brigade commander, General

Mercer, fell mortally wounded. Mr. Kirk was also in the battle of Brandywine, in September, 1777, in which his Captain, Chilton, was killed, as was Major Lee, of his regiment; he was likewise in the battle of Germantown and wintered at Valley Forge. His term of enlistment for two years expired in the spring of 1778, and he received his discharge. All the people of the New River Valley, who bear the name of Kirk, and many others who do not, are the descendants of this family. John Kirk represented Giles County in the House of Delegates of Virginia in the years of 1818-19, and was also Sheriff of that county.

THE LYBROOKS.

The progenitor of this family came from Holland (1) to Pennsylvania. The original name was Leibroch, but Anglicized into Lybrook. The first and only one of this name that sought and found a home in the New River Valley was Philip Lybrook, who came from Pennsylvania between 1748 and 1755, locating at the mouth of Sinking Creek, in what is now the County of Giles, then Augusta. He did not come with the Draper's Meadows settlers in 1748, as he is not mentioned, nor does his name appear in connection with that settlement or the people who made it until August 7th, 1755, the day before the butchery of the Draper's Meadows settlers by the Indians, when young Preston had been sent by his uncle, Colonel Patton, over to Lybrook's to get him to help with the reaping of the grain. Mr. Lybrook is again mentioned by Hale, in his "Trans-Alleghany Pioneers," in connection with the retreat of the Indians with their prisoners, taken at Draper's Meadows, and the leaving of the head of Philip Barger at Lybrook's. It may be mentioned in connection with the remarkable escape and tramp of Mrs. Ingles from Big Bone Lick, in Kentucky, up the New River to Adam Harman's at the Gunpowder spring, that she

(1). George Lybrook was killed by a runaway horse, about 1835, at a point about one half mile south of Pearisburg, Va.

would not have stopped two miles below at Lybrook's; she had
been taken to Lybrook's by the Indians on their retreat, and
there would seem to be no reason why she should not have
sought shelter at Mr. Lybrook's. The only reasonable conclusion is that either Lybrook had become fearful of the Indians
and had gone away to a place of greater safety, or that Mrs.
Ingles, in her worn and enfeebled condition, had lost all knowledge of the locality of Lybrook's cabin, lost her bearings, and
that in avoiding the high cliff of rocks jutting into the river
just below the mouth of Sinking Creek, had been compelled to
leave the river, keeping, however, the general course thereof
along the hills, and in this way reached the river at a point
above Lybrook's without knowing exactly where she was. There
is no information obtainable that Mr. Lybrook had abandoned
his settlement between the dates referred to; in fact, there is
no other mention of him until the year of 1774, though, beyond
doubt, he had been visited by John Snidow, from Pennsylvania,
in 1765, as Snidow's family settled near him in 1766. The
Lybrook-Chapman-Snidow fort stood at the extreme upper end
of what is known as the "Horse Shoe" farm, a short distance
below the mouth of Sinking Creek. In the early days of
August, 1774, there had been made known to the settlers that
Indians were prowling around. John Chapman was away from
home that day, Saturday, the 6th day of August, that information was conveyed to his family that Indians were in the neighborhood. Mrs. Chapman gathered her children and such of
the household goods as they could carry, crossed the river and
struck for the fort, and as they passed through the little bottom above the mouth of Little Stoney Creek they found the
fresh remains of a hog that had just been killed by the Indians;
this tended to hasten their pace and they reached the fort in
safety. Mr. Lybrook and an Irishman by the name of Mc-
Griff were cultivating a small crop of corn at the mouth of
Sinking Creek, had erected a couple of cabins in which their
respective families resided; these men treated the statement
that Indians were in the neighborhood as idle stories. On the

MAJ. SAMUEL E. LYBROOK

Great Grandson of Philip, the Settler.

morning of Sunday, the 7th, some of the young people from
the fort, among them the Snidows, went up to Philip Lybrook's,
where during the day six Indians attacked the young people
in and about the river, and also Mr. Lybrook in his little mill
on the Spring branch. They killed a young woman by the name
of Scott, and five small children of Lybrook and Mrs. Snidow,
wounded Mr. Lybrook in the arm, captured three small boys,
and ran a foot race after John Lybrook, eleven years old, who
escaped to his father's house.

Mr. Philip Lybrook had a number of children, but it is only
proposed to follow John and his descendants. Opposite this
page is the photograph of Major Samuel E. Lybrook, a great
grandson of the elder Philip, the settler, and grandson of John,
who outran the Indian. John lived and grew to manhood and
old age. When he was about twenty-five years old he fell in
love with Annie Chapman, daughter of John and Sallie Abbott
Chapman. Annie had another lover in the person of James
French, son of Matthew, whom she had agreed to marry; the
day of the wedding was fixed, the license procured and the
wedding supper cooked, the minister present to perform the
ceremony, all the invited guests had arrived, save one—and
that was John Lybrook—who arrived, however, about dark.
He rode up, hitched his horse, walked in and made enquiry for
Annie, and having found her in a room with her bridesmaids,
enquired, "Annie are you ready?" She replying in the affirma-
tive, walked out with him, sprang on his horse behind him, and
off they went for the home of John's father, leaving James
weeping and disconsolate. John seems to have had a license
also, at any rate he captured Jimmy's girl, and married her,
as the marriage bond shows under the name of Annie Chapman.
The marriage bond bears date January 11th, 1787, and the
marriage bond authorizing her marriage to James French is
dated January 1st, 1787. John Lybrook and Annie, his wife,
had a number of children, among them Philip, the first surveyor of Giles County, and a man of prominence in his day.
He married Miss Marrs and they had quite a large family of

sons and daughters; of his sons, David Johnston Lybrook went to Australia at an early day, dying there some five or more years past; a son, Major Samuel E., who resides in Giles County, and who married Miss Jennie Chapman; a son, John, of Montgomery County, who is the father of John Barger Lybrook, of Washington, D. C., an employee in the office of the Inter-State Commerce Commission.

John Lybrook, who escaped from the Indian in 1774, by jumping a ravine twelve feet wide, became a famous hunter and brave, bold Indian fighter; serving for several years in the various forts along the New River Valley frontier under Captain John Floyd, and Lieutenant Christian Snidow. Mr. Lybrook lived to about the age of eighty years.

THE M'CLAUGHERTYS.

This family is of Scottish origin, and about 1688, with the large tide of emigration then moving from Scotland to Ireland, on account of religious persecution and other causes, emigrated to County Down, from whence sprang the American representatives of that family. James McClaugherty, of County Down, Ireland, married Agnes McGarre, and came with his family to America in the year 1786, settling at Sweet Springs (now Monroe County, West Virginia). In 1809 he started with his family to Tennessee, and on reaching New River found a heavy flood of water had carried away all the boats within reasonable reach, and he stopped at the New River, settling where the late James Floyd McClaugherty and family resided for many years. The sons of James McClaugherty and Agnes, his wife, were James, John and Hugh, and one daughter, Jane. On May 8th, 1813, in crossing New River, Mr. McClaugherty, his wife, Agnes, and daughter Jane were drowned.

John, the son of James, married Miss Dingess, daughter of Peter Dingess, and they had a family of sons and daughters. James, the son of James, married Miss Sallie Mullins, and they had sons, James, John and William, and daughters.

Captain John McClaugherty became a prominent figure in the affairs of Giles County, and was for long years a magistrate, Deputy Clerk, Sheriff, and Deputy Sheriff; lived a long life of usefulness, dying at the age of about ninety-three. John, son of James McClaugherty, married Phœbe Hale, a daughter of Captain Edward Hale, and they had sons, John, Joseph H., Nelson H., Edward, who died in the Confederate military service; D. W., and Robert C., and a daughter, who married Dr. Evan H. Brown; another, who married W. F. Heptinstall; another who married Mr. Fillinger, and another, who married Charles A. Deaton.

James Floyd McClaugherty, son of Captain John, married Miss Martha Cunningham, and had sons, John, George and Robert, and a daughter, Sallie, who married George Walker; John died young and unmarried.

Charles W., son of Captain John, married first, Miss Anne Kyle, second, Mrs. Shanklin; by his first wife he had sons, Robert and J. Kyle; Robert died young; a daughter, Henrietta, married Charles W. Walker, and Virginia married John Adair, of New River.

THE M'COMASES AND NAPIERS.

In 1776 John McComas and his brother-in-law, Thomas h. Napier, came from western Maryland to the New River Valley. McComas was of that bold, adventurous, Scotch-Irish stock that feared no danger, and was always anxious to get away from restraints of all kinds, and to be free and happy. McComas and Napier first took up their abode at what is now known as Ripplemeade, but shortly removed to the territory where Pearisburg, Virginia, now stands, and as a protection against the Indians, built in connection with the Halls Fort Branch on the land lately owned by Mr. Charles D. French, and which is about three-fourths of a mile to the southeast of Pearisburg. McComas very soon afterward entered and surveyed some lands around or near the location referred to; and in 1782,

the land where Judge Philip W. Strother now resides, or a part
thereof, was taken up and surveyed by Moredock O. McKensey,
and afterward conveyed to Thomas H. Napier.

The first or elder David Johnston died in 1786; his will bears
date in July of that year, and John McComas is one of the subscribing witnesses to that instrument. John McComas and his
wife had a considerable family of children; among the sons
were: Elisha, David, Jesse, John, William and Moses, and
there were several daughters. John McComas, the elder, died
in Giles County, Virginia. Elisha McComas, son of the elder
John, and who is referred to as General Elisha, obtained his
title after he went to Cabell County, being commissioned a
Brigadier General of militia. He married in January, 1791,
Annie French, daughter of Matthew, of Wolf Creek, and removed to Cabell County about 1809. His brothers, or some of
them, preceded him by seven or eight years, and settled on the
Guyandotte and Mud River waters, then in Kanawha County,
Cabel not being created until 1809. It will be noted that
Elisha was there in 1810, either in Guyandotte or vicinity, for
he is made, by the act of the Legislature creating that town, one
of the trustees, as well as a trustee of Barboursville in 1813.
David McComas, son of the elder John, married Miss Bailey, a
daughter of the elder Richard. David died early, leaving a
widow and one son, James, the latter the ancestor of the Mercer
McComas', viz: Archibald, Eli and others.

General Elisha McComas and his wife had sons, David, William and James, and daughters, one of whom married John
Shelton, and another married .... Keenan, from whom
descended Patrick Keenan McComas, the eccentric lawyer of
Logan County, West Virginia.

David, the son of General Elisha, married Cynthia French,
daughter of Captain David and Mary Dingess French, and he
became a distinguished Judge; was a member of the General
Court of Virginia; Judge of the Kanawha Circuit Court, and
was at one time a State Senator from the Kanawha District.
He was born about 1795 and died in Giles County, Virginia, in

1864. He was a jolly man, full of wit and humor, but a most negligent man about his dress. Some good stories of his life as a judge have been preserved, and are worth relating. As has been said, he was Circuit Judge; his circuit was a large one, and his mode of travel was on horseback. Before he started on his circuit his wife made up and arranged his clothing for the trip, which often lasted for weeks, and on his return his wife would search his saddle bags for his soiled clothes, frequently finding none; he had simply, by his forgetfulness, left them at his boarding houses. On one occasion, when he was about to start off for his courts, his wife prepared for him and packed in his saddlebags a dozen new shirts, and enjoined upon him that he should exercise prudence in taking care of the same. On his return, on examination by his wife of the saddlebags, she found not a single shirt, whereupon she said: "Just as I expected, Mr. McComas, you have brought back no stop throwing off shirts until he had unburdened himself of eleven. His wife and himself, while he was Circuit Judge and lived in Charleston, made a visit to his relations in Cabell County, and after they had made the rounds, he remarked to his wife, "Well, we must go and see old brother . . . ." to which his wife inquiringly said, "Mr. McComas, isn't he in the poorhouse?" "Yes," said the Judge, "but there is no difference between him and myself; he is on the county and I am on the state." While Judge McComas was in the Senate of Virginia, it is said that he made the first straightout secession speech that up to that time had been made in Virginia. He and his wife left no children.

William McComas, son of General Elisha, married Miss Ward, lived for some years at Malden, in Kanawha County, and while living there in 1832 was elected to the Congress of the United States. He was a member of the Virginia Secession Convention of 1861. William McComas and his wife had the following children: Elisha W., Hamilton, William Wirt, Mat, and Benjamine Jefferson, and a daughter, Irene, who married Major McKendree. Elisha W. was in the Virginia Convention of 1850-1, and was also Lieutenant Governor of Virginia, afterward dying at Fort Scott, Kansas.

Hamilton, an eminent lawyer of St. Louis, Missouri, was killed by Indians in New Mexico; Benjamine Jefferson, a lawyer of distinction and a Captain in the Confederate service, died at Barboursville, West Virginia, and George J. McComas, a prominent lawyer of Huntington, West Virginia, is his son.

Dr. William Wirt McComas married Sarah M. French, daughter of Captain Guy D., and Araminta Chapman French; he was an eminent physician, and at the beginning of the Civil war raised in Giles County a company of artillery, which he led into the service, and at the battle of South Mills, North Carolina, April 19th, 1862, he was slain, leaving his widow and two small children, Guy F., and Minnie, surviving him. The Napiers removed from Giles County to Cabell about the time of the emigration of the McComases.

THE MEADOWS FAMILY.

Two representatives of this family came to the New River Valley after the surrender of Cornwallis at Yorktown. The exact date of their coming cannot be fixed with certainty, but was about 1782 or 1783. Jacob Meadows came from the County of Rockingham, in the Valley of Virginia, and was a neighbor of the elder John Peters, who came to the New River Valley in 1782. It appears by the application of Jacob Meadows for a pension made in 1832, that in 1781 he served in the Virginia militia under Captain Coker, in the regiment commanded by Colonel William Noll; his first service was for three months, during which time he was engaged in a number of skirmishes with the British in and around Norfolk and Portsmouth; the last three months he served as a substitute for Adam Hansberger, and was at the battle of Yorktown, serving in LaFayette's corps. John Peters, who gives his affidavit of the service performed by Jacob Meadows, shows that he saw him at Yorktown, serving as a soldier. Jacob Meadows settled on lower

East River, and is the ancestor of the Meadows family in that vicinity.

The other Meadows was Josiah, who came from the County of Bedford, Virginia. He, too, was an American soldier, having served for two or more periods; a part of the time on the frontier against the Indians, and another part in the American army against the British. The facts here stated are taken from his declaration made for pension in 1832, when he was seventy-four years of age. He enlisted in the early spring of 1778, under Captain Joseph Renfroe, and marched with his company to Jarrett's Fort, on Wolf Creek, now in the County of Monroe, where the company was divided, and part thereof, he among the number, was sent to Keeney's Fort, on the Greenbrier, where he was stationed at the time of the attack made by the Indians on Donnally's Fort. Upon the expiration of the term for which he enlisted he again entered the service in the company of Captain Isaac Taylor, and with his company and regiment, the latter commanded by Colonel John Montgomery, marched through the Holstein country to the Indian town at Chicamauga, which they destroyed; from thence going to the Illinois country, under Colonel George Rogers Clark. After his return he was with a portion of the American army that had charge of the British prisoners captured at Yorktown. Mr. Meadows was a Baptist minister in the last years of his life; locating on the north of the Bluestone, and among his sons were Josiah and John Meadows. From this Josiah Meadows, the soldier, has descended the large family of that name in Mercer and adjoining counties.

The name Meador came later, whether it originated from Meadows is not definitely known, but is altogether probable. Closely connected with this Meadows family is that of Lilley, whose first representative in the New River Valley was Robert, who came from Franklin County, Virginia, and who lived for a few years about the mouth of East River, settling there in about 1790; then locating in the North Bluestone section where many of his descendants now live. He was long a magistrate of Mercer County. The first Josiah Meadows, the American soldier, was the great-grandfather of Hon. R. G. Meador, of Mercer County.

THE M'DONALDS.

The name suggests its Scottish origin, and Glencoe as the original home of the family. After the close of the Revolution of 1688 many of the Scottish clans continued in arms for King James against William and Mary. In August, 1691, the government of William and Mary issued a proclamation offering amnesty to such insurgents as should take the oath of allegiance on or before the 31st day of December then next ensuing. All the chiefs submitted within the prescribed time, except the aged Macdonald of Glencoe, whose clan inhabited or lived in the pass of Glencoe. He went to Fort William on December 31st and offered to take the oath, but the officer in command, not having authority to administer it, referred the matter to the Sheriff, before whom Macdonald took the oath on January 6th, 1692; this, however, did not satisfy the adherents of King William, who determined to avail themselves of this unintentional delay to effect the destruction of the clans. On February 12th a body of 120 soldiers, commanded by Campbell, murdered Macdonald and two of his attendants, and so wounded his wife that she died the next day. About forty persons were killed that night. Detachments of soldiers sent to guard the outlets of the valley arrived too late, and many of the clans escaped half naked to the mountains, where a considerable number of the women and children perished of cold and hunger —("McCauley's His. of England, Vol. IV").

Shortly after this massacre, supposed to have been between 1692 and 1700, Bryan McDonald and Mary Combs McDonald, with their family, having first migrated to Ireland, came from thence to America, and settled at or near New Castle, Delaware, then in the Province of Pennsylvania, and presently purchased of William Penn, the proprietor, a large and valuable tract of land. Bryan McDonald and family came, in 1756, to the Virginia Valley, having been preceded some years earlier by two of his sons, Joseph and Edward. In a battle with the Indians, in 1761, near Amsterdam, in what is now Botetourt County, Edward, a bright and promising young lawyer, was killed. He left four daughters, two of whom married Campbells, one married Greenway, and one a Russell. Their descendants are numerous, prominent and influential people; one of them, David Campbell, was Governor of Virginia; William went to Tennessee; Dr. Edward McDonald Campbell and Judge John A. Campbell were their descendants. The Russells lived in southwest Virginia, and the Greenways in Lynchburg and Baltimore.

Joseph McDonald married Miss Elizabeth Ogle, whose ancestors had come from Castle Ogle, Northumberland County, England. They, the Ogles, came to England with William the Norman. Joseph McDonald, who was born April 4th, 1722, after his marriage came, in 1763, over the Alleghanies and settled in what is now Montgomery County, then Augusta. He died in 1809. In the American Revolution he served in Captain Kirkpatrick's company. He had six sons in the American army; Richard was a Major, Edward was a Captain, and Alexander served in Captain Thompson's company. Powder for the patriot army was manufactured on his farm, and a government tannery established, as well as provisions gathered there. All these supplies had to be largely, if not altogether, transported to the army on horses, and this proved a dangerous business, on account of Indian forays. Captain Edward McDonald was in the border wars against the Indians, and in scouting expeditions toward the Ohio.

Joseph McDonald had ten children in the following order as to ages: Bryan, who married Mary Bane; John, who married, first Miss Sawyers, second Miss Cannaday; Joseph, who married Nancie Sawyers; Edward, who married Keziah Stephens; Richard, who married Mrs. Mary Martin; Alexander, who married Elizabeth Taylor, niece of President Taylor; William, who married Ursula Huff, daughter of Dr. Huff; Elizabeth, who

married Samuel Ingram; Jonas, who married Elizabeth Foster;
James, who married, first Elizabeth New, second Mary Flour-
noy. The descendants of Joseph McDonald have scattered
over many states of the Union, and have held many prominent
positions, many of them able and distinguished persons. A
great many of them were slain, or died, in the war between the
states.

Joseph McDonald Sanders, a bright young lawyer of Mercer
County, West Virginia, who served eight years as judge of the
9th Judicial Circuit of West Virginia, and who was recently elevated to the bench of the Supreme Court of Appeals of West
Virginia, is a great-great-grandson of Joseph McDonald, and
great-grandson of Edward McDonald and Keziah Stephens Mc-
Donald.

During the American Revolution one David Hughes, formerly of North Carolina, and a Tory, while scouting through the
wilderness country toward the Ohio River, discovered that
beautiful body of valuable land on the Clear Fork of Guyandotte, in the now County of Wyoming. He informed the above
mentioned Edward McDonald of his discovery, with whom he
agreed for one blanket and a rifle gun to show him this land,
which he did, and in 1780 McDonald entered and surveyed the
same; and in 1802, together with his son-in-law, Captain James
Shannon, removed to the Guyandotte Valley and took possession of his valuable property; his son-in-law, Captain Shannon,
settling a few miles away on the Big Fork of the Guyandotte.
When Captain Shannon took possession of his land he found
still standing on the bottoms the Indian wigwams.

Edward McDonald had several sons and daughters. The
sons, Joseph, William and Stephen, settled on the lands given
them by their father out of the homestead. One daughter married Captain James Shannon; one Captain Thomas Peery; one
Augustus Pack; one William Chapman. Joseph McDonald
married Nancy Chapman, daughter of Isaac Chapman and his
wife, Elian Johnston Chapman, and their children were Sallie,
who married John Sanders; Juliett, who married John Tif-

"GREEN HILL"

The old MacDonald Homestead, built about the close of Revolutionary war.

fany; Elizabeth, who married John Anderson, and Nancy, who married Lewis McDonald. W. W. McDonald, of Logan, married Miss Scaggs; Lewis, the son of Joseph, married, first Miss McDonald, second Miss Keffer. John C., Floyd and Colonel Isaac E. were never married; the two former died in the army during the Civil war. Colonel Isaac E. lived on the McDonald homestead, in Wyoming County, until 1876, when he purchased, by exchange, the valuable farm of Mr. George Pearis George, on Bluestone, in Tazewell County, Virginia. Colonel Isaac E. was a member of the Virginia Legislature in 1861, and of the West Virginia Senate for several years.

The family of William McDonald, son of Edward, consisted of one son, Edward, who married a Miss Black, of Montgomery County, and daughters, of whom one married Harmon Newberry, one William G. Mustard, one Zachary T. Weaver, and one Captain Robert H. Bane.

Stephen McDonald's family went west many years ago. He had two sons, Andrew McDonald and Crockett McDonald; the latter married Miss Ellen Hall, then of Princeton, West Virginia. He died several years ago, leaving three children, two sons and a daughter, who, with their mother, live in the state of Kansas. Joseph, William and Stephen all died about the beginning of or during the Civil war. Colonel Isaac E. died a few years ago, leaving the major part of his valuable estate to his nephew, Walter McDonald Sanders, who also died some two or three years ago, leaving a widow and three or four infant children, who, with their mother, reside on the Bluestone farm.

Before closing this sketch of the McDonald family it is desirable to present a photograph of the oldest dwelling of that family now standing in Virginia, which is at Greenhill, in Montgomery County.

THE PACKS.

The progenitors of this family now in this section of the

country were on the New River, about the mouth of Indian Creek, as early as 1763. Pack, Swope and Pittman, hunters, discovering Indian signs, started, one for the Jackson's River, and the others for the Catawba settlements, to warn the people, but the Indians had traveled faster than the hunters and the warning did not reach them. The given name of this hunter, Pack, is not obtainable; it is probable that he was the ancestor of the Samuel who was born in Augusta, in 1760, as members of this family, soon after 1764, are found along the New River between the mouth of the Greenbrier and Indian Creek. A history of this family, from the Pack MSS., is interesting and is here inserted:

A Mr. Pack and several sons came to Jamestown, from England, with the early settlers on the James. Owing to the hardships encountered there they went back to England; later, however, three of the sons returned to this country; two of them went to the South, and the other remained in Virginia. There were born to the last mentioned Pack two sons, one of whom was named Samuel, who was born in 1760, in Augusta County. He had seven sons, whose names were: John, Matthew, Samuel, Bartley, Lowe, William and Anderson; the daughters were: Betsey, who married Jacob Dickison; Polly, who married Joe Lively, and Jennie, who married Jonah Morriss.

John and Bartley settled at Pack's Ferry, now Summers County; Matthew died on the west side of New River, opposite Pack's Ferry; Samuel settled on Glade Creek, in what is now Raleigh County; Lowe lived on Brush Creek, in what is now Monroe County; William went West; Polly Lively and Betsey Dickison lived in Monroe; Jennie Morriss moved to Missouri.

John, the son of the above named Anderson Pack, was taken prisoner on Flat Top Mountain during the Civil war, and Colonel Hayes, afterward President of the United States, claimed relationship with John and told him that his wife's mother was a Pack (this was Jennie, who married Jonah Morriss), and by reason of this John was allowed the privilege of the camp.

John Pack, who lived at Pack's Ferry, had great trouble with the Indians; he frequently had to plow with his rifle strapped to his shoulder. After friendly relations were secured with the Indians, an old Indian came to John Pack's house one day and told him that on one occasion he conceived the idea to steal two of John's little girls, and when he saw them coming he hid in an old stump to capture them as they came by, but that they were in the course of a foot race when they came up, and they passed so quickly that he could not catch them.

Alderman Pack, an ancestor of the above mentioned Packs, was a member of Parliament during Cromwell's time, and he moved that body to confer the title of Protector on Cromwell. There is authority for saying that a Mr. Pack, an English General, who fought in the Peninsula campaign and in France and Portugal against Napoleon, was one of the ancestors of the Packs who came to America and settled on New River. Mrs. Emily Landgraff, who lived near Pack's Ferry, said that she had seen her grandfather, Samuel Pack, the first Samuel, and that he was an old gentleman of the English type, who dressed in the frock coat and knee breeches peculiar to the Eighteenth century and that he wore a cue.

The aforesaid John Pack, who married Jane Hutchinson, was the father of the following named children: Samuel, who married Harriet French; Rebecca, who married Robert Dunlap; Archibald, who married Patsey Peck; Polly, who married Richard Shanklin; Rufus, who married Catharine Peters, and Julia, who married Elliott Vawter.

Samuel Pack and his wife, Harriet French Pack, who was a daughter of Captain David French, had four sons and one daughter; the sons were: Captain John A., who married Miss Mary Gooch; Allen C., who married Miss Sue Lugar; Samuel, who married Miss Sallie Douthat; Charles D., who died unmarried; the daughter, Minerva, married Dr. John W. Easley. Samuel Pack, who married Harriet French, was a lawyer by profession, and long practiced in Giles and adjoining counties.

THE PECK FAMILY.

This family comes of German stock. Jacob Peck, born in Germany, in 1696, came to America, first locating in Pennsylvania, and then removed to the Valley of Virginia and settled in the neighborhood of where the city of Staunton is now situated, prior to 1744. He married, about the year last mentioned, Elizabeth, a daughter of the elder Benjamine Burden, who had come to America as the agent of Lord Fairfax to look after his large landed estate in the Northern Neck of Virginia. Benjamine Burden, on his coming to the country, first visited the Virginia capitol at Williamsburg, where he met some of the sons of John Lewis, who had then recently located in the Valley, and he went with them to their home. On a hunting expedition with the sons of Lewis he captured a white Buffalo calf which he presented to Governor Gooch; whereupon the Governor ordered certificate to be issued to Burden, authorizing him to locate 100,000 acres of land on the rivers James and Sherando, which he did, securing a large and valuable body of James River bottom lands, now in the County of Botetourt, then Orange.

Benjamine Burden, the elder, died about 1743, and by his will he gave the James River lands to his five daughters, one of whom was Elizabeth, who afterward became Mrs. Jacob Peck. There was a long litigation over this land between Peck and wife and Harvey, a full history of which can be seen by reference to the reported case in the Court of Appeals of Virginia, 1st Munford's R. 518-28. Jacob Peck and his wife died before the litigation ended, which was in 1810; the suit was decided for them, and their children received the land, moved to it, and became citizens of Botetourt County. The children of Jacob and Elizabeth Burden Peck were Jacob, John, Joseph and Hannah, the latter marrying Peter Holm.

This name Burden is frequently spoken of as Borden or Burton. One of these three sons of Jacob Peck was the father of Benjamine Peck, who settled on the Catawba or Sinking Creek about 1785. This Benjamine Peck, grandson of the first

Jacob, and great-grandson of the elder Benjamine Burden, had sons John, Jacob, Benjamine and Joseph. John married Elizabeth Snidow, a daughter of Colonel Christian Snidow. Benjamine married Rebecca Snidow, also a daughter of Colonel Christian Snidow. Jacob married Malinda Givens, of Botetourt. This name Givens appears in the list of persons located between 1738-43, in Beverly Manor near Staunton.

John Peck and his wife, Elizabeth Snidow Peck, had the following sons: William H., Christian L., Joseph A., Dr. Erastus W. and Charles D., and daughters: Mary, who married Benjamine Burden Peck; Margaret, who married Charles L. Pearis; Clara, who married John H. Vawter; Josephine, who married .... Phillips; Ellen, who married Dr. Robert B. McNutt; Martha, who married Judge John A. Kelley; and another daughter, who married Edwin Amos.

William H. Peck and family removed to Logan County, West Virginia; Joseph A. and family removed to Texas; Christian L. died in Giles County, but left a family, among them a son, Charles Wesley, who died in the service of his country, and sons Erastus and John H., who were gallant Confederate soldiers, receiving in battle severe wounds, from which the former has never recovered.

Dr. Erastus Peck was thrice married and left some children, among them, Amos Peck, Miss Josie Peck and the wife of Walter V. Peck. Charles D., who married Miss Thomas, had but one son who attained his majority, John K.; a daughter, Lucretia, who married Dr. D. W. McClaugherty; another, Maggie, who married Judge Hugh G. Woods; another, Clara, who married J. Kyle McClaugherty; another, Fannie, married John Adair, and Rachael married Mr. Fulton.

Benjamine Burden Peck and wife had six sons: Pembroke P., Charles L., James H., Jacob A., Erastus H., and B. Wallace, the latter yielding up his life for his country in the battle of Gettysburg. Mr. Phillips and family went to Alabama. Judge John A. Kelley and family lived in Smyth County, Virginia. Charles L. Pearis and wife had but one child, a daughter,

Electra, who married Dr. Charles W. Pearis. Dr. Robert B. McNutt and wife had three sons, viz: John W., Joseph P., and Charles R.; and daughters, Josie, who died young; Mary, who married Colonel James B. Peck; Neta, who married George B. Sinclair.

John H. Vawter and wife had several children; among the sons are: Charles E. and Lewis A., and daughters, Josephine, who married B. Frank Sweeney; another who married Lewis Peck; Virginia, who married William Farrier. Benjamine Peck and his wife, Rebecca Snidow Peck, had four sons, viz: William H., Christian S., Frank, John S. and Andrew J., and daughters, Eliza, who married James Sweeney; Mary, who married William Farrier, and Margaret, who married John A. Calfee.

Jacob Peck and his wife, Malinda Givens Peck, had the following children, viz: Benjamine Burden, who married Mary Peck; Wm. G., who died unmarried; Elisha G., who married Margaret Peters; Daniel R., who died unmarried; George Harrison, who married Sarah J. Handley; James Preston, who married Elizabeth Scott; Jacob H., who married Ann Handley; Patsey C., who married Archibald Pack; Rhoda E., who married James McClaugherty; Louisa S., who married Lewis Payne, and Rebecca, who married John A. Peters.

THE PEARIS FAMILY.

The ancestors of this family were Huguenots, who fled from France, stopping temporarily in Barbadoes, thence about 1710, to South Carolina, locating on an island about five miles from Port Royal, to which they gave the name "Paris Island." This name is sometimes spelled "Pearris," again "Paris," and "Pearis"; the modern spelling being Pearis. The settler was Alexander Pearis (Parris), who became quite a distinguished man in the early days of the history of South Carolina. Opposite this page is the photograph of the late Captain George W.

CAPT. GEO. W. PEARIS

Grandson of Col. Geo. Pearis, the Settler.

Pearis, a grandson of the New River settler, Colonel George Pearis.

Judge McCrady, in his History of South Carolina under the Proprietary Government, 1670-1719, gives considerable prominence to Colonel Alexander Pearis, whom he shows to have been Commissioner of Free Schools, Commissioner for Building Churches, Member of House of Commons, of which Colonel Wm. Rhett was Speaker; as a military officer and one of the judges to try pirates, and as commander of militia in the Revolution of 1719. Colonel Alexander Pearis had a son, Alexander, who made some conveyance of property in 1722-26. Alexander Pearis, Jr., had a son, John Alexander, who likewise had a son, John Alexander, as shown by his will probated August, 1752. The last mentioned John Alexander had a son, Robert, who spelled his name as did his father, John Alexander "Pearis." This Robert Pearis died about 1781; he had a daughter, Malinda, who married Samuel Pepper, who removed to the New River Valley prior to 1770, and located at the place where, about 1780, he established a ferry, and which place has since been known as Peppers. His two brothers-in-law, George and Robert Alexander Pearis, sons of the preceding Robert, came, with him, or about the same time. At the date of the coming of Pepper and the Pearises, in fact, before that date, there lived in the neighborhood where Pepper located, a gentleman by the name of Joseph Howe, who had some pretty daughters, and it did not take long for these young Huguenots to fall in love with these girls, at least with two of them. An examination of the Pearis Bible discloses that George Pearis was born February 16th, 1746, and was married to Eleanor Howe February 26th, 1771. Robert Alexander Pearis was probably two years younger than his brother George. He married also a daughter of Joseph Howe, and about 1790 removed with his family to Kentucky and settled in what is now Bourbon County, and from whom it is said the town of Paris, in that county, is named. He had a son who in the early history of that state was a member of its Legislature. George Pearis remained in the vicinity of Pepper's Ferry until the spring of 1782; prior to this time he had been made a Captain of one of the militia companies of the County of Montgomery.

On the advance of the British army into the Carolinas, in the fall of 1780, there was a Tory uprising in Surry County, North Carolina, of such formidable proportion as to impel General Martin Armstrong, comanding that military district, to call on Major Joseph Cloyd, of the Montgomery County militia, to aid in its suppression. About the 1st day of October, 1780, Major Cloyd with three companies of mounted men, one of which was commanded by Captain George Pearis, marched to the State of North Carolina, where he was joined by some of the militia of that state, augmenting his force to about 160 men, with which he, on the 14th day of the month, attacked the Tories at Shallow Ford of the Yadkin, defeating them with a loss of fifteen killed and a number wounded; Major Cloyd had one killed and a few wounded, among them Captain Pearis, severely, through the shoulder. This fight cleared the way for the crossing of General Green's army at this ford, which the Tories were seeking to obstruct. Captain Pearis returned home wounded, and in addition to his suffering from his wound had the misfortune to lose his wife by death in a few days after his return, she dying on November 14th. Captain Pearis' wound disabled him from performing further military service, and having purchased from Captain William Ingles, about the year of 1779, for seventy pounds sterling (about $350.00), the tract of 204 acres of land on New River—whereon is now situated Pearisburg station on the line of the Norfolk & Western Railway, and which land was known for years as the Hale and Charleton tracts—he, in the spring of 1782, removed thereto, erecting his dwelling house at a point nearly due south of the residence of Mr. Edward C. Hale, and a little to the southeast of where the road from Mr. Hale's house unites with the turnpike. Two or three years after Captain Pearis made his location, he had a ferry established across the New River, and kept a small stock of goods, and later kept public entertainment.

On October 5th, 1784, he married Rebecca Clay, daughter of Mitchell Clay. The children of Colonel George Pearis and his wife, Rebecca Clay Pearis, were: George N., Robert Alexander, Samuel Pepper, Charles Lewis; their daughters, Rebecca, Julia, Rhoda, Sallie and Eleanor.

Colonel George N. Pearis married Elizabeth Howe, daughter of Major Daniel Howe; Robert Alexander Pearis married Miss Arbuckle, of Greenbrier County; Samuel Pepper Pearis married Rebecca Chapman, daughter of Isaac and Elian Johnston Chapman; Charles Lewis Pearis married Margaret Peck, daughter of John and Elizabeth Snidow Peck; Rebecca married John Brown, they went to Texas about 1836, leaving a son, George Pearis Brown, who lived for a number of years in Mercer County; Julia married Colonel Garland Gerald; Rhoda married Colonel John B. George; Sallie married Baldwin L. Sisson, and Eleanor married Captain Thomas J. George.

The children of Colonel George N. Pearis and his wife, Elizabeth Howe Pearis, were: Captain George W., who never married, died in 1898 at the age of nearly eighty-nine years; Colonel Daniel Howe, who married Louisa A. Johnston; Rebecca, who married George D. Hoge; Nancy, who married Archer Edgar; Ardelia, who married Daniel R. Cecil, and Elizabeth, who married Benjamin White. Robert Alexander Pearis and his wife had no children, and after the death of said Robert Alexander, his widow married Colonel McClung.

The children of Colonel Garland Gerald and Julia Pearis Gerald, his wife, were: Sons, Thomas, Robert, Pearis, Garland T.; a daughter, Rebecca, married Dr. Edwin Grant; Louisa married James M. Cunningham; Mary married ......; Fannie married a Mr. Yost; Virginia died in Texas, unmarried; Ophelia, married ....

The children of Colonel John B. George and Rhoda Pearis George were: George Pearis George, who married Sarah A. Davidson; Jane, who married Judge Sterling F. Watts. The names of the children of Captain Thomas J. George and wife are as follows, viz: A. P. G. George, W. W. George, Robert, and John; the daughters, Larissa, who married Jacob A. Peck; Matilda, who married a Mr. Austin, and Rebecca, who married George W. Jarrell.

Charles Lewis Pearis and his wife, Margaret Peck Pearis, had but one child, a daughter, Electra, who married Dr. Charles W. Pearis, and they had no children.

As already stated, John Brown and family went to Texas prior to 1836; some of his older sons were soldiers in the Texan army. Brown settled in that part of the state that became Collin County. George Pearis Brown, the son of John, remained in Virginia; he married a Miss Mahood, a sister of the late Judge Alexander Mahood, and he and his wife left numerous descendants, among them the wife of Mr. Robert Sanders, the wife of Edward A. Oney, the wife of M. W. Winfree, a son, Cornelius, who was killed on the retreat of the Confederates from the battlefield at Clark's house, May 1st, 1862.

The elder Colonel George Pearis, the settler, was long a magistrate of Montgomery and Giles Counties, and sat in the courts of both counties, and was for a term the Presiding Magistrate of the latter county. The first court of the County of Giles was held in a house belonging to him, and the land for the county buildings and town was given by him and the town of Pearisburg took its name from him. He died on November 4th, 1810, and his ashes repose in the burying ground on the farm on which he died, on the little hill just southwest of Pearisburg station. His widow married Philip Peters and she died April 15th, 1844.

THE PETERS FAMILY.

John and Christian Peters were of a German family of that name, who had located in the Valley of Virginia shortly after 1732. The place of the settlement was in the now County of Rockingham. The inscription on the tombstone of Christian Peters shows that he was born October 16th, 1760, and died October, 1837; it is possible that John was older. In 1781 the

British army under Lord Cornwallis invaded Virginia, finally fixing its base of operation at Yorktown. In May of the year mentioned, the Governor of Virginia called out the militia of the state, placing them under the command of General Nelson, who joined and became a part of General LaFayette's corps, then operating against the army of Cornwallis. John and Christian Peters obeyed the call of the Governor and served through the campaign, and were at the surrender of Cornwallis at Yorktown, on October 19th; the militia was then disbanded and returned to their homes. The war, now regarded as ended, and the services of the militia no longer needed, John and Christian Peters, with their families, together with their brother-in-law, Charles Walker, in the spring of 1782, left their Valley homes, crossed the Alleghanies, and located in the New River Valley; John, on the farm on which Mr. Charles D. French now resides, and Christian where the village of Peterstown, named from him, is now situated. The two or three years immediately following the surrender of Cornwallis brought over the Alleghanies swarms of people, and while many of them went to Kentucky, a goodly number halted in the New River Valley.

John Peters married Miss Simms, of that part of Rockingham that afterwards became Madison County. Christian Peters married Miss Katharine Belcher, of Rockingham, who spoke the German language, and kept in her house her German Bible.

The following are the names of the children of John Peters and wife: Elijah, William, John, Philip, Christian; and daughters, one who married Henry Bailey; and Frances, who married Captain Christianos H. A. Walker, son of Charles, heretofore mentioned.

The families of Conrad Peters, Captain John Peters, of Peterstown, and that of the late James M. Byrnside are descendants of Christian Peters.

John Peters, Jr., the son of the settler, and who married Sallie Clay, daughter of the elder Mitchell, was the Captain of

a company in the war with Great Britain of 1812; was long a
Magistrate, and represented Giles County in the Legislature.
The names of the sons of Captain John Peters and his wife,
Sallie Clay Peters, are as follows: Oliver C. Peters, long an
honored citizen of Giles County, dying at a ripe old age; An-
drew J. Peters, Thompson H. Peters, William P. Peters, Jacob
Peters, Augustus C. Peters; and two daughters by the second
marriage, one of whom married Andrew Johnston, and Miss
Jane, who never married. The grandsons and descendants of
Captain John Peters were among the best, truest and bravest
Confederate soldiers that fought for the South, among them
James M. Peters, William D. Peters, John D. Peters and Wil-
liam H. Peters.

THE SHANNONS OF NEW RIVER VALLEY.

The Shannons came from Ireland at a period anterior to the
beginning of our war for Independence, and located in what
is now the County of Amherst, in Virginia, then probably Albemarle County. Samuel, the New River Valley settler, came
with his family over the Alleghanies in 1774, and located at
the place now called Poplar Hill, in the then County of Fincastle, now Giles County. After a residence of ten years, and
after the marriage of his oldest son, whose name was Thomas,
he, in the spring of 1784 (Shannon MSS.), with his family,
except Thomas and his wife, who remained, removed to a point
near whereon now stands the city of Nashville, Tennessee.

Thomas married Miss Agnes Crowe, and continued in possession of the Poplar Hill property, which is still in the hands of
his descendants. He became a man of prominence in civil and
military affairs; was long a Magistrate of Giles County, Sheriff
thereof, and a Representative in the Legislature. In the
month of February, 1781, the British army advanced northward through the Carolinas toward Virginia, and Colonel
William Preston, the military commandant of the Montgomery
troops, and of which Joseph Cloyd was Major, called out the

forces to go to the help of the American army commanded by
General Greene. Thomas Shannon was the Captain of the
Middle New River Company, in which one Alexander Marrs
was a Lieutenant, and among the members thereof were Thomas
Farley, Isaac Cole, Matthew French, John French, Joseph
Hare, Edward Hale, the Clays, and others. Captain Shannon
and his company joined the battalion at the New River Lead
Mines about the middle of February, 1781, and on the 18th
day of that month the command under Colonel Preston and
Major Cloyd, 350 strong, marched to the Haw River section of
North Carolina, in the vicinity of which was the army of General Greene, as was that of Lord Cornwallis. Being in a
strange country, and not being advised of the positions of the
respective armies, Preston's men went into camp, finding themselves the next morning between the combatants, and close by
the British pickets. Colonel Preston had been ordered to report to General Pickens, and was on his way thither when he
halted and camped between the armies. On the 2nd day of
March Lee's Legion and Preston's battalion had a spirited encounter with Tarleton's cavalry, inflicting upon it considerable
loss. Again on the 6th of March, at Wetzel's Mills, Pickens'
command, including Preston's and Cloyd's men, had quite a
battle with the British advance. General Pickens retreated to
Guilford Court House, where the troops of Preston and Campbell, under Colonel William Campbell, were posted on the
American left, and put up a good fight. They were attacked
by Colonel Tarleton, who led the British right wing, and he
says in his "His. of His Southern Campaign," that his troops
were badly hurt by the Backwoodsmen from Virginia; that
"they were behind a fence, and stood until the British infantry,
with their bayonets, climbed the fence." Captain Shannon
lived to the age of ninety years, leaving a son, Thomas, who
married Julia Allen, and their children are: Thomas, Joseph,
James R., all three of whom are dead; William R., who married a Miss Bush; Nancy, now dead, who married John Henderson Bane; Eliza, who married James B. Miller; and Samuel B.,

who resides on the old homestead. The second Thomas Shannon served as a Magistrate in his county, and sat as a member of the County Court for long years, and was more than once a member of the Virginia Legislature. At the beginning of the Civil war in 1861 he was reckoned the wealthiest man in Giles County. His sons were all gallant Confederate soldiers.

Opposite this page is seen the photograph of Mr. William R. Shannon, the great-grandson of the settler.

THE SMITHS OF NEW RIVER.

This family is here designated as of "New River," otherwise it might not be known to what family of Smiths reference is made, and hence, they are styled "The Smiths of New River." Isaac Smith was a soldier of the American Revolution, and served with the corps of LaFayette at Yorktown. He lived in that part of Rockingham County now embraced in Madison. The territory in which it is supposed and believed that he was born was then Augusta County, and was still Augusta when, in about 1770, he married Miss Simms. After the battle of Yorktown and the return of the Virginia militia to their homes Mr. Smith, together with several of his neighbors and relations, in the year of 1782, passed over the Alleghanies into the New River Valley. Mr. Smith was brother-in-law to John Peters and Larkin Stowers, and they, together with Christian Peters, Charles Walker and others, came to New River. Smith settled on the Long Bottom on New River, nearly opposite the place of settlement of John Peters. Among the sons of Isaac Smith were: Ezekiel, Benjamine, and William, the latter born in 1774. Ezekiel went to Texas before the war for its independence, was captured by the Mexicans and kept a prisoner for five years. His son, French C. Smith, a man of talent and brilliancy, followed his father to Texas, and became a prominent figure in that state, having been the Whig candidate for Governor, but was defeated by General Sam Houston, the Democratic candidate, by a large majority. Benjamine Smith

WM. R. SHANNON

Grandson of Thomas Shannon, the Settler.

lived in the County of Mercer and had several sons—among them Theodore, who went West—Thomas, and Allen. Dr. French W. Smith, of Bluefield, and Judge Charles W. Smith, of Princeton, West Virginia, are the grandsons of Benjamine Smith.

Captain William Smith married a Mrs. Neal, whose maiden name was Dingess, a daughter of Peter Dingess, a Revolutionary soldier, who served in Trigg's battalion of Montgomery County artillery in LaFayette's corps at the battle of Yorktown.

Opposite page 454 will be seen the photograph of Captain William Smith, taken when he was a very old man. He lived to about the age of eighty-four. Mr. John B. Smith, of Willowton, in Mercer County, is a son of Mr. Benjamine Smith, and was a heroic and devoted Confederate soldier.

THE SNIDOWS OF NEW RIVER VALLEY.

This family is of German origin and the first of the family to come to America was Christian Snyder, who landed at Philadelphia in 1727. The record kept at the port of Philadelphia of the arrival of emigrants does not disclose that Christian brought a family with him; if he had done so the same would have been recorded. He no doubt was a young man at the time, and had crossed the ocean to seek his fortune in the New World. The spelling of this name is no index as to who he was, as the original German spelling, is Schneider. It is spelled as originally also Snyder, Snider, Snido, and Snidow. There is, however, something in the use among these German people of the given name; as the same given names in families are handed down from one generation to another. In this family the name Christian seems to have been handed down for more than a hundred years. When, or who Christian Snidow married is not now known, but there came in 1765 to New River, from Pennsylvania, John Snidow, who had married Elizabeth Helm; he came to see the country, and visited Philip Lybrook at the mouth of Sinking Creek. It is likely, in fact more than probable, that Lybrook had been his neighbor in Pennsylvania. The circumstances show that he had made up his mind to settle in the New River Valley, as he went back to Pennsylvania and the next year, 1766, started for the New River with his family, and on the way was taken suddenly and violently ill and died. His widow, Mrs. Elizabeth, with her children, some of them very small, made her way to Philip Lybrook's, or to his neighborhood. The exact place of her settlement is difficult to locate, but from circumstances it is believed that she made her home near the mouth of Sinking Creek, in what is now Giles County. Mrs. Snidow's family consisted of five sons and three daughters; the sons, Philip, Christian, John, Theophilus, and Jacob; daughters, Barbara, and two small girls, killed by the Indians in 1774.

Philip married Barbara Prillman, Christian married Mary Burke, Jacob married, first, Clara Burke, second, Miss Pickelsimon, and third, Mary Hankey; John was killed, being thrown from a horse; Theophilus, when quite a lad, was captured by the Indians in 1774, and after being detained in captivity a number of years returned in bad health, and soon died; Barbara, the daughter, married Jacob Prillman, of Franklin County. Among the children of Barbara Prillman Snidow, was Christian, called the Blacksmith, to distinguish him from his uncle, Colonel Christian.

The children of Colonel Christian Snidow and his wife, Mary Burke Snidow, were: Sons, John, Lewis, and William H.; the daughters were, Elizabeth, Mary, Rebecca, Clara, Nancy and Sallie. John married Rachael Chapman, daughter of Isaac and Elian Johnston Chapman; their children were, Christian, James H., David J. L., Elizabeth, Mary, Elian C., and Ellen J.

Lewis Snidow married Barbara, the daughter of the blacksmith, Christian, and his wife, Sarah Turner Snidow; their children are, William Henry Harrison and George Lewis; the latter married Josephine Snidow; the former unmarried. After

CAPT. Wm. SMITH

Born 1774, Died 1859.

the death of Lewis Snidow his widow, Barbara, married Jacob Douthat, by whom she had several children.

William H. Snidow married Adeline Chapman, daughter of John Chapman; the names of their children are: John Chapman Snidow, now dead; James Piper Snidow and Annie, the latter now dead, and who married Dr. Harvey G. Johnston.

Elizabeth, the daughter of Colonel Christian Snidow, married John Peck, of Giles County; Mary married Major Henry Walker, of Botetourt, later of Mercer County; Rebecca married Benjamine Peck, of Monroe County; Clara married Conrad Peters, of Monroe County; Nancy married James Harvey, of Monroe County; Sallie married Haven Bane, of Giles County. Among the descendants of John Peck and his wife, Elizabeth, are, in part the Pecks of Giles, the Vawters of Monroe, the Kelleys of Smyth, the McNutts of Mercer, and the Pecks of Logan County, West Virginia.

Some of the descendants of Major Henry Walker and wife reside in Mercer County; the descendants of Benjamine Peck reside in Monroe, Mercer, Giles, and in the State of Kansas. The descendants of James Harvey and wife reside in Monroe County, among them, the Adairs of Red Sulphur, and the family of the late Allen Harvey.

Colonel Christian Snidow, when quite a young man, was a lieutenant in Captain John Floyd's company, and did service in Barger's, Snidow's and Hatfield's forts, and in scouts and skirmishes with the Indians. His father-in-law, Captain Thomas Burke, born 1741 and died 1808, and whose wife's given name was Clara, was also a Captain in the Indian wars, and at one time in command at Hatfield's Fort. Colonel Christian Snidow was for long years a Justice of the Peace, in both Montgomery and Giles Counties; was Sheriff of Giles County, and frequently represented the same in the House of Delegates of Virginia. Among his descendants were some of the best and bravest soldiers in the Confederate army.

THE NEW RIVER STRALEYS.

Jacob Straley (German, Strahle) was a German, born at Frankfort-on-the-Main, in Germany; his wife was Susan Barbor, whom he married in Germany, and came directly after his marriage to America, in 1758, and found his way to James River, where the city of Lynchburg now stands. Jacob Straley had a brother John, who came over to America with him, and they are supposed to have landed in New York; John had a wife and several children.

Jacob came South with other emigrants to Virginia, and John went into Pennsylvania; separating, they lost sight of each other and seem never to have heard of each other after their separation. Jacob, as before stated, found his way to where Lynchburg now stands; there he bought land of his brother-in-law, Jacob Lynch, and here the children of Jacob Straley and his wife, Susan, were born, to-wit: Andrew, Elizabeth, Catherine and Jacob. Jacob Straley and his wife Susan both died and were buried at Lynchburg. Andrew was twice married, but had no family; he was a soldier of the American Revolution, and Jacob, his brother, a youth of about sixteen at the close of the Revolution, served in what was called the Reserves, or Home Guards. Elizabeth married a man by the name of Caldwell, by whom she had two or three children; her husband died, she then married a man by the name of Marshall Burton, by whom she had a son called Isaac, who married a Snodgrass, and who left a son, Green, living now in Giles County, and three daughters, Lucretia, who married McCauley; Sallie, who married Albert, and the name of the husband of Jane is not known. Catherine Straley, daughter of the elder Straley, went to Kentucky.

Jacob Straley, son of the elder Jacob, was a brickmason by trade, and about the year of 1782 came to New River, in what is now Giles County, and in June, 1785, married Martha French, daughter of Matthew and Sallie Payne French, by whom he had nine sons and two daughters. His sons were: James, Daniel, John, David, Charles, Jacob, French, Joseph and Leland; the daughters were Sallie and Nancy. James married Betsey Vaught, Daniel married Mary French, John married Betsey Wilson, Charles married Betsey McComas, Jacob L. married Eliza Bergen, French died unmarried; Joseph married Jane Brown, David married Elizabeth Perkins, Leland died young and unmarried, Sallie married Isaac French, and Nancy married Edward Morgan.

James Straley and his wife had one son, Madison, and six daughters: Martha, who married Joseph Summers; Talitha, who married Hampton Brown; Almira, who married George C. Stafford; Rebecca, who married James H. Wilburne; Serilda, who married John Stafford, and Maharald, who married James P. Thorn.

Daniel Straley and his wife, Mary, had two sons and two daughters; the sons were James F. and Jacob C., both of whom died childless; Julia T. married Colonel James M. Bailey, of Mercer County, and by him had five children, two sons and three daughters. The sons, Gaston C. and Daniel M., and daughters, Lizzie, died unmarried; Belle, married James D. Honaker, and Alice married a Mr. Lee.

Sallie F. married Elijah Bailey and had two children, Robert H. and Mary J.

John Straley and Elizabeth, his wife, had two sons and six daughters; the sons, Charles D. and Harrison W.; the daughters, Louisa, married Claudius Burdett; Araminta, married Elijah Bailey; Dorcas, married Benjamine Tinsley; Martha, married Andrew J. Davis; Harriet, married J. McThompson; Valeria, married John Q. Spangler. Charles D. Straley died in 1890, unmarried; Louisa has a large family; Dorcas, Araminta and Martha have no children; Harriet has two children; Valeria has three living children. Harrison W. Straley, now dead, married Delia A. Byrnside, who died in May, 1888, and by her he had four children who reached their majority.

Charles Straley, by his wife Betsey, had nine children, and by his second marriage with Miss Warneck, whom he married in the State of Illinois, had one son, Hugh. Charles Straley removed to Texas, where he died.

Jacob Lynch Straley and his wife, Eliza, had three children, all daughters. Margaret married a Mr. Eldridge, of Tennessee; Caladonia married Joseph Taylor, and Sallie married David C. Straley, son of Joseph. Jacob L. Straley was a minister of the Methodist Church. Joseph Straley and his wife Jane had but two children, William D. and David C.

David Straley and Elizabeth, his wife, had two sons and three daughters. The sons were: Granville P. and David B., the latter dying young; the former is a lawyer by profession, and lives in Maury County, Tennessee. The daughters, Martha T., married Dr. George A. Long, now dead; Mary, married Girard Willis, of Chattanooga, Tennessee, both being now dead. Sallie married Mr. Anderson, and they live in South Carolina.

Sallie Straley married Isaac French, and had two children: Harvey and Elizabeth, both dead. Harvey never married; Elizabeth married Oscar F. Johnston.

Nancy Straley, who married Edward Morgan, had four sons and three daughters; the sons are, Rufus, John, Newton, and Joseph; and the daughters, Martha, who married Mr. Noffsinger; Virginia, who married Richard Gilliam, and Sallie, who died young and unmarried. This Straley people have been quiet, law-abiding and unpretentious, never seeking public position, always ready and serving their friends, especially their relations. Three of the sons of Jacob Straley and his wife, Martha French Straley, served in the war of 1812; they were James, Daniel and John. Our Civil war, 1861-5, produced from their ranks some magnificent soldiers, among them Captain Jacob C., son of Daniel, who led, as Captain, a company in the 17th Virginia regiment of cavalry; he was bold and fierce on the field of battle, and rode boldly into the thickest of the conflict and abreast the storm as if on parade. His courage was not exceeded by that of any man who ever drew sabre.

HARRISON W. STRALEY

Grandson of Jacob Straley, the Settler.

There is presented opposite this page the photograph of Harrison W. Straley, the great-grandson of the emigrant.

THE WITTENS, OF TAZEWELL.

This was a Saxon family from Wittensburg, in Prussia, and a part of the family emigrated to America at a very early day and located in Maryland, about the time of the first white settlements therein. They were neighbors to the Cecils, with whom they married and intermarried for long years. A few years prior to 1771 Thomas Witten, whose wife was a Cecil, and who, with his family, had removed to the neighborhood of Fredericktown, Maryland, came along the Valley of Virginia and over the Alleghanies, living for a year or two at the large spring on Walker's Creek near what is now known as the William Allen farm, and becoming close neighbors of Samuel W. Cecil, who had come from Maryland. The Wittens decided to move to the Clinch, and on the 16th day of March, 1771, they located on that stream; Thomas settled at the Crab Orchard, west of the present Court House of Tazewell; James near what is now Pisgah Church, and Jerry at a point west of the Court House. James Witten, born near Fredericktown, in 1759, married Rebecca Cecil, and William Cecil married Nancy Witten. The Wittens are among the most prominent citizens of Tazewell County; several of them having been honored with important civil positions. Mr. J. W. M. Witten was a Senator in the Virginia Legislature, and also represented Tazewell in the House of Delegates. Upon information derived from Mr. James R. Witten, Governor Greenup, of Kentucky, son of John, of the Clinch Valley, was born near what is now known as Pisgah Church, in Tazewell County. It is said that James Witten carried the first negro slaves into what is now Tazewell County.

APPENDIX D.

THE FOLLOWING is a list of the persons who have represented Tazewell County in the House of Delegates of Virginia from 1800 to 1905, inclusive:

1800-1—Thomas Witten and David Ward.

1801-2—Thomas Witten and David Ward.

1802-3—Henry Bowen and John Grills.

1803-4—Henry Bowen and James Thompson.

1804-5—William Neal and James Thompson.

1805-6—Andrew Peery and James Thompson.

1806-7—Andrew Peery and James Thompson.

1807-8—John Cecil and James Thompson.

1808-9—John Cecil and James Thompson.

1809-10—John Ward and James Thompson.

1810-11—John Ward and James Thompson.

1811-12—John Ward and J. D. Peery.

1812-13—Reece B. Thompson and James Thompson.

1813-14—Reece B. Thompson and James Thompson.

1816-17—John B. George and Reece B. Thompson.

1817-18—John B. George and Thomas Harrison.

1818-19—Thomas Peery and John B. George.

1819-20—Harvey P. George and William Gillespie.

1820-21—Harvey P. George and William Shannon.

1821-22—John B. George and J. C. Davidson.

1822-23—John B. George and William Thompson.

1823-24—John B. George and John Ward.

1824-25—John B. George and Thomas Peery.

1825-26—John B. George and .... Deskins.

1826-27—John B. George and .... Deskins.

1827-28—John B. George and John Ward.

1828-29—Thomas J. George and William Barnes.

1829-30—William Barnes and Thomas J. George.

After 1830, one delegate every two years.

1831-33—Robert Gillespie.   1833-34—Robert Gillespie.

1834-35—Harvey George.

1835-36—J. W. M. Witten.

1836-37—Robert Gillespie.

1837-38—J. W. M. Witten.

1838-39—Addison Crockett.

1839-40—James C. Spotts.

1840-41—James C. Spotts.

1841-42—Henry Bowen.

1842-43—James C. Spotts.

1843-44—Alexander Harrison.

1844-45—Harvey G. Peery.

1845-46—Samuel Laird.

1846-47—Thomas H. Gillespie.

1847-48—Thomas H. Gillespie.

1848-49—Harvey George.

1849-50—Harvey George.

1850-51—J. W. M. Witten.

1851-52—J. W. M. Witten.

1852-53—Robert Davidson.

1853-54—Harvey George.

1854-55—William M. Gillespie.

1855-56—John M. Witten.

1856-57—Hamilton R. Bogle.

1857-58—George W. Deskins.

1858-59—Harvey George.

1859-60—Harvey George.

1860-65—Reese T. Bowen.

1866-68—George W. Deskins.

1869-73—Henry Bowen.

1873-77—William P. Cecil.

1877-83—James R. Witten.

1883-85—William G. Mustard.

1885-87—James Bandy.

1887-89—W. L. Moore.

1889-91—John W. Crockett.

1891-93—J. Howe Sawyers.

1893-95—Andrew M. Peery.

1895-97—James W. Smith.

1897-99—W. B. Spratt.

1899-1901—Joseph S. Moss.

1901-03—W. L. Moore.

1903-05—J. Powell Royal.

---o---

APPENDIX E.

A LIST of attorneys for the Commonwealth for Giles County from 1806 to 1905:

Henley Chapman.

A. G. Pendleton.

J. J. Wade.

James D. Johnston.

W. H. Stable.

F. W. Mahood.

James B. Peck.

David J. Chapman.

George W. Easley.

Gordon T. Porterfield.

W. J. Henson.

John W. Williams.

James F. Ross.

Martin Williams.

William B. Snidow.

APPENDIX F.

THE FOLLOWING is a list of field officers who commanded Confederate organizations, in which were men from the New River Valley, upper Bluestone and Clinch:

Fourth Regiment, Virginia Infantry (Stonewall Brigade)—

Colonels: James F. Preston.
                 William Terry.
                 Charles A. Runald.

Lieutenant Colonels: Lewis T. Moore.
                 Robert D. Gardner.

Majors: Albert G. Pendleton.
                 Joseph F. Kent.
                 Matthew D. Bennett.

Seventh Virginia Regiment of Infantry—

Colonels: James L. Kemper.
                 Walter T. Patton.
                 Charles C. Flowerree.

Lieutenant Colonels: Walter T. Patton.
                 Charles C. Flowerree.
                 Lewis B. Williams.

Majors: Walter T. Patton.
                 Charles C. Flowerree.
                 Aylett A. Swindler.

Eighth Regiment, Virginia Cavalry—

Colonels: Albert G. Jenkins.
                 James M. Corns.

Lieutenant Colonels: Albert G. Jenkins.
                 Walter H. Jennifer.
                 Henry Fitzhugh.
                 Thomas P. Bowen.
                 Alphonso W. Cook.

Majors: P. M. Edmundson.

Henry Fitzhugh.

Thomas P. Bowen.

Fourteenth Regiment, Virginia Cavalry—

Colonels: Charles Thorburn.

James Cochran.

Lieutenant Colonels: Robert Augustus Bailey.

John A. Gibson.

Majors: George Jackson.

Frank B. Eakle.

Sixteenth Regiment, Virginia Cavalry—

Colonel: Milton J. Ferguson.

Lieutenant Colonel: William Graham.

Major: James H. Nounnan.

Seventeenth Regiment, Virginia Cavalry—

Colonel: William H. French.

Lieutenant Colonel: William C. Tavener.

Major: Frederick F. Smith.

Twenty-second Regiment, Virginia Cavalry—

Colonel: Henry S. Bowen.

Lieutenant Colonel: John T. Radford.

Major: Henry F. Kendrick.

Thirty-fourth Virginia Cavalry Battalion—

Lieutenant Colonel: Vincent A. Witcher.

Majors: William Stratton.

John A. McFarland.

Twenty-second Regiment, Virginia Infantry—

Colonels: C. T. Thompkins.

George S. Patton.

William A. Jackson.

Andrew R. Barbee.

(FIELD OFFICERS—Cont'd.)

Lieutenant Colonels: John C. McDonald.

Robert Augustus Bailey.

Isaac N. Smith.

Twenty-third Virginia Infantry Battalion—

Lieutenant Colonels: Clarence Derrick.

William P. Cecil.

Majors: David S. Hounshell.

William Blessing.

Twenty-fourth Regiment, Virginia Infantry—

Colonels: Jubal A. Early.

William R. Terry.

Peter J. Hairston.

Lieutenant Colonels: Peter J. Hairston.

Richard L. Maury.

Majors: J. P. Hammett.

J. A. Hambrick.

W. W. Bentley.

Twenty-sixth Virginia Infantry Battalion—

Colonel: Charles A. Crump.

Lieutenant Colonels: Powhatan R. Page.

James C. Councill.

George M. Edgar.

Richard Woodrum.

Patrick H. Fitzhugh.

Joshua L. Garnett.

Majors: William R. Perrin.

William H. Wheelwright.

Twenty-seventh Regiment, Virginia Infantry—

Colonels: W. W. Gordon.

Andrew J. Griggsby.

Lieutenant Colonels: John Echols.

James K. Edmundson.

Lieutenant Colonels: Charles Haynes.

Daniel M. Shriver.

Majors: Philip F. Frazer.

Elisha F. Paxton.

Twenty-eighth Regiment, Virginia Infantry—

Colonels: Robert T. Preston.

William Watts.

Robert C. Allen.

Lieutenant Colonels: William L. Wingfield.

Samuel B. Paul.

Majors: Nathaniel C. Willson.

Michael P. Spessard.

Twenty-ninth Regiment, Virginia Infantry—

Colonels: Alfred C. Moore.

James Giles.

Lieutenant Colonels: Alexander Haynes.

William Leigh.

Edwin R. Smith.

Majors: Isaac White.

Ebenezer Bruster.

W. R. B. Hoone.

Thirtieth Virginia Infantry Battalion—

Lieutenant Colonel: J. Lyle Clark.

Major: Peter Otey.

Thirty-sixth Regiment, Virginia Infantry—

Colonels: John McCausland.

Thomas Smith.

Lieutenant Colonels: William E. Fife.

Reid L. Wiber.

Benjamine Linkous.

Majors: Thomas Smith.

William E. Fife.

(FIELD OFFICERS—Cont'd.)

Forty-fifth Regiment, Virginia Infantry—

Colonels: Henry Heth.
                       William H. Brown.
                       William E. Peters.

Lieutenant Colonels: Edwin Harman.
                       Benjamine F. Ficklin.
                       William H. Werth.

Majors: Gabriel C. Wharton.
                       William Sanders.

Fifty-first Regiment, Virginia Infantry—

Colonels: Gabriel C. Wharton.
                       Augustus Foresberg.

Lieutenant Colonels: John P. Wolf.
                       James Massie.
                       George A. Cunningham.

Majors: William A. Yonce.
                       Stephen M. Dickey.
                       William T. Akers.
                       David S. Hounshell.
                       Peter Otey.

Fifty-fourth Regiment, Virginia Infantry—

Colonel: Robert C. Trigg.

Lieutenant Colonels: John J. Wade.
                       Henry A. Edmundson.
                       William B. Shelor.

Majors: John S. Deyerle.
                       Austin Harman.
                       James C. Taylor.

Sixtieth Regiment, Virginia Infantry—

Colonels: William E. Starke.
                       Beuhring H. Jones.

Lieutenant Colonels: John C. Summers.

William A. Swank.

William A. Gilliam.

George W. Hammon.

J. W. Spaulding.

James L. Corley.

Majors: Jacob N. Taylor.

James W. Sweeney.

William S. Rowan.

Sixty-third Regiment, Virginia Infantry—

Colonel: James M. French.

Lieutenant Colonels: David C. Dunn.

C. H. Lynch.

John J. McMahon.

Sixty-fourth Regiment, Virginia Infantry (mounted)—

Colonels: A. L. Pridemore.

Campbell Slemp.

Lieutenant Colonel: James B. Richmond.

Major: Henry Gray.

Beckley's Cavalry Battalion: Colonel, **Henry Beckley.**

————o————

APPENDIX G.

A ROLL of Company D, Seventh Regiment of Virginia Infantry (Giles County company):

OFFICERS.

Captains: James H. French.

Joel Blackard.

Robert H. Bane.

Lieutenants.

Eustace Gibson.	William A. Anderson.
Joel Blackard.	John W. Mullens.
E. M. Stone.	E. R. Walker.
Thomas S. Taylor.	

(COMPANY D, 7TH REGIMENT—Cont'd.)

Non-Commissioned Officers.

B. P. Watts.

William D. Peters.

T. N. Mustain.

J. B. Young.

J. C. Hughes.

A. L. Fry.

J. W. Hight.

Privates.

Akers, David C.

Akers, George W.

Albert, William R.

Bish, Daniel

Bane, Allen M.

Bane, Joseph E.

Barrett, Jesse

Bolton, Alexander

Burton, Travis

Carr, William H.

Collins, James M.

Crowford, John R.

Croy, James B.

Cole, James

Dulaney, B. E.

Dulaney, M. J.

Darr, T. P.

Dudley, John S.

Douthat, William H.

Davenport, Thomas

Davis, David

Eaton, E. S.

East, E. D.

East, J. W.

Eggleston, Joseph

Eggleston, James M.

Farley, F. H.

Fortner, William C.

Fortner, James H.

Frazier, J. T.

Frazier, William

Frazier, Creed D.

French, William A.

French, A. J.

French, J. S. W.

Gardner, J. H.

Gordon, Frances M.

Griggsby, Andrew J.

Hale, Charles A.

Hale, John A.

Hale, H. J.

Hare, John D.

Hare, Isaac

Henderson, James B.

Henderson, John

Hoge, B. L.

Hughes, James

Hurt, James J.

Hurt, George W.

Jones, John F.

Johnston, M. S.

Johnston, George

Johnston, David E.

Knowl, George

Lee, C. N. J.

Lewy, Henry

Lewy, Joseph

Layton, W. H.

Lindsey, James
Leffler, P. H.
Meadows, Anderson
Meadows, John
Meadows, B. P.
Morris, N. J.
Minnich, George A.
Minick, John H.
Manning, A. D.
Merrix, Raleigh
Mays, T. P.
Martin, John Q.
Martin, John H.
Muncey, W. W.
Mullins, George C.
Nye, James J.
Pack, A. C.
Palmer, John
Peck, Charles W.
Sarver, John W.
Sarver, D. L.
Southern, Josephus
Shannon, S. B.

Shannon, Joseph C.
Snidow, W. H. H.
Sublett, John P.
Sublett, William T.
Skeens, L. R.
Skeens, Joseph
Sumner, A. L.
Stafford, Thomas J.
Stafford, William H.
Stafford, R. M.
Thompson, A. J.
Thompson, Adam
Thompson, Alonzo
Vass, W. R. C.
Vass, Lee E.
Wiley, Lewis N.
Wilburn, G. L.
Wilburn, H. J.
Wilburn, William I.
Yager, E. Z.
Young, Thomas
Young, Isaac
Young, Jesse B.

TABLE.

Whole number of enlisted men 121
Number promoted to field officers 1
Number killed in battle 13
Number died of wounds 4
Number wounded 52
Number wounded more than once 10
Number died of disease 13
Number discharged on account of wounds 27
Number on detached service 5
Number transferred to other companies 5
Number deserted 10

A ROLL of Company F, 24th Virginia Regiment of Infantry (Giles County company) :

OFFICERS.

Captains :   William Eggleston.
              Thomas Haden.
              George A. Porterfield.
              B. W. Hines.

Lieutenants.

Charles D. Peck.   James P. Snidow.
George H. Weiseger.   William Haden.
W. H. Payne.   Lewis Bane.

Non-Commissioned Officers.

J. H. Peck.   Jacob Albert.
Thomas Haden.   Lloyd Hiden.
James Surface.   Edward Carter.

Privates.

Albert, Jacob A.   Echols, Henderson
Albert, George   Echols, Jerimah
Albert, James   Fisher, Daniel
Albert, Harvey   Harless, Russell H.
Atkins, John   Hutchenson, Joseph
Atkins, Robert   Hutchenson, Van
Adams, Tim   Gerald, Robert
Adams, Jesse   Jeter, Henry
Angel, E. B.   Keister, John
Beller, Andrew   Kissinger, H. H.
Beller, Daniel   Lucas, Samuel L.
Barger, William   Lucas, J. C.
Brewer, Jesse   Lucas, Christian
Blunt, James   Lucas, William
Dowdy, Absalom   LaFon, Paris
Doss, Zack   LaFon, Enoch
Dimond, Thomas J.   Link, Henry
Epling, Anderson   Link, William H.
Epling, Floyd   Manning, James

Manning, John
Manning, Tobias
Munsey, Tunis
Munsey, John
Moser, Jacob
Martin, George
Martin, Shafer
Meridith, Chapman
McCroskey, Miles
Morgan, Charles
Price, Samuel
Price, John
Price, Robert
Price, James
Price, George
Payne, Jack
Payne, Erastus
Pare, Perrin
Poole, John
Poole, Alson
Porterfield, George
Porterfield, David
Porterfield, Gordon
Porterfield, Lewis

Rutlege, Harrison
Smith, William
Smith, Benjamine
Smith, Emanuel
Snidow, George L.
Surface, Jack
Surface, Christian
Stanley, Henley
Sanders, Henry
Sanders, Gustavus
Sanders, Joseph
Sibold, Luther
Stafford, J. G.
Trainer, Van
Trainer, Clell
Webb, W. F.
Webb, William
Weiss, John
Wingo, John K.
Williams, J. M.
Williams, Floyd S.
Wysong, Joseph
Weiss, Dock

A ROLL of Company H, 36th Virginia Infantry (Giles County company) :

OFFICERS.

Captains: A. J. Porterfield.
James F. Hare.

Lieutenants.

Absalom Kirk.
James F. Hare.

T. W. Leftwich.
Green B. Chandler.

Non-Commissioned Officers.

Green B. Chandler.
W. H. Beller.

(COMPANY H, 36TH REGIMENT—Cont'd.)

Noah H. Criner.

James H. Vaught.

James A. R. Kirk.

B. N. Snidow.

James E. Rowlett.

Thomas Hale.

Privates.

Atkins, Moses L.

Albert, Ballard

Benton, James

Bishop, J. E.

Booth, Abijah (1)

Bradley, Andrew

Burton, Henry

Burton, A. D.

Blankenship, James

Blankenship, Daniel

Blankenship, Ben

Caldwell, F. H.

Cumbee, G. M.

Croy, Isaac

Croy, Michael

Chapman, John

Conley, John

Chandler, M.

Duncan, Joseph

Darr, S. H.

Dowdy, Edward

Dowdy, E. F.

Doss, John R.

Dowdy, John

Davis, Thomas

Epling, Lewis

Epling, Elias

Epling, L. A.

Echols, H. B.

Echols, W. S.

Farley, James

French, Jerimah

Ferrell, Michael

Ferrell, E. J.

Hupp, Perry

Harless, George

Hutchenson, Wm.

Hunter, D. B.

Hunter, Harrison

Hale, Charles

Hale, Daniel P.

Hale, James W.

Kindry, Peter

Kindry, William

Kerr, John

Kerr, T. M.

LaFon, D. V.

LaFon, E. C.

LaFon, J. C.

LaFon, W. H. C.

Lambert, James

Lucas, George A.

Long, Isaac

Lucas, James E.

Lucas, M.

McCroskey, David

Lucas, Samuel L.

Martin, James A.

Lucas, Thomas

Martin, Richard

(1).   Abijah Booth died while a prisoner at Camp Chase, Ohio.

Martin, Mitchell
Mattox, George
McGinley, Michael
Porterfield, B. F.
Porterfield, C. C.
Porterfield, J. B.
Porterfield, W. L.
Price, David K.
Price, Christian
Price, John R.
Price, J. W.
Price, C. L.
Price, Jonathan
Pool, Harrison
Pool, John
Rock, John
Smith, A. J.
Smith, J. H.
Sarver, Henley
Sanders, G. W.
Stump, J. C.
Tawney, William
Tabor, W. J.

Terry, Joseph
Terry, William
Turpen, James P.
Vaught, C. L.
Vaught, Henry
Vaught, John
Vaught, Ransom
Vaught, Rufus
Vaught, William R.
Vaught, William T.
Wingo, A. G.
Wheeling, A. C.
Williams, A. R.
Williams, James E.
Williams, John C.
Williams, J. A.
Williams, F. G.
Williams, G. H.
Williams, John H.
Williams, W. D.
Williams, John M.
White, James
Worley, J. D.

Total number officers and men 123
Number killed 7
Number wounded 3
Number died 5

A ROLL of McComas' battery (Giles County company):

OFFICERS.

Captains: W. W. McComas.
David A. French.

Lieutenants.

W. W. Powell.
W. J. Fizer.
Daniel W. Mason.

Thomas A. Mahood.
William H. Smith.

(m'comas' battery—Cont'd.)
Non-Commissioned Officers.

Woodram, J. N.
Peters, James N.
Wilburn, Gordon L.
Francis, David

Charlton, E. W.
Walker, J. M.
Jordon, O. F.

Privates.

Anderson, W. A.
Allison, J. C.
Austin, George
Broderick, H. W.
Breen, M. N.
Bailey, Benjamine
Bailey, Harrison
Bailey, John
Bailey, Joseph
Bailey, Preston
Bailey, Walker
Bailey, Boston
Bailey, James
Brotherton, T. M.
Barnett, A. M.
Blankenship, Oscar
Bean, John
Burton, Isaac
Burton, H. P.
Burton, B. H.
Burton, John W.
Burton, Elias
Boyd, John
Crawford, Calvin C.
Crawford, Isaac
Crawford, James
Croy, E. L.
Charlton, J. W.
Charlton, C. W.

Clyburn, H. C.
Caldwell, William
Collins, Henry
Collins, Hoge
Collins, J. R.
Carbaugh, William
Conley, Isaac
Crawford, D. M.
Crawford, Charles
Crawford, W. M.
Carper, J. W.
Chapman, A. A.
Duncan, E. G.
Douthat, C. T.
Davis, Elijah
Day, Joshua
Davis, Landon
Davidson, George F.
Davidson, Daniel
Dedamore, William
Dennis, George C.
Davenport, Isaac
Easley, George W.
Evans, Henry
Ellis, Henry
Ellis, James
French, Rufus A.
French, Isaac E.
French, William A.

Fizer, Michael

Fizer, H. K.

Frazier, David M.

Frazier, J. K.

Farley, T. C.

Foster, Berry

Fortner, A. G.

Foster, William K.

Gibson, Eustace

Gautier, Ballard

Gitt, W. R.

Hearn, William

Haldron, James M.

Hale, Edward C.

Hicks, Henry

Hurley, Hugh

Hare, Joseph

Hoback, J. T.

Harman, William

Harman, Lewis

Hobbs, W. S.

Ingraham, John

Johnston, James

Johnston, O. P.

Johnston, Adam

Johnston, Isaac E.

Johnston, J. D.

Jones, H. T.

King, John

King, Giles

Kirby, Peter

Kelley, William

Kelley, Thomas F.

Kelley, C. A.

Lucas, M. K.

Lambert, Charles

Manning, G. A.

Moye, Newton

Moser, John E.

Morgan, Luther

McClaugherty, Charles

McDaniel, S. P.

McDonald, Lewis

Martin, George

Meadows, John

Mahood, F. P.

McClanahan, D. M.

McClanahan, Thomas

McFadden, Charles

Mahood, R. C.

Mahood, E. T.

Mahood, C. B.

Nabors, John

Overstreet, John

O'Keeffee, John

O'Donald, John

Oliver, Joseph

Peters, Jacob L.

Peters, Charles C.

Peters, William H.

Pack, Charles E.

Pack, Samuel H.

Pack, Allen C.

Perdue, James

Perdue, McHenry

Pauley, George

Payne, John R.

Peck, E. W.

Phillips, J. R.

Preston, John

Rutlege, Charles

Rutlege, David

(M'COMAS' BATTERY—Cont'd.)

Repass, I. M.
Rogers, Jacob
Rice, John
Robinson, D. C.
Stafford, M.
Stafford, E. W.
Snidow, D. J. L.
Snidow, John D.
Stover, Henry
Sarver, William J.
Tucker, A. L.
Tucker, Robert
Thompson, Adam
Thomas, John
Underwood, Andrew
Underwood, H.

Underwood, Lindsey
Vass, W. A.
Vass, Thomas
Woodyard, W. S.
Woodyard, William
Woodyard, Milton
Woods, William P.
Williams, J. W.
Williams, Charles
Williams, Samuel
Watkins, James
Weese, Jacob
Watts, B. P.
Walker, C. W.
Walker, George D.
Wade, W. C.

TABLE.

Total number of officers and men 176
Number killed 5
Number died of wounds and disease 7
Number wounded 13
Number discharged 31

ROLL of Captain Andrew Gott's Company I, 36th Virginia Regiment of Infantry:

OFFICERS.

Captain Andrew Gott.

Lieutenants.

James E. Bane.
James K. Shannon.

L. P. Johnston.
J. M. Henderson.

Sergeants.

Wm. H. Stafford.
Winton Eaton.
John Ayers.

E. F. Starrett.
A. J. Bane.

Corporals.

Crockett Hughes.   Thomas Turner.
John Floyd Johnston.   Wm. Henderson.

Privates.

Bane, W. H.   Martin, W. K.
Bane, Wilson   Oliver, John
Bland, J. M.   Price, Crockett
Bland, W. H.   Price, Stewart
Burton, John   Robinson, Charles
Carr, Joseph B.   Robinson, George
Conley, John   Rye, Hiram
Carden, Andrew   Shelton, W. J.
Eaton, Jos. C.   Stafford, John R.
Gott, Andrew Jr.   Stafford, Flemming
Hedrick, John   Stafford, James E.
Hetherington, Christy   Stafford, David C.
Hetherington, Augustus   Stafford, Hugh J.
Hodge, Harvey   Stafford, Mitchell
Hammon, John D.   Stafford, Floyd
Hamlin, ...   Stafford, Marcus L.
Johnston, Elbert J.   Snidow, Ballard
Johnston, Joseph   Sands, James
Johnston, Isaac   Stinson, William
Johnston, Stafford   Stephens, Daniel
Johnston, Hugh   Shepherd, Henry
Kirk, Harrison   Turner, Crockett
Kirk, Christian   Tickel, Peter
Lawson, Dotson   Tickel, Solomon
Lee, John   Wiley, John
Miller, James B.   Wiley, Samuel
Meadows, Samuel   Williams, Preston
Meadows, John T.   Williams, James
Meadows, Sampson   Weisinger, R. B.
Meadows, Willis   Wilburn, J. H.
Martin, James   Wohlford, Thomas

Incomplete list of Captain Wm. H. Dulaney's company of Giles County Reserves of the 4th Battalion in Col. Robt. T. Preston's brigade:

Captain, Wm. H. Dulaney.

Lieutenants.

W. W. Powell.   Samuel Brown.

Privates.

Cunningham, George   Simpkins, William
Caperton, Lewis   Snidow, Christian
Conley, Skidmore   Shumate, Anderson
Dulaney, D. E.   Thompson, Pearis
Dickinson, ...   Thompson, Frank
Gusler, James   Vest, William
Lucus, Samuel   Woods, John Hudson
Meadows, John   Worley, John
McClaugherty, William   Wingo, James
Porterfield, Harvey   Wingo, Parker
Simpkins, Thomas

ROLL of Company H, 60th Virginia Regiment of Infantry (Mercer County company):

OFFICERS.

Captains: John A. Pack.
            John M. Bailey.
            Rufus A. Hale.

Lieutenants.

John M. Bailey.   George W. Belcher.
Rufus A. Hale.   Leftwich Bailey.
James M. Bailey.   Daniel F. Austin.

Sergeants.

Oscar J. Emmons.   Thomas M. Shrewsberry.
Geo. D. Bailey.

Corporals.

Council W. Bailey.   Andrew G. Belcher.

Privates.

Absher, Samuel J.
Bailey, Jamison
Bailey, Allen C.
Bailey, Geo. P.
Bailey, Samuel J.
Bailey, Edwin A.
Bailey, Pembroke
Bailey, Wm. C.
Bailey, Jonathan S.
Bailey, Daniel M.
Bailey, Uriah A.
Bailey, Cornelius W.
Bryant, Samuel
Burton, Elias
Belcher, Alexander
Belcher, Henderson
Belcher, Obediah J.
Belcher, Middleton F.
Boggess, Nimrod
Carr, Jesse G.
Caldwell, Madison A.
Cooper, Wm. A.
Cooper, Jas. L.
Crawford, W. H.
Calfee, Henry
Calfee, Jno. A.
Caperton, O. H.
Cooper, Alexander
Carr, Jas. S.
Deweese, Andrew
Dillon, Ballard P.
Dillon, Jesse
Dillon, Jeff.
Dillon, Wm.
Farmer, W. H.

Farmer, A. B.
French, W. K.
Fletcher, Anderson
Farmer, Jno. D.
Falkner, W. D.
Falkner, Chas. L.
Glen, Wm.
Godfrey, Thomas
Graham, David E.
Gilmore, Chas.
Grim, Jas.
Hurst, Jas. H.
Hurst, Armistead A.
Helton, Jeremiah
Hodge, Haywood
Hodge, Wm.
Hetherington, J. T.
Hodge, Geo. W.
Hager, Russell
Herndon, W. H.
Hartwell, Jno. L.
Hale, Chas. A.
Hubbard, Sam. G.
Hudson, Jno. L.
Jones, W. H.
Jones, Jno. H.
Johnston, Adam W.
Johnston, Jas. E.
Jones, Isaac
Jones, James
Justice, Henry D.
Kirk, W. H.
Karr, Jas. S.
Karr, Giles R.
Karr, Jesse G.

(Company H, 60th Regiment—Cont'd.)

Karr, Jos. T.
Kahle, Jno. B.
Lusk, Mathew E.
Lusk, Reece T.
Maxey, Augustus
Martin, Samuel
McComas, Rufus
Martin, Jos. H.
McPherson, Andrew
Poe, Jesse
Privett, Geo. R.
Reed, Chas. A.
Reed, Wm. A.
Reece, Jno. H.
Runyon, Richard
Runyon, John
Shannon, Samuel D.
Shannon, Jno. R.
Saddler, Jas. S.
Saunders, Wm. I.
Saunders, David N.
Shrader, Samuel W.
Shrader, Jas. McH.
Shrader, Henry A.
Shrewsberry, N. L.
Shutt, Jno. W.
Shrewsberry, T. M.

Thompson, Gordon
Taylor, Jno.
Taylor, James
Taylor, William
Tracey, Edward G.
Thornton, W. R.
Tuggle, Lewis
Tuggle, Jno.
Trail, Lewis A.
Underwood, J. A.
Underwood, Jesse
Williams, Jno. A.
Walker, Underwood
Walker, Burrill U.
Whorley, Chas.
Whittaker, Byrd
Whittaker, Jno. T.
Whittaker, Franklin
Whittaker, W. D.
Wimmer, Jas. F.
Wilson, Jesse P.
Wilson, Jno. A.
Wall, Henry D.
Worrell, Fleming S.
Walker, Geo. C.
Wright, Jno. J.
White, William F.

Names of members of Company H, 60th Virginia Regiment Infantry, who were killed in battle, died of wounds or disease, to-wit:

Dillon, Ballard P.,   Oct. 1, 1861, of fever.
Dillon, William,   Nov. 17, 1861, of fever.
Crawford, Wm.,   1861, of camp fever.
Lusk, M. E.,   Nov. 2, 1861, of camp fever.

Martin, Jos. H.,	Nov. 14, 1861, of camp fever.
Saddler, James,	Oct. 30, 1861, of camp fever.
Shrewsberry, Logan T.,	Oct. 21, 1861, of camp fever.
Shrewsberry, N. L.,	Oct. 25, 1861, of camp fever.
Shrewsberry, Thos. M.,	Nov. 13, 1861, of camp fever.
Trail, Lewis A.,	Oct. 27, 1861, of dysentery.
Shrader, Samuel W.,	Nov. 27, 1861, of fever.
Wall, Henry D.,	Dec. 4, 1861, of fever.
Lusk, Reece T.,	Dec. 20, 1861, of fever.
Reade, Chas. A.,	Dec. 5, 1861, of consumption.
Walker, Underwood,	April 1, 1862, of consumption.
Dillon, Samuel W.,	July 10, 1862, from wounds received June 30th, 1862.
Poe, Jesse,	July, 1862, from wounds received June 30th, 1862.
McComas, Rufus,	July 9, 1862, from wounds received June 30th, 1862.
Walker, George C.,	Oct. 14, 1862, from wounds received June 30th, 1862.
Bailey, James (Lieu't.)	Dec. 15, 1861, of fever.
Helton, Jeremiah,	June 12, 1863, of fever.
Wilson, Jno. A.,	May 9, 1864, killed in battle of Cloyd's farm.
Gussler, Henry,	May 9, 1864, killed in battle of Cloyd's farm.
Thompson, Gordon,	May 9, 1864, killed in battle of Cloyd's farm.
Runyan, Richard,	May 31, 1864, wounds received at Cloyd's farm.
Bailey, Pembroke,	July 24, 1864, killed battle of Hernstown.
Runyan, John,	Aug. 17, 1864, killed at Winchester.
Belcher, Middleton F.,	Sept. 19, 1864, wounded at Winchester.

(MEMBERS OF COMPANY H KILLED, ETC.—Cont'd.)

Boggess, Nimrod,	Sept. 19, 1864, killed at Winchester.
White, Wm. F.,	Sept. 19, 1864, killed at Winchester.
Peters, Thaddeus S.,	Oct. 9, 1864, wounds received battle Leetown, Aug. 25, 1864.
Wimmer, Jas. F.,	Oct. 19, 1864, wounds received at Fisher's Hill, 22nd Sept., 1864.
Bailey, Geo. D.,	Oct. 19, 1864, killed battle of Cedar Creek.
Karr, Jos. T.,	Oct. 26, 1864, wounds received battle Cedar Creek.
Worrell, Flemming S.,	Dec. 7, 1864, died of gastritis.
Hager, Russell,	Nov. 9, 1864, wounds received in battle of Winchester, Sept. 19th, 1864.

It appears that thirty-six of this company died of wounds, disease, or were killed in battle. The roll of this company is compiled from the original, made by Captain Rufus A. Hale, and on which appears the names of thirty-eight men marked as deserters, and whose names do not herein appear, as several of those so marked did not go over to the enemy, but united with other Confederate commands and served faithfully to the end of the war, and hence it would be wrong to brand and hand down to posterity their names as deserters.

ROLL of Captain Alexander Pine's company of Mercer County Reserves, composed of men between 45 and 50 years, and boys between 16 and 18 years. This company served for some time in the trenches around Richmond in the fall of 1864:

Bailey, Samuel J.	Bailey, Daniel M.
Bailey, Cornelius W.	Belcher, Anderson A.
Bailey, Enos	Belcher, Daniel P.

Bailey, Uriah A.
Calfee, William
Calfee, Augustus B.
Calfee, Houston
Chatting, George
Carper, Ballard
Clamore, James
Ferguson, John (Orderly Sgt.)
Hurst, Armstead A.
Hearn, Levi
Hubbard, Samuel G.
Hutchinson, Allen
Jones, Wm. H.
Jones, Isaac
Kahle, Jno. B.
Mills, Benjamin
Mills, George
Miller, Floyd

McBride, John
Neeley, William
Neeley, E.
Oxley, Sanford (Lieutenant)
Petrey, Jacob
Phillips, John
Stinson, Charles
Stinson, Loraine (2d Lieut.)
Shorter, James
Shorter, Philip
Stewart, Vest
Stovall, Levi (1st Lieut.)
Shutt, Jno. W.
Tracey, R. J.
Trail, Jacob
Trail, Samuel M.
Weeks, Bert
Walker, Burrill U.

This company was attached to the 4th Battalion Virginia Reserves, commanded by Col. Wallace. A number of Capt. Pine's company were transferred to Company H, 60th Va. Regt. of Infantry.

A ROLL of Company G, 24th Regiment of Virginia Infantry (Mercer County company):

OFFICERS.

Captains: Robert A. Richardson.
Hercules Scott.
Benjamine P. Grigsby.

Lieutenants.

Benjamine G. McNutt.
William Mc Calfee.
John A. Douglass.

Rufus G. Rowland.
Harvey M. Calfee.

Privates.

Abshire, Winston
Austin, R. T.

Abshire, James A.
Alvis, D. M.

(COMPANY G, 24TH REGIMENT—Cont'd.)

Bailey, Edward

Bailey, G. C.

Bailey, Robert H.

Bailey, G. F.

Bailey, N. B.

Bailey, Festus

Bowling, William

Burroughs, Charles

Brown, John A.

Brown, Thomas C.

Belcher, William McH.

Belcher, George P.

Bird, Blueford W.

Batchelor, Robert

Cooper, A. L.

Cooper, R. C.

Cooper, C. W.

Cook, Squire

Coeburn, John .

Calfee, Milton H.

Calfee, French

Carbaugh, Wm. T.

Calloway, James

Cox, Jordon

Deeds, John F.

Douglass, John A.

East, Alexander

Easter, John

French, B. P.

French, David

Fellers, Zechariah

Foley, Marshall

Faulkner, Hugh M.

Farley, William

Flick, J. M. N.

George, Robert A.

Grigsby, B. P.

Grim, Peter

Gore, G. H.

Herndon, William H.

Heptinstall, Leslie

Holston, A. J.

Hearn, Andrew

Hearn, James

Hopkins, James T.

Hill, George

Hambrick, Joseph

Hall, James

Harris, George A.

Hale, Luther C.

Johnson, James H.

Johnson, Dennis

Johnson, Addison

Justice, Henry D.

Kinney, James

Karnes, Isaac

McNutt, B. G.

McNutt, John W.

McClaugherty, M. H.

McClaugherty, Albert

Mahood, William A.

Mahood, F. W.

Motley, R. D.

Mullins, F. M.

Mills, James H.

Manning, Tobias

Monroe, James M.

Oney, Isaac A.

O'Daniel, William

Peters, Thaddeus

Peck, B. Wallace
Parker, George W.
Prillaman, Stephen
Perkins, James A.
Reese, Manly
Reynolds, Wm. M.
Rowland, R. G.
Saunders, M. B.
Saunders, Gordon L.
Smith, Allen
Smith, John M.
Smith, Wm. N.
Stovall, Joseph
Smiley, George W.
Shumate, R. H.
Schmitz, George B.

Snead, James
Stuart, William
Toney, George W.
Thompson, J. M.
Thompson, H. C.
Thomas, John P.
Thomas, Jeff
Thomas, James
Turner, Wm. H.
Vermillion, Levi V.
Vest, Crawford
Wright, John
White, H. G.
White, H. M.
Whittaker, A. J.
Whittaker, Boston

A ROLL of Company I, 59th Regiment of Virginia Infantry (Mercer County company):

OFFICERS.

Captain, William B. Dorman.

Lieutenants.

C. D. Straley.
James M. McCue.

J. C. Straley.

Non-Commissioned Officers.

William L. Bridges.
D. H. Carr.
J. W. Thompson.
J. L. Walker.
Benjamine P. Grigsby.

Thomas C. Gooch.
J. H. Peck.
W. W. George.
James O. Cassady.

Privates.

Bailey, John H.
Bailey, A. C.
Bailey, Daniel P.
Bailey, Wilson L.
Barbor, H. B.

Belcher, Hugh I.
Belcher, Rufus K.
Blankenship, Robert
Brian, Albert P.
Brian, William H.

(COMPANY I, 59TH REGIMENT—Cont'd.)

Bray, Thomas

Brunty, Ransom

Bowling, Lee

Bowling, Thomas J.

Burnside, A. J.

Carper, William

Calfee, George

Calfee, Davis

Calfee, Henry

Caldwell, M. C.

Caldwell, W. H.

Caldwell, Andrew

Davidson, Henry P.

Dangerfield, Owen

Daniely, W. J.

Davis, A. J.

Davis, Gabriel

French, Ballard P.

French, James H.

Fletcher, William H.

Fletcher, Charles

Gallier, Jack

Gibson, James

Godfrey, Thomas

Gooch, Benjamine P.

Grimm, Isreal

Grimm, Peter

Graley, Isaac

Graley, Henry

Heptinstall, W. F.

Haden, J. E.

Holly, Wm. H.

Holly, W. S.

Hall, ...

Harris, Wm. A.

Harless, N. B.

Hudson, Robert M.

Jones, Nathan

Jones, Fleming

King, Wm. R.

Lavender, Henry

Lilley, J. K.

Lowman, John

Martin, Hardin K.

Martin, French

Martin, H. W.

Martin, John

Martin, Wm. H.

Martin, Henry

Miller, George C.

Miller, George W.

McKenzie, Hiram

Morgan, Wm. H.

Murrill, Drury T.

Oney, Ambrose

Oney, Edward A.

Parker, Giles

Perkins, J. J.

Peters, Elijah

Robinson, John H.

Robinson Rufus

Rowland, Kinsie

Rowland, Rufus G.

Smith, Gaston

Smith, Ballard P.

Spade, Samuel

Tabor, George O.

Thompson, Syms

Thompson, Samuel

Underwood, Isham

Underwood, Jesse
Underwood, Peter
Worrell, Fleming

Walker, Wm.
White, James
White, Ballard P.

NOTE.—This was the second company organized in Mercer County and united with the 59th Virginia regiment of Infantry, of the Wise Legion, under the command of General Henry A. Wise. This command served for some time in western Virginia about the Gauley Dogwood Gap and on Sewell Mountain. It was afterward transferred to eastern North Carolina and captured at the battle of Roanoke Island. On the return of these men from captivity, their term of enlistment having expired, they joined themselves to various Confederate commands.

A ROLL of Company A, 17th Virginia Cavalry Regiment (Mercer County company):

OFFICERS.

Captains: William H. French.
J. W. Graybeal.

Lieutenants.

Wm. B. Crump.
Edward McClaugherty.
Judson Ellison.

W. A. Reid.
Robert Gore.
LaFayette Gore.

Men of the Line.

Austin, A. G.
Anderson, A. J.
Anderson, David
Alvis, B.
Brown, William
Brown, P. R.
Brown, Joseph
Burnside, Jackson
Burgess, James
Butler, Joel A.
Boling, James
Bolin, J. J.

Bolin, F. A.
Bolin, A. H.
Bolin, G. S.
Bolin, U. A.
Barbor, H. B.
Belcher, Floyd
Brian, G. H.
Brian, Robert
Brian, Albert P.
Batchelor, Robert
Campbell, James
Campbell, Henry

(COMPANY A, 17TH REGIMENT—Cont'd.)

Campbell, Lewis

Campbell, Wm. A.

Clemmens, John

Clemmens, James

Crawford, G. W.

Caldwell, G. W.

Caldwell, Manilius

Caldwell, Morton

Calfee, A. J.

Calfee, Albert B.

Davis, P.

Easter, James

Easter, C. W.

Fanning, A. J.

French, Allen

French, Milton H.

French, Wm.

Fletcher, Wm. H.

Faulkner, Hugh

Faulkner, George

Foley, Marshall

Foley, Barnet

Flowers, John

Foster, G. W.

Foster, James

Foster, Robert

Farley, Jackson

Gore, H. S.

Gibson, Leroy

Hall, Wm.

Holroyd, W. M.

Hunt, Eli W.

Hunt, G. W.

Hunt, Arnold

Haldren, Samuel

Haldren, G. W.

Haldren, Ballard

Hatcher, Henry

Hatcher, Jackson

Hatcher, Green

Higginbotham, Henry

Higginbotham, G. L.

Lowman, John

Lane, Charles

Means, Charles

Martin, H. E.

Martin, Daniel

Martin, Francis

Martin, Joseph

Martin, J. D.

Monroe, J. W.

Massie, Thomas

Meadows, Harry

Massie, Jefferson

McClaugherty, Joseph

McClaugherty, John

McClaugherty, Nelson

Nash, Albert

Neeley, William

Newkirk, J. R.

Newkirk, William

Nelson, John

Nelson, Lewis

Pennington, Levi

Pennington, G. L.

Prince, Floyd

Prince, Lee

Pettry, William

Pettry, H. F.

Patton, ...

Ratcliffe, Cook
Reed, G. W.
Reed, Clark
Redman, Robert
Redman, William
St. Clair, William
St. Clair, Daniel
St. Clair, E. W.
St. Clair, Bluford
St. Clair, Green
Shorter, W. A.
Shorter, G. W.
Snead, James
Sweeney, William
Stafford, W. H.
Shrewsberry, Johnson
Shrader, Robert
Tucker, ...
Thompson, Philip

Thomley, Thomas
Thompson, Joseph
Thompson, Allen
Thornton, William
Virmillion, J. R.
Virmillion, S. T.
Walker, John
Woodall, John R.
Woodall, W. A.
Woodall, M. F.
Wright, John
Wiley, Hugh
Wiley, Bird
Wiley, J. A.
Wiley, James L.
Weatherford, Samuel
Williams, Andrew
Wood, J. A.

FRENCH'S MERCER COUNTY BATTERY.

OFFICERS.

Captain, Napoleon B. French.

Lieutenants.

John J. Maitland.
Edward G. Tracey.
Theodore Smith.

B. G. McComas.
John A. Douglass.
Charles R. Boyd.

CHAPMAN'S VIRGINIA BATTERY (Monroe County company):

OFFICERS.

Captain, Beirne Chapman.

Lieutenants.

Reed
Henderson
Thrasher

Smith
Campbell

(CHAPMAN'S VIRGINIA BATTERY—Cont'd.)

Non-Commissioned Officers.

Cephalis Black.

William T. Patton.

M. M. Balentine.

R. Davidson.

William Dickerson.

J. G. Stevens.

Charles Heeney.

Dr. E. F. Raymond.

Privates.

Argabright, J. L.

Arnett, Jesse

Andrews, H. M.

Andrews, William

Andrews, Charles

Armstrong, Henry

Alderson, J. W.

Briggs, Miles

Bostic, James

Burns, Matthew

Boyd, Matthew

Ballentine, Andrew

Ballentine, John

Burdett, James

Beamer, Matthew

Beamer, Bird

Banks, Clem

Bran, Robert

Bennet, J. W.

Bradley, George

Clark, Aaron

Coiner, John

Christie, Allen

Christie, Newton

Cummings, Robert

Davidson, Ferdinand

Daugherty, John

Daugherty, William

Dickson, Charles

Dickson, Robert

Dungan, Robert

Ellison, Charles

Ellis, Jacob

Ellis, W. H.

Ellis, John

Ford, James

Foster, Jacob

Groves, Alexander

Gray, John

Gray, Alexander

Griffey, Robert

Huffman, George

Hoylman, Francis

Hogsett, B. F.

Hogsett, H. M.

Hogsett, William

Hogsett, Washington

Halstead, Allen

Halstead, Henry

Hill, A. J.

Hines, James

Hines, J. W.

Hamilton, Houston

Hoke, J. H.

Honaker, Ike

Hicks, Samuel

Humphrey, Berry
Hurt, Garland
Holderlee, W. H.
Kirby, James
Keaton, Cole
Kiser, Bogle
Layton, Frank
Lynch, Hugh
Lemon, Frank
Lowe, John
Lewis, Thomas
Loudermilk, James
Lee, Mason
Lynch, Henderson
McGhan, Mack
McDowell, Andrew
Mays, Robert
Moran, James
Matheney, George
Mann, Thomas
Mann, Clark
Mann, Kenley
Mann, John
Miller, Wilson
McGee, John
Morris, John
McRay, William
Meeks, H. A.
Meeks, Harrison
Morgan, John
Minner, Dick
McNeer, W. R.
Neel, Henry
Neel, A. A. P.
Parker, J. N.
Pyles, John

Pyles, Henry
Pharr, Dian
Peck, Jacob
Pitzer, Henry
Pitzer, Wink
Robison, William
Robison, James
Robison, Dick
Robinson, Samuel
Reed, Joseph
Riffe, John
Riffe, Samuel
Swoope, Wm. L.
Stevens, J. A.
Smith, Wash
Smith, Josiah
Smith, Lorenso
Shaver, William
Shumate, William
Shumate, Harry
Saunders, William
Selvey, William
Stuart, James
Sams, Andrew
Sams, Dock
Sams, Hugh
Sawyers, Jesse
Stull, Dan
Spangler, John
Simpson, Jacob
Stickley, John
Sively, Charles
Tracey, J. J. H.
Upton, J. H.
Vance, Adam
Vance, David

(CHAPMAN'S VIRGINIA BATTERY—Cont'd.)

Vance, Rice
Vance, Henry
Vance, Cape
Vine, George
Vans, Tavern H.
Vaught, Miles

Walters, J. W.
Walker, Charles
Walker, Newton
Young, J. C.
Young, George
Young, William

A ROLL of Bryan's Virginia Battery, in which a number of Monroe County and New River Valley men served:

OFFICERS.

Captain, Thomas A. Bryan.

Lieutenants.

Giles A. Fowlkes.
William Steele.

William H. Jennings.
Mosheim Tabler.

Non-Commissioned Officers.

William A. Francis.
John T. Simms.
A. J. Patton.
G. W. Branham.
M. W. Humphreys.
A. A. McAllister.
Otho Crebbs.
B. F. Irons.

Judson Howell.
Wm. A. Burdett.
N. A. Dunbar.
H. C. Campbell.
John D. McCartney.
George W. Earley.
William R. Leach.
George W. Wetzel.

Privates.

Alexander, Henry
Alexander, M. J.
Allen, G. W.
Allen, Hugh
Allen, John
Allen, N. R.
Alvis, ...
Arnold, Alexander
Arthur, Charles M.
Bell, A. M.

Beckett, Michael
Bland, Alexander
Boyd, George A.
Boyd, F. A.
Boyd, R. A.
Branham, John H.
Bryan, Walter
Bugg, G. W.
Burdett, John K.
Burnes, James T.

Bush, Harvey
Calfee, J. A.
Campbell, A. N.
Campbell, Daniel
Campbell, John E.
Campbell, John P.
Campbell, W. H. H.
Campbell, Wm. P.
Caperton, Hugh
Carroll, James
Carter, Wm. A. Sr.
Carter, Wm. A. Jr.
Chewning, Stephen
Clark, James F.
Clark, Preston
Collins, Edward
Collins, Philip
Connell, M. S.
Ceelican, Thomas McL.
Croghan, Timothy
Crosier, J. L.
Crosier, J. M.
Crosier, T. B.
Crosier, W. B.
Crowder, L. V.
Cumins, Jack
Davis, Charles M.
Dehart, James R.
Dehart, John
Dehart, Michael A.
Dehart, William C.
Debins, Daniel
Doland, Andrew
Doland, Mark
Dooley, James A.
Doswell, R. M.

Duffy, John H.
Dunbar, C. W.
Dunbar, James M.
Dunbar, John A.
Dunbar, R. S.
Dunbar, Thomas E.
Dunbar, W. M.
Dunn, B. P.
Dunn, Rufus K.
Dunsmore, J. A.
Dunsmore, W. H.
Erskine, Madison H.
Fisher, James T.
Fisher, John I.
Foster, David W.
Fox, I. L.
Francis, John A.
Fullen, Wm. H.
Glover, John H.
Glover, William P.
Graves, John W.
Hall, Joseph
Hall, Robert
Handley, J. A.
Hebberman, ...
Honaker, E. S.
Huffman, G. S.
Huffman, Tim L.
Hughes, ...
Humphreys, C. A.
Humphreys, John W.
Irons, William Y.
James, W. H. H.
Jennings, Petrie
Kelley, Dennis
Kershner, James H.

(BRYAN'S VIRGINIA BATTERY—Cont'd.)

Kershner, M. M.

King, William A.

Kissinger, Erastus

Knightstep, W. C.

Kountz, Samuel

Landridge, Thos.

Lawhorn, James

Lawhorn, Joseph

Leach, A. U. G.

Leach, Cornelius

Leach, A. Y.

Leach, Joshua

Leach, Wm. R.

Lewis, John E.

Lewis, John T.

Long, N. B.

Lynch, John

McClaugherty, George E.

McClearn, Alexander

McClowney, J. K.

McCreery, W. H.

McDowell, R. D.

McMahon, A. J.

Manning, Dennis

Martin, Thomas

Martin, Thomas S.

Meadows, E. B.

Meredith, L. D.

Miller, T. J.

Miller, Wm. G.

Morgan, Thomas A.

Mourn, G. W.

Murdeck, James L.

Murrill, Charles H.

Murrill, Thomas B.

Neal, A. P.

Neal, John L.

Nelson, John F.

Nicholas, John

Nickell, George T.

Obenchain, C. E.

Parker, D. R. P.

Parker, R. Y.

Parker, W. H. H.

Patton, A. D.

Patton, John C.

Patton, John J.

Patton, Napoleon

Patton, Wallace

Pearis, George D.

Ramsey, James W.

Ramsey, John

Reaburn, R. A.

Reaburn, W. H.

Riley, Timothy

Ripley, J. L.

Robertson, Frank

Robertson, B. H.

Robinson, Alexander

Rusk, M. M.

Russell, Walter

Saunders, James

Scott, William

Shanklin, C. A.

Shanklin, H. S.

Sheppard, Joel G.

Shields, Wm. H.

Shumate, R. A.

Smith, Alexander

Smith, Pat

Spade, Brice M.

Spade, W. C.

Stack, Thomas

Steele, John

Steele, Lewis M.

Steele, M. G.

Steele, Thomas B.

Stephens, C. I.

Snyder, Alexander

Tabler, J. N.

Teass, Thomas A.

Thomas, D. R.

Thomas, G. W.

Thompson, George H.

Tipton, W. H.

Tolbert, Charles

Tomlinson, A. N.

Tomlinson, James P.

Tomlinson, Joseph

Tomlinson, W. C.

Vance, Adam

Vass, Charles

Walker, C. W.

Wallace, John A.

Wallace, John J.

Wallace, Wm. A.

Watson, A. J.

Weaver, Aylett

Weaver, John C.

Witten, Guy M.

Wickline, J. A.

Wickline, S. D.

Williams, S. B.

Williams, George W.

Williams, James

Williams, Wm. P.

Wiseman, Charles A.

Wiseman, John A.

Woodson, A. A.

Woolwine, A. P.

Wiley, Perry

Wiseman, John L.

Young, George

Young, Josiah

A ROLL of Company D, 23rd Virginia Battalion of Infantry, commanded by Colonel Clarence Derrick (Tazewell County company):

OFFICERS.

Captains: William P. Cecil, promoted to Major.

D. B. Baldwin.

Lieutenants.

Thomas W. Whitt.

David J. Gillespie.

W. M. Witten.

James Gillespie.

Oscar F. Barnes.

James H. Harding, Adjutant.

Hugh Dillon, Fife Major.

John Whetsel, Drum Major.

(COMPANY D, 23RD VIRGINIA BATTALION—Cont'd.)

Orderly Sergeants.

David J. Daugherty.　　David A. Edwards.
Thomas P. Brewster.

Flag Bearers.

John W. Daniels.　　Benjamine White.
Fred Smiley.　　A. J. Sweeney.

2nd, 3rd and 4th Sergeants, Corporals and Privates.

Agner, William
Ayers, Isaac
Ayers, B. F.
Asberry, John
Asberry, Madison
Brown, W. J.
Bowman, Arch
Bowman, Samuel P.
Barnes, John
Brown, Wm.
Carter, John
Carter, Smith
Carter, James
Cooley, Joseph
Conley, Isaac
Cook, B. K.
Doughton, Enos
Doughton, Mitchell
Doughton, George
Doughton, Andrew
Dillion, Henderson
Dillion, Osborne
Dillion, Thomas P.
Dixon, John
Dailey, W. W.
Faddis, John
George, James H.

Gray, James
Gillespie, Robert
Gillespie, George W.
Gillenwalters, James
Hunter, James
Hankins, Richard
Higginbotham, M. N.
Helton, Buch
Hooker, Wm.
Hall, John
Hall, James
Hall, Thomas
Haldron, A. J.
Hensley, Wm.
Mathena, John
Marrs, David W.
Mitchell, Eli
Moore, Robert M.
Newton, James
Newton, Wm.
Pack, Jordan
Puckett, James
Price, Wm.
Pack, John
Quicksell, Harman
Rollins, Davidson
Rollins, Emsley

Redwine, Joseph

Rollins, Wm.

Rader, Wm. E.

Ratcliff, Richard S.

Ratcliff, Howard

Ratcliff, Henderson

Smith, C. D.

Spotts, Campbell

Spence, Jonas

Spence, Wm.

Spence, James

Sparks, Jonas

Sergent, Wm.

Sergent, Johnston

Shannon, Powell

Steele, Montague

Sweeney, I. J.

Vest, James

Vaughan, Jeff

Waldron, M. A.

Whitt, Alfred

Witten, Thomas

Whitt, Montague

Whitt, Elias A.

White, Benjamine

White, James A.

White, Osborne

White, Joseph

Whitt, James A.

White, John

White, Arch

White, John Jr.

Young, Charles

Young, John B.

NOTE.—This company was engaged in the following actions and battles: Cotton Hill, W. Va., Dickenson, McCoys, Fort Donelson (five days fight), Fayetteville, Montgomery's Ferry, Camp Piatt, Charleston, Pack's Ferry, Lewisburg, New Market, Berryville, Shepherdstown, Dry Creek, Monocacy, Opequon, Winchester, Strasburg, Middletown, Fisher's Hill, Fort Harrison, Cold Harbor, Snicer's Gap, Atlee's Station, Lacy Springs, Kernstown. This company had 33 men wounded, 10 killed, 10 captured, and 7 died of disease. Osborne Dillion was captured in McDowell County, West Virginia, and brought to a place now known as Roseville, near Pocahontas, Virginia, tied to a tree and shot.

COMPANY H, of the 8th Virginia cavalry regiment, commanded by Captains George W. Spotts, John C. McDonald, Thomas P. Bowen and Henry Bowen, was composed in part of the following named Mercer County men, to-wit:

Lieutenant, Jacob A. Peck.

(COMPANY H, 8TH VIRGINIA CAVALRY—Cont'd.)
Privates.

Alvis, Fel

Alvis, James

Alvis, John

Bailey, A. J.

Bailey, Rufus K.

Bailey, Rufus

Bailey, Festus

Bailey, Clinton

Belcher, Henry D.

Belcher, Philip

Belcher, Waddy

Blankenship, Wm.

Calfee, H. S.

Calfee, John

Cassady, R. P.

Clowers, Daniel

Crawford, Reuben

Deweese, Andrew

Duncan, Wm.

George, Robert A.

Godfrey, John D.

Hale, John E.

Higginbotham, J. H.

Higginbotham, Allen

Hight, James H.

Karnes, James A.

Kesterson, Frank

McClananhan, Charles

McNutt, Joseph P.

McPherson, Jacob

McPherson, James

McThompson, John

Mills, James R.

Painter, Wm. L.

Reed, Hiram

Shrader, Robert

Smith, Wm. B.

Stickleman, Thomas

Stovall, John Q.

Tiller, J. P.

Thompson, H. B.

Thompson, Patrick

Thompson, Thomas W.

Thompson, Wm. H.

Underwood, Peter

Walker, Wm.

Wilson, John

THE FOLLOWING is a list of officers who commanded various organizations from Tazewell County which served in the Confederate army:

COMPANY D, 23RD VIRGINIA BATTALION OF INFANTRY.

Captains, Wm. P. Cecil, D. B. Baldwin; Lieutenants, James Gillespie, David J. Gillespie, Montague Whitt, Wm. M. Witten, Milburn W. Barrett, Thomas L. Whitt, Oscar F. Barnes, who served at one time Sergeant Major of said battalion. Captain

Wm. P. Cecil was promoted to Major and commanded for a while the said battalion, and he was succeeded by Major David S. Hounshell. At the reorganization of the army, Lieutenant Colonel Clarence Derrick, a graduate of West Point, became Lieutenant Colonel and commander of said battalion. Captain Wm. Blessing, of Company A, was promoted to Major, and James A. Harding was appointed Adjutant.

45TH VIRGINIA REGIMENT OF INFANTRY.

Colonels, Henry Heth, Wm. E. Peters, Wm. H. Brown; Lieutenant Colonel Edwin H. Harmon; Captains, Joseph Harrison, Charles A. Fudge, John H. Whitley, John Thompson, Henry Yost, T. V. Williams, James H. Peery. Lieutenants, B. W. Williams, Henry S. Higginbotham, Robert Wingo, Robert A. Winston, Robert G. Baldwin, R. A. Taylor, Norman Bailey, Henry Davidson, Preston Croft, Joseph H. Bane, W. C. Williams, Charles P. Gillespie, James P. Whitman, James W. Smith, John Thompson, and Henry E. Maxwell.

DERRICK'S BATTALION.

Captains, George Gose, Frank Peery; Lieutenants, S. H. Skelton, H. G. Peery.

29TH VIRGINIA REGIMENT OF INFANTRY.

Captains, Archibald Peery, Rufus Britton, Ebb Brewster, the two latter afterwards promoted to Majors; Lieutenants, P. Barnes, P. Croft.

22ND REGIMENT OF VIRGINIA CAVALRY.

Colonel, Henry S. Bowen; Lieutenant Colonel, ... Radford; Captains, Bailey Higginbotham, W. W. Brown; Lieutenants, Samuel Brooks, Wesley Hall.

16TH REGIMENT OF VIRGINIA CAVALRY.

Colonel, Milton J. Ferguson; Lieutenant Colonel, Wm. L. Graham; Captains, Jonathan Hankins, Robert Taylor, Wm. Edward Peery; Lieutenants, M. L. Linkous, Wm. Elswick,

M. W. Barrett, Henderson Plummer, Wm. Bailey, W. H. H. Witten, John H. Wood, John Whitley, S. J. Thompson, Ferd S. Dunn.

8TH REGIMENT OF VIRGINIA CAVALRY.

Captains, George W. Spotts, John C. McDonald, Thomas P. Bowen, Henry Bowen; Lieutenants, Joseph S. Moss, J. H. Abbott, A. J. Tynes (afterwards promoted to Captain).

34TH VIRGINIA CAVALRY BATTALION.

Colonel, Vincent A. Witcher; Captains, Elias V. Harman, David G. Sawyers, John Yost.

50TH REGIMENT OF VIRGINIA INFANTRY.

Captain, Frank W. Kelly. There were two companies of Tazewell County Reserves at the battle of Saltville, one commanded by Captain Samuel L. Graham, and the other by Captain Starnes.

UNITED STATES CENSUS, 1790 TO 1900, SHOWING THE POPULATION OF THE COUNTIES OF MONTGOMERY, MONROE, TAZEWELL, GILES AND MERCER.

COUNTIES	1790	1800	1810	1820	1830	1840	1850	1860	1870	1880	1890	1900
Montgomery	13223	9044	8409	8733	12306	7405	8359	10617	12556	16098	17742	15852
Monroe		4188	5444	6680	7798	8422	10204	10757	11124	11501	12429	13130
Tazewell		2127	3007	3916	5749	6290	9942	9920	10791	12861	19899	23384
Giles			3745	4521	5274	5307	6570	6888	5895	8794	9090	10793
Mercer						2243	4222	6819	7064	7467	16002	23022

INDEX.

H.

I.

J.

CPSIA information can be obtained
at www.ICGtesting.com
Printed in the USA
LVHW080145041222
734538LV00004B/29

9 781296 719258